OXFORD THEOLOGICAL MONOGRAPHS

OXFORD THEOLOGICAL MONOGRAPHS

PETER MARTYR VERMIGLI AND PREDESTINATION
The Augustinian Inheritance of an Italian Reformer
Frank A. James III (1998)

EARLY ISRAELITE WISDOM
Stuart Weeks (Paperback: 1999)

ZADOK'S HEIRS
The Role and Development of the High Priesthood in Ancient Israel
Deborah W. Rooke (2000)

UNIVERSAL SALVATION
Eschatology in the Thought of Gregory of Nyssa and Karl Rahner
Morwenna Ludlow (2000)

ANGLICAN EVANGELICALS
Protestant Secessions from the Via Media, *c.*1800–1850
Grayson Carter (2001)

CHRISTIAN MORAL REALISM
Natural Law, Narrative, Virtue, and the Gospel
Rufus Black (2001)

KARL RAHNER AND IGNATIAN SPIRITUALITY
Philip Endean (2001)

EZEKIEL AND THE ETHICS OF EXILE
Andrew Mein (2001)

THEODORE THE STOUDITE
The Ordering of Holiness
Roman Cholij (2002)

HIPPOLYTUS BETWEEN EAST AND WEST
The Commentaries and the Provenance of the Corpus
J. A. Cerrato (2002)

FAITH, REASON, AND REVELATION IN THEODORE BEZA
Jeffrey Mallinson (2003)

Frontispiece: Detail from title page of Richard Hooker, *Of the Lawes of Ecclesiasticall Politie*, 1593. Reproduced by kind permission of the Bodleian Library, University of Oxford [illegible]

Frontispiece: Detail from title page of Richard Hooker, *Of the Lawes of Ecclesiasticall Politie*, 1593. Reproduced by kind permission of the Bodleian Library, University of Oxford, Ref. G 5.2(1,2) Th.

Richard Hooker and Reformed Theology

A Study of Reason, Will, and Grace

NIGEL VOAK

OXFORD
UNIVERSITY PRESS

OXFORD
UNIVERSITY PRESS

Great Clarendon Street, Oxford OX2 6DP

Oxford University Press is a department of the University of Oxford.
It furthers the University's objective of excellence in research, scholarship,
and education by publishing worldwide in

Oxford New York

Auckland Bangkok Buenos Aires
Cape Town Chennai Dar es Salaam Delhi Hong Kong Istanbul
Karachi Kolkata Kuala Lumpur Madrid Melbourne Mexico City Mumbai
Nairobi São Paulo Shanghai Taipei Tokyo Toronto

Oxford is a registered trade mark of Oxford University Press
in the UK and in certain other countries

Published in the United States
by Oxford University Press Inc., New York

First published 2003

British Library Cataloguing in Publication Data
Data available

Library of Congress Cataloging in Publication Data
Data applied for

ISBN 0-19-926039-7

1 3 5 7 9 10 8 6 4 2

Typeset by Newgen Imaging Systems (P) Ltd., Chennai, India
Printed in Great Britain
on acid-free paper by
Biddles Ltd, Guildford & King's Lynn.

To my Parents and Daniela

Two things there are which troble greatly these later times, one that the Church of Rome cannot, another that Geneva will not erre.

Richard Hooker, *Autograph Notes*, 4: 55.4–6

ACKNOWLEDGEMENTS

This study began life as a thesis for the Faculty of English Language and Literature at the University of Oxford, for which in part I received an M.Phil. in 1994. It then grew to become a larger thesis, within the same faculty, for which I received a D.Phil. in 1999. I am most grateful to Professor John Carey, my first supervisor, for his kind assistance throughout these two stages. By his perceptive and logical analysis he was able to help me to refine my arguments, as they headed ever further into the realms of theology and philosophy. I am equally grateful for the generous assistance that my second supervisor, Professor Diarmaid MacCulloch of the Faculty of Theology of the University of Oxford, gave me in the later years of the D.Phil. and in the process of transforming the doctoral thesis into this book. With his profound knowledge of the sixteenth century he helped me in particular to give my work some of the contextualization that it was previously lacking, and also to realize the importance of discussing Hooker's views on religious authority.

I am much indebted to the two examiners of my doctoral thesis, Professor Peter Lake and Dr Peter McCullough, for the helpful comments they made during my viva voce. It was especially a pleasure to meet Professor Lake in person, whose work on Hooker I have always found stimulating over the years.

My thanks are also due to Professor Sir Anthony Kenny and Dr Dominic Perler, who both advised me concerning Aquinas's philosophy of mind, and particularly concerning the role of the will in relation to the reason. I likewise wish to thank Dr Ward Jones for inviting me to give a paper on Hooker's philosophy of mind and action before the Ockham Society, and for the stress he so rightly placed on the role of belief-formation in Hooker's work.

It is important, furthermore, to acknowledge my debt to the work of the editors of *The Folger Library Edition of The Works of Richard Hooker*. This book would be much the poorer were it not for their joint efforts, both in terms of making Hooker's entire surviving corpus reliably available to modern scholars, and by giving it a critical apparatus which is so much more accessible than that of Keble. I should also like to thank the staff of the Bodleian

Library and the British Library for their help over the years, and in particular for the patient assistance of Mr Richard Bell over interlibrary loans.

Since good ideas seldom reach fruition without some financial backing, I am deeply grateful to the British Academy for the scholarship that supported my M.Phil. and the initial part of my D.Phil., and at the same time to my parents, who most generously helped me financially, and in so many other ways, during these years of study.

I should also very much like to thank Ms Claudia Simon for her help with several Latin translations, and Mr Charles Gibbons for his advice on a range of philosophical problems. The Revd Stuart Richards has inspired me greatly over the years in our pleasurable conversations in the pub about theology, and I am also very grateful for the benefit of his knowledge of the Greek language. Last but far from least, I should like to thank my wife Dr Daniela Havenstein for the care with which she has twice read through my work and made numerous invaluable suggestions, and for the loving patience with which she has consistently supported my work on Hooker.

N.V.

London
May 2002

CONTENTS

ABBREVIATIONS

Works of Hooker

AN	*Autograph Notes to the Christian Letter*
Answer	*Master Hooker's Answer to the Supplication that Master Travers made to the Counsell*
Cert.	*A Learned and Comfortable Sermon of the Certaintie and Perpetuitie of Faith in the Elect*
DF	*The Dublin Fragments*
Jude 1	*The First Sermon Upon Part of S. Judes Epistle*
Jude 2	*The Second Sermon Upon Part of S. Judes Epistle*
Just.	*A Learned Discourse of Justification, Workes, and How the Foundation of Faith Is Overthrowne*
Lawes	*Of the Lawes of Ecclesiasticall Politie*
LL	*A Latin Letter*
Pred.	*Notes toward a Fragment on Predestination*
Pride	*A Learned Sermon of the Nature of Pride*
Remedie	*A Remedie Against Sorrow and Feare, delivered in a funerall Sermon*
SFP	*A Sermon Fragment on Proverbs 3.9–10*

Other Works

ACL	Anonymous, 'A Christian Letter of Certaine English Protestantes... unto that Reverend and Learned man, Maister R. Hoo[ker]', in *The Folger Library Edition of The Works of Richard Hooker*, iv. 1–79
'Defence'	John Whitgift, 'The Defence of the Answer to the Admonition', in *The Works of John Whitgift*, ed. J. Ayre, i–iii
Ecclesiastical Discipline	Walter Travers, *A Full and Plaine Declaration of Ecclesiasticall Discipline owt of the word of God*, trans. T. Cartwright
Folger	*The Folger Library Edition of The Works of Richard Hooker*, ed. W. S. Hill, i–vii

Inst.	John Calvin, *Institutes of the Christian Religion*, ed. J. T. McNeill, trans. F. L. Battles
'A Just and Temperate Defence'	William Covel, 'A Just and Temperate Defence of the Five Books "Of Ecclesiastical Polity" Written by Mr. Richard Hooker', in *Hooker's Ecclesiastical Polity and Other Works*, ed. B. Hanbury, ii. 439–568
OA	*Iacobi Arminii . . . Opera Theologica*
OC	*Ioannis Calvini Opera Quae Supersunt Omnia*, ed. G. Baum, E. Cunitz, and E. Reuss
OS	*Joannis Calvini Opera Selecta*, ed. P. Barth and G. Niesel
OED	*The Oxford English Dictionary*, 2nd edn.
PL	*Patrologiae Cursus Completus*, Series Latina, ed. J. P. Migne
Replye	Thomas Cartwright, *A Replye to an answere made of M. Doctor Whitegifte againste the admonition to the Parliament*
The Rest of the Second Replie	Thomas Cartwright, *The Rest of the Second Replie agaynst maister Whitgifts second Answer*
RHCCC	*Richard Hooker and the Construction of Christian Community*, ed. A. S. McGrade
ScG	Thomas Aquinas, *The Summa Contra Gentiles of Saint Thomas Aquinas*, trans. English Dominican Fathers
The Second Replie	Thomas Cartwright, *The Second Replie of Thomas Cartwright: against Maister Doctor Whitgiftes second answer, touching the Church Discipline*
ST	Thomas Aquinas, *Summa Theologiae*, Latin text with English trans., Blackfriars edn.
STC	*A Short-Title Catalogue of Books Printed in England, Scotland, & Ireland and of English Books Printed Abroad 1475–1640*, 2nd edn., rev. W. A. Jackson, F. S. Ferguson, and K. F. Pantzer

'Supplication' Walter Travers, 'A Supplication made to the Privy Council by Master Walter Travers', in *The Folger Library Edition of The Works of Richard Hooker*, ed. W. S. Hill, v. 189–210.

A NOTE ON THE TEXT

Quotations from printed books dating from the sixteenth and seventeenth centuries have had the long s, the v and u, the j and i, and all ligatures standardized to modern usage. All contractions have also been expanded. Quotations from the Bible have been taken from the Geneva version, in line with Hooker's own usual practice.[1]

All quotations from works by Hooker are taken from the modern *Folger* edition, as is the dual reference system for citing the *Lawes*. This reference system is designed to aid those readers who have access only to Keble's widely available nineteenth-century edition, and may be summarized as follows: volume number in the *Folger* edition; colon; page number(s) and line number(s) in the *Folger* edition; Hooker's note number, where relevant; line number in Hooker's note, where relevant; open bracket; book number of the *Lawes*; chapter number (Hooker's); section number (Keble's); close bracket. For example: *Lawes*, 1:57.2–12 (I.1.2).

[1] See *The Geneva Bible. A Facsimile of the 1560 Edition* (Madison, 1969). See also William P. Haugaard, 'Introduction: The Preface', *Folger*, vi. 64.

A NOTE ON RELIGIOUS TERMINOLOGY

Any discussion of religion in late sixteenth-century England requires some description of the opposing groups within the Church at that time. This task has been complicated by the fact that the traditional binary pairing of 'Anglican' and 'puritan' is now generally considered unsatisfactory, since 'Anglican' is, in this context, an anachronism that carries with it many connotations inapplicable to the then Reformed consensus in the English Church. 'Puritan' is itself not an entirely satisfactory term, but most historians have been reluctant to dispense with it entirely; although it was a term of abuse, it was at least current in the period. A study of Hooker's theology is not, however, the place for a detailed discussion of such terminological controversies. The important point is that the reader know how religious terms are being used, not that that use be here defended in detail. Peter Lake has examined these issues in depth, and has provided both a careful definition of the term 'puritan', and the suggestion that 'conformist' be used as an accompanying term for those on the right of the English Church in this period. His definitions, taken from his book *Anglicans and Puritans?*, are adopted throughout the length of this study, as is his useful definition of the term 'presbyterian':

In what follows 'presbyterian' will be used to refer to those men who can be shown to have espoused or defended the presbyterian platform of church government. The term 'puritan' is used to refer to a broader span of opinion, encompassing those advanced protestants who regarded themselves as 'the godly', a minority of genuinely true believers in an otherwise lukewarm or corrupt mass. It is therefore used as a term of degree, or relative religious zeal rather than as a clear-cut party label. Thus, while all presbyterians were puritans, not all puritans were presbyterians and the usage adopted here is designed to reflect that. The term 'conformist' is used to refer not to all those who can in some sense be said to have conformed to the rites and ceremonies of the English church, but only to those men who chose to make a polemical fuss about the issues of church government and ceremonial conformity and who sought to stigmatize as puritans, those less enthusiastic about such issues than themselves.[2]

The terms 'Calvinist' and 'Reformed' also require some comment. They have often been considered synonymous in the past, and some writers use them interchangeably. 'Calvinist' has, however, recently been considered a misleading term, as it places too much weight on the influence of Calvin in a tradition that has, both in the sixteenth and in subsequent centuries, been influenced by many theologians, and which is far from being monolithic. 'Reformed' is now increasingly preferred as the more satisfactory, inclusive alternative.[3] This is especially important if Arminianism is considered as a branch of the Reformed tradition, for Arminius differed profoundly from Calvin as regards the nature of the divine and human wills and the doctrine of predestination.[4] The primary emphasis in this book is on the Reformed tradition from its Reformation origins up until the rise of Arminianism in the seventeenth century: in other words, the Reformed theological context in which Hooker wrote, and which existed in the period immediately after his death. As a consequence, the writers cited in this book to illustrate ideas closely associated with the Reformed tradition are all from this period: primarily Calvin, Thomas Cartwright, and the anonymous writers of the *Christian Letter*, but also other theologians such as John Whitgift, William Perkins, Walter Travers, and Martin Bucer. It is of course open to critics to observe that the Reformed tradition developed significantly in later centuries, with the inevitably complex picture that emerges from

[2] Peter Lake, *Anglicans and Puritans? Presbyterian and English Conformist Thought from Whitgift to Hooker* (London, 1988), 7. See also Lake, 'Defining Puritanism—again?', in F. J. Bremer (ed.), *Puritanism: Transatlantic Perspectives on a Seventeenth-Century Anglo-American Faith* (Boston, Mass., 1993), 3–29.

[3] See Patrick Collinson, 'England and International Calvinism 1558–1640', in M. Prestwick (ed.), *International Calvinism* (Oxford, 1985), 214–15; Alister E. McGrath, *Christian Theology. An Introduction* (Oxford, 1994), 60–1. For a discussion of the origin of the classification 'Reformed', see Jaroslav Pelikan, *Reformation of Church and Dogma (1300–1700)* (Chicago, 1983), 183–7.

[4] For conflicting assessments of the relation of Arminianism to the Reformed tradition, see Carl Bangs, 'Arminius as a Reformed Theologian', *The Heritage of John Calvin: Heritage Hall Lectures 1960–1970*, ed. J. H. Bratt (Grand Rapids, Mich. 1973), 213–21; Richard A. Muller, *God, Creation, and Providence in the Thought of Jacob Arminius: Sources and Directions of Scholastic Protestantism in the Era of Early Orthodoxy* (Grand Rapids, Mich. 1991), 269, 281–5.

such an all-embracing perspective. None the less, it is believed that the conclusions of this book, while primarily directed at Hooker's relation to the Reformed tradition of his day, are also very broadly true of his relation to Reformed theology more generally.

Introduction

For well over a century Richard Hooker (1554–1600), master of the Temple Church in London and author of the famous *Of the Lawes of Ecclesiasticall Politie*, was to the casual observer a decidedly uncontroversial figure. Up until the last twenty years scholarly debates on various aspects of his theology and political theory left unruffled the generally perceived significance of his treatise and of his place in the English Church. Hooker, it was argued, was the first systematic defender of Anglicanism, setting out in Elizabeth I's reign the Church's position as a *via media* between Roman Catholicism and Reformed Protestantism. In the specific context of his day, he acted as an advocate for the Anglican mainstream of the Church of England against the puritans, standard-bearers of an alien Calvinist or Reformed theology.[1] Even if it was not always accepted that Hooker was explicitly commissioned by Archbishop Whitgift for this task, it was certainly assumed that he was articulating the establishment position, though in a philosophical manner that gave his work a validity untempered by its specific literary and theological origins.[2]

Such stability belies the fact that, from a historical perspective, this picture of Hooker has been far from universally accepted. Michael Brydon and Diarmaid MacCulloch have mapped out the disturbing fluidity of Hooker's reputation from the time of his death up until the mid-nineteenth century.[3] It was the Oxford

[1] For use of the terms 'Calvinist' and 'Reformed', see A Note on Religious Terminology.

[2] For classic expressions of this position, see e.g. Francis Paget, *An Introduction to the Fifth Book of Hooker's Treatise of the Lawes of Ecclesiastical Polity* (Oxford, 1899; 2nd edn. 1907); Vernon Stanley, *Richard Hooker* (London, 1907); Marie Stephanie Stueber, 'Richard Hooker's Place in the History of Renaissance Christian Humanism' (Ph.D. thesis, St Louis Univ., 1954); J. S. Marshall, *Hooker and the Anglican Tradition: An Historical and Theological Study of Hooker's Ecclesiastical Polity* (London, 1963); Arthur S. McGrade, 'Hooker's *Polity* and the Establishment of the English Church', *Richard Hooker: Of the Laws of Ecclesiastical Polity*, ed. A. S. McGrade and B. Vickers (London, 1975), 11–40; Louis Weil, 'The Gospel in Anglicanism', S. Sykes and J. Booty (eds.), *The Study of Anglicanism* (London 1988), 66–71; Aidan Nichols, *The Panther and the Hind. A Theological History of Anglicanism* (Edinburgh, 1993), 37–50.

[3] See Michael A. Brydon, 'The Evolving Reputation of Richard Hooker: An Examination of Responses to the *Ecclesiastical Polity*, 1640–1714' (Ph.D. thesis, Univ. of

Movement, drawing on earlier Laudian notions, that firmly cemented Hooker's position as the first systematic defender of a mainstream Anglican *via media*, hostile to Reformed theology and Roman Catholicism alike. Yet in the early seventeenth century, although Hooker quite swiftly became established as an authority whom people wished to cite, he was claimed as much by solidly Reformed theologians such as Joseph Hall, as by those of the religious persuasion of William Laud.[4] If Hooker was seen as a figure of the mainstream Church of England, much depended upon how that mainstream was defined by the interested parties concerned. In the past twenty years, as the old consensus over Hooker has crumbled, there has been a significant return to such polarized attitudes, as critics now disagree profoundly over the most central aspects of his theology. Yet this recent debate has brought with it a renaissance in Hooker scholarship, with at least one specialist book appearing annually over the last few years. Such interest has been fuelled by Hooker's perceived importance as an advocate of Anglican values, at a time when many people are seeking a substantive, philosophically grounded understanding of this concept. Numerous writers have appealed to Hooker for support, thus further emphasizing the contentiousness of the subject, as reinterpreting Hooker has for some again become a way of reinterpreting Anglicanism.[5]

The recent critical debate over Hooker needs to be seen in the context of wider developments in the understanding of the Elizabethan and Jacobean Church; developments that are now widely known and discussed, but that it is still important to review in brief. The old view that the theological establishment in this period was composed primarily of churchmen adhering to an Anglican *via media* between Rome and Geneva has come under

Durham, 1999), 2, 8, 21, 26–56, 193–4; Diarmaid MacCulloch, 'Richard Hooker's Reputation', *English Historical Review* 117 (2002), 773–812.

[4] See Brydon, 'The Evolving Reputation of Richard Hooker', 26–56; MacCulloch, 'Richard Hooker's Reputation'.

[5] See e.g. Egil Grislis, 'The Anglican Spirituality of Richard Hooker', *Toronto Journal of Theology* 12 (1996), 35–45; Nigel Atkinson, *Richard Hooker and the Authority of Scripture, Tradition and Reason* (Carlisle, 1997), pp. xii, 132; John Booty, *Reflections on the Theology of Richard Hooker: An Anglican Addresses Modern Anglicanism* (Sewanee, Tenn., 1998), 198–9; Paul F. M. Zahl, *The Protestant Face of Anglicanism* (Grand Rapids, Mich. 1998), 2–5, 72, 78–80; Bryan D. Spinks, *Two Faces of Elizabethan Anglican Theology: Sacraments and Salvation in the Thought of William Perkins and Richard Hooker* (Lanham, Md., 1999), pp. xiii, 8–9, 158–60, 169–75; Nigel Atkinson, 'Hooker's Theological Method and Modern Anglicanism', *The Churchman* 114 (2000), 40–70.

heavy attack in the last twenty years. Through the formative work of Patrick Collinson, Dewey D. Wallace, and others, the critical consensus has undergone a dramatic change.[6] Reformed theology is no longer identified squarely with puritanism, as if it remained essentially the province of marginal groups, divorced from the mainstream of the English Church in this period. It now appears that most of the educated churchmen who held positions of any significance under Elizabeth and James I were fundamentally Reformed in their theological outlook: Bullinger, Calvin, and Peter Martyr, for instance, were all well respected in England, and widely held as figures of religious authority. Puritans existed at the periphery of the establishment not because they were Reformed *per se*, but because the more advanced reformation that they wished to see in the English Church, and in the piety of English men and women, was unacceptable to many of their peers, and above all to the monarchs of the day.[7] The predominant tensions in the Church were thus between people of varying shades of Reformed opinion, and between them and Roman Catholicism, whether latent at home or resurgent abroad. Superimposing Anglicanism onto the Elizabethan and Jacobean Church is thus now widely seen as an anachronistic act of revisionism, attractive principally to those who, like the members of the Oxford Movement, wish to deny Reformed theology its central place in the early post-Reformation history of the English Church.

Such developments in Tudor and Stuart historiography pose an immediate problem for traditional Hooker scholarship. Given that the Church establishment under Elizabeth and James I is now seen as imbued with Reformed theology and values, it is no longer credible to see Hooker in the old sense as the mainstream defender

[6] See e.g. Patrick Collinson, *The Religion of Protestants: The Church in English Society 1559–1625* (Oxford, 1982); Dewey D. Wallace Jr., *Puritans and Predestination: Grace in English Protestant Theology, 1525–1695* (Chapel Hill, NC, 1982); Collinson, 'England and International Calvinism 1558–1640', 197–223; Borden W. Painter, 'Anglican Terminology in Recent Tudor and Stuart Historiography', *Anglican and Episcopal History* 56 (1987), 237–49; Lake, *Anglicans and Puritans?*; Nicholas Tyacke, *Anti-Calvinists. The Rise of English Arminianism c. 1590–1640* (Oxford, 1987; repr. pbk 1990); Diarmaid MacCulloch, *The Later Reformation in England 1547–1603* (Basingstoke 1990), 60–72; Peter Lake, 'Predestinarian Propositions', *Journal of Ecclesiastical History* 46 (1995), 110–23. For a dissenting opinion, see Peter White, *Predestination, Policy and Polemic: Conflict and Consensus in the English Church from the Reformation to the Civil War* (Cambridge, 1992).

[7] For further remarks on the use of the term 'puritan', see A Note on Religious Terminology.

of an Anglican *via media*, though that has not prevented some recent writers from continuing to do so. Hooker cannot on the one hand have philosophically articulated the establishment position of a Reformed English Church, and on the other have been a proto-Laudian Anglican. Either one must accept that only one of these two views is basically correct, and the other a historical misconception, or one must somehow arrive at a compromise that incorporates both these uneasy polarities. It is not surprising, therefore, that much recent Hooker criticism should have divided along just these lines. Unfortunately, works adopting a conciliatory approach have tended to agree uncritically with both these views of Hooker, so developing an unacknowledged paradox rather than a satisfactory synthesis.[8] This, of course, only adds to the division in Hooker studies, and emphasizes the importance of understanding the positions of those critics who take such very different views on Hooker and his enigmatic work.

Of these recent critics, none has had a greater impact than Peter Lake. His analysis of Hooker in *Anglicans and Puritans? Presbyterians and English Conformist Thought from Whitgift to Hooker* spans only one chapter, but is of such density and sophistication that it is not easily summarized. In many respects his argument here is a development of the old understanding of Hooker as an Anglican theologian, radically reinterpreting this notion in the light of the new appreciation for the Elizabethan and Jacobean Calvinist or Reformed consensus. Rather than seeing Hooker as a conservative defending the establishment *via media*, Lake sees him as an innovator, profoundly remodelling the conformist[9] arguments of such men as John Whitgift and John Bridges to reflect the Church's Catholic heritage, and so forging a new theological synthesis that eventually became Anglicanism. Lake even goes so far as to call Hooker the inventor of Anglicanism, though he observes that Hooker must be seen as giving voice to lines of theological movement that were quietly present in late sixteenth-century England.[10] He unequivocally sees this proto-Anglicanism as a hostile response to the dominant Calvinist theology of the day, and all the significant points he makes about Hooker's theology in

[8] See e.g. Booty, *Reflections on the Theology of Richard Hooker*, esp. 111, 158; Philip B. Secor, *Richard Hooker: Prophet of Anglicanism* (Tunbridge Wells, 1999), 220, 244, 298, 302, 305.

[9] For the use of the term 'conformist', see A Note on Religious Terminology.

[10] See Lake, *Anglicans and Puritans?*, 225–9.

this study are seen as antagonistic to views widely held by Calvinist writers. Lake considers Hooker's theology in breadth as well as depth, so the list of these points is a long one. It encompasses, in particular, a relatively benign view of original sin, and a high estimation of human abilities, leading to the belief that humans can work with grace to merit salvation, and to perform works of supererogation for a specific heavenly reward. Contrition is seen as important for claiming Christ's merits, and Lake goes so far as to speculate that in his opposition on various fronts to Calvinist doctrines of predestination, Hooker may have accepted that election occurred on the basis of foreseen merits. The capacities of human reason are also emphasized rather than denied, especially as regards the validation and interpretation of Holy Scripture, in contrast to the characteristically Calvinist belief that the Holy Spirit has a primacy in these activities that quite displaces reason. Lake also argues that Hooker had a positive evaluation of ceremonies, rituals, and prayer that set him quite at odds with Calvinist theology, and that he consequently placed less emphasis on the role of sermons, so focal to Calvinist piety.[11] Various subsidiary arguments might also be adumbrated, but this is the core of Lake's complex view of Hooker in *Anglicans and Puritans?*, and what constitutes Hooker's claim to have been the inventor of Anglicanism. It gives to Hooker a role of tremendous significance in the history of the English Church, but in the context of current concerns about Anglican identity, it also makes him a fiercely contentious figure.

Lake's work has been well received in certain quarters, but few writers have attempted a further exploration of this conception of Hooker.[12] With the exception of highly traditional studies, this has rather left the ground open for those critics who view Hooker in an entirely different light, and who argue that if Elizabethan England was a time of Reformed consensus, then Hooker should indeed be seen as a defender of the orthodox values of his day.

[11] Ibid. 145–97.

[12] But see e.g. W. Speed Hill, Review of Peter Lake, *Anglicans and Puritans? Presbyterian and English Conformist Thought from Whitgift to Hooker*, *Seventeenth-Century News* 47 (1989), 39–40; Debora Shuger, ' "Society Supernatural": The Imagined Community of Hooker's *Lawes*', in C. McEachen and D. Shuger (eds.), *Religion and Culture in Renaissance England* (Cambridge, 1997), 136; P. G. Stanwood, 'Richard Hooker's Discourse and the Deception of Posterity' in N. Rhodes (ed.), *English Renaissance Prose: History, Language and Politics* (Tempe, Ariz., 1997), 77.

Unlike in the case of Lake, no one critic has been the definitive initiator of this understanding of Hooker, but Dewey D. Wallace's *Puritans and Predestination: Grace in English Protestant Theology, 1525–1695* contains a highly formative assessment of Hooker in this light, and is an appropriate place to begin. Drawing on earlier studies, and placing particular emphasis on the early tractates and sermons, Wallace regards Hooker as a theologian whose views differed in various respects from many of his English contemporaries, but were not such as to take him outside of the bounds of the Reformed tradition.[13] He mentions in connection with this three areas where Hooker has been seen in the past as differing from Reformed theology; namely his sacramentalism and his doctrines of predestination and justification.[14] Wallace accepts that Hooker placed a greater emphasis upon sacramental piety, ritual, and tradition than most of his fellow Englishmen, but unlike Lake in *Anglicans and Puritans?* observes that 'it is difficult to see that he departed from the formulations of Calvin regarding them', given the sacramental aspects of Calvin's own theology. With respect to predestination, Wallace bases his view on an article by Michael T. Malone, which argues that Hooker's ideas on this subject were semi-Calvinist and semi-Arminian.[15] Both these conclusions have been broadly affirmed in the more extensive recent studies of W. David Neelands (which contains the finest discussion to date of Hooker and predestination) and Bryan D. Spinks.[16] Finally, Wallace cites a study by C. F. Allison which argues, somewhat obliquely, that Hooker's theory of justification

[13] See Wallace, *Puritans and Predestination*, 76–7, 219. See also Gerald R. Cragg, *Freedom and Authority: A Study of English Thought in the Early Seventeenth Century* (Philadelphia, 1975), 98–100.

[14] Richard Bauckham also identifies Hooker's sacramentalism and his doctrines of predestination and justification as the pre-eminent areas in which Hooker's thought was characterized by the development of essentially Calvinist ideas. See Richard Bauckham, 'Richard Hooker and John Calvin: A Comment', *The Journal of Ecclesiastical History* 32 (1981), 33. See also P. D. L. Avis, 'Richard Hooker and John Calvin', *The Journal of Ecclesiastical History* 32 (1981), 19–28; Peter White, 'The *Via Media* in the Early Stuart Church', in K. Fincham (ed.), *The Early Stuart Church, 1603–1642* (Basingstoke, 1993), 214.

[15] See Michael T. Malone, 'The Doctrine of Predestination in the Thought of William Perkins and Hooker', *Anglican Theological Review* 52 (1970), 117.

[16] See W. David Neelands, 'The Theology of Grace of Richard Hooker', D.Th. thesis, Trinity College and the University of Toronto (1988), 134–290; Spinks, *Two Faces of Elizabethan Anglican Theology*, 109–75.

by faith alone was thoroughly Calvinist.[17] This conclusion has also been ringingly endorsed in a more recent and more analytical study: Alister E. McGrath's *Justitia Dei: A History of the Christian Doctrine of Justification.* As its title suggests, this well-known book does a good deal more than discuss Hooker's theology, and McGrath's treatment is naturally confined to this one subject. Yet it would be hard to underestimate the significance of McGrath's short study, as in a little over a page he makes out a strong case that Hooker's views on justification were similar to those of Luther and Calvin.[18] Given the centrality of the issue in late sixteenth-century theology, this is powerful evidence indeed of the overall cast of Hooker's theology, and squares poorly with Lake's views on merit and human co-operation with God, especially as Lake does not consider Hooker's theory of justification. The significance of all this for an understanding of the early Church of England is far from lost on McGrath, who goes on to be sharply critical of John Henry Newman's attempts to construct an Anglican *via media* over justification, pointing out how thoroughly Reformed the early Church of England theologians were over this matter.[19]

Lake's understanding of Hooker in *Anglicans and Puritans?* has been addressed more directly by other recent critics, most notably W. J. Torrance Kirby and Nigel Atkinson.[20] Their contention is that Hooker set out to defend the 'magisterial' or 'orthodox' Reformed consensus against radical groups such as the puritans, who had distorted the English Church's Reformed heritage. In the nineteenth century, however, Hooker was appropriated by the Oxford Movement as a defender of an Anglican *via media* that was falsely projected back into the past, and it is only in recent years, they argue, that it has been possible to separate him from such

[17] See C. F. Allison, *The Rise of Moralism: The Proclamation of the Gospel from Hooker to Baxter* (London, 1966), 3, 201. See also Philip E. Hughes, *Faith and Works: Cranmer and Hooker on Justification* (Wilton, Conn., 1982), 44.

[18] See Alister E. McGrath, *Iustitia Dei: A History of the Christian Doctrine of Justification*, 2nd edn. (Cambridge, 1998), 291–3, 297, 313.

[19] See McGrath, *Iustitia Dei*, 308–21.

[20] See W. J. Torrance Kirby, *Richard Hooker's Doctrine of the Royal Supremacy* (Leiden, 1990); 'Richard Hooker as an Apologist of the Magisterial Reformation in England', *RHCCC*, 220–32; 'Richard Hooker's Theory of Natural Law in the Context of Reformation Theology', *Sixteenth Century Journal* 30 (1999), 681–703; Nigel Atkinson, *Richard Hooker and the Authority of Scripture, Tradition and Reason.*

historical accretions. Both writers explicitly discuss questions of human nature, reason, original sin, and merit, comparing Hooker's work with major Reformers such as Calvin, Luther, Bullinger, and Melanchthon. Their conclusions are, of course, wholly different from those of Lake, and indeed Atkinson is openly critical of Lake's *Anglicans and Puritans?*. For Atkinson the reinterpretation of Hooker is evidently part of a wider agenda, in that he sees it in terms of a reclamation of the English Church's Reformed heritage, which is also an appropriation of its present theological role and position. Other writers, such as Spinks, have also attempted to gain insight into Anglican identity through the reinterpretation of Hooker, but have argued less radically that in seeing him as a Reformed writer we come to appreciate the divided nature of the English Church, which has important Reformed as well as Catholic roots.[21] In either case, however, the Hooker here described is really quite at odds with the proto-Laudian Anglican depicted in Lake's *Anglicans and Puritans?*.

Lake has now modulated his position as a result of this recent criticism. He continues to argue, as in *Anglicans and Puritans?*, that Hooker in the *Lawes* made a radical attack on a broad series of beliefs and practices that were central to Elizabethan Reformed or Calvinist theology. He emphasizes, however, the breadth and diversity of the Reformed tradition, which must be carefully distinguished from this tradition as it was localized in the English Church. As a result, he accepts the argument made by Kirby amongst others that 'the sources for much of Hooker's thought were thoroughly Reformed', and while he continues to define Hooker as a forerunner of Laudianism and Arminianism he is now content to describe Hooker's thought as 'in some sense "Reformed" '.[22]

Kirby and Atkinson have also opened up another, though closely related, avenue in the Reformed reinterpretation of Hooker, by looking at the vital question of religious authority. The traditional Anglican view of Hooker on this subject, which is still very widely accepted, is that Hooker upheld the joint authority of scripture, reason, and tradition in religious matters, in that order. Lake does not discuss this matter explicitly, but in his remarks on the relation

[21] See n. 5 above.

[22] See Peter Lake, 'Business as Usual? The Immediate Reception of Hooker's *Ecclesiastical Polity*', *Journal of Ecclesiastical History* 52 (2001), 469, 484–5.

of reason to scripture in *Anglicans and Puritans?* he does nothing to suggest that this view is in need of modification. Kirby and Atkinson, however, argue that scripture is alone a religious authority for Hooker in matters of Christian doctrine, firmly identifying him with the Reformed (and indeed more generally Protestant) principle of *sola scriptura*.[23] Atkinson indeed goes so far as to identify Hooker with the concomitant Reformed notion that Holy Scripture is self-authenticating on the internal witness of the Holy Spirit.[24] If this is correct then this is yet further strong evidence of the overall Reformed tenor of Hooker's theology, as it would distance him thoroughly from what is often seen by proponents of the view of Anglicanism as a *via media* between Roman Catholicism and Reformed Protestantism as the central tenet of Anglican self-understanding.

It would, though, be a mistake to see in the present Reformed understanding of Hooker a total break with earlier twentieth-century criticism. The clearest precursor of such writers as Kirby and Atkinson is the little-known Robert Kavanagh, whose 1944 doctoral thesis went unpublished and consequently little read. Most unusually for his day, Kavanagh aligns Hooker closely with Reformed theology, and above all with Calvin, on such topics as human nature, grace, merit, and natural law. He particularly stresses Hooker's conception of the total depravity of the human reason and will, which are redeemed, for Christians, only by divine grace, and so enabled to function aright.[25] Kavanagh's ideas entered the mainstream through the work of Egil Grislis, yet in this process they underwent a subtle but significant change. Grislis retains the idea that Hooker accepted the total depravity of human nature, which can be redeemed for Christians only by divine grace. Yet while Grislis argues that Hooker was grounded in Reformed theology, especially that of Calvin, he for the most part portrays Hooker as a *via media* figure, rather than as wholeheartedly

[23] See Kirby, 'Richard Hooker as an Apologist of the Magisterial Reformation in England', 227, 230; 'Richard Hooker's Theory of Natural Law in the Context of Reformation Theology', 702–3; Atkinson, *Richard Hooker and the Authority of Scripture, Tradition and Reason*, esp. 92–3.

[24] See Atkinson, *Richard Hooker and the Authority of Scripture, Tradition and Reason*, 93, 108.

[25] See Robert Kavanagh, 'Reason and Nature in Hooker's Polity' (Ph.D. thesis, Univ. of Wisconsin, 1944), 78, 86–104, 159, 164.

Reformed.[26] Critics who have been influenced by Grislis in these matters have tended to retain this portrait of Hooker's theological position,[27] with the consequence that it is only in the recent work of Kirby and Atkinson that ideas truly close to Kavanagh's have again become current. None the less, one can see in this process that the conception of Hooker as, at least in part, a Reformed theologian, has a long history, stretching well back into the early twentieth century, and as MacCulloch has shown, dating back in fact to the early seventeenth century. Perhaps one should conclude from this that if Lake's picture in *Anglicans and Puritans?* of Hooker as a proto-Laudian Anglican draws on much older studies of Hooker as an opponent of Reformed theology, writers such as Wallace, McGrath, Kirby, Atkinson, and perhaps now Lake himself, also have behind them a not inconsiderable critical tradition, identifying Hooker with Reformed theology.

One point on which most recent writers are now agreed, it is clear, is that the significance of Hooker's theology, for both the Elizabethan and Jacobean Church, and through that to the Church of England today, is undoubtedly to be assessed in relation to Reformed theology. Whether Hooker was a theologian of the Reformed tradition, or whether he constructed his theology in hostile reaction to Reformed theology, it is now accepted as essential that his views be related to what was the mainstream religious tradition in the England of his day. This is an approach strongly endorsed by this study, which will attempt, in its exploration of Hooker's complex relationship with Reformed theology, to understand why Hooker should have elicited such diverse responses on this issue. It will be contended that the most satisfactory interpretation of Hooker is a synthesis between these opposing views, for both contain in them much that is true about Hooker's theology.

[26] See Egil Grislis, 'Richard Hooker's Image of Man', *Renaissance Papers 1963*. (The Southeastern Renaissance Conference, 1964), 75–84; 'The Role of *Consensus* in Richard Hooker's Method of Theological Inquiry', in R. E. Cushman and E. Grislis (eds.), *The Heritage of Christian Thought: Essays in Honor of Robert Lowry Calhoun* (New York, 1965), 70–8; 'The Hermeneutical Problem in Richard Hooker', in W. S. Hill (ed.), *Studies in Richard Hooker: Essays Preliminary to an Edition of his Works* (Cleveland, 1972), 165–78; 'The Assurance of Faith According to Richard Hooker', *RHCCC* 246, 249.

[27] See e.g. Robert K. Faulkner, 'Reason and Revelation in Hooker's Ethics', *The American Political Science Review* 59 (1965), 681, 688, 690; Paul E. Forte, 'The Achievement of Richard Hooker, 1554–1600' (Ph.D. thesis, State Univ. of New York at Buffalo, 1980), 175, 177, 209, 211; 'Richard Hooker's Theory of Law', *The Journal of Medieval and Renaissance Studies* 12 (1982), 144–5.

In particular, by understanding the development of Hooker's religious ideas, many of these problems can be unwoven. At the last analysis, however, this book will side heavily with Lake's approach to Hooker in *Anglicans and Puritans?*, for while it is in need of revision and elaboration, it is nevertheless broadly accurate in its portrait of his theology, and indeed of its general significance in relation to the Reformed tradition.

The rich diversity of approaches to Hooker here described requires some explanation, and this is probably to be found as much in the nature of Hooker's literary output, as in a study of the critics themselves. One problem that has not infrequently clouded Hooker scholarship is that critics usually assume that his theology did not develop significantly over time. Reference may be made, perhaps, to his more conciliatory attitude to the Roman Catholic Church in the *Lawes*, as opposed to his earlier writings, but nothing that would suggest a more profound change. Even the old theory, now largely discredited, that Hooker's definition of law in Book 1 of the *Lawes* does not tally with his use of the concept in the last three books, did not assume that Hooker changed his mind, but rather that he was guilty of rhetorical guile. Yet not all critics have viewed Hooker in this way. John Keble, for instance, was sufficiently embarrassed by the Reformed nature of Hooker's opinions on election in *The First Sermon Upon Part of S. Judes Epistle* that he questioned its authenticity, and remarked that if it were genuine, as is now accepted, it must be seen as a work of his youth.[28] More recently, Richard Bauckham has commented on Hooker's 'theological development' away from certain aspects of Calvinist theology, and Patrick Collinson has observed that: 'Hooker started off in the mainstream and subsequently diverted from it'.[29] As this study will show, there is, in fact, a complex process of development across the breadth of his work, and it is vital that the reader be aware of this if Hooker's theology is to be properly appreciated. Critics who assume that Hooker's remarks in one of his writings are representative of his views as a whole need to be careful to ensure that he did not take a different

[28] See John Keble, Editor's Preface, in Richard Hooker, *The Workes of . . . Mr. Richard Hooker*, 7th edn., ed. J. Keble, rev. R. W. Church and F. Paget (Oxford, 1888), vol. i. lv–lvi.

[29] See Richard Bauckham, 'Hooker, Travers and the Church of Rome in the 1580s', *Journal of Ecclesiastical History* 29 (1978), 37; Patrick Collinson, 'Hooker and the Elizabethan Establishment', *RHCCC* 154–6.

approach elsewhere. On no topic can this be more plainly seen than that of justification, where critics have almost invariably analysed the early tractates, and completely ignored his later writings; a serious oversight that will be explored in detail in Ch. 4. Plainly, then, excerpts from Hooker's work need to be seen in the context in which they were written, and individual works in the context of his output as a whole. This approach may seem self-evident, but it has been adopted all too seldom by Hooker's commentators. Yet it is not only a lack of sensitivity to context and development that has caused problems in interpreting Hooker. His work contains discussions of numerous complex theoretical issues, for he was fond of analysing the fundamental theological and philosophical principles underlying the specific topics with which he was concerned. In this he showed himself a good son of medieval scholasticism. Yet although it is now widely recognized that scholastic ideas were embraced by many Reformed writers,[30] their acceptance in the sixteenth century was qualified, and depended very much on the purpose for which they were used. The scholastic predestinarianism of Beza and William Perkins, for instance, should by no means be taken as implying that medieval scholasticism had been completely rehabilitated in Reformed theology. Hooker was careful not to develop scholastic ideas too extensively in the *Lawes*, but he was still accused in a contemporary publication of burying the Gospel under pagan philosophy.[31] As it is, Hooker tends to mention highly important scholastic concepts in a most abbreviated form, sometimes so obliquely that the reference is easily lost. He thus avoids some of the more technical aspects of scholastic philosophy, but in so doing his views can be difficult to grasp, and extensive analysis and cross-comparisons can be necessary to establish his views. Yet above and beyond all this, there can be no doubt that Hooker is most obscure in expressing his ideas on certain subjects. His lack of elaboration about grace in the *Lawes*, for instance, has caused critics to look to his late manuscripts for clarification about his opinions on this issue. Yet although he discusses grace at length in these papers, it can scarcely be said that he does so with perfect clarity. Such complications compound together to make Hooker a difficult writer to

[30] See Charles B. Schmitt, *John Case and Aristotelianism in Renaissance England* (Kingston, 1983), 61–76.

[31] See *ACL* 4: 64–71.

master, and do much towards explaining the controversies that beset his work. Perhaps it is not so wholly surprising when these problems are considered, that Lake, McGrath, Kirby, and Atkinson, amongst many others, have disagreed so profoundly about the very nature of Hooker's theology.

Such textual difficulties make it particularly important that the reader has a general grasp of the whole range of Hooker's literary output. It seems highly desirable, therefore, now to undertake such a general survey, and to describe in brief the nature and historical context of each of his works. Hooker's writing falls into three distinct categories—tractates and sermons, the *Lawes*, and manuscript responses to attacks on the *Lawes*—respectively published in vol. v, vols. i–iii, and vol. iv of the Folger Library Edition. Hooker's surviving sermons, and tractates based on sermons, number only ten, and three of these are mere fragments. The great majority of the sermons that he would have written in his ministerial charges have simply not survived. The *Two Sermons Upon Part of S. Judes Epistle* probably date from 1582 or 1583, when he was still at Corpus Christi College in Oxford pursuing his quite successful academic career.[32] Only three of the others can be dated with any certainty, but they are the most important of this collection, coming from 1585–6, in the first two years of Hooker's fateful tenancy of the Mastership of Temple Church, ministering to the influential lawyers of Middle and Inner Temple.[33] These works, *A Learned and Comfortable Sermon of the Certaintie and Perpetuitie of Faith in the Elect, A Learned Discourse of Justification, Workes, and How the Foundation of Faith Is Overthrowne*, and *A Learned Sermon of the Nature of Pride*, served in part to provoke Hooker's fellow minister at the Temple, Walter Travers, into the controversy that eventually came before the Privy Council and the then Archbishop of Canterbury, John Whitgift. Travers was one of the most prominent presbyterians in the Church of his day, second only to Thomas Cartwright in authority and influence.[34] As is well

[32] On the date of these sermons, see Laetitia Yeandle, 'Textual Introduction: *Two Sermons Upon S. Judes Epistle*', *Folger*, v. 1–3.

[33] See Laetitia Yeandle, 'Textual Introduction: *A Learned and Comfortable Sermon of the Certaintie and Perpetuitie of Faith in the Elect*', *Folger*, v. 59; 'Textual Introduction: *A Learned Discourse of Justification, Workes, and How the Foundation of Faith Is Overthrowne*', *Folger*, v. 83; 'Textual Introduction: *A Learned Sermon of the Nature of Pride*', *Folger*, v. 299.

[34] For an account of the controversy, see Egil Grislis, 'Introduction to Commentary', *Folger*, v. 641–8. For remarks on the use of the term 'presbyterian', see A Note on Religious Terminology.

known, he had applied for the position of Master himself on Richard Alvey's demise, having previously been taken on as a reader to support the ailing incumbent. As the Temple Church is a royal peculiar, Whitgift could not personally reject the appointment of Travers, whose presbyterianism and general advanced Protestantism did not endear him to the Archbishop. Whitgift did, however, lobby the Queen on behalf of his own candidate, Nicholas Bond, one of her personal chaplains; Travers gained the powerful support of William Cecil, and so eventually the little-known Hooker was appointed as a compromise option. Many of the congregation, however, liked Travers and his advanced views, so he was retained as reader to be a thorn in Hooker's side. The three surviving sermons/tractates of these years contain discussions on assurance, grace, and Roman Catholicism that Travers found highly unorthodox, even heretical. He criticized Hooker's theories in his own afternoon sermons, and for such unruliness lost his post as reader, but his appeal to the privy council forced Whitgift to adjudicate between the theological differences of the two men. Various documents survive from these proceedings, including Hooker's reply to Travers's defence of himself to the Privy Council, *Master Hookers Answer to the Supplication that Master Travers made to the Counsell.* The papers show that Whitgift was far from fully vindicating Hooker, especially as regards Hooker's lenient attitude to the salvation of Roman Catholics, but his support was sufficient to leave Hooker in sole charge of the Temple Church.

Hooker left the Temple Church in 1591, and although he held ecclesiastical appointments at Salisbury cathedral, Netheravon, and Boscombe, these appear to have been largely absentee: in all probability Hooker was based in London up until 1595, working on his *magnum opus, Of the Lawes of Ecclesiasticall Politie.* As modern research has shown, financial and other pressures forced Hooker to publish the work in parts: the preface and Books 1–4 in 1593 and Book 5 in 1597, while the last three books made it into print only long after his death: Books 6 and 8 in 1648, and Book 7 finally in 1662.[35] The last three books are unfinished, or perhaps rather incomplete; there is good evidence that Hooker did finish them, perhaps as early as 1593, although he may well have continued

[35] On the early publishing history of the *Lawes*, and the textual problems presented by the various books, see *Folger*, vi.

revising them up until his death in 1600. Certainly much of Book 6 has been lost, as autograph notes by two of Hooker's former students on what was clearly a more extensive version of the book show.[36] None the less, the surviving *Lawes* is a coherent whole, which develops a carefully focused argument from start to finish. A general summary of its contents, however, requires first some comment on the literary context of the work. As any reader acquainted with anything more than brief excerpts from these books should be aware, the *Lawes* is a controversial work, plainly designed to rebut the theological arguments of Thomas Cartwright and Walter Travers, both specifically as regards presbyterianism, and more generally as regards a spectrum of broadly puritan religious positions. Thus the *Lawes* is concerned with far more than Church discipline, but also with such matters as the relationship of reason and revelation, the concept of the Christian Church, and the justification for Church of England rituals and practices, among much else besides. It is but a part, although by far the most enduring, of the Admonitions controversy, which has long been the province of the historical specialist. The controversy has been capably discussed by a number of recent writers, and there is no need to enlarge upon the subject here.[37] Suffice to say that from the publication of the original anonymous *An Admonition to Parliament* in 1572, attacking episcopacy and various perceived abuses in the Church, the controversy widened into a series of theological exchanges between Cartwright, who defended the *Admonition*, and Whitgift. The *Lawes* is in many respects a development of Whitgift's arguments against Cartwright, though just how radical that development was depends upon which critics one believes. For Kirby and Atkinson, for instance, for whom the *Lawes* is an attack on puritan theology from the perspective of Reformed orthodoxy, that development is presumably to be seen in terms of Hooker's greater sophistication; Whitgift was himself, after all, a thoroughly Reformed theologian. For Lake, however, Cartwright and Travers are in some respects foils to Hooker's larger objective: he views the *Lawes* in *Anglicans and Puritans?* as: 'a sort of sleight

[36] See Arthur S. McGrade, 'Introduction: The Last Three Books and Hooker's Autograph Notes', *Folger*, vi. 233–47.

[37] See e.g. Lake, *Anglicans and Puritans?*; M. E. C. Perrott, 'Richard Hooker and the Problem of Authority in the Elizabethan Church', *The Journal of Ecclesiastical History* 49 (1998), 29–45.

of hand whereby what amounted to a full-scale attack on Calvinist piety was passed off as a simple exercise in anti-presbyterianism'.[38] Thus although it is easy for critics to agree on the anti-presbyterianism of the *Lawes*, its ultimate purpose remains highly contentious. For the reader largely unfamiliar with the *Lawes*, the following highly condensed overview may serve as a basic introduction. Yet this goes little way to establishing the final significance of Hooker's great work, which will be dealt with again only very much later in this book.

The preface to the *Lawes* contains a strongly polemical attack on presbyterians, and puritans within the English Church more generally, while Book 1 contains a general discussion of Hooker's first principles, especially as concerns the nature of law. Through developing the argument that humans are governed by a diversity of different laws, in Book 2 he attempts to rebut the charge that Holy Scripture is the sole repository of divinely sanctioned laws for human action. Book 3 then extends this into an attack on the notion that Holy Scripture describes the only divinely sanctioned discipline to be used within the Christian Church. Books 4 and 5 are concerned with rituals and ceremonies used within the English Church: Book 4 defends, in general terms, practices also used by Roman Catholics from the charge that they are tainted with popery and should therefore necessarily be abandoned, while the huge fifth book examines such rituals and ceremonies on an individual and comprehensive basis. In the last three books Hooker turns his attention to specific questions of Church discipline, developing the more general arguments he has made in the earlier volumes. The sixth book contains little of the discussion of Church elders that Hooker evidently did pen, and now consists mostly of a somewhat peripheral discussion of repentance. Book 7 deals with episcopacy, leaving the final book to discuss the politically contentious issue of the English monarch's headship of the Church. The *Lawes* is thus, as modern critics are fond of pointing out, not a theological *summa*, either of Reformed or supposedly 'Anglican' opinions. It is a book with a specific polemical purpose, even if enigmatically part of that purpose remains unclear.

The third category of Hooker's writing dates from the last two years of his life, before his death after a short illness in 1600. He

[38] See Lake, *Anglicans and Puritans?*, 239.

was then minister of Bishopsbourne in Kent, a position he occupied from 1595 onwards. In 1599, a tract entitled *A Christian Letter* was published anonymously, attacking Books 1–5 of the *Lawes*, and accusing Hooker of holding opinions contrary to the Thirty-Nine Articles. Hooker's copy of this tract survives in Corpus Christi College, Oxford, including his own autograph notes, and these make for interesting reading. He then started to prepare a defence of his published work, which now resides in manuscript in Trinity College, Dublin, but which he did not live to complete. He made a series of notes to answer the *Christian Letter* as regards the subject of predestination, as seems to have been his usual practice when writing the *Lawes*, and then wrote parts of a draft of the defence itself, now known as the *Dublin Fragments*.[39] The significance of these works is twofold. First, Hooker was forced to elaborate on various aspects of the *Lawes* where his views were considered to be heretical by the *Christian Letter*, and this is obviously of great interest to the Hooker scholar. Some critics now give almost more weight to what Hooker says in these fragments than to the *Lawes* itself, on the grounds that Hooker is here giving his final and expanded views on the important subjects concerned. Secondly, these manuscripts contain the last surviving works of Hooker's pen, after a writing career spanning some seventeen or eighteen years, from the age of 28 to 46. One would expect to find some development in Hooker's theological opinions over such a span of years, and what may be fairly termed his 'late' writings are immensely valuable in what they say about his views in the two years prior to his death.

Bearing in mind the complexities inherent in Hooker's writing, and the nature and context of each of his works, we may now return to consider the points of contention in the recent debates about his theology. Looking at the criticism of McGrath, Lake, Kirby, and Atkinson in particular, we have so far singled out the following issues as being of central importance: the capacities of human reason and will, including the extent to which humans are free in their actions; the relationship of humans to God, especially through divine grace; the nature of justification; and the religious authority of scripture, reason, and tradition. Of these, the most important from a modern-day standpoint is probably the question

[39] See John E. Booty, 'Introduction', *Folger*, vol. iv. pp. xxviii–xxxviii.

of authority, as this crucial matter continues to act as a radical divide between different Christian groupings. Yet all these issues, more or less directly, revolve around the central problem of human nature—of what it is to be human—and of how humans relate to God. Problems of authority arise because humans are perceived to have difficulty in accessing divine truth. Yet the wellspring of this difficulty is the sinfulness of human nature, and in particular (from the perspective of scholastic psychology) the capacities, or incapacities, of the human will and reason. The same may be said of justification, especially as regards questions of merit or demerit; people require divine salvation, in whatever form it takes, because of their nature as sinful human beings. In assessing human nature from a Christian standpoint, however, it is vital to examine how humans relate to God, due to the belief that human behaviour, and human nature itself, can be modified or transformed by divine grace. Grace works to help achieve for humans ends that they would not otherwise obtain, even if these ends are not necessarily salvific. One of the key questions in sixteenth-century theology was the extent to which humans are capable of performing specific actions with or without God's aid; of whether, in fact, humans have any merit for the good deeds that they perform. This is precisely to enquire into the manner in which human reason, human will, and divine grace relate to one another. This book is written in the belief that these three areas are the most important for understanding Hooker's theology, and for resolving many of the controversies that beset Hooker scholarship today. They are a cluster of problems fundamental to Christian theology as a discipline, and this demonstrates that Hooker was concerned with far more than a series of obscure disputes relevant only to late sixteenth-century England. In this respect it is perhaps fitting that critics have argued over the general tenor of Hooker's theology, as being hostile to Reformed theology or in fact Reformed, for Hooker was at heart concerned with questions of such an overarching nature.

It will be noticed that two other areas in which Hooker's relation to Reformed theology has attracted comment in recent years have been left out of the previous paragraph: his doctrine of predestination (in which he was probably notionally situated somewhere between Calvin and Arminius) and his sacramentalism. Without denying the significance of these subjects, they will not be examined further, since they are not in themselves primarily concerned with the relationship between reason, will, and grace that forms the focus of this study. They are, of course, intimately related to reason, will, and grace in a secondary sense, for instance because predestination raises questions of human freedom and the efficacy of grace, and sacramentalism is closely concerned with the graces that are associated with the sacraments. None the less, in these instances, it is human freedom, the efficacy of grace, and the nature of sacramental graces that are the proper objects of this study, and not predestination and sacramentalism themselves. Reference will, however, be made to the work of critics in these areas in the course of the final concluding assessment of Hooker's relation to Reformed theology.

If one is to tackle these issues, it is wise to shadow Hooker's own methodology in the *Lawes*, for he appreciated the great value of mapping out philosophical first principles before discussing specific theological problems. Given that we wish to understand Hooker's attitude to human nature, and to a series of closely related questions, it is vital first to examine his philosophy of mind and action; for this is precisely how Hooker proceeded himself, in Book I of the *Lawes*. The philosophical principles that he adumbrates in this initial volume have fundamental ramifications for his theology in the *Lawes* as a whole, for he sets out there his view of how the human mind operates. Chapters 1 and 2, in the first part of this volume, will, therefore, analyse respectively Hooker's philosophy of mind and his philosophy of action, not merely in the *Lawes*, but in his work as a whole. While these issues may at times seem highly technical and abstract, it should be borne in mind that they are of central relevance to the discussion that is to follow.

The second part of this volume will then examine how human nature, and specifically the human reason and will, relate to divine grace. This discussion is split into three broad parts. As one would expect of a sixteenth-century theologian, Hooker makes a radical distinction between grace as it relates to Christians and to non-Christians. The difficult problem of reprobate Christians is never really discussed in detail in his work, and we need not be concerned with it here. In this context, Christians are distinguished by the fact that they receive the graces of justification and sanctification, which have a profound impact on human nature and how God and humans relate to one another. By exploring Hooker's views on non-Christians, however, who lack such transforming graces, it is easier to examine his attitude to unredeemed human nature, and so to explore such issues as original sin, and the corruption of the human will and reason. Many of the scholarly debates on these subjects can be resolved by an adequate understanding of Hooker's views on the relationship between the Holy Spirit and non-Christians, and this will be the focus of the third chapter of this volume.

The fourth chapter will concentrate on the reason and the will of (elect) Christians, examining at first Hooker's theories of justification and sanctification. This will provide an opportunity for a discussion of the critical controversies surrounding these issues, and above all of the disagreement between Lake, McGrath, Kirby, and Atkinson over the contentious subject of merit. From there the chapter will move on to examine Hooker's views on the operations of the Holy Spirit more generally, as this is a question central to an understanding of the *Lawes*, and to Lake's Hooker criticism. By looking at how reason, will, and grace interact with each other as regards the verification and interpretation of Holy Scripture, one comes to the polemical heart of Hooker's theology, which provides a perfect springboard for a final discussion of his views on the religious authority of scripture, reason, and tradition.

Each of these four chapters will draw on the whole range of Hooker's writing, though with an eye to the specific context of individual passages, and to any developments in Hooker's theology over the course of time. An important exception will, however, be made in the case of the 'late' works, which have never really received the kind of careful analysis that they require, especially the difficult and ambiguous first essay of the *Dublin Fragments*. Where the matter of grace is concerned, it is not helpful at this present time if they are discussed alongside all the other works of Hooker's pen. Apart, therefore, from the general philosophical questions examined in Part I, and certain other areas, such as justification and sanctification, where it is also felt that the interpretative issues are not so clouded, these writings will be examined only in the fifth, and final, chapter. In this way this volume will close with a discussion of Hooker's most mature theological opinions on reason, will, and grace, as articulated in manuscript in the last two years of his life.

Hooker's writings give the impression that he was an essentially conservative person, nostalgic for the past and suspicious of change, even while at the same time he was deeply committed to some of the radical developments brought about by the Reformation. The tensions that resulted from this uneasy combination can be seen in the evolution of his approach to Reformed theology, the tradition that he was schooled in by his tutor at Corpus Christi College, the famous puritan divine, John Rainolds. As the recent scholarly debates have made abundantly clear, Hooker's theology must be understood in relation to the dominant theological tradition of his day. Much of the analysis in this study will, therefore, be thoroughly comparative in nature, and the second part in particular will attempt to trace, in this relationship, the growth of Hooker's own distinctive theological stance. For it is only when the full complexity of his relation to Reformed theology is appreciated that it becomes possible to resolve many of the recent critical controversies, and indeed to do justice to Hooker, as a conservative who paradoxically came to occupy a remarkably individual, innovative position, at a time of transition in the English Church.

Part I

Reason and Will

And if any complaine of obscuritie, they must consider, that in these matters it commeth no otherwise to passe then in sundry the workes both of art and also of nature, where that which hath greatest force in the very things we see, is notwithstanding it selfe oftentimes not seene. The statelinesse of houses, the goodlines of trees, when we behold them delighteth the eye; but that foundation which beareth up the one, that root which ministreth unto the other nourishment and life, is in the bosome of the earth concealed: and if there be at any time occasion to search into it, such labour is then more necessary then pleasant both to them which undertake it, and for the lookers on.

Lawes, 1:57.2–12 (I.1.2)

1
Philosophy of Mind

The topic of this chapter is Hooker's conception of the basic structure and workings of the human mind, or to put the matter somewhat more expansively, of the nature of the human ability to reason, desire, and imagine. Questions of a more applied philosophical and theological orientation, such as how defective human actions result in sin, and how grace interacts with the human mind, will be left to later chapters. For the moment it is necessary to concentrate on more fundamental and abstract problems concerning the human mind, which are central to the nature of Hooker's theology. The understanding of Hooker presented in this book is founded on the arguments made in this chapter; an observation that is equally valid for the *Lawes* as regards its first volume.

Hooker's philosophy of mind was thoroughly scholastic in its orientation, as will become clear from the analysis of his work in this chapter. However much scholastic theories of the mind may differ in points of substance, they tend to share very basic common features, most notably the tendency to see the mind in terms of the interaction of such discrete faculties or powers as the reason, the will, the (sensitive) appetite, and the imagination/fancy. These are but four of the most important faculties/powers out of the many that might be named, and they have other variant English titles (which will be looked at later), but these are the ones that primarily will be concentrated on in this chapter. This is due to the fact that they relate most directly to Hooker's views on human nature, with which we will be concerned in the rest of this book. Hooker's attitude towards other mental faculties or powers, and to other aspects of philosophy of mind will thus not be examined here.

In elaborating his views on the mental faculties[1] that interact in the processes of human thought, Hooker did not in general go

[1] It is unncessary in this context to discuss whether Hooker 'attributed continuous actuality to the soul's powers', and considered them to be separate faculties. For the purposes

into the sort of technical philosophical detail of many of his medieval scholastic predecessors. This is for reasons that, as has been observed, are entirely characteristic of this work. His *magnum opus*, the *Lawes*, despite its comprehensiveness, is not a theological *summa*, and he had to be careful in his presentation of scholastic ideas, which were accepted only to a limited degree in the England of his day, and not by all. As a result many of the scholastic concepts that he does articulate are expressed briefly, and are to some extent scattered throughout his work, needing careful analysis before a detailed overall picture can emerge. In order to facilitate an understanding of his scholastic philosophy of mind, therefore, it is highly desirable to analyse his views alongside those of another scholastic writer, who expresses similar ideas in a more expansive and lucid way. The choice of such a writer is, though, more contentious than it might at first appear. The principal literary source for Hooker's ideas on philosophy of mind would appear to be the most obvious contender, but this merely serves to beg the question. Aristotle was, of course, the ultimate source for many scholastic ideas on the mind, and Hooker certainly quotes him on the topic; but Aristotle was seen through the lens of later scholastic commentators, and it is more appropriate in this context to choose a scholastic writer closer in time to Hooker's own work. It is here that Aquinas recommends himself, as he has been almost universally considered to be the prime source for Hooker's scholasticism since at least the work of A. P. D'Entrèves and Peter Munz earlier last century.[2] Yet the arguments of these scholars connecting Hooker so intimately to Aquinas are quite dubious, in philosophy of mind as in other areas.[3] Munz, for instance, traces

of convenience, however, a faculty-based terminology will be used henceforth. See Katharine Park, 'The Organic Soul', in C. B. Schmitt, Q. Skinner, and E. Kessler (eds.), *The Cambridge History of Renaissance Philosophy* (Cambridge, 1988), 467–8.

[2] See Alexander Passerin D'Entrèves, *The Medieval Contribution to Political Thought* (Oxford, 1939), 117–35; D'Entrèves, *Natural Law. An Introduction to Legal Philosophy* (London, 1951), 64–78; Peter Munz, *The Place of Hooker in the History of Thought* (London, 1952), 46–64, 175–93. For later writers who have compared Hooker's philosophy of mind with that of Aquinas, see most especially: H. F. Kearney, 'Richard Hooker: A Reconstruction', *The Cambridge Journal* 5 (1952), 304–5; Stueber, 'Richard Hooker's Place in the History of Renaissance Christian Humanism', 335–51; Grislis, 'Richard Hooker's Image of Man', 73–5; Neelands, 'The Theology of Grace of Richard Hooker', 120, 301–45; Lee W. Gibbs, 'Introduction: Book I', *Folger*, vi. 105–8.

[3] For strong criticism of the arguments of D'Entrèves, Munz, and others for connecting the views of Aquinas and Hooker on the subjects of rationalism and law, see Nigel Voak,

a whole series of parallels between Book I of the *Lawes* and various writings of Aquinas, but most of these concern scholastic commonplaces that could equally have been culled from the work of many other scholastic writers.[4] That Hooker has been repeatedly compared with Aquinas on these points perhaps says more about the clarity of Aquinas's style and thought, and the accessibility of translations of his work to modern critics, than it necessarily does about Hooker's debt to the great Dominican. When the two writers are compared on anything more than superficial terms, then one is at least as much struck by the differences in their respective philosophies of mind as one is by the similarities. None the less, the accessibility of Aquinas remains a powerful argument for using him in a comparative analysis, and so it is with some reluctance that he will be used in this chapter for that purpose, in two carefully defined ways. As was noted above, scholastic theories of the mind tend to share very basic common features, and as regards these commonplaces it is not particularly crucial which scholastic writer Hooker be compared with. A more extensive examination of Hooker's philosophy of mind would probably seek to compare Hooker with a variety of writers in these areas, but given the limited space available here Aquinas is a very practical choice, as long as the general nature of the comparisons being undertaken is borne in mind. If, however, one scratches below the surface of scholastic philosophy of mind then one rapidly encounters complex philosophical debates, over which there is a great variety of opinion. The only issue where we need pursue matters to this depth regards the faculty of the will, because Hooker's views on this topic set him at odds with many of his contemporaries, and are of the utmost significance from the perspective of this study. Here Hooker differed profoundly from Aquinas, a fact that has not been recognized in the past; though as we shall see, it is another matter to enquire whether Hooker was conscious of this philosophical divide. It is essential that Hooker's views on the will be compared with several different writers, and so Duns Scotus and Calvin have been chosen to supplement Aquinas here. Duns Scotus illustrates the ideas of a

'Reason, Will and Grace in the Works of Richard Hooker' (D.Phil. thesis, Univ. of Oxford, 1998), 51–83.

[4] See Munz, *The Place of Hooker in the History of Thought*, 175–93.

writer near in time to Aquinas, but whose theory of the will is much closer to that of Hooker. Calvin, despite his complex and largely negative attitude to scholasticism, does to some extent adopt a scholastic framework for discussing philosophy of mind, and he has been chosen as he demonstrates the views of an extremely influential Reformed contemporary of Hooker, whose ideas on the will are in certain limited respects a good deal closer to those of Aquinas than they are to those of Hooker and Duns Scotus. The debates between these four writers over the nature of the human will, and what is understood by the notion of human freedom, are at the root of many of the issues with which this book is concerned. It will be seen by the end of this chapter how in his philosophy of mind Hooker fundamentally divided himself from the view of human freedom characteristic of Reformed philosophy and theology in his day, with ramifications that echo through his thought as a whole.

Reason

Thomas Aquinas

We can begin this selective study of the mental faculties by looking at the reason, intellect, or understanding (as this faculty is variously known in English), approaching the basics of Hooker's views by first examining, by way of example, the most general aspects of Aquinas's own theories. Aquinas, in fact, distinguishes between two entirely different powers of the intellect, of which only the receptive intellect (*intellectus possibilis*) need concern us here. The agent intellect (*intellectus agens*) deals with the abstraction of universal ideas from particular sense-experiences, an epistemological issue which we have excluded from our general survey. The receptive intellect is responsible for the ratiocination of these universal ideas, and this is very much to our purpose. Significantly, Aquinas observes that while the agent intellect is an active faculty, having the power to transform sense-experiences, the receptive intellect is passive, having only the power to undergo change as a result of the universal ideas it receives. This has important implications for his views on human liberty, as we shall later see.[5]

[5] See *ST* I.79.2–3; Anthony Kenny, *Aquinas on Mind* (London, 1993), 42–7.

Aquinas divides the operations of the receptive intellect itself into two different categories,[6] the first of which concerns the understanding or apprehension of simple ideas (*intelligentia indivisibilium*). Such simple ideas are generalized abstractions of individual things, and according to Anthony Kenny, correspond roughly to linguistic definitions. For instance, apprehension of the idea of a painting is similar to comprehension of what the word 'painting' signifies.[7] It is fundamental to Aquinas's view of the human mind that there can be no possibility of error in this process of simple apprehension.[8]

The second type of operation concerns the process of reasoning, whereby affirmative and negative judgements (*compositio et divisio*) are made about particular propositions.[9] For example, on seeing a painting in a gallery ascribed to Turner, I might affirm that the painting was indeed by him. It is here, however, that the intellect becomes capable of error; the painting might, for instance, be a forgery.[10] The only exceptions to this rule concerning human error are the first principles of practical and theoretical reasoning, such as that 'the part is smaller than the whole', which Aquinas considers to be habits (*habitus*) of the receptive intellect. As with the apprehension of simple ideas, he argues that the mind cannot be mistaken over such principles, and necessarily assents to these basic truths.[11]

These two types of operation are both concerned with knowing intelligible truth, which is for Aquinas the defining activity of the intellect.[12] It is noteworthy, though, that truth and falsehood are for him interchangeable with good and evil, for as he observes: 'Good and true each include the other. For truth is a good thing, otherwise we would not desire it, and good is something true, otherwise we should not know about it.'[13] This serves to indicate the intrinsically moral nature of the intellect and the reasoning process

[6] See *ST* I.79.8; Kenny, *Aquinas on Mind*, 47. [7] See Kenny, *Aquinas on Mind*, 48.

[8] See *ST* I.85.6.

[9] See ibid. I.85.5: the intellect 'must necessarily either combine one apprehension with another or separate them, or else it must go from one combination or separation to another (which is the process of reasoning)': necessare habet unum apprehensum alii componere vel dividere; et ex una compositione vel divisione ad aliam procedere, quod est ratiocinari.

[10] See ibid. I.85.6. [11] See ibid. I.85.6; I-II.53.1; I-II.57.2. On habits, see p. 70 below.

[12] See *ST* I.79.8.

[13] Ibid. I.79.11 ad. 2: verum et bonum se invicem includunt. Nam verum est quoddam bonum, alioquin non esset appetibile, et bonum est quoddam verum, alioquin non esset intelligibile.

for Aquinas. As Robert Hoopes has argued, Aquinas did not have a concept of the amoral, discursive faculty of modern science:[14] rather, his intellect may be termed 'right reason', a faculty capable of establishing moral truths with as much objective certainty as was then attached to the principles of Euclidean geometry.[15]

Richard Hooker

Hooker's account of the ratiocinative faculty is basically the same as Aquinas's account of the receptive intellect, though it is also characteristically less systematic.[16] Hooker also splits its operations into two categories, as may be seen by looking at two passages where he describes how the function of Holy Scripture is to impart knowledge of Christian doctrine.[17] In these passages he argues that the process by which theologians pursue their enquiries into revealed truth is methodologically no different from that used by philosophers as regards natural truth. In both cases people reason from first principles through to demonstrative conclusions. Yet whereas the natural first principles are self-evident, the principles of faith can only be grasped by someone who accepts the revealed nature of Holy Scripture. Scripture, Hooker notes, leaves 'an *apprehension* of thinges divine in our understandinge', which would seem to be analogous to simple apprehension of the natural world, in that neither can be broken down into simpler units of apprehension. The sentences or propositions of Holy Scripture then function as first principles, which can be used in a similar manner to natural first principles 'to procure our assent unto such conclusions as the industrie of right discorse doth gather from them'. Such 'assent' would logically need to occur after those processes that are for Hooker the distinguishing marks of rationality; the ability to comprehend 'differences of time,

[14] See Robert Hoopes, *Right Reason in the English Renaissance* (Harvard, 1962), esp. 3–4, 73–85.

[15] See Kenny, *Aquinas on Mind*, 56–7. This is, rather inevitably, a highly simplified account of the nature of right reason.

[16] One may note, however, Faulkner's observation that Hooker has no concept of *synderesis* or *synedesis* in his account of the reason. See Faulkner, 'Reason and Revelation in Hooker's Ethics', 685. Hooker also has no equivalent of Aquinas's agent intellect, no doubt due to the fact that his works are not concerned with such issues of epistemology.

[17] See *Lawes*, 2:84.31–85.24 (V.21.3); 2:290.6–31 (V.63.1). See also *Lawes*, 1:229.33–230.2 (III.8.11). For a discussion of the first passage with regard to these operations, see Stueber, 'Richard Hooker's Place in the History of Renaissance Christian Humanism', 368–9.

affirmations, negations, and contradictions in speech'.[18] Hooker's conception of the processes of '*apprehension*' and 'assent' would seem, therefore, to be analogous to Aquinas's notion of *intelligentia indivisibilium* and *compositio et divisio*. The only difference is that whereas Aquinas defines the first principles of natural reasoning as habits of the receptive intellect, Hooker supposes that these principles are grasped by an act of simple '*apprehension*'.[19] This is an illogical move on Hooker's part, and one that will be discussed in detail in Ch. 4, regarding the subject of faith.[20] Hooker does however, like Aquinas, use different terms to describe the ratiocinative faculty in the acts of apprehension and assent; 'the understanding' relates to the act of apprehension, and 'the reason' to the act of assent.[21] These appear to be the equivalent respectively of Aquinas's 'intellect' (*intellectus*) and 'reason' (*ratio*), which are both powers of the receptive intellect.[22]

Both apprehension and assent are evidently for Hooker concerned with the knowledge of intelligible truth.[23] Yet, as with Aquinas, truth and falsehood are for him interchangeable with good and evil. As he observes, 'Goodnesse is seene with the eye of the understanding. And the light of that eye, is reason,' and 'our naturall faculty of reason... [is] able to judge rightly betweene truth and error, good and evill'.[24] Characteristically for his period, therefore, Hooker believed that ethics was an objective science, on

[18] See *Lawes*, 1:75.25–7 (I.6.3).

[19] See ibid. 2:290.23–4 (V.63.1): 'principles of that kinde are apprehended'. Cf. Covel, 'A Just and Temperate Defence', 484.

[20] See pp. 197–9.

[21] See *Lawes*, 1:78.3–4 (I.7.2); 1:80.8–14 (I.7.6); 2:85.5–6 (V.21.3); 2:290.24–5 (V.63.1). Cf. Covel, 'A Just and Temperate Defence', 484. Hooker does not, however, always use these two terms in this technical sense, sometimes for instance using 'understanding' to relate to the act of assent. See e.g. *Lawes*, 2:3.27–4.1 (V.Ded.5).

[22] See *S.T.* I.79.8.

[23] Joseph Devine and W. David Neelands both argue that 'assent' is an act of the will. See Joseph G. Devine, 'Richard Hooker's Doctrine of Justification and Sanctification in the Debate with Walter Travers 1585–1586' (Ph.D. thesis, The Hartford Seminary Foundation, 1976), 275–6; Neelands, 'The Theology of Grace of Richard Hooker', 36–7. This cannot, however, be the case, since 'assent' is an act in which the mind acknowledges something to be true, which is the function of the reason, and not the will. Nevertheless, this error is quite comprehensible, for 'assent' is an act of the reason which does presuppose an act of the will. This relationship is not direct, for otherwise humans would be able to choose what they believe. Rather, the will can direct the reason to concentrate on particular things, and so can have an indirect impact on the reasoning process. When this influence is malign, defective action and/or belief-formation will occur, as is described in the next chapter. See also Kenny, *Aquinas on Mind*, 48–9; Daniel Westberg, *Right Practical Reason: Aristotle, Action, and Prudence in Aquinas* (Oxford, 1994), 200, 254.

[24] See *Lawes*, 1:76.21–3 (I.6.5); 1:78.3–4 (I.7.2). See also ibid. 1:84.11 (I.8.3).

a level with natural scientific enquiry. Thus, as a number of critics have observed before,[25] he evidently considered reason to be a moral instrument, and in fact he uses the term 'right reason' himself to describe its intrinsic nature.[26]

WILL

We must now depart from the level of scholastic commonplace to examine in some depth the views of Hooker, Aquinas, Duns Scotus, and Calvin on the will. A superficial comparison between Hooker and Aquinas on this subject might have noted that both writers assert the existence of this faculty, and associate it, at least in part, with human freedom and the act of choice. This is certainly true, but it is far from being the whole truth, and if we wish to appreciate the significance of Hooker's views on human nature, we need first to know exactly what he understood by the concept of freedom. In order to do this, we must look in detail at his theory of the will, and see it in the context of the ideas of a variety of scholastic opinions on this mental faculty.

Thomas Aquinas

Beginning with the work of Aquinas, it is probably fair to say that there is an inherent problem for some readers in grasping the nature of his views on the will, so counter-intuitive are his rationalist ideas in the light of later voluntarist theories, which came in time to be the dominant scholastic models of the human mind. As we shall see, even later Dominican philosophers who believed they were being faithful to Aquinas often tended to look at his writing through a voluntarist lens, so it is vital to examine his ideas apart from the later pervasive influence of Duns Scotus. When this is done, the distance between the philosophy of mind of Hooker and Aquinas becomes quite starkly apparent.

One should note, initially, that the will (*voluntas*), for Aquinas, 'means rational appetite' (*voluntas nominat rationalem appetitum*); it is *not* the faculty of free choice *per se*.[27] The act of choice (*electio*), and

[25] See Munz, *The Place of Hooker in the History of Thought*, 64; Hoopes, *Right Reason in the English Renaissance*, 123–31; Marshall, *Hooker and the Anglican Tradition*, 81; W. Speed Hill, 'The Doctrinal Background of Richard Hooker's *Laws of Ecclesiastical Polity*' (Ph.D. thesis, Harvard Univ., 1964), 174–8.

[26] See *Lawes*, 1:79.9–16 (I.7.4).

[27] See *ST* I-II.6.2 ad. 1 and Kenny, *Aquinas on Mind*, 42, 59.

the freedom of so doing, are for Aquinas only a part of the activities of the will, and they are not its essential characteristics.[28] The will for him is fundamentally a faculty of appetite or desire, but of a specifically intellectual kind, for it can only desire those things that are presented to it by the intellect.[29] The key to understanding his theory of the will lies in grasping the precise nature of this presentation. Aquinas observes that 'appetite is a passive power, born to be moved by a thing apprehended'.[30] As regards the will and the intellect, this is most accurately expressed in terms of causation. As Aquinas explains, 'that will-act which turns towards an object proposed to it as being good, that is, as being reasonably subordinate to the end, is "materially" one of will, but "formally" one of reason'.[31] Acts of the will are thus given their formal content by previous acts of the intellect: in other words, the intellect decides upon the object of the will's act, and the will then proceeds to desire in accordance with that decision. It is emphatically not the case, as so many writers have assumed, that the will can choose between those objects presented to it by the intellect. That would be an essentially voluntarist account of the mind, directly opposed to Aquinas's rationalist theory of the will.

As regards Aquinas's views on the freedom of the mind, it is important to note that the traditional Latin term that he and his fellow scholastics used to discuss this topic was *liberum arbitrium*, which does not contain the Latin word for the will, *voluntas*. Indeed *liberum arbitrium*, which means 'free choice' or 'free decision', was not always associated with the will, and J. B. Korolec has documented the ways in which it was variously regarded as, for instance, a power of the intellect, a power separate from both intellect and will, and a disposition of the mind.[32] Aquinas, however, does identify *liberum arbitrium* with the will, since he sees it as

[28] Others acts of the will are termed by Aquinas wishing (*velle*), intention (*intentio*), consent (*consensus*), use (*usus*), and enjoyment (*fruitio*). See Westberg, *Right Practical Reason*, 119–20, 131.

[29] See *ST* I.80.2.

[30] See ibid. Potentia enim appetitiva est potentia passiva, quae nata est moveri ab appreheso. See also I.83.3; I-II.13.1; I-II.14.1 ad. 1; I-II.19.3; Vernon J. Bourke, *Will in Western Thought* (New York, 1964), 53, 59; Thomas Gilby, 'Appendix One', *ST* xvii. 216–17; Westberg, *Right Practical Reason*, 56, 59, 85–6, 110, 113, 239.

[31] See *ST* I-II.13.1: ille actus quo voluntas tendit in aliquid quod proponitur ut bonum, ex eo quod per rationem est ordinatum ad finem, materialiter quidem est voluntatis, formaliter autem rationis.

[32] See J. B. Korolec, 'Free Will and Free Choice', in N. Kretzmann, A. Kenny and J. Pinborg (eds.), *The Cambridge History of Later Medieval Philosophy* (Cambridge, 1982), 629–41.

a function of choice (*electio*), itself an act of the will. As he notes, we say that we have such freedom 'when we can adopt one course and reject another: this is to choose'.[33] This must, however, be understood in terms of his theory of the will as a passive power, the act of which is formally specified by the intellect. Choice, as he notes, implies an act of comparison, whereby one thing is preferred over another.[34] Yet the will is itself incapable of comparisons, for that is the function of the intellect:

> No sense power embraces the diversity that reason does, it simply perceives one sort of thing. And so according to that one thing the movement of sense appetite is determined. But reason relates to many things and so intellectual appetite, that is to say will, can be moved by any of many things, and is not necessarily moved by any one of them.[35]

The freedom that resides in the act of choice is thus the result of the non-necessity of prior acts of the intellect, in that the intellect is capable of making a variety of different judgements regarding the goodness of specific objects.[36] The will is, by itself, unable to choose, because it is unable to compare, so making it dependent upon the intellect for its freedom of choice. This might be thought to make *liberum arbitrium* a cognitive power. Since, however, Aquinas identifies *liberum arbitrium* with choice, which he defines as an act of desire, he still sees *liberum arbitrium* as a power of the will. As Thomas Gilby has observed, for Aquinas the intellect dictates the object of choice, but choice only occurs when the will breaks its suspense and desires the means presented to it.[37] Nonetheless, *liberum arbitrium* is clearly, for Aquinas, a power of the will only in a sharply qualified sense.

This obviously raises the question as to in what sense the will is free *as regards its own act.* A terminological distinction is useful here, as there are a variety of different methods of defining this

[33] See *ST* I.83.3: quod possumus unum recipere alio recusato, quod est eligere.

[34] See ibid. I.83.3 ad. 3.

[35] Ibid. I.82.2 ad. 3: vis sensitiva non est vis collativa diversorum sicut ratio, sed simpliciter aliquid unum apprehendit. Et ideo secundum illud unum determinate movet appetitum sensitivum. Sed ratio est collativa plurium, et ideo ex pluribus moveri potest appetitus intellectivus, scilicet voluntas, et non ex uno ex necessitate.

[36] See ibid. I-II.17.1 ad. 2. See also Alan Donagan, 'Thomas Aquinas on Human Action', *Cambridge History of Later Medieval Philosophy*, 652–3; Kenny, *Aquinas on Mind*, 79–80.

[37] See Gilby, 'Appendix One', 216–17.

freedom.[38] The two definitions that are relevant in this context are usually known as *liberty of spontaneity* and *liberty of indifference*. Liberty of spontaneity concerns human wanting; we are free when we do something if and only if we do it because we want to do it. Liberty of indifference concerns human power; we are free in an action if and only if it is in our power not to do it. The first, but not the second, is compatible with causal determinism. To give an example, if my behaviour is determined such that I must commit a particular action, but I nevertheless want to commit that action, then I have liberty of spontaneity, even though I have no liberty of indifference.

For Aquinas the will is only free when it is not coerced into a particular line of action, although he does add that by its nature the will necessarily seeks for happiness. As the following lines demonstrate, therefore, Aquinas accepted that the will has liberty of spontaneity:

> An agent cause imposes necessity when it applies force to the point where one cannot act otherwise. Necessity of this type is called coercion.
>
> Now necessity of coercion is totally incompatible with willing. For we call violent whatever is against the bent of a thing. But the movement of the will is a sort of bent towards something. And so just as something is called natural because it accords with a natural bent, so a thing is called voluntary when it accords with the bent of the will. And just as it is impossible for anything to be at once violent and natural, it is equally impossible for anything to be coerced, or subject to violence, and yet be voluntary.[39]

Aquinas nowhere suggests, however, that the will has liberty of indifference; not surprisingly, since the object of its act is specified by the judgement of the intellect. The will is, therefore, not free to choose between a series of objects presented to it by the intellect,

[38] See Anthony Kenny, 'Descartes on the Will', *The Anatomy of the Soul: Historical Essays in the Philosophy of Mind* (Oxford, 1973), 97–8; Tomis Kapitan, 'Free Will Problem', in R. Audi (ed.), *The Cambridge Dictionary of Philosophy* (Cambridge, 1995), 280–2.

[39] See *ST* I.82.1: Ex agente autem hoc alicui convenit, sicut cum aliquis cogitur ab aliquo agente ita quod non possit contrarium agere. Et haec vocatur necessitas coactionis. Haec igitur coactionis necessitas omnino repugnat voluntati. Nam hoc dicimus esse violentum, quod est contra inclinationem rei. Ipse autem motus voluntatis est inclinatio quaedam in aliquid. Et ideo sicut dicitur aliquid naturale quia est secundum inclinationem naturae, ita dicitur aliquid voluntarium quia est secundum inclinationem voluntatis. Sicut ergo impossibile est quod aliquid simul sit violentum et naturale, ita impossibile est quod aliquid simpliciter sit coactum, sive violentum, et voluntarium.

but rather freely chooses the one particular object presented to it, which the intellect has specified.[40] *Liberum arbitrium* thus consists for Aquinas precisely in the will's liberty of spontaneity with respect to the previous determinations of the intellect. When one considers that the (receptive) intellect is also, like the will, a passive faculty, then one can see why Anthony Kenny should have labelled Aquinas a 'soft determinist'.[41] For although Aquinas does argue that the will is genuinely free, it would seem that the passivity of both will and intellect renders this freedom effectively compatible with causal determinism.

A further, and very important aspect of Aquinas's soft determinism can be seen in some of his remarks on the relation between the human mind and God. The particular issue in question concerns the widely held scholastic belief that the human mind, as a non-material thing, needs to be moved to act by God, the First Mover, as it is unable to actuate itself. It should be noted that, according to this theory, divine aid is required for all mental actions, whether upright or sinful, and is a basic ontological necessity.[42] Yet given that all mental acts are actuated by God, it becomes pertinent to ask whether this divine aid is consonant with the notion of human freedom, and if so, in what sense. Aquinas addresses these points in these two passages, asserting the compatibility of *liberum arbitrium* and divine determinism:

were the distinction between necessary and contingent causes to be introduced merely by the secondary causes engaged, it would be marginal to God's intending and willing, a conclusion that does not answer to the situation.

This is better described by invoking the very effectiveness of the divine will. From a fully effective cause in operation an effect issues not only as to the fact that arrives but also as to the mode of its coming and being... Since God's will is of all causes the most effective, the consequence is that not only those things come about which God wills, but also that they come about in the manner that God wills them to.

God wills some things to become real necessarily, and others contingently, in order to furnish the full equipment of the universe. Accordingly for some he has designed necessary causes which cannot fail, from which effects result necessarily, and for others defectible and contingent causes

[40] See *ST* I.80.2; I.82.2 ad. 3; I-II.17.1 ad. 2; Bourke, *Will in Western Thought*, 69; Westberg, *Right Practical Reason*, 35, 82, 217.

[41] See Kenny, *Aquinas on Mind*, 77–8; Kapitan, 'Free Will Problem', 281.

[42] See *ST* I-II.109.1.

from which effects result contingently. Hence the ultimate reason why some things happen contingently is not because their proximate causes are contingent, but because God has willed them to happen contingently, and therefore has prepared contingent causes for them.

Free decision spells self-determination because man by his free decision moves himself into action. Freedom does not require that a thing is its own first cause, just as in order to be the cause of something else a thing does not have to be its first cause. God is the first cause on which both natural and free agents depend. And just as his initiative does not prevent natural causes from being natural, so it does not prevent voluntary action from being voluntary but rather makes it be precisely this. For God works in each according to its nature.[43]

Since the divine will is perfectly efficacious, whatever God desires will unfailingly be accomplished. Yet, according to Aquinas, God can determine whether a created effect occurs necessarily or contingently, with the result that God can move a created will efficaciously while preserving its contingent freedom. It should be noted that the efficaciousness of the divine will is internal to the divine aid given to the created will; Aquinas rejects any notion that God consults in some manner the created will before moving it into action. This would seem to raise the question as to how God can preserve contingent human freedom, if God consults only himself with regard to his determinations, and God desires intrinsically efficaciously. Aquinas, however, appears untroubled by this

[43] Ibid. I.19.8: quia si distinctio contingentium a necessariis referatur solum in causas secundas, sequitur hoc esse praeter intentionem et voluntatem divinam; quod est inconveniens. Et ideo melius dicendum est quod hoc contingit propter efficaciam divinae voluntatis. Cum enim aliqua causa efficax fuerit ad agendum, effectus consequitur causam, non tantum secundum id quod fit, sed etiam secundum modum fiendi vel essendi.... Cum igitur voluntas divina sit efficacissima, non solum sequitur quod fiant ea quae Deus vult fieri, sed et quod eo modo fiant quo Deus ea fieri vult. Vult autem quaedam fieri Deus necessario, quaedam contingenter, ut sit ordo in rebus ad complementum universi. Et ideo quibusdam effectibus aptavit causas necessarias quae deficere non possunt, ex quibus effectus de necessitate proveniunt; quibusdam autem aptavit causas contingentes defectibiles ex quibus effectus contingenter eveniunt. Non igitur propterea effectus voliti a Deo eveniunt contingenter quia causae proximae sunt contingentes, sed propterea quia Deus voluit eos contingenter evenire contingentes causas ad eos praeparavit; I.83.1 ad. 3: liberum arbitrium est causa sui motus, quia homo per liberum arbitrium seipsum movet ad agendum. Non tamen hoc est de necessitate libertatis, quod sit prima causa sui id quod liberum est; sicut nec ad hoc quod aliquid sit causa alterius requiritur quod sit prima causa ejus. Deus igitur est prima causa movens et naturales causas et voluntarias. Et sicut naturalibus causis, movendo eas, non aufert quin actus earum sint naturales, ita movendo causas voluntarias non aufert quin actiones earum sint voluntariae, sed potius hoc in eis facit. Operatur enim in unoquoque secundum ejus proprietatem. See also I.22.2, 4; I.49.2; I.105.4.

matter, leaving it as a divine mystery to trouble later theologians. None the less, one can see why, as a result of these theological issues, Kenny should have termed Aquinas a soft determinist. For while Aquinas does indeed assert that the human will is truly free in its actions, this is evidently compatible for him with the concept of divine causal determinism.[44] Duns Scotus was not alone, of Aquinas's contemporaries and successors, in feeling that such a theory was effectively destructive of the notion of human freedom, and in his efforts to oppose determinism he developed a new theory of the will, which we shall consider next.

John Duns Scotus

Like Aquinas, Duns Scotus defines the will (*voluntas*) as a rational appetite, but the apparent similarity ends when one enquires what he understands by this.[45] For unlike Aquinas, who sees the will as being a passive power, Duns Scotus observes that the will is, in different ways, both passive and active; and, as we shall see, it is the latter aspect that is the key to his philosophy of mind. The will is passive, for Duns Scotus, in that, by definition, it has an appetite for goodness presented to it by the intellect; this constituting an ontological necessity of its nature. Yet, he argues, the will is also completely undetermined, in the sense that it is intrinsically free to choose between any objects that the intellect presents to it:[46]

> For a power or potency is related to the object in regard to which it acts only by means of some operation it elicits in one way or another, and there is only a twofold generic way an operation proper to a potency can be elicited. For either [1] the potency of itself is determined to act, so that so far as itself is concerned, it cannot fail to act when not impeded from without; or [2] it is not of itself so determined, but can perform either this act or its opposite, or can either act or not act at all. A potency

[44] See Kenny, *Aquinas on Mind*, 77–8. See also Bernard J. F. Lonergan, *Grace and Freedom: Operative Grace in the Thought of St. Thomas Aquinas*, ed. J. P. Burns (London, 1971), 95, 103–5, 116; Calvin Normore, 'Future Contingents', *Cambridge History of Later Medieval Philosophy*, 366; John F. Wippel, *Metaphysical Themes in Thomas Aquinas* (Washington, DC, 1984), 255–63.

[45] See Bernadine M. Bonansea, 'Duns Scotus' Voluntarism', in J. K. Ryan and B. M. Bonansea (eds.), *John Duns Scotus, 1265–1965* (Washington, DC, 1965), 86.

[46] See Efrem Bettoni, *Duns Scotus: The Basic Principles of his Philosophy*, trans. and ed. B. Bonansea (Washington, DC, 1961), 82; Bonansea, 'Duns Scotus' Voluntarism', 86–8.

of the first sort is commonly called 'nature,' whereas one of the second sort is called 'will.'[47]

It is this intrinsic freedom (a freedom he describes in general as *liberum arbitrium*) that makes the will an active faculty, and is, for Duns Scotus, even more essential to its nature than the appetite for goodness. For, he argues, although the will is unable to desire evil *per se*, it is still free to choose not to desire goodness at any given time, and this is sufficient in his opinion to conserve its freedom in the choice of the good.[48]

This definition of the will is fundamentally different from that of Aquinas, for it gives to the will itself the ability to make opposite decisions about a given object. It will be recalled that although Aquinas identifies *liberum arbitrium* with the will, he locates the root of this freedom in the ability to make opposite judgements about a given object, which he ascribes to the (receptive) intellect, itself a passive faculty. Duns Scotus in fact accepts the correlation Aquinas makes between *liberum arbitrium* and reasoned decision, but in so doing he significantly redefines the nature of rationality. For, he argues, if rationality is defined as the ability to make opposite judgements about a given object, then only the will can in an unqualified sense be considered as a rational faculty:[49]

But if 'rational' is understood to mean 'with reason,' then the will is properly rational, and it has to do with opposites, both as regards its own act and as regards the acts it controls. And it has to do with opposites not in the way that a nature, like the intellect, acts, which has no power to determine itself in any other way. But the will acts freely, for it has the power of self-determination. Properly speaking, however, the intellect is not a potency with regard to external things, because if it does have to

[47] '*Quaestiones in Metaphysicam IX*', q. 15, *Duns Scotus on the Will and Morality*, selected and trans. Allan B. Wolter (Washington, DC, 1986), 150–1: Non enim potentia ad obiectum circa quod operatur, comparatur nisi mediante operatione quam elicit, et hoc sic vel sic. Iste autem modus eliciendi operationem propriam non potest esse in genere nisi duplex: aut enim potentia ex se est determinata ad agendum, ita quod quantum est ex se, non potest non agere quando non impeditur ab extrinseco; aut non est ex se determinata, sed potest agere hunc actum vel oppositum actum, agere etiam vel non agere. Prima potentia communiter dicitur 'natura,' secunda dicitur 'voluntas'.

[48] See Frederick Copleston, *A History of Philosophy*, ii. *Mediaeval Philosophy* (London, 1950), 539; Bonansea, 'Duns Scotus' Voluntarism', 87–8, 90–3, 96.

[49] See Bettoni, *Duns Scotus*, 86; Allan B. Wolter, *The Philosophical Theology of John Duns Scotus* (Ithaca, NY, 1990), 163.

do with opposites, it cannot determine itself, and unless it is determined, it is unable to do anything extra.[50]

This leads Duns Scotus to the conclusion, quite alien to the Thomist perspective, that the intellect 'is rational only in the qualified sense that it is a precondition for the act of a rational potency'.[51] The will is thus intrinsically a rational appetite for Duns Scotus, rather than extrinsically as for Aquinas.

It should be evident from the material that we have so far considered that Duns Scotus, as well as making *liberum arbitrium* an intrinsic power of the will, conceives of this freedom in a quite different sense from Aquinas. This is not to say that there are no points of convergence, and indeed both writers, as one would expect, accept that the will has liberty of spontaneity, or freedom from coercion. As Duns Scotus observes on this topic: 'I say that where man is concerned, no human act, properly speaking, can be coerced, for it is a contradiction for the will to be simply forced to will. According to Bk. III of the *Ethics*, "Violence occurs where the moving principle is outside and the person himself contributes nothing." '[52] Clearly, though, Duns Scotus sees the freedom of the will as being more radical than simple freedom from coercion, given that he argues that the will is self-determined, and the object of its act is neither specified by the intellect nor by any other mental faculty. In fact, as we have seen, he observes that the will 'can perform either this act or its opposite, or can either act or not act', and this is in essence to ascribe to the will an indeterminacy with regard to objects presented to it by the intellect.[53] It is this intrinsic

[50] '*Quaestiones in Metaphysicam IX*', q. 15, *Duns Scotus on the Will and Morality*, 156–7: Si autem intelligitur 'rationalis' [ut] 'cum ratione,' tunc voluntas est proprie rationalis, et ipsa est oppositorum tam quoad actum proprium quam quoad actus inferiorum, et non oppositorum modo naturae, sicut intellectus non potest se determinare ad alterum, sed modo libero potens se determinare. Et ideo est potentia, quia ipsa aliquid potest, nam potest se determinare. Intellectus autem proprie non est potentia respectu extrinsecorum, quia ipse, si est oppositorum, non potest se determinare, et nisi determinetur, nihil extra poterit.

[51] Ibid. 156–7: solummodo autem secundum quid rationalis, inquantum praeexigitur ad actum potentiae rationalis.

[52] '*Ordinatio IV*', dist. 29, *Duns Scotus on the Will and Morality*, 174–7: Dico quod coactio non cadit proprie in homine in aliquo actu humano. Contradictio enim est voluntatem simpliciter cogi ad actum volendi, quia cum 'violentum,' ex *III Ethicorum*... 'sit cuius principium est extra, non conferente vim passo!'

[53] For further details concerning the freedom of the will in Duns Scotus, see Bonansea, 'Duns Scotus' Voluntarism', 88; William A. Frank, 'Duns Scotus' Concept of Willing Freely: What Divine Freedom Beyond Choice Teaches Us', *Franciscan Studies* 42 (1982), 77.

liberty of indifference in the will that most decisively separates Duns Scotus's voluntarist philosophy of mind from the rationalist theory of Aquinas. While, therefore, Kenny calls Aquinas a soft determinist for reconciling causal determinism with human freedom, Duns Scotus can accurately be described as a metaphysical libertarian[54] for refusing to accept such a compatibilist philosophy, and for insisting that *liberum arbitrium* and determinism are diametrically opposite concepts.

Duns Scotus does, though, like so many other scholastics, concur with Aquinas in believing that the aid of God, the First Mover, is necessary to actuate all human mental processes. Given the soft determinism of Aquinas's model, it is important to ask how Duns Scotus's views on the will are reflected in his approach to this philosophical subject. As one would expect, Duns Scotus is unable to accept the view that God can make a created will act contingently, as this seems to him to remove the created will's liberty of indifference with respect to God. None the less, he does, of course, allow that God always wills efficaciously, and this would seem to threaten the human freedom that he is so eager to conserve. He evolves, therefore, the theory that God and the created will are partial causes of acts of the created will, both necessary if such an act is to occur. Both causes act contingently, and in this way the determinism associated with natural causes is avoided: 'In us, that is, in the will, there is contingency that stems both from ourselves and from God. In some other things, however, there is necessity of themselves but contingency on the part of God... But in every effect or thing willed by us as such there is no necessity but only contingency.'[55] The divine and the created will co-operate with each other simultaneously, there being no precedence at all in point of time, and God in no way determining the contingency of the resulting act. While, therefore, for Aquinas, the divine grace is intrinsically efficacious in that God alone determines the nature of the act produced, for Duns Scotus the divine grace is extrinsically

[54] For the use of this term, see Kapitan, 'Free Will Problem', 281.

[55] '*Reportatio 1A*', 39–40, quoted in William A. Frank, 'Duns Scotus on Autonomous Freedom and Divine Co-Causality', *Medieval Philosophy & Theology* 2 (1992), 162: in nobis, i.e., in voluntate, a se et a Deo est contingentia. In aliquibus autem ⟨aliis⟩ necessitas est a se, sed contingentia ex parte Dei... sed in omnibus in effectibus vel rebus a nobis volitis in quantum huiusmodi, nulla est necessitas sed tantum contingentia. See also 142–64; Wolter, *Philosophical Theology of John Duns Scotus*, 315–33.

efficacious: the will of God is unfailingly accomplished, but the contingent nature of the act it brings about is essentially determined by the created will.[56] Duns Scotus thus ensures that his philosophy of mind is genuinely 'libertarian', in that the created will has liberty of indifference not only with respect to the world, but also with respect to God. Yet in so doing, he engages in a similar type of mysticism to that found in Aquinas's approach to this topic. For he offers no solution as to how God can know what sort of aid to give the created will in the instant of choice, and this latent problem was also to pass down into later centuries, causing considerable dissension in its wake.[57]

Later Roman Catholic Controversies

The theory of the will as a passive power was condemned by the bishop of Paris, Stephen Tempier, in 1277, three years after Aquinas's death, on the grounds that it led to determinism. The voluntarist theory of the active will, espoused by Duns Scotus, became prevalent from the late thirteenth century onwards, as the rationalism of Aquinas and some of his contemporaries was largely left behind.[58] By the sixteenth century many Dominican theologians who considered themselves orthodox Thomists, such as Cardinal Thomas de Vio Cajetan, were able to interpret Aquinas in a generally voluntarist sense.[59] Yet the widespread acceptance that the will had liberty of indifference with respect to the intellect and the other mental faculties by no means necessarily entailed a rejection of the soft determinism of Aquinas. Many Dominicans continued to argue that the divine will determined the operation of created wills, although in a manner compatible with human freedom. The debate became famously inflamed in late sixteenth-century Spain when the Jesuit Luis de Molina undertook to rebut the determinism he saw as inherent in much of the philosophy and theology of his day. He developed the notion, found in Duns Scotus, that God wills extrinsically efficaciously in a manner that preserves the created will's liberty of

[56] See Wolter, *Philosophical Theology of John Duns Scotus*, 333.

[57] See Frank, 'Duns Scotus on Autonomous Freedom and Divine Co-Causality', 163–4.

[58] See Copleston, *A History of Philosophy*, ii. *Mediaeval Philosophy*, 538–41; Efrem Bettoni, *Duns Scotus*, 81–6; Bourke, *Will in Western Thought*, 11, 77–88; Korolec, 'Free Will', 637, 641.

[59] See Westberg, *Right Practical Reason*, 123–5.

indifference with respect to God, while he also attempted to show how God can know what sort of aid to give the created will in the moment of choice. Spanish Dominicans, such as Domingo Bañez, reacted vigorously to these developments, concurring with Aquinas that the created will is not indifferent with respect to God and that God wills intrinsically efficaciously, while nevertheless making the voluntarist assertion that the created will does have liberty of indifference with respect to the natural world.[60] What is apparent from this sophisticated controversy is that the Roman Catholic Church in the sixteenth century contained within it widely opposing attitudes to the human will, with the Dominicans in general more accepting of certain aspects of divine determinism than the Franciscans or Jesuits. An understanding of this complex picture is vital for dispelling the view, sometimes held, that while Lutheran and Reformed theology was then supposedly committed to divine determinism, Roman Catholic theology in the sixteenth century was in some way essentially libertarian. The obverse of this is that, just as the deterministic aspects of certain strands of Roman Catholic thought need to be emphasized, so one must appreciate those elements in sixteenth-century Reformed theology that assert the existence, in whatever manner, of the liberty of the human will. In this respect Calvin is a most illuminating and ambivalent figure, whom we turn to examine now.

John Calvin

Calvin had a profound influence on the Reformed view of the will and human freedom, and it is noteworthy in this context that his philosophy of mind, like many of his successors, was less absolutely deterministic, and more nuanced, than is sometimes thought. He rejected the extreme language concerning human bondage then characteristic of Lutheranism, and adopted an approach that is revealing as much for its similarities to that of Aquinas and his fellow

[60] See Joseph Pohle, 'Molinism', *The Catholic Encyclopedia* (New York, 1911), x. 437–40; Anton C. Pegis, 'Molina and Human Liberty', *Jesuit Thinkers of the Renaissance* (Milwaukee, 1939), 82–120; F. L. Sheerin, 'Molinism', *New Catholic Encylopedia* (New York, 1967), ix. 1011–13; Normore, 'Future Contingents', 378–81; Alfred J. Freddoso, 'Introduction', in Luis de Molina, *On Divine Foreknowledge* (*Part IV of the Concordia*), trans. with an introduction and notes by A. J. Freddoso (Ithaca, NY, 1988), 26–8.

Dominicans as for its evident differences.[61] Although he was highly suspicious of scholasticism, often damning it for replacing the Gospel with Aristotle, he was prepared to employ scholastic philosophical concepts where they accorded with his purposes. This is certainly true of his handling of philosophy of mind, which appeared as a subject to interest him only modestly, but where he understood the value of establishing basic philosophical principles if one is to discuss human psychology and behaviour with any rigour.[62]

Although Calvin broadly accepts the commonplace scholastic picture of the mental faculties outlined in this chapter, his treatment of the subject is sufficiently unorthodox to take him outside the mainstream of traditional scholastic philosophy of mind. In his initial examination of the topic in the *Institutes*, he mentions with approval the opinion of philosophers that there are three appetitive faculties in the human soul; namely the will, the concupiscible appetite, and the irascible appetite.[63] Due, though, perhaps to his concern for the practical ramifications of philosophy of mind, rather than for the philosophy itself, he decides to adopt a considerably simpler version of this theory. He argues that the human soul should be seen as having only one appetitive faculty, which he interchangeably calls the appetite (*appetitus*) or the will (*voluntas*), and into which he conflates all three of the traditional scholastic appetitive faculties:

But let us rather choose a division within the capacity of all, which cannot be successfully sought from the philosophers. For they, while they want to speak with utter simplicity, divide the soul into appetite and understanding, but make both double... The former part (I mean the appetitive) they... divide, into will and concupiscence; and as often as appetite, which they call βούλησις, obeys reason, it is ὁρμή; but it becomes πάθος when the appetite, having thrown off the yoke of reason, rushes off to intemperance. Thus they always imagine reason in man as that faculty whereby he may govern himself aright.

We are forced to part somewhat from this way of teaching because the philosophers, ignorant of the corruption of nature that originated from the penalty for man's defection, mistakenly confuse two very diverse states of man. Thus let us, therefore, hold—as indeed is suitable

[61] See Seán F. Hughes, 'The Problem of "Calvinism": English Theologies of Predestination c.1580–1630', in S. Wabuda and C. Litzenberger (eds.), *Belief and Practice in Reformation England: A Tribute to Patrick Collinson from his Students* (Aldershot, 1998), 238, 247–8.

[62] See *Inst.* I.xv.6.

[63] See *Inst.* I.xv.6. See also p. 61 below.

to our present purpose—that the human soul consists of two faculties, understanding and will. . . . Again, for the term 'appetite,' which they prefer, I substitute the word 'will,' which is more common.[64]

Having made this distinction, Calvin goes on to make the perfectly orthodox observation that it is the responsibility of the appetite or will to follow the dictates of the reason; an ability, he observes, that was within the capacity of prelapsarian humans, but which has been greatly vitiated by the Fall.[65] Original sin, he notes, has corrupted this faculty, causing it largely to ignore the reason, and to follow instead those goods desired by the exterior senses:

But man does not choose by reason and pursue with zeal what is truly good for himself according to the excellence of his immortal nature; nor does he use his reason in deliberation or bend his mind to it. Rather, like an animal he follows the inclination of his nature, without reason, without deliberation. Therefore whether or not man is impelled to seek after good by an impulse of nature has no bearing upon freedom of the will. This instead is required: that he discern good by right reason; that knowing it he choose it; that having chosen it he follow it.[66]

Since the exterior senses will desire some objects that would be repugnant to right reason, such behaviour will inevitably end in being sinful. It should be noted, though, that from a traditional scholastic perspective, the behaviour that Calvin is describing here would not be considered metaphorically brutish, but rather quite

[64] *Inst.* I.xv.6–7 (*OS* 3:184–5): Sed nos divisionem potius eligamus infra omnium captum positam, quae certe a philosophis peti non potest. Nam illi dum simplicissime loqui volunt, animam dividunt in appetitum et intellectum; sed utrunque faciunt duplicem. . . . Illum quoque (appetitum dico) in voluntatem, et concupiscentiam partiuntur, ac βούλησιν quidem esse quoties rationi appetitus, quem ὁρμήν appellant, obtemperat: πάθος autem fieri ubi excusso rationis iugo, ad intemperiem excurrit. Ita semper in homine rationem imaginantur qua se recte moderari queat. Ab hac docendi ratione paulum discedere cogimur: quia philosophi, quibus incognita erat naturae corruptio quae ex defectionis poena provenit, duos hominis status valde diversos perperam confundunt. Sic ergo habeamus, subesse duas humanae animae partes, quae quidem praesenti instituto conveniant, intellectum et voluntatem. . . . Rursum pro appetitus nomine, quod illi malunt, voluntatis nomen, quod usitatius est, usurpo. See also II.ii.2.

[65] See ibid. I.xv.8. For a fuller discussion of Calvin's views on the nature of the postlapsarian will and reason, see pp. 150–56 below.

[66] *Inst.* II.ii.26 (*OS* 3:269): Homo vero, nec id quod vere sibi bonum sit, pro naturae suae immortalis excellentia, ratione deligit, ut id studio persequatur: nec rationem adhibet in consilium, nec mentem intendit: sed sine ratione, sine consilio, naturae inclinationem, instar pecudis, sequitur. Nihil ergo hoc ad arbitrii libertatem, an homo sensu naturae ad bonum appetendum feratur: sed hoc requiritur, ut bonum recta ratione diiudicet, cognitum eligat, electum persequatur.

literally action befitting an animal. Aquinas and Duns Scotus, for instance, both argue that the senses can only influence the will via the mediation of the reason. In this respect, all human behaviour, however influenced by the impulses of the senses, is fundamentally rational. The direct influence that Calvin posits, in which reason is wholly displaced by the senses, would for them pertain to the actions of a mad person, or an animal devoid of reason; a point we shall return to later, in Hooker's evaluation of the will. In Calvin's essentially practical understanding of the mind, however, where the will and the concupiscible and irascible appetites are conflated together, the point that he is making here is that in a way sinful humans are mad, as they have abandoned the divinely influenced rationality of their prelapsarian nature. The philosophical sophistication of the traditional scholastic position is set aside by Calvin for a more direct message about the sinfulness of human nature.

Calvin's chief concern in his practical approach to philosophy of mind is to analyse the freedom, or lack of freedom, belonging to the human will. He displays marked hostility to the scholastic term *liberum arbitrium*, as he associates it with the view that people are themselves free to choose between good and evil, something he considers beyond the capacity of sinful human nature. None the less, he is not opposed to all definitions of this term, which demonstrates that he did to some extent accept the concept of the liberty of the human will. As he observes in the *Defensio Sanae et Orthodoxae Doctrinae de Servitute et Liberatione Humani Arbitrii*:

> Now as far as the term [*liberum arbitrium*] is concerned I still maintain what I declared in my *Institutes*, that I am not so excessively concerned about words as to want to start an argument for that cause, provided that a sound understanding of the reality is retained. If freedom is opposed to coercion, I both acknowledge and consistently maintain that choice is free, and I hold anyone who thinks otherwise to be a heretic.[67]

[67] John Calvin, *The Bondage and Liberation of the Will. A Defence of the Orthodox Doctrine of Human Choice against Pighius*, ed. A. N. S. Lane, trans. G. I. Davies (Grand Rapids, Mich., 1996), 68 (*OC* 6:279): Ego vero, quantum ad vocem pertinet, adhuc profiteor, quod in mea Institutione testatus sum, non adeo me superstitiosum esse in verbis, ut eius causa velim contentionem aliquam movere: modo rei intelligentia sana maneat. Si coactione opponitur libertas, liberum esse arbitrium, et fateor, et constanter assevero: ac pro haeretico habeo, quisquis secus sentiat. See also *Inst.* II.ii.7.

The type of human freedom that Calvin unequivocally does accept is liberty of spontaneity, or freedom from coercion, something he makes very clear some lines later on in the same treatise:

> But since Pighius is always craftily confusing coercion with necessity, when it is of the greatest importance for the issue under discussion that the distinction between them be maintained and carefully remembered, it is appropriate to note how the following four [claims] differ from one another: namely that the will is free, bound, self-determined, or coerced. People generally understand a free will to be one which has it in its power to choose good or evil, and Pighius also defines it in this way. There can be no such things as a coerced will, since the two ideas are contradictory. But our responsibility as teachers requires that we say what it means, so that it may be understood what coercion is. Therefore we describe [as coerced] the will which does not incline this way or that of its own accord or by an internal movement of decision, but is forcibly driven by an external impulse. We say that it is self-determined when of itself it directs itself in the direction in which it is led, when it is not taken by force or dragged unwillingly. A bound will, finally, is one which because of its corruptness is held captive under the authority of evil desires, so that it can choose nothing but evil, even if it does so of its own accord and gladly, without being driven by any external impulse.
>
> According to these definitions we allow that man has choice and that it is self-determined, so that if he does anything evil, it should be imputed to him and to his own voluntary choosing. We do away with coercion and force, because this contradicts the nature of the will and cannot coexist with it. We deny that choice is free, because through man's innate wickedness it is of necessity driven to what is evil and cannot seek anything but evil.... For where there is bondage, there is necessity. But it makes a great difference whether the bondage is voluntary or coerced.[68]

[68] See Calvin, *The Bondage and Liberation of the Will*, 69 (*OC* 6:280): Sed quoniam astute Pighius cum necessitate coactionem perpetuo confundit, quarum discrimen tenere et diligenter meminisse, plurimum ad propositam quaestionem refert, haec quatuor quid inter se differant, observare convenit: voluntatem aut liberam esse, aut servam, aut spontaneam, aut coactam. Liberam voluntatem vulgo intelligunt, et sic Pighius quoque definit, quae bonum aut malum eligere habeat in sua potestate. Coacta voluntas nulla esse potest, quum alterum alteri repugnet. Verum docendi causa, quid significet, dicendum est, ut intelligatur quid sit coactio. Eam ergo sic vocamus, quae non sponte sua, nec interiore electionis motu, inclinatur huc vel illuc, sed externo motu violenter fertur. Spontaneam dicimus, quae ultro se flectit, quocunque ducitur, non autem rapitur, aut trahitur invita. Serva postremo voluntas est, quae propter corruptionem sub malarum cupiditatum imperio captiva tenetur, ut nihil quam malum eligere possit, etiam si id sponte et libenter, non externo motu impulsa, faciat. Secundum has definitiones homini arbitrium concedimus, idque spontaneum, ut, si quid mali facit, sibi ac voluntariae suae electioni imputare debeat. Coactionem et violentiam tollimus, quia pugnet cum natura voluntatis, nec simul consistat. Liberum autem negamus, quia propter ingenitam homini pravitatem ad malum necessario feratur, nec nisi

This important passage says a good deal about Calvin's attitude to liberty. Although he accepts that the will by definition has liberty of spontaneity, or freedom from coercion, he does not equate this here with the will being conceptually free. This is because in this passage he associates free will, or *liberum arbitrium*, with the power to choose between good and evil. He denies that the fallen human will possesses such liberty of indifference with respect to the objects of choice, since he views this will as being bound by necessity to make evil choices. He concludes, therefore, that humans sin voluntarily, but also of necessity. Yet as we have seen, he is prepared to accept a redefinition of *liberum arbitrium* in terms of liberty of spontaneity, and redefined in this way, *liberum arbitrium* is evidently compatible for him with necessity. This is not so very far from the position of Aquinas that freedom and determinism are compatible, showing that contrary to some writers, Calvin should, like Aquinas, be seen as a soft determinist, rather than as an upholder of absolute, or hard determinism. The language of the two writers serves to obscure this similarity, however, for while Aquinas emphasizes human freedom, Calvin emphasizes human bondage. For Aquinas liberty of spontaneity is a vital philosophical concept and the essence of human freedom, whereas Calvin can see little point in bestowing upon it the 'proud name' (*superbo titulo*) of *liberum arbitrium*.[69] Given such grudging support for human free will on Calvin's part, it is no wonder that he has often been misinterpreted on this issue.[70]

It would, however, be a simplification to state that Calvin believed the human will lacks liberty of indifference *per se*. Clearly, for a start, Calvin viewed the will as indifferent with regard to the judgements of the reason; in this respect he is very far from being a rationalist in the Thomist sense of the term.[71] More generally, his attitude to the will varies depending upon the type of human condition that he is addressing. The above remarks on the necessity of human sinfulness apply only to unredeemed post-lapsarian humans; admittedly, for Calvin, the great majority of humanity.[72]

malum appetere queat . . . Ubi enim servitus, illic necessitas. Sed plurimum interest, voluntariane sit servitus, an coacta. For a similar Reformed interpretation of human freedom, see *The Second Helvitic Confession*, ch. 9, in A. C. Cochrane (ed.), *Reformed Confessions of the 16th Century* (London, 1966), 237–40.

69 See *Inst.* II.ii.7 (*OS* 3:249).

70 See A. N. S. Lane, 'Did Calvin Believe in Freewill?', *Vox Evangelica* 12 (1981), 72, 78–80, 86.

71 Ibid. 73.

72 See *Inst.* II.ii.1–7; II.iii.5; Lane, 'Did Calvin Believe in Freewill?', 78.

He readily accepts, though, that before the Fall Adam was free to choose between good and evil, even though Adam lacked the grace to persevere: 'But it was because his will was capable of being bent to one side or the other, and was not given the constancy to persevere, that he fell so easily. Yet his choice of good and evil was free.'[73] Calvin also, at times, appears to allow that, through the operation of grace, redeemed Christians have a limited ability to choose freely between good and evil.[74] It must be said, though, that he makes little of this liberty of indifference with respect to the world, and good and evil, as he is so aware of the overall determinism that for him governs the human will. Grace, in his opinion, totally dictates Christian behaviour, so that all commendable actions must be ascribed to God alone, without any recourse to notions of human co-operation or merit. The divine determinism that Calvin sees as governing Christian behaviour is, of course, but a part of his wider attitude to human behaviour, both before and after the Fall, since he firmly asserts that the human will has no liberty of indifference with respect to God.[75] He is critical, for instance, of the view that the help that humans receive from the First Mover, necessary to actuate the will, is not determining in its nature. As he observes in the *Institutes*:

> Let them now say that man is moved by God according to the inclination of his nature, but that he himself turns the motion whither he pleases. Nay, if that were truly said, the free choice of his ways would be in man's control. Perhaps they will deny this because he can do nothing without God's power. Yet they cannot really get by with that, since it is clear that the prophet and Solomon ascribe to God not only might but also choice and determination.[76]

The grace that actuates the human will also determines the nature of the resulting human choice, according to Calvin. In another

[73] *Inst.* I.xv.8 (*OS* 3:186): sed quia in utranque partem flexibilis erat eius voluntas, nec data erat ad perseverandum constantia, ideo tam facile prolapsus est. Libero tamen fuit electio boni et mali. See also *Inst.* II.iii.13; Calvin, *The Bondage and Liberation of the Will*, 70; Lane, 'Did Calvin Believe in Freewill?', 73.

[74] See Lane, 'Did Calvin Believe in Freewill?', 83–4.

[75] See ibid. 73–5, 84–5.

[76] *Inst.* I.xvi.6 (*OS* 3:196): Dicant nunc, hominem a Deo moveri secundum naturae suae inclinationem, ipsum autem convertere motum quo visum fuerit. At si id vere diceretur, penes hominem foret viarum suarum arbitrium. Negabunt forte, quia nihil sine Dei potentia valeat. At quum Prophetam et Solomonem constet non potentiam modo, sed electionem quoque ac destinationem Deo attribuere, nequaquam se expediunt.

passage from the *Institutes*, he appears to equate this position with the view that the divine will is always efficacious (*efficax*), in the sense that its choices are unfailingly performed: 'He does not move the will in such a manner as has been taught and believed for many ages—that it is afterward in our choice either to obey or resist the motion—but by disposing it efficaciously.'[77] As we have seen, however, both Duns Scotus and Molina accept that the will of God is efficacious in this manner, so this position is not in itself necessarily determinist. Calvin's hostility here is much more relevant to the type of opinion held, for instance, by Hooker, as we shall shortly see. Nonetheless, from other statements that he makes, it is evident that Calvin considers that the divine will is intrinsically efficacious, in that God not only infallibly moves the created will, but also exclusively determines the nature of its motion: 'We do indeed teach that man is so acted upon by the grace of God that he nevertheless [also] acts at the same time, but he acts in such a way that the effectiveness of the action is and remains entirely in the control of the Spirit of God.'[78] The view that this efficacious aid controls or determines the resulting human action is far closer to the Dominican position of a writer such as Aquinas or Bañez, than it is to Molina or Duns Scotus. Like the Dominicans, Calvin asserts that human behaviour is in a sense contingent and free, but this does not obscure the fact that ultimately all finite causes are determined by the infinite divine will.[79] As he observes, in his most detailed discussion of this matter, *De Aeterna Dei Praedestinatione*:

Augustine's word, that the will of God is the necessity of things, always seems at first hearing to be a hard saying. But he adds by way of explanation that God made inferior causes in such a way that out of them that of which they are the causes is possible but not necessary. But the higher

[77] Ibid. II.iii.10 (*OS* 3:285): Ac voluntatem movet, non qualiter multis seculis traditum est et creditum, ut nostrae postea sit electionis, motioni aut obtemperare aut refragari: sed illam efficaciter afficiendo.

[78] Calvin, *The Bondage and Liberation of the Will*, 172 (*OC* 6:351): Hominem sic quidem docemus agi Dei gratia, ut tamen simul agat: sic tamen ipsum agere, ut penes Dei spiritum tota sit ac maneat actionis efficacia. See also *Inst.* I.xvi.8; I.xviii.1; II.iv.7; John Calvin, *Concerning the Eternal Predestination of God*, trans. J. K. S. Reid (London, 1961), 162, 174–85.

[79] See Hughes, 'The Problem of "Calvinism"', 236, 242, 247.

remote causes He hides in Himself, so that out of them what He makes possible by them is necessary.[80]

None of this is to deny that there are significant points of departure between Calvin and the Dominicans, both in terms of substance and also, most particularly, of expression. At the last analysis, however, both sides accept a form of soft determinism in which liberty and necessity are compatible, and this sets them sharply at odds with theologians such as Duns Scotus and, as we shall see, Hooker, who defend the reality of metaphysical libertarianism.

Richard Hooker

We are now finally in a position to look at Hooker's views on the will, and to appreciate their significance in the light of traditional scholastic and contemporary Reformed ideas on the subject. Given the assertion that Aquinas's philosophy of mind is quite distinct from later voluntarist developments, it may now seem less surprising to argue that Hooker differed radically from Aquinas in this area. In order to establish this clearly, though, and to place his theories in relation to those of the other writers we have examined, we must look in some detail at his various writings.

The principal discussion of the will in Hooker's work occurs in ch. 7 of Book 1 of the *Lawes*, entitled '*Of mans will which is the thing that lawes of action are made to guide*.'[81] It is noteworthy, however, that the will is only mentioned on the thirtieth line of text in the *Folger* edition. The chapter opens by promising a discussion of how humans know 'things unsensible as are to be knowne that they may be done'; this is the realm, therefore, of the practical reason. Attention then quickly shifts to the question of how the mind is stirred into motion. The answer is found to be the desire for some end, but as yet Hooker does not identify this desire with the will, nor the knowledge of that end with the reason. Instead, the discussion moves on to examine the freedom of this desire, and in the process the term 'choice' is introduced. 'Choice' is defined in part as the ability 'to will one thing before another', so that 'to will', 'to

[80] Calvin, *Concerning the Eternal Predestination of God*, 178 (*OC* 8:360): Durum primo statim auditu videtur illus Augustini, quod Dei voluntas sit rerum necessitas. Item quod subiicit explicandi gratia, quod sic causas inferiores condiderit Deus ut ex illis esse illud, cuius causae sunt, possit, sed non necesse sit: altiores autem et remotas sic in se absconderit, ut ex eis esse necesse sit, quod ex illis fecit, ut esse possit. See also *Inst.* I.xvi.9; III.xxiii.8.

[81] See *Lawes*, 1:77.1–81.23 (I.7.1–7).

choose', and 'to desire' would all appear to be synonymous. All desire assumes that one thing is preferred instead of another, and since willing and choice are both acts of desire they must be identical. Hooker then specifies the object of this desire, stating it to be that good which is comprehended by the reason. Reference is then made to '*Knowledge* and *Will*', and a further definition of choice occurs: 'will in things tending towards any end is termed *Choice*'. Since will is a form of desire, and Hooker has previously argued that all desire presupposes some end, this again means that he equates an act of will with an act of choice.

The structure of this opening discussion is most interesting, for rather than mentioning the will from the start, Hooker first introduces the concepts of intellectual desire and freedom of choice that are integral to his definition of the will. This serves to highlight the importance of this definition, as the powers of the will are given more initial prominence than the name of the faculty itself. In defining the will as a rational appetite or desire, Hooker follows both Aquinas and Duns Scotus, as we have seen. His fundamental identification of the will with the freedom to choose, however, puts him firmly in the voluntarist camp with Duns Scotus; a philosophical allegiance that we shall explore further in the next few pages.

Having discussed the nature of choice, Hooker goes on to explain that there is another 'inferiour naturall desire' called 'appetite', and he is careful to differentiate it from the will by referring to the objects of each. As he states:

> But of one thing we must have speciall care, as being a matter of no small moment, and that is, how the will properly and strictly taken, as it is of things which are referred unto the ende that man desireth, differeth greatly from that inferiour naturall desire which we call appetite. The object of appetite is whatsoever sensible good may be wished for; the object of wil is that good which reason doth leade us to seeke.[82]

Both faculties by their very nature desire goodness, but not of the same kind. The appetite is directed to those things which the sense organs indicate to be good; for instance, eating and drinking. The will is directed to good as it is comprehended by the reason, and as Hooker then emphasizes, to nothing else: 'neyther is any other

[82] *Lawes*, 1:78.10–16 (I.7.3).

desire termed properly will, but that where reason and understanding, or the shew of reason prescribeth the thing desired'. This further emphasizes the fact that the will is, for Hooker, a faculty of intellectual desire: one could not, therefore, will irrationally, in the sense of choosing something that was not first comprehended by the reason. Hooker thus adopts the traditional scholastic position on this subject, in line with both Duns Scotus and Aquinas, but in complete contrast to the simplified view found, for instance, in Calvin's *Institutes*. Whether Hooker had Calvin's work specifically in mind here is unclear, but the disagreement between them is evident.

Some critics might argue, though, that Hooker contradicts himself on this point, for he also states in the next lines that 'appetite is the wills sollicitor'. If the object of all acts of the will must be comprehended by the reason, then the appetite cannot directly solicit the will; this would reintroduce the possibility of irrational choice, since the reason could be totally ignored. There are several passages in Hooker's work that are suggestive of such an irrational model, and they will receive treatment later in this chapter. For the moment, however, two quotations will suffice. In *A Learned Sermon of the Nature of Pride* Hooker describes an irrational person, the Babylonian, in whom 'wilfulnes tyrannized over reason, and brutish sensuality over will'.[83] This could be taken as suggesting that the appetite solicits the will directly. Rather than concluding that Hooker had no firm position over this matter, however, it is useful to look at another passage from the seventh chapter of Book I of the *Lawes*.[84] Here Hooker describes how the appetite, being provoked by 'Sensible goodnesse', then proceeds to solicit the will: 'Now pursuit and refusall in the will do follow, the one the affirmation, the other the negation of goodnes, which the understanding apprehendeth, grounding it selfe upon sense.' The reason (or understanding) thus apprehends the appetite's desires, so that the will can act on the basis of them. Thus the appetite solicits the will only via the mediation of the reason. Given the commonplace nature of this scholastic theory, it would seem reasonable to suppose that this was Hooker's general position as regards the interaction of

[83] See *Pride*, 5:314.22–3.

[84] See *Lawes*, 1:80.6–11 (I.7.6). See also 1:79.20–7 (I.7.5); Grislis, 'The Role of *Consensus* in Richard Hooker's Method of Theological Inquiry', 75.

these three faculties, even though his words are sometimes open to other interpretations.

We have seen that Hooker follows the voluntarist ideas of Duns Scotus in defining the will in terms of the freedom to choose. In his principal discussion of the will in ch. 7 of Book I of the *Lawes*, Hooker gives an exposition on human freedom even before mentioning the faculty of which it is a power: the will is by definition the faculty of *free* choice, and he must first establish the nature of that freedom before he can discuss the will itself. We must now, therefore, examine Hooker's concept of free will, beginning with his remarks in the vital seventh chapter. The fact that the English term, 'free will', designates the will as the source of human freedom, unlike the neutral Latin term *liberum arbitrium*, says much about the ascendance that voluntarist philosophy of mind gained over competing theories in the late Middle Ages. Hooker's use of the term alone hints at the voluntarist caste of his philosophy of mind.[85] In ch. 7 of Book I he begins his exposition by drawing a direct parallel between human and divine freedom. Theologians in Hooker's day treated the liberty of God with immense seriousness, which demonstrates the importance of human freedom as a concept for him.[86] He then observes that as humans we are not constrained in the manner of natural agents, since we have the 'power to leave the things we do undone'. Similarly, he observes that choice can only be said to exist when 'the thing which we take be so in our power that we might have refused and left it'. Both these definitions, in terms of a negative 'power' of choice, clearly refer to liberty of indifference; the freedom to act or not to act in

[85] For Hooker's use of the term, see e.g. *Lawes* 1:62.29 (I.2.6). For accounts of Hooker's belief in free will, see e.g. Gunnar Hillerdal, *Reason and Revelation in Richard Hooker* (Lund, 1962), 25; George W. Morrel, 'The Systematic Theology of Richard Hooker' (Th.D. thesis, Pacific School of Religion, 1969), 76; Gibbs, 'Introduction: Book I', *Folger*, vi. 103.

[86] This makes it all the more strange that Hooker should have argued, in *A Learned Discourse of Justification*, that 'The heresie of freewill was a milstone about the pelagians neckes' [*Just.* 5:143.16–9]. The freedom of the will is one of the cornerstones of the *Lawes*, and one can only assume that Hooker refined his opinions about this subject between 1586, when he wrote the sermons that make up this tractate, and the years running up to 1593 when the first four books of the *Lawes* were published. It may be that the formation of his opinions on common grace was instrumental in this matter, allowing him to adopt a more nuanced attitude towards the will as it is influenced and uninfluenced by divine aid. See pp. 100–12 below. Kavanagh attempts to reconcile this passage from the tractate with the *Lawes*, but his argument is unpersuasive. See Kavanagh, 'Reason and Nature in Hooker's Polity', 78.

any given case. Hooker also argues in the same passage that people only act through desire; mere apprehension of a good does not cause motion, since we must prefer to act rather than to leave an action undone. This would appear to describe liberty of spontaneity; the freedom that consists in humans wanting to act in a particular manner, as opposed to being coerced into action. Both types of liberty are related by Hooker to the act of choice or desire, and are, therefore, fundamental to his conception of the human will.

Further statements on the will's liberty of indifference can be found in other parts of Hooker's work. There is, for instance, that passage in Book I of the *Lawes* which so annoyed the anonymous writers of the *Christian Letter*: 'There is in the will of man naturally that freedome, whereby it is apt to take or refuse any particular object whatsoever being presented unto it.'[87] Similarly, in *A Learned Sermon of the Nature of Pride*, Hooker describes how people are not 'by any such necessity tyed naturally unto any certain determinate mean to obtein their end by but that they may if they will forsake it'.[88] Finally, in the *Dublin Fragments*, Hooker speaks explicitly of the 'indifferencie' of the will, and notes that this faculty has 'a kinde of authoritie and power to take which part itselfe listeth in a contradiction, and of twoe oppositt effects, to give being unto eyther'.[89] This general espousal of the will's liberty of indifference is a significant point of disagreement between Hooker, Aquinas, and Calvin, though Hooker does join them in accepting one particular limitation upon the will, in that this faculty necessarily desires the good.[90]

It is worthwhile returning at this point to Hooker's definition of the will as an intellectual desire, for it is now clear from the above that Hooker did not, unlike Aquinas, consider this desire to be passive. It is precisely because the will has liberty of indifference that it is an active power, and the object of its act is not determined by the intellect. To make this point entirely transparent, one may again quote a passage from the seventh chapter of Book I

[87] See *Lawes*, 1:79.27–9 (I.7.6). For a fuller discussion of this controversial passage, and of Hooker's commentary on it in the *Dublin Fragments*, see pp. 296–7, 306. See also *Lawes*, 1:187.12–15 (II.8.1). [88] See *Pride*, 5:311.11–3.

[89] See *DF* 4:101.24–6; 4:127.1–10. See also 4:101.10–13 and pp. 298–9 below. Hooker uses 'indifferency' here in the third sense listed by the *OED* (the earliest use of which is given as 1552): '3. Indetermination of the will; freedom of choice; an equal power to take either of two courses. †**liberty of indifferency**, freedom from necessity, freedom of the will.'

[90] See *Lawes*, 1:82.1–5 (I.8.1).

of the *Lawes*, where Hooker discusses how the will is solicited by the appetite via the mediation of the understanding. As he then observes: 'Now pursuit and refusall in the will do follow, the one the affirmation, the other the negation of goodnes, which the understanding apprehendeth, grounding it selfe upon sense.'[91] The will can, therefore, choose to reject that good which has been apprehended by the understanding, and thus the object of its act is not determined in the manner suggested by Aquinas's rationalist model of the mind.

There are, however, two passages in the *Lawes* that could be taken as suggesting a passive view of the will, contrary to the rather overwhelming evidence to the contrary. In the first passage, which has been quoted above, Hooker observes that the will is a faculty of intellectual desire: 'neyther is any other desire termed properly will, but that where reason and understanding, or the shew of reason prescribeth the thing desired'.[92] The key word is 'prescribeth', since this could be taken as suggesting that the object of the will is determined by the reason. 'Prescribe', in this sense, means 'to write or lay down as a rule or direction to be followed', the second definition listed by the *OED*. Yet an alternative meaning was also current in Hooker's day; 'to describe beforehand'. This is the first definition listed by the *OED*, and the one that would seem to be the more appropriate in this context. In this sense the will can only choose those objects that have been described by the reason, which is nothing other than an assertion that all choice must be rational. Given that Hooker argues that the will has liberty of indifference, this second interpretation is obviously to be preferred.

In the second passage, Hooker could be taken as arguing that the will necessarily desires the greatest good that has been comprehended by the reason. As he observes, 'All particular things, which are subject unto action, the will doth so farre forth incline unto, as reason judgeth them the better for us, and consequently the more avayleable to our blisse.'[93] Taken literally, this would mean that the problem of defective action and belief-formation is in fact one of knowledge; if the subject correctly understands the

[91] See *Lawes*, 1:80.8–10 (I.7.6). See also e.g. 1:78.6–10 (I.7.2); 2:233.30–234.4 (V.55.8); Grislis, 'The Role of *Consensus* in Richard Hooker's Method of Theological Inquiry', 75.

[92] See *Lawes*, 1:78.24–6 (I.7.3).

[93] See ibid. 1:82.5–7 (I.8.1).

greatest available good, he or she will necessarily desire it, which means that people sin only through ignorance. This is a Socratic explanation for human behaviour, and (with the solitary exception of someone who experiences the Divine Vision)[94] it is not the model Aquinas adopts when arguing for the passivity of the will. Given that Hooker is explicit about the will's liberty of indifference, his meaning in this passage is presumably merely that the will is dependent upon the reason if it is to make a correct choice. As he notes, 'If reason erre, we fall into evill', since a person who does not know the good is unlikely to choose it.[95] Ignorance is not, for Hooker, the only source of defective action and belief-formation, something that will be examined in detail in the next chapter.

None of the material we have looked at so far definitely establishes that Hooker was a metaphysical libertarian like Duns Scotus in his philosophy of mind, for as we have seen, Dominicans such as Bañez argued that the human will has liberty of indifference with respect to the world but not with respect to God. Calvin also at times comes close to this position, as regards the wills of redeemed Christians. We need, therefore, to look at Hooker's views on whether the human will is ultimately determined by the divine will. This is a matter that he explores only in the *Dublin Fragments*, leaving to some extent open the question of whether he once held other ideas. It would, though, be surprising if Hooker had held a contrary opinion when writing the *Lawes*, as both works agree in other respects as regards the freedom of the human mind.

Hooker's stance in the *Dublin Fragments* is quite clear, in that the will of God in no way determines human behaviour, or conflicts with human liberty of choice:

Prescience, predestination and grace impose not that necessitie by force, whereof man in doing good hath all freedome of choice taken from him. If prescience did impose any such necessitie, seeing prescience is not only of good butt of evill, then must wee grant that *Adam* himselfe could not chose but sinne, and that *Adam* sinned not voluntarily, because that which *Adam* did ill, was foreseene. If predestination did impose such necessitie, then was there nothing voluntarie in *Adams* well doing neyther, because what *Adam* did well was predestinated; Or if Grace did impose

[94] See *ST* I.82.2. [95] See *Lawes*, 1:82.7–8 (I.8.1).

such necessitie, how was it possible that *Adam* should have done otherwise then well, being soe furnished as he was with grace?[96]

Hooker rejects the notion here that necessity is in some sense compatible with human freedom; unsurprisingly, since as we have seen, he explicitly mentions liberty of indifference in these writings.[97] Prescience or foreknowledge does not determine human behaviour, he argues, and neither does predestination itself. As he goes on to observe in the lines that follow, predestination presupposes the fact that free choice is a part of human nature, and hence that 'grace conteyned under the purpose of predestinating man may perfect and doeth, butt cannot possiblie destroye the libertie of mans will'.[98] Logically, therefore, the human will is free to accept or to reject divine grace, and indeed Hooker states this himself some pages later: 'the providence of God bestoweth not in this present life, grace soe neerely illustrating goodnes, that the will should have noe power to decline from it. Grace is not therefore here given in that measure which taketh away possibilitie of sinning, and soe effectuallie mooveth the will, as that it cannot.'[99] Hooker allows that the elect angels and the saints in glory are not able to sin, though he does not mention whether he agrees with Duns Scotus that they nevertheless retain freedom of the will.[100] He does argue, though, that in this present life the grace of God can be resisted, which implies that humans have liberty of indifference with respect to God, as well as to the world. It may be objected at this point that humans cannot logically be free to reject the aid of the First Mover, necessary to actuate all human

[96] *DF* 4:102.13–23. See Charles M. Thornburg, 'Original Sin, Justification and Sanctification in the Thought of Two Sixteenth Century English Divines: John Jewel and Richard Hooker' (Ph.D. thesis, The Hartford Seminary Foundation, 1975), 145–6; Neelands, 'The Theology of Grace of Richard Hooker', 172–6.

[97] See p. 55 above.

[98] *DF*, 4:102.32–103.2. It is not easy to reconcile this view with his assertion, for instance, in the *Notes towards a Fragment on Predestination* that 'God knows by reason that Peter having been chosen should have to be saved before He knew that he would have the merits through which he was to be saved' (*Prius ratione scit Deus Petrum electum fore salvandum quam sciat ipsum habiturum merita per quae salvandus est*). (See *Pred.* 4:85.11–14.) Such a theory of the predestination of the elect might be thought to require some concept of determinism. Hooker is attempting, though, in different parts of his late works, both to assert that predestination to life is wholly attributable to God, and that humans have liberty of indifference. Given the problem of squaring this theological circle, one can appreciate why not all his statements on these two subjects seem to be philosophically compatible.

[99] *DF* 4:104.32–105.8. See also 4:112.22–3; 4:136.26–30.

[100] See Bonansea, 'Duns Scotus' Voluntarism', 94–5.

thought, which we have considered in connection with Hooker's predecessors: one cannot reject that without which choice itself would be impossible, so it might be claimed that Hooker could perhaps still, for all that he says in the *Dublin Fragments* about the rejection of grace more generally, be a soft determinist. Yet by arguing that predestination does not contradict human liberty of indifference Hooker in effect answers this objection, for if predestination in general does not determine human choice then it cannot be the case that the particular aid of the First Mover does. Hooker may, therefore, justly be termed a metaphysical libertarian, a position that sets him sharply at odds with Calvin and sixteenth-century Reformed theology more generally, as well as with Aquinas and many sixteenth-century Dominicans. All the writers that have been considered here believe in the existence of human freedom, but they by no means believe in it in the same way. When the fine detail is considered the radical differences emerge, and Hooker is found to stand on the opposite side from many of his Reformed contemporaries, with such Jesuit writers as Molina and Suárez. Hooker's position in the Reformed England of his day is even plainer when one considers the views of theologians rather less subtle than those that have been reviewed so far: it was, for instance, the opinion of no less an author than John Whitgift, writing in 1574, that: 'The doctrine "of free-will," because it is an enemy to the grace of God, must needs be of itself a damnable doctrine.'[101] Hooker's understandable caution in openly opposing what were commonplace Reformed ideas, to be examined further in Ch. 5, meant that it was Arminius and not he who championed the movement against soft determinism in the Protestant churches. Arminius's assertions that humans can resist divine grace, and that human freedom is incompatible with divine determinism, have close parallels in Hooker's work.[102] Whether if Hooker had lived longer his impact on the Reformed tradition would have been more profound is something we cannot know.

This study of the will has compared and contrasted Hooker's position with that of several of his predecessors: this does not

[101] See Whitgift, 'Defence', 189.

[102] See 'A Declaration of the Sentiments of Arminius on Predestination, Divine Providence, the Freedom of the Will, the Grace of God, the Divinity of the Son of God, and the Justification of Man before God', *The Works of James Arminius*, ed. J. Nichols (London, 1825–75), i. 600 (*OA* 122): 'I believe, according to the Scriptures, that many

necessarily mean that where there are points of agreement, these earlier writers were Hooker's direct source. More work will need to be done in this field, and it may be ultimately that there is insufficient evidence in his surviving work for critics to make any very definite attributions. Curiously, this may even be true conversely of Hooker's relation to Aquinas's philosophy of mind. Despite the considerable differences between their respective voluntarist and rationalist theories, Aquinas was, as we have seen, interpreted by sixteenth-century Dominicans such as Cajetan in a generally voluntarist manner. It was Cajetan's famous edition of the *Summa Theologiae*, replete with exhaustive marginal commentary, that Hooker himself used.[103] Despite his differences from the Dominicans in various important respects, therefore, Hooker may well have made use of Aquinas when shaping his own philosophy of mind, even though one can no longer accept the view of Munz that he followed him throughout. Hooker was not an original thinker as regards the human will, though his views were highly advanced in the Reformed England of his day, but to which writers he directly owes his ideas is for the moment a decidedly clouded question.

(Sensitive) Appetite

Having surveyed some of the complex controversies surrounding the will, we may now return to the level of scholastic commonplace and look at two further mental faculties in less depth, both

persons resist the Holy Spirit and reject the grace that is offered' (Quantum enim ad hoc; juxta Scripturas credo, quod multi *Spiritui S. resistunt, & gratiam oblatam repellunt*); 'The Apology or Defence of James Arminius', *The Works of James Arminius*, i. 688 (*OA* 141): 'But they say, "It is possible for one and the same event to be necessary and contingent in different respects—*necessary* with regard to the First Cause, which is God,—and *contingent* in respect to second causes."... The necessity or contingency of an event is to be estimated, not from one cause, but from all the causes united together... But since none of those causes is *the total cause* of that event, and since all of them united together form *the total cause*, the thing ought itself to be accounted and declared to have been done from that total cause, either *necessarily* or *contingently*' (Sed dicunt, unum eundemque *eventum* posse *diverso respectu* esse *necessarium & contingentem*; *Necessarium respectu primae causae, qua est Deus, & contingentem respectu secundarum causarum.... Necessitatem* vel *contingentiam eventus* non ex *una causa*, sed ex *omnibus simul iunctis* esse aestimandam... sed quum nulla earum causarum sit *causa totalis istius eventus*, sed *omnes simul iunctae totalem faciant causam*, ex illa totali causa vel *necessario* vel *contingenter* facta esse statui & dici debet res ipsa). See also Carl Bangs, *Arminius: A Study in the Dutch Reformation* (Nashville, 1971), 343.

[103] See John E. Booty, 'Introduction: Book V', *Folger*, vi. 207; *Lawes*, 2:260.g (V.60.6).

of which play a significant role in Hooker's understanding of human nature, and hence in this study. The first of these, the (sensitive) appetite, we have already touched upon in relation to Hooker.[104] Hooker usually refers to it simply as the 'appetite', and notes that it desires those goods which are apprehended by the sense-organs (hence it is sometimes referred to as the *sensitive* appetite, in contraposition to the *intellectual* appetite or will).[105] It is a passive power, and its object is determined by this act of apprehension. As he observes, 'appetite, can neyther rise at the conceipt of a thing indifferent, nor yet choose but rise at the sight of some things'.[106] This is the orthodox scholastic position, though as we have seen, it is a view not shared by Calvin. Aquinas's general position is as might be expected, however, precisely the same as Hooker's, although he does add the further common scholastic distinction that the sensitive appetite (*appetitus sensitivus*) may be divided into the irascible and concupiscible powers.[107]

Imagination/Fancy

The principal other faculty that Hooker mentions in his work is the imagination, or fancy; he uses these two terms interchangeably, as Aquinas does his equivalent terms, *imaginatio* and *phantasia*.[108] Marie Stueber has argued implicitly that the views of these two theologians are the same as regards this faculty.[109] Yet while her evidence is quite persuasive, she perhaps simplifies what is a rather complex picture. One may start by examining the opinions of Aquinas, who views the imagination as one of the interior senses. A sense is defined by him as a passive power that has the ability to undergo change through the action of a sense-object.[110] Some senses are external, such as sight, the organ of which is the eyes, while others are internal, such as the imagination, the organ of which is housed somewhere in the brain.[111] The imagination has several different functions. The first concerns the retention of

[104] See pp. 52–3 above.

[105] See *Lawes*, 1:78.10–14 (I.7.3). Hooker does sometimes speak of the 'sensuall' appetite. See e.g. *Pride*, 5:314.18.

[106] See *Lawes*, 1:78.18–19 (I.7.3).

[107] See *ST* I.80.2; I.81.1–2. As regards the commonplace nature of this view of the (sensitive) appetite, see Park, 'The Organic Soul', 464–71.

[108] See *ST* I.78.4.

[109] See Stueber, 'Richard Hooker's Place in the History of Renaissance Christian Humanism', 340–3.

[110] See *ST* I.78.1; Kenny, *Aquinas on Mind*, 33–4.

[111] See *ST* I.84.7.

particular forms, or phantasms (*phantasmata*), which have been received, albeit indirectly, from the five exterior senses.[112] Thus, for instance, it can store the forms of the smell and taste of a particular apple. It is also capable of rearranging these forms, in whatever manner is desired. Aquinas gives as an example the individual forms of gold and a mountain, from which 'we compose the single form of a golden mountain which we have never seen'.[113] The imagination has, however, one other crucial function: the processes of reasoning can only occur, Aquinas argues, with reference to these particular forms. As he explains: 'As anyone can experience for himself, if he attempts to understand anything, he will form images for himself which serve as examples in which he can, as it were, look at what he is attempting to understand.'[114] To give an example, if one wished to consider the best way to cross a river, one would use a variety of forms housed in the imagination, such as those of water, a river-bank, and so on. The processes of thought require, therefore, a continual interaction between the higher rational powers and the imagination.

As regards Hooker's theory of the imagination, the passage that Stueber cites from the *Lawes* is worth quoting in full:

> The minde while wee are in this present life whether it contemplate, meditate, deliberate, or howsoever exercise it selfe, worketh nothinge without contineuall recourse unto imagination the onlie storehowse of witt and peculiar chaire of memorie. On this anvil it ceaseth not daye and night to strike; by meanes whereof as the pulse declareth how the hart doth worke, so the verie thoughtes and cogitations of mans minde be they good or bad doe no where sooner bewray them selves, then through the crevesses of that wall wherewith nature hath compassed the celles and closettes of phancie. In the forehead nothinge more plaine to be seene then the feare of contumelie and disgrace. For which cause the scripture (as with great probabilitie it may be thought) describeth them marked of God in the forehead whome his mercie hath undertaken to keepe from finall confusion and shame.[115]

The first two definitions of 'wit' in the *OED* refer respectively to 'the mind' and to the faculty of 'thinking and reasoning', so

[112] See *ST* I.78.4; Kenny, *Aquinas on Mind*, 37.

[113] See ibid. I.78.4: componimus unam formam montis aurei quem nunquam vidimus.

[114] See ibid. I.84.7: quia hoc quilibet in seipso experiri potest, quod quando aliquis conatur aliquid intelligere, format aliqua phantasmata sibi per modum exemplorum, in quibus quasi inspiciat quod intelligere studet. See also Kenny, *Aquinas on Mind*, 94–6.

[115] *Lawes*, 2:306.32–307.13 (V.65.7).

it might initially seem that the imagination is here described as a memorative faculty that stores the ideas of the reason. Hooker does, however, quote several passages from Aristotle's *De Anima* in a footnote appended to this paragraph, and these suggest a rather different interpretation of this word. Ronald Bayne translates these quotations as follows:

> Thought is either the presentation of an image or not independent of such presentation.
>
> The faculty of representing images of sense exists in irrational animals; but the faculty of representing images for deliberation only in animals that reason.
>
> Thus then the reason, while employing as its materials the images of sense, grasps from among them general ideas; and in the same manner as it determines for itself within these images what is to be pursued and what avoided, so also outside the actual perception of these objects it is, when engaged merely with the images of sense, stirred to action.[116]

These passages make it clear that Hooker did conceive of the imagination as a faculty that can represent sense images, which can then subsequently be used in deliberation. 'Witt', therefore, would appear in this context to mean 'sense', the third definition of this word listed in the *OED*. Although Hooker does not quote Aristotle on the memorative function of the imagination, he does emphasize this power himself. Thus he would appear to be in accordance with Aquinas, as well as Aristotle and scholastic theory more generally, over the function of imagination as a storehouse of sensory forms that can be used for deliberation.[117]

Stueber detects an additional point of similarity between the views of the two theologians, in that she sees in Hooker's reference to 'phancie' the creative power of the imagination which Aquinas speaks of, as being able to rearrange sensory forms.[118] Hooker's argument would seem, however, to be of a quite different

[116] Ibid., 2:307.r.1–5 (V.65.7): *Τὸ νοεῖν ἢ φαντασία τις ἢ οὐκ ἄνευ φαντασίας* Arist. de Anim. l. I. c. I. *Ἡ μὲν αἰσθητικὴ φαντασία καὶ ἐν τοῖς ἀλόγοις ζῴοις ὑπάρχει, ἡ δὲ βουλευτικὴ ἐν τοῖς λογιστικοῖς*. 1.3. c. II. *Τὰ μὲν οὖν εἴδη τὸ νοητικὸν ἐν τοῖς φαντάσμασι νοεῖ· καὶ ὡς ἐν ἐκείνοις ὥρισται αὐτῷ τὸ διωκτὸν καὶ φευκτὸν, καὶ ἐκτὸς τῆς αἰσθήσεως ὂν, ὅταν ἐπὶ τῶν φαντασμάτων ᾖ, κινεῖται*. 1.3 c.7.; John E. Booty, 'Commentary: Book V', *Folger*, vi. 757–8.

[117] See *Lawes*, 2:310.21–4 (V.65.11). As regards the commonplace nature of this view, see Park, 'The Organic Soul', 464–71.

[118] See Stueber, 'Richard Hooker's Place in the History of Renaissance Christian Humanism', 340–2.

nature. What he observes here is that, since all thought makes use of the imagination, an observation of that faculty's workings would indicate the nature of thought at a given time. The imagination can itself be indirectly observed by studying a person's 'forehead', since it is adjacent to the organ in which the imagination is housed; as he phrases it, 'wherewith nature hath compassed the celles and closettes of phancie'. Thus, for example, a person considering death may recall the form of a grave, and his or her face will show fear. Yet since this process can occur without the need for rearranged images to be created, Stueber would appear to be mistaken in her claim that Hooker describes here a creative power of the imagination, as Aquinas does in the *Summa Theologiae*.

In order to discuss the other way in which Hooker speaks of the imagination, it will first be necessary to consider one final faculty of the mind; the common sense (*sensus communis*). Aquinas lists it as being one of the four internal senses, like the imagination.[119] He observes that its purpose is to receive information (albeit indirectly) from the five external senses, and then to apprehend the differences between those things that they have each perceived. Thus, for instance, it can discern the difference between white and sweet. It is also through this faculty that we are conscious that we are using our external senses; for instance, knowing that we are seeing. Hooker, however, appears to use the term in two ways; one loose, and the other technical. As regards his non-technical usage, in one particular passage he observes how some matters are best determined by those persons possessing a certain practical experience, rather than by speculative reasoning. He gives as an example the notion that an artisan, rather than a philosopher, may best know when a fire is sufficiently hot that it can purify gold. This practical knowledge, which Hooker here calls 'common sense', would appear, as Lee W. Gibbs argues, to be contrasted with more speculative philosophy.[120] Hooker's other usage is more scholastic: 'The rule of naturall agents which worke after a sort of their owne accord, as the beasts do, is the judgement of common sense or phancy concerning the sensible goodnes of those objects wherwith

[119] See *ST* I.78.4, esp. ad. 2; Kenny, *Aquinas on Mind*, 37–8. Similar theories can again be found in many other writers. See Park, 'The Organic Soul', 464–71.

[120] See *Lawes*, 1:76.23–32 (I.6.5); Lee W. Gibbs, 'Commentary: Book I', *Folger*, vi. 494.

they are moved.'[121] Common sense is here described as a faculty capable of comparative judgements, by which animals are able to direct themselves and make 'choices' about those goods that they perceive. This would make it similar to another of Aquinas's internal senses, the *vis aestimativa* (humans possess a superior quasi-rational faculty, called the *vis cognitativa*). This power allows animals to assess the goodness of objects that have been perceived by the senses, beyond the goodness of immediate sensory pleasure. As Aquinas observes, 'a bird collects straw, not because it pleases its senses, but because it needs it for building its nest'.[122] Hooker's phrase, 'the sensible goodnes of those objects', is somewhat vague, but it would appear to refer to some such estimative, judicial power.[123]

Since Hooker uses 'common sense' and 'phancy' interchangeably in the above passage, one may conclude that he also sometimes speaks of the fancy, or imagination, in non-scholastic terms as a judicial power of the sensitive part of the soul. Thus, for example, he complains about the conclusions the '*common sort*' reach concerning their election, when their '*phancie . . . hath once throughlie apprehended the Spirit to be author of their perswasion concerning discipline*'.[124] In another passage, he speaks of people whose fear makes them irrational, so that they 'try all thinges which phancie offereth'.[125] Hooker is, therefore, able to undermine the way in which such people reach judgements concerning their religious beliefs, by locating the origin of this process in a quasi-rational, as opposed to a fully rational, faculty of the soul.[126]

Hooker, one may now state, usually adopts a commonplace scholastic approach towards the faculties of the sensitive part of the soul, like that to be found in Aquinas's work. Occasionally, however, Hooker departs significantly from this scholastic model,

121 *Lawes*, 1:84.22–5 (I.8.4).

122 See *ST* I.78.4: avis colligit paleam, non quia delectat sensum, sed quia est utilis ad nidificandum; Kenny, *Aquinas on Mind*, 36–9. This theory was, again, widely held: see Park, 'The Organic Soul', 464–71.

123 See Stueber, 'Richard Hooker's Place in the History of Renaissance Christian Humanism', 339, although she does not use this passage to evaluate Hooker's usage of the term 'phancy'.

124 See *Lawes*, 1:18.8–14 (Pref.3.11).

125 See ibid. 2:28.2–9 (V.3.1).

126 See also ibid. 1:141.28–9 (I.16.7); 3:174.4–5 (VII.6.7). Note that this process does not make human thought irrational, in the sense that decisions are made without the participation of the reason. See *Lawes*, 2:3.22–4.1 (V.Ded.5), where Hooker speaks of 'fancie' corrupting, but not replacing, rational judgement.

and uses terms such as 'common sense' in a rather loose, non-technical manner.

Closing Comments

At this point it seems desirable to make some closing comments on how these faculties should relate to one another in a correctly ordered mind. Hooker gives a concise summary of this relationship in *A Learned Sermon of the Nature of Pride*: 'the orderly disposition of the mind of man should be this, perturbations and sensuall appetites all kept in aw by a moderate and sober will; will in all things framed by reason; reason directed by the law of god and nature'.[127] The will should desire that good advocated by the reason, while the desires of the appetite should be moderated by the will.[128] The imagination, when considered as a faculty capable of quasi-rational judgements, should also presumably be kept in check by the will. The reason should itself conform to the divine reason, the precepts of which are laid out in divine and natural law. Aquinas's theory is of course virtually identical, except with regard to Hooker's non-scholastic treatment of the imagination, although it is expressed in terms of his rationalist philosophy of mind.[129] It is perhaps most easily summarized by looking at his definitions of the four cardinal virtues. The intellect, he argues, should be subject to the law of God, which yields the virtue of prudence. The object of the will's desire is of course determined by the intellect, but when the intellect specifies that the greater good be pursued (and the will desires accordingly), this yields the virtue of justice.[130] Finally, the concupiscible and irascible powers of the sensitive appetite must both be subject to the will, which yields the virtues of temperance and fortitude respectively. Both these models assume, therefore, an identical hierarchy in the correctly ordered mind, even though they differ in their conception of the will. There is, however, nothing surprising about this fact, for scholastic theories of the mind, whether rationalist or voluntarist, were in general agreement on this basic model for correct action and belief-formation. Much more complex, though, is the question of how to explain defective action and

[127] *Pride*, 5:314.16–20. See also *Lawes*, 1:86.29–87.13 (I.8.6); 1:225.24–6 (III.8.8).

[128] See *Lawes*, 2:197.18–198.2 (V.48.10).

[129] See *S.T.* I-II.61.2; I-II.85.3.

[130] See Westberg, *Right Practical Reason*, 160–4.

belief-formation, which are such a common and important aspect of sinful human nature. For Hooker's views on this matter, and how his theories on the freedom of the will transpose themselves to the problem of human error, one must look in detail at his philosophy of action, and this is the subject of the next chapter.

2

Philosophy of Action: Defective Action and Belief-Formation

Having looked at Hooker's conception of the human mental faculties in Ch. 1, it is now possible to broaden the enquiry somewhat and analyse his philosophy of action. Given that we wish to understand his views on human nature, we need to examine his theory of how the mental faculties interact in the processes of human behaviour. At the end of the previous chapter we saw the ideal hierarchical relationship that should, according to Hooker, exist between the faculties of the mind. This simple model tells us relatively little, however, about his philosophy of action, as it is in the processes of error that the complexity of the mind is revealed. Since we ultimately want to compare Hooker's views on human nature with those characteristic of the Reformed tradition in general, and of Calvin in particular, it is especially important that we see how in his opinion sinful human behaviour originates, as Reformed theology places such weight on the sinfulness of post-lapsarian humanity. It is for this reason that this chapter will concentrate on the defective aspects of human action, with special emphasis on the topic of belief-formation, which was of considerable philosophical and rhetorical interest to Hooker.

It should be noted that the following discussion is of a general philosophical nature, and will examine how error occurs in the minds of human beings as a species. As will be argued in Part II, the ultimate explanation for Hooker as to why certain errors are made closely pertains to a lack of divine grace on the part of particular individuals. For instance, in Hooker's opinion, the status of Holy Scripture as divine revelation, and the existence of God, can both be proved demonstrably to be true. People who do not accept these facts, in his view, do so because they lack respectively sanctifying and common grace. Fundamentally, however, the immediate causes of error are the same in both cases, as indeed they are, for Hooker, in all examples of defective action and belief-formation;

one or more of the mental faculties has failed to function aright. It is the purpose of this chapter to enquire into the nature of these processes, and to examine the general repercussions this has for Hooker's view of human nature. More specific questions concerning the effect of grace upon the human mind, and the extent to which Christians and non-Christians are actually capable of choosing and knowing, as well as correctly believing in the good, will be addressed later, in Chs. 3, 4, and 5.[1]

In analysing Hooker's views on this subject it is convenient to use a scholastic distinction employed by Aquinas, but not present in Hooker's own work. Aquinas, like many scholastic theologians, distinguishes between sins of malice, sins of ignorance, and sins of passion, depending upon whether the mental faculty primarily responsible for the sin is, respectively, the will, the intellect, or the sensitive appetite.[2] Hooker's examples of defective action and belief-formation can be similarly divided, which makes it easier to appreciate the theoretical basis behind his position.

One may begin with sins of malice, attributable primarily to the will, which form a small but significant proportion of the examples of defective action considered by Hooker. As the name suggests, such sins are committed deliberately, when a person knows what he or she should do, but purposely chooses to do something else. Hooker does note that people cannot choose evil *per se*, since the will necessarily desires happiness. Rather, as he observes, the will chooses evil because of 'the goodnes which is, or seemeth to be joyned with it', thus preferring the lesser over the greater good.[3] If something appeared to be purely evil, therefore, it could not be desired.

Both the cases of malice discussed by Hooker in Book I of the *Lawes* are associated with vicious customs. The following passage contains the first example, taken from ch. 7:

> Hereby it commeth to passe, that custome inuring the mind by long practise, and so leaving there a sensible impression, prevaileth more then reasonable perswasion what way so ever. Reason therfore may rightly discerne the thing which is good, and yet the will of man not incline it

[1] Hooker appears to adopt a traditional definition of knowledge as justified true belief. See *Lawes*, 1:223.9–17 (III.8.6) where he implicitly equates knowledge of God with justified true belief in God. See also Paul K. Moser, 'Epistemology', *Cambridge Dictionary of Philosophy*, 233–5.

[2] See *ST* I-II.76–8 and A. C. O'Neil, 'Sin', *Catholic Encyclopedia*, xiv. 9.

[3] See *Lawes*, 1:80.3 (I.7.6).

selfe therunto, as oft as the prejudice of sensible experience doth oversway. Nor let any man think that this doth make any thing for the just excuse of iniquity. For there was never sin committed, wherein a lesse good was not preferred before a greater, and that wilfully.[4]

Customs 'inure' the mind, causing the will to choose in a particular manner. There may be a play here on another meaning of 'inure' current at about that time—to 'burn in' or 'brand'—since Hooker notes that this process leaves a 'sensible impression'.[5] This would appear to be an implicit reference to the scholastic theory of habits, mentioned by Hooker several times in his work. Habits incline specific mental faculties towards particular objects, and their strength increases or decreases depending upon how often such objects are desired or considered. Customs, as Hooker describes them, evidently involve such a repetitious action, whereby the will becomes inclined to act in a certain way.[6] In the example given above, vicious customs induce the will to act contrary to the greater good that has been recognized by the reason, which constitutes a sin of malice. One should note, however, that Hooker implies that this action is still free, for he considers it to be blameworthy, and as he remarks elsewhere, when we are constrained to act we are not to be held responsible for what we do.[7]

The other case of malice mentioned by Hooker in Book I of the *Lawes* is based on the passage in Matthew where Jesus berates the people of Jerusalem for their intransigence: 'sometimes the very custome of evil making the hart obdurate against whatsoever instructions to the contrary, as in them over whom our Saviour spake weeping, *O Jerusalem, how often and thou wouldst not?*'[8] 'Hart' here is presumably a synonym for the will, since it connotes a form of desire, and Hooker tends to associate customs/habits with the

[4] See *Lawes*, 1:80.18–26 (I.7.6–7).

[5] See *OED*, 'Inure', *v.* 2, first definition. The earliest occurrence listed by the *OED* is 1619.

[6] On the subject of habits, see *Lawes*, 2:290.20–4 (V.63.1); 2:291.19–24 (V.63.2); 3:8.4–8 (VI.3.2); 3:54.29–30 (VI.5.4); *DF* 4:110.h; 4:127.27–128.2; *Just.* 5:129.19–130.12. Cf. *ST* I-II.50.5; I-II.52.3; I-II.54.3; I-II.63.2. It is noteworthy that Hooker, unlike Aquinas, always assigns habits to the will, apart from faith which he regards as a habit of the reason, and that he never speaks of habits of the appetite. As he observes in the *Dublin Fragments*, paraphrasing the contents of a chapter in Augustine's *Confessions*: 'good and evil habits bind the will' (habitus boni et mali necessitant voluntatem). He thus joins Augustine in making lust a habit of the will, unlike Aquinas who sees it as a habit of the sensitive appetite. See *ST* II-II.153.1; Lawrence Manley, *Convention 1500–1750* (Cambridge, Mass., 1980), 91.

[7] See *Lawes*, 1:94.7–95.5 (I.9.1), and Appendix, p. 328.

[8] *Lawes*, 1:81.4–7 (I.7.7).

faculty of intellectual desire, the will.[9] Moreover, the appetite cannot itself choose to act contrary to the 'instructions' of (what is presumably) the reason, whereas this is the prerogative of the will. Hooker in this passage, therefore, again blames the will's deliberate choice of the lesser good on a vicious custom or habit.

Turning now to look at sins of ignorance, which are primarily attributable to the reason, these would at first appear to be more insidious than sins of malice. A person can, after all, avoid sins of malice simply by choosing the greater good, however difficult this choice may be; yet when a person is ignorant of the greater good, he or she is most unlikely to choose it. The principal problem here is laziness; people either do not bother to enquire into the truth, or do so with insufficient diligence.

Before considering the question of diligence, it is important to establish just how certain the reason must be about the truth in order to fulfil its responsibilities. Hooker mentions this matter in Book I of the *Lawes*, but provides a somewhat ambiguous answer:

> if reason have taught it rightly to be good, yet not so apparently that the mind receiveth it with utter impossibility of being otherwise; still there is place left for the will to take or leave. Whereas therfore amongst so many things as are to be done there are so few, the goodnes wherof reason in such sort doth or easily can discover; we are not to marvaile at the choyce of evill, even then when the contrary is probably knowne.[10]

In this passage Hooker makes an important distinction between probable and infallible knowledge. In order to understand this it is worth spending some time looking at his theory of certainty, especially as this subject is also central to his ideas on religious authority, to be examined later in Ch. 4.

THEORY OF CERTAINTY

Although Hooker argues that humans can through reason gain knowledge of the truth, he does observe that they cannot always do so with the same degree of certainty. There are, in fact, he argues in the *Lawes*, four levels of certainty pertaining to objects

[9] See n. 6 above. For a fuller discussion of Hooker's references to the 'hart', see Ch. 4 n. 226.
[10] *Lawes*, 1:80.11–8 (I.7.6).

that the human mind can know.[11] It will be advisable to start by looking at the second level of certainty and then proceed to the third and fourth: the first (and most certain) level will be left until last, as it has some unusual properties that separate it from the other three.

The second level of certainty Hooker calls 'plaine aspect and intuitive beholding',[12] and it can be split into two categories. The first, 'plaine aspect', concerns sense-data, where he shows his opposition to the sceptical argument that we can have no true knowledge of empirical reality. This can most clearly be seen from his exchanges with Walter Travers in the Temple controversy, where Travers accused him of teaching that '*the assurance of that we beleeve by the word, is not so certeyne as of that we perceyve by sense*'.[13] In response, Hooker observes that: 'if tenne men do all looke uppon the moone, every one of them knoweth it as certenly to be the moone as another: But many beleevinge one and the same promis all have not one and the same fulnesse of perswasion.'[14] No one looking at the moon will doubt its identity, Hooker argues, because information provided by the external senses is wholly sure. Thus, in the case of sight, a person does quite literally plainly behold the truth, and cannot be mistaken. This category of certainty would appear to concern the apprehension of simple ideas, and is the responsibility of the understanding, which, as has been noted in the previous chapter, cannot err in its activities.[15]

The other category, 'intuitive beholding', is more metaphorical, concerned as it is with 'The maine principles of reason'. These are the first principles of reasoning, which are self-evident to the mind, and do not require proof. Hooker gives examples of speculative first principles, such as '*a part of anything is lesse then the whole*',

[11] This subject has received much attention from Hooker critics. See e.g. Hillerdal, *Reason and Revelation in Richard Hooker*, 97, 99, 113–14, 117; Hill, 'The Doctrinal Background of Richard Hooker's *Laws of Ecclesiastical Polity*', 265; Grislis, 'The Hermeneutical Problem in Richard Hooker', 178–9; Rudolph Almasy, 'The Purpose of Richard Hooker's Polemic', *Journal of the History of Ideas* 39 (1978), 260; Neelands, 'The Theology of Grace of Richard Hooker', 111; Atkinson, *Richard Hooker and the Authority of Scripture, Tradition and Reason*, 92–4. On this topic more generally, see Henry G. Van Leeuwen, *The Problem of Certainty in English Thought 1630–1690* (The Hague, 1963), 14, 20–5, 29–32; Ian Hacking, *The Emergence of Probability: A Philosophical Study of Early Ideas about Probability, Induction and Statistical Inference* (Cambridge, 1975), 12–46; Barbara J. Shapiro, *Probability and Certainty in Seventeenth-Century England* (Princeton, 1983), 77.

[12] See *Lawes*, 1:179.11–12, 20 (II.7.5). See also *Cert.* 5:69.24–6.

[13] See 'Supplication', 5:200.5–11.

[14] *Answer*, 5:236.30–237.2.

[15] See pp. 30–1 above.

and practical first principles, such as '*the greater good is to be chosen before the lesse*', '*God to be worshipped,*' and '*Others to be used by us as we our selves would by them.*'[16]

The third level of certainty, 'strong and invincible demonstration', is defined by Hooker in terms of an argument which '*being proposed unto any man and understood, the mind cannot choose but inwardly assent*'.[17] It is thus concerned with the processes of reasoning, and is a conclusion logically and necessarily deduced from first principles. As such it is infallibly certain, and when the reason comprehends the process of deduction, it necessarily assents to the conclusion. Hooker gives several examples, one of which is the following, taken from Matthew 16: 26: 'For a man to winne the world, if it be with the losse of his soule, what benefite or good is it?'[18]

The fourth, and least certain level, 'greatest probability', remains when it is impossible to base an argument purely on first principles.[19] Conclusions reached in this manner may be forceful, but the reason does not assent to them necessarily once the process of deduction has been understood. As Hooker observes, with regard to the possibility of error, '*As for probabilities, what thing was there ever set downe so agreeable with sound reason, but some probable shewe against it might be made?*'[20] Of particular interest amongst the examples he gives of probable reasoning are *adiaphora*, or indifferent points of theology, which he argues are not matters of Christian doctrine because by definition only probable proofs can be adduced for their validity. In such cases we are not bound by our faith to believe, he notes, but may rather 'lawfully doubt and suspend our judgement, inclyning neyther to one side nor other'.[21] Hooker mentions in this context several such *adiaphora*, one of which is the perpetual virginity of the Virgin Mary after the birth of Christ. As William Haugaard has observed, this was 'an undisputed teaching with a heavy weight of tradition', and was accepted by such sixteenth-century Reformers as Luther, Zwingli, and Calvin.[22] It is not a matter of doctrine, however, in

[16] See *Cert.* 1:70.9–11; *Lawes*, 1:85.6–86.9 (I.8.5); 2:290.6–24 (V.63.1). For Hooker's views on whether the acceptance of first principles relates to the reason's act of apprehension or assent, see pp. 197–8 below.

[17] See *Lawes*, 1:33.19–20 (Pref.6.6); 1:179.12–16 (II.7.5). See also 2:39.9–10 (V.8.2); 2:85.14–24 (V.21.3); 2:290.6–9 (V.63.1)

[18] See ibid. 1:85.15–86.4 (I.8.5).

[19] See ibid. 1:179.16–18 (II.7.5). See also 2:39.11–14 (V.8.2).

[20] See ibid. 1:33.27–9 (Pref.6.6).

[21] See ibid. 1:179.25–180.8 (II.7.5).

[22] See William P. Haugaard, 'Commentary: Book II', *Folger*, vi. 546.

Hooker's opinion, because there are no demonstrative arguments attesting to its truth. Hooker also includes long-standing Church traditions in this fourth level of certainty: the basis for this will be examined in detail at the end of Ch. 4.

Finally, one may look at the first, and most certain level, which concerns Christian doctrine. Hooker looks in most detail at this type of certainty in his early tractate, *A Learned and Comfortable Sermon of the Certaintie and Perpetuitie of Faith in the Elect*, where he observes that 'That which wee know ether by sense or by most in fallible demonstration is not so certain as the principles articles and conclusions of Christian fayth.'[23] He explains what he understands by this by making a scholastic threefold distinction between different classes of certainty, quite different from the ones we have considered so far.[24] Of the first two of these three classes he observes the following:

> Certainty of evidence wee call that, when the mind doth assent unto this or that; not because it is true in it selfe, but because the truth therof is cleere, because it is manifest unto us. Of thinges in them selves most certain, except they be also most evident, our persuasion is not so assured as it is of thinges more evident although in themselves they be lesse certayn. It is as sure if not surer that there be sprites as that there be men: but wee are more assured of these then of them because these are more evident.[25]

Hooker here describes certainty of evidence in terms of proofworthiness, or the degree to which it is manifest to us that something is true. The three types of certainty that have been considered above, 'plaine aspect and intuitive beholding', demonstrative reasoning, and greatest probability, all fall within this definition, as subtypes of certainty of evidence. Hooker also speaks in this passage, however, of certainty attaching to things 'in them selves', which may be termed 'intrinsic certainty'. His example, regarding humans and spirits, points to a metaphysical distinction concerning perfection and mutability. Spirits, being higher in the celestial hierarchy of perfection than humans, may be said to be more 'certain', which logically leaves God as the most certain

[23] *Cert.* 5:69.24–6. See also *Lawes*, 1:126.18–24 (I.14.2); 2:39.8–9 (V.8.3) and cf. *ST* II-II.4.8.

[24] This distinction is to be found, for instance, in Aquinas's *De Veritate*, 14.1. See Egil Grislis, 'Commentary', *Folger*, v. 700.

[25] *Cert.* 5:70.1–8. The third class of certainty, certainty of adherence, will be examined in the proper context of the divinely infused habits of faith and love, in Ch. 4, pp. 244–6.

thing of all. As Aquinas, for instance, observes, the less something is prone to change the more intrinsically certain it is.[26] It is for this reason that Hooker argues in the *Lawes* that the Word of God is more certain than the objects of sense-data, as Holy Scripture reflects the certainty of the Divine Being: 'that which we see with our eies is not thought so sure as that which the scripture of God teacheth; because wee hold that his speech revealeth there what himselfe seeth, and therefore the strongest proofe of all, and the most necessaryly assented unto by us (which do thus receive the scripture) is the scripture.'[27] Yet although Hooker finds Holy Scripture more intrinsically certain than sense-data, he finds sense-data more evidentially certain. This is again the point that provoked Travers in the Temple controversy, and it is worth quoting Hooker's words from the *Answer to the Supplication* for a second time, but now at greater length:

Yea I taughte as he [Travers] hym self I truste woulde not denye that the thinges which God doth promys in his worde are surer unto us then any thinge we touche handle or see, but are we so sure and certeyne of them? if we be, why doth God so often prove his promises unto us as he doth by argumentes taken from our sensible experiences? We must be surer of the profe then of the thinge proved, otherwise it is no profe. Howe is it that if tenne men do all looke uppon the moone, every one of them knoweth it as certenly to be the moone as another: But many beleevinge one and the same promis all have not one and the same fulnesse of perswasion?[28]

Hooker repeats the maxim that 'We must be surer of the profe then of the thinge proved, otherwise it is no profe' in *A Learned and Comfortable Sermon of the Certaintie and Perpetuitie of Faith in the Elect*, and it reveals much about the nature of his theology.[29] No matter how intrinsically certain any aspect of Christian doctrine may be, he finds, it is only as evidentially certain as the proofs adduced in its favour allow. For this reason God in Holy Scripture attempts to convince humans of Christian doctrine by arguments based on sense-data, because the evidential certainty of sense-data is so high. The same point can be seen in Book I of the *Lawes*, in a

[26] See *ST* II-II.4.8.

[27] *Lawes*, 1:179.20–5 (II.7.5). Hooker also accepted that infallible revealed knowledge could be known intuitively, though one should note that his example concerns no less a person than St Paul. See *Lawes*, 1:31.10–13 (Pref.6.3).

[28] *Answer*, 5:236.23–237.2.

[29] See *Cert.* 5:70:19–20.

passage where Hooker distinguishes between doctrines 'necessarye unto salvation' that are expressly stated in Holy Scripture, and other such doctrines that can rationally be deduced from it:

In like sort, albeit scripture do professe to conteyne in it all things which are necessarye unto salvation; yet the meaning cannot be simplye of all things that are necessarye, but all things that are necessarye in some certaine kinde or forme . . . Further, there hath bene some doubt likewise, whether *conteining in scripture* do import expresse setting downe in plaine tearmes, or else *comprehending* in such sort that by reason we may from thence conclude all things which are necessary. Against the former of these two constructions, instance hath sundrie wayes bene given. For our beliefe in the Trinitie, the Coeternitie of the Sonne of God with his Father, the proceeding of the Spirit from the Father and the Sonne, the dutie of baptizing infants, these with such other principall points, the necessitie wherof is by none denied, are notwithstanding in scripture no where to be found by expresse literall mention, only deduced they are out of scripture by collection. This kind of comprehension in scripture being therfore receyved, still there is doubt how far we are to proceed by collection before the full and complete measure of things necessarie be made up. For let us not thinke that as long as the world doth indure, the wit of man shal be able to sound the bottome of that which may be concluded out of the scripture, especially if things conteined by collection do so far extend, as to draw in whatsoever may be at any time out of scripture but probablie and conjecturallie surmised. But let necessary collection be made requisite, and we may boldlie denye that of all those things which at this day are with so great necessitie urged upon this Church under the name of reformed Church discipline, there is any one which their bookes hetherto have made manifest to be conteyned in the scripture.[30]

Hooker observes here that some Christian doctrines such as 'the Trinitie, the Coeternitie of the Sonne of God with his Father, the proceeding of the Spirit from the Father and the Sonne, the dutie of baptizing infants' need to be deduced from Holy Scripture, as they are not mentioned expressly within it. That they are nevertheless Christian doctrines 'necessarye unto salvation' stems from the fact that, by definition, they can be extracted from Holy Scripture by 'necessary collection', as opposed to what can be 'but probablie and conjecturallie surmised': in other words, by a process of demonstrative, as opposed to mere probable, reasoning. These doctrines are because of this, however, no more evidentially certain

[30] *Lawes*, 1:125.32–127.3 (I.14.2). See also 1:184.24–185.7 (II.7.9).

than demonstrative reasoning, in spite of their absolute intrinsic certainty: from this it follows that someone not accepting or understanding the principles underlying this reasoning process would not admit them to be true. As regards doctrines 'necessarye unto salvation' which are to be found in Holy Scripture 'by expresse literall mention', the fact that they do not need to be ascertained through a demonstrative argument suggests that their evidential certainty is higher. Hooker may well here be tacitly comparing doctrines expressly mentioned in Holy Scripture, such as the resurrection of Jesus, with the process of 'intuitive beholding' by which a person apprehends or assents to natural first truths. If this is so then this comparison is metaphorical, for as Hooker argues, all rational human beings accept natural first principles, whereas Christians alone, because they believe that Holy Scripture is the Word of God, accept the divine first principles in Holy Scripture.[31] Even doctrines to be found 'by expresse literall mention' in Holy Scripture are, indirectly, no more evidentially certain than the evidence proving that Holy Scripture is the Word of God, and (as will be examined in Ch. 4) Hooker considers the strongest proof in this regard to be demonstrative reasoning.[32]

It is perhaps in part because of this reliance on demonstrative reasoning that Hooker ascribes the religious doubts of Christians to the difficulties that imperfect humans have in evaluating the evidence for Christian doctrine. It should also be remembered in this regard that most Christians are not theologians, and will not be in a position to reason about such matters demonstrably: they will as a consequence have less evidential certainty for their (instrinsically certain) religious beliefs. As Hooker observes, in *A Learned and Comfortable Sermon of the Certaintie and Perpetuitie of Faith in the Elect*:

I conclud therefore that wee have lesse certaintie of evidence concerning thinges beleeved then concerning thinges sensibly or naturally perceyved. Of these who doth doubt at any time, of them at some tyme who doth not? I will not here alledge the sundry confessions of the perfeitest that have lived upon earth concerning their great imperfections this way, which if I did I should dwell to longe upon a matter sufficiently knowen to every fayth full man that doth know him selfe.[33]

[31] For further analysis of Hooker's conception of divine first principles and demonstrative conclusions in Holy Scripture, see p. 197.

[32] See pp. 227, 253–5.

[33] *Cert.*, 5:70.23–30.

The argument here is identical to that found in the *Answer to the Supplication*, that no one seeing the moon will doubt its existence, but the promises of God are only evidentially as sure as the proofs that human reasoning can adduce in their favour. Human reasoning is, therefore, absolutely essential as regards the evidential certainty of Christian doctrine for Hooker; a vital notion that will be returned to later when considering his views on religious authority.[34]

One may now return to the subject of defective action and belief-formation, and to the passage from Book I of the *Lawes* regarding the certainty with which the reason should ascertain the truth.[35] From the above analysis it is easier to see the logic behind Hooker's remark that there are very few cases in which reason 'doth or easily can discover' the good with infallible certainty. Very few arguments, particularly regarding practical matters, can be based logically on first principles. Daniel Westberg gives as an example the statement that 'the economy is slowing down because taxes are still too high', which would be impossible to verify in this manner.[36] Hooker prizes such reasoning very highly, but also implicitly acknowledges its rarity, when he observes that 'one demonstrative reason' is of more authority than the judgements of 'ten thousand generall Councels'.[37] Most questions must be resolved by probable arguments, and it is one of Hooker's basic positions in his dialogue with the presbyterians that this is perfectly satisfactory, 'in defect of proofe infallible'.[38] The reason, therefore, is responsible for ascertaining the truth with sufficient surety such that the good may be chosen; it is only rarely required to be infallibly certain.

Hooker's own conclusion in Book I of the *Lawes* regarding infallible knowledge is very strange, however, for he argues that in such cases the will necessarily desires in accordance with reason. If this is taken literally then it would again point to a Socratic theory of defective action and belief-formation, where humans sin because they do not sufficiently understand the truth.[39] It has previously been pointed out that Hooker's conception of the will directly opposes this notion, and this can now be illustrated by reference to infallible knowledge. '*God to be worshipped*' is, Hooker

[34] See pp. 254–6. [35] See p. 71. [36] See Westberg, *Right Practical Reason*, 199.
[37] See *Lawes*, 1:180.20–9 (II.7.5). [38] See ibid. 1:180.29–32 (II.7.5).
[39] See pp. 56–7 above and Westberg, *Right Practical Reason*, 37.

states, one of the first principles of practical reasoning. Since first principles are intuitively certain, the understanding thus necessarily assents to this truth. Yet Hooker is under no illusion in his work that people who know that God should be worshipped always choose to do so; people have liberty of indifference, and can in theory do as they please. The sins of malice discussed previously demonstrate clearly how the will can disobey the reason, and this must be true even when the reason is infallibly sure. One must conclude, therefore, that Hooker either nodded when writing these lines, or failed to make his meaning sufficiently clear.

It is now appropriate to look at some cases of sin through ignorance mentioned by Hooker, in order to understand where errors arise. Interestingly enough, the two clear examples of such sin to be found in the *Lawes* are both connected with vicious customs, in a similar manner to sins of malice. In the first case, from Book 1, Hooker examines how people come to be ignorant of natural law, and in particular the law forbidding idolatry. As he observes, quoting from Wisdom 14: 15–16:

> I denie not but lewde and wicked custome, beginning perhaps at the first amongst few, afterwards spreading into greater multitudes, and so continuing from time to time, may be of force even in plaine things to smother the light of naturall understanding, because men will not bend their wits to examine, whether things wherewith they have bene accustomed, be good or evill. For examples sake that grosser kind of heathenish idolatrie, whereby they worshipped the verie works of their owne hands, was an absurditie to reason... The cause of which senselesse stupiditie is afterwards imputed to custome. *When a father mourned grievously for his sonne that was taken away suddainly, he made an image for him that was once dead, whom now he worshippeth as a God, ordeining to his servants ceremonies and sacrifices. Thus by processe of time this wicked custome prevailed, and was kept as a law.*[40]

Custom causes the activities of the reason to be stifled, and people believe without rationally considering their beliefs. The same is true in the second case of ignorance, to be found in the preface, except that here the people concerned show a distorted sense of intelligence:

> *Pythagoras, by bringing up his Scholers in the speculative knowledge of numbers, made their conceipts therein so strong, that when they came to the contemplation of things*

[40] *Lawes*, 1:91.30–92.22 (I.8.11).

naturall they imagined that in every particular thing they even beheld as it were with their eyes, howe the elementes of number gave essence and being to the workes of nature. A thing in reason impossible; which notwithstanding through their misfashioned preconceipt, appeared unto them no lesse certaine, then if nature had written it in the verie foreheads of all the creatures of God.[41]

The Pythagoreans corrupt the correct process of reasoning, in that they treat their '*misfashioned preconceipt*' concerning numbers as if it were a first principle, and proceed to deduce from it false conclusions. What they fail to do is to consider their assumptions, and to realize that they are not based on first principles themselves. This is very much an archetypal model of defective action and belief-formation for Hooker, which he uses to explain how people (especially his presbyterian opponents) can reason carefully and yet reach false conclusions. This is one explanation why the first book of the *Lawes* contains so much theoretical material, in that Hooker does not wish to base his own theology on premises that he has not explored.[42] Most of his examples of such errors, however, concern sins of passion, and will be dealt with later in this chapter. In the case of the Pythagoreans, as with the idolaters, errors would appear purely to arise from ignorance attributable to a vicious custom. Since customs are habits, and Hooker tends to associate habits with the will,[43] this would suggest that the explanation why people fail to reason diligently is because the will has become corrupted, and does not direct the reason to find the truth. Put simply, people do not choose to reason diligently. To confirm this interpretation, and to examine Hooker's views on whether the reason can in some sense be corrupt itself, one needs to return to the chapter '*Of mans will*' in Book 1 of the *Lawes*.

Towards the end of this chapter, having looked at how customs influence the mind, Hooker makes the following remarks about diligence: 'There is not that good which concerneth us, but it hath evidence enough for it selfe, if reason were diligent to search it out. Through neglect thereof, abused wee are with the shew of that which is not, somtimes the subtilty of Satan inveagling us as it did Eve.'[44] Hooker then gives two additional examples of defective

[41] *Lawes*, 1:16.12–9 (Pref.3.9). [42] See ibid. 1:57.6–16 (I.1.2). [43] See n. 6.

[44] See *Lawes*, 1:80.29–81.1 (I.7.7). Cf. 1:240.2–8 (III.10.1); Grislis, 'The Role of *Consensus* in Richard Hooker's Method of Theological Inquiry', 70. See also *Cert.* 5:78.5–10; 5:80.20–1.

action and belief-formation, but as they are not sins of ignorance they are analysed elsewhere.[45] The example quoted here is interesting, however, as no explanation is given for the lack of diligence on Eve's part, except the subtlety of Satan. There is no suggestion that Eve had acquired a vicious habit, or was influenced by passion, but simply that she was lazy in her reasoning. Hooker subsequently emphasizes, though, that there can be no excuse for such behaviour, which must mean that it is voluntary, and under the command of the will. He then makes the will's role in reasoning explicit in his ensuing remarks:

> The search of knowledg is a thing painful and the painfulnes of knowledge is that which maketh the will so hardly inclinable thereunto. The root hereof divine malediction whereby the instruments being weakned wherewithall the soule (especially in reasoning) doth worke, it preferreth rest in ignorance before wearisome labour to knowe. For a spurre of diligence therefore wee have a naturall thirst after knowledge ingrafted in us. But by reason of that originall weaknes in the instruments, without which the understanding part is not able in this world by discourse to worke, the very conceipt of painefulnesse is as a bridle to stay us. For which cause the Apostle who knew right wel, that the wearines of the flesh is an heavy clog to the will, striketh mightely upon this key, *Awake thou that sleepest, Cast off all which presseth downe, Watch, Labour, strive to go forward and to grow in knowledge.*[46]

Hooker describes the will here as being responsible for the search for knowledge, and applies Paul's exhortations regarding diligence to this faculty. He also notes that humans have a natural thirst for knowledge, and since thirst is a form of desire, this must apply to the will as well. People are not, then, he evidently feels, ignorant by necessity, but because they freely choose not to discover the truth. This means that sins of ignorance, while pertaining primarily to the reason, are also the responsibility of the will; not surprisingly, since Hooker emphasizes that sin is by definition a voluntary activity.[47]

The above passage is also important in that it shows that, in Hooker's opinion, original sin has made the reasoning process arduous. There is, however, a striking difference between the explanation he gives for this here, and the one he provides in his

[45] See pp. 69–71 and n. 63 below.

[46] *Lawes*, 1:81.10–23 (I.7.7).

[47] See p. 70 and Appendix, p. 328. See also John G. Hughes, 'The Theology of Richard Hooker' (Ph.D. thesis, Univ. of Leeds, 1979), 32.

late works. In this passage from the *Lawes*, Hooker does not argue that the reason itself has become corrupted, but rather that the 'instruments' of reasoning have. The instruments are associated by Hooker with the 'flesh', and in a footnote he quotes Wisdom 9: 15 on how '*A corruptible body is heavie unto the soule, and the earthly mansion keepeth down the mind that is full of cares.*' The function of this quotation would appear to be to illustrate a dualist distinction between the body and the soul. In scholastic philosophy of mind, and in Aristotelian psychology more generally, the will and the reason are identified with the immaterial soul, and the lesser sensitive and vegetative faculties with the body.[48] This is the logic behind Hooker's observation that the imagination is housed in an organ near the forehead; it is a physical faculty, located in a particular place, unlike the reason and the will. As regards the 'instruments' without which, according to Hooker, the 'understanding part' cannot work, these would seem to refer to the imagination, since as we have seen in Ch. 1, all reasoning requires the use of phantasmata housed in this faculty.[49] This argument is supported by the fact that Hooker observes that the 'understanding part' is not able to reason without the 'instruments' 'in this world'. Aquinas argues that the reason and the will are in themselves capable of thought in the afterlife, without the aid of the lower sensitive powers.[50] Hooker would appear here to agree, implicitly suggesting that the imagination is not required by the immaterial 'understanding part' in the world to come. He is not arguing in this passage, therefore, that the reason itself is corrupted by original sin, but rather the imagination (and perhaps the sensitive faculties more generally). This would in itself be a sufficient explanation for why reasoning has become a difficult process, given that the reason must make use of the forms stored in this faculty. In the late works, however, Hooker blames the reason directly for ignorance, and observes that original sin has corrupted it and made it slothful:

> Wee have therefore a will, the nature whereof is apt and capable as well to receive the good as the evill; butt sinne is fraudulent, and beguileth us with evill under the shewe of good, sloth breeding carelesnes, and our originall corruption sloth in the power of reason, which should discerne betweene the one and the other.[51]

[48] See e.g. *ST* I.75.2–3; I.77.8. [49] See p. 63. [50] See *ST* I.84.7; I.89.

[51] *DF* 4:107.22–6. See also *AN* 4:18.6–24; *DF* 4:105.21–4; 4:108.14–15; 4:108.30–2; 4:109.3–4.

His initial inclination in the *Lawes*, therefore, was to exonerate the reason from the taint of corruption. One can only speculate that the accusations of Pelagianism made by the *Christian Letter* persuaded him to become more cautious in his late works. Yet in both the late works and the *Lawes*, he emphasizes that this corruption is not so debilitating that through diligence a person cannot discover the truth. In the *Lawes* he quotes Paul on how knowledge can be arrived at through labour, despite the corruption of the 'instruments' of reasoning. In the late works he argues that the reason 'has in itself sufficiently all good by which it can prove itself to a man who is painstaking and diligently pays heed' (*Habet tamen omne bonum satis quidem in se quo probare se possit homini . . . sedulo diligenterque attendenti*).[52] Original sin, therefore, requires the will to be more resolute than would otherwise have been necessary, in directing the reason to inquire after the good. In fact, as will be seen, Hooker does not belittle the difficulty of such diligence, and argues that common and sanctifying grace are in different ways essential if it is to occur. Yet this does not change his position that ignorance is a voluntary condition, the result of laziness on the part of the will: as such, a person could theoretically choose to avoid sin, despite the fact that original sin has made arduous the reasoning process.

To come now finally to sins of passion, which pertain primarily to the appetite (though also, as we shall see, to the imagination), it is noticeable that most of the cases mentioned by Hooker concern the subversion of the reasoning process. In fact, most of the examples in Hooker's work of people forming false beliefs deal with the malign influence of the appetite on the reason and the will. Perhaps this is not surprising, given the nature of the beliefs that Hooker wishes to explain. His principal interest is in the belief-formation process of people deeply concerned about religion, which cannot easily be ascribed to sins of malice or of ignorance. Sins of malice pertain only to action, since one cannot simply choose to form a false belief contrary to what one knows to be right. Sins of ignorance are principally the result of laziness, and in most cases Hooker is clearly aware that this cannot be said of the people whom he wishes to criticize. Given his theory of the

[52] See *AN* 4:18.10–12; John E. Booty, 'Commentary', *Folger*, iv. 194. Trans. from Latin by Ronald Bayne.

mind, therefore, it was logical that he would see the appetite as ultimately to blame for such cases of defective belief-formation.

The model that Hooker employs for sins of passion is best illustrated by his description of how heretics of the patristic period formed their religious beliefs. As he observes: 'obstinatlie following their owne ambitious or otherwise corrupted affections, in stead of framing their wills to maynteyne that which reason taught, they bent their wits to finde how reason might seeme to teach that which their wills were set to maynteyne.'[53] The will fails to reject the inordinate desires of the appetite, and is instead itself persuaded to desire in accordance with them. The will then directs the reason to find arguments for why this object of desire should be chosen, which the reason proceeds to do. Sensitive desire unreasonably influences intellectual desire, and intellectual desire distorts the reasoning process. The result, as Hooker describes it, is that 'wee studdy to deceive ourselves', assiduously finding arguments for things we want to believe.[54] Yet with such a '*misfashioned preconceipt*' such people will inevitably go astray, since their reasoning is not based on first principles or the available evidence, but simply on their malign sensual desires.

There are many examples in Hooker's work of heretics whose beliefs have been influenced adversely by their appetites: Aërius opposes episcopacy due to his ambitious pride, and to his failure to obtain promotion; Arius through envy and resentment, and failure to obtain promotion, comes to deny the co-equality and co-eternity of the Son with the Father; Pelagius through his sour disposition is critical of priestly attire; Tertullian through sourness and choler comes to support Montanism, and its severe attitudes to such matters as feast days and fasting.[55] The Anabaptists are described in a similar manner, with regard to their consideration of whether polygamy should be practised. '*Glad and faine they were to have it so*,' Hooker observes, '*which verie desire was it selfe apt to breede both an opinion of possibilitie, and a willingnesse to gather argumentes of likelihood that so God him selfe would have it.*'[56] They do not, therefore,

[53] *Lawes*, 1:225.24–8 (III.8.8). Cf. *Pride*, 5:314.20–3. See also Debora K. Shuger, *Habits of Thought in the English Renaissance: Religion, Politics, and the Dominant Culture* (Berkeley and Los Angeles, 1990), 259.

[54] See *DF* 4:105.24–5.

[55] See *Lawes*, 3:199.9–21 (VII.9.1); 2:166.7–20 (V.42.2); 2:123.22–6 (V.29.2); 1:164.3–165.8 (II.5.7); 3:76.8–15 (VI.6.6). It is interesting to note that Tertullian's affections are described as causing him to make an error with regard to natural law, since he incorrectly charges those who wear garlands with breaking this law.

[56] See ibid. 1:48.10–13 (Pref.8.11).

consider abstractly whether God permits polygamy, but on the basis of desires which are presumably sexual in origin, search for reasons for something they merely wish to find true. Atheists are also described in such terms; Hooker conceives of them as mere hedonists, intent on reaping 'what sensuall profitt or pleasure soever the world yealdeth'.[57] Since God condemns such 'base desires' as these, they reject him, and 'studie howe to perswade them selves that there is no such thinge to be knowne'.

Amongst the many other examples which might be given, one of the most significant concerns Calvin's position on presbyterianism. In the preface to the *Lawes* Hooker commends Calvin for establishing this discipline in Geneva, but not for his subsequent attempt to universalize the practice, and impose it on all other Churches.[58] In so doing, Hooker suggests, Calvin showed an immoderate love for the discipline he had created, wishing to believe that it was of divine ordination. '*Nature*', Hooker notes, '*worketh in us all a love to our owne counsels.*'[59] When people proceeded to contradict Calvin on this matter, this sharpened his '*wit to dispute, to argue, and by all meanes to reason for it*'.[60] Such love of one's own opinions cannot pertain to the will, since Hooker notes that this self-love was the cause of Calvin's beliefs on presbyterianism, and one cannot simply choose what to believe. Hooker is, moreover, not accusing Calvin of a sin of malice, of deliberately going astray. Rather, it would appear that this self-love is here defined in a scholastic sense as a selfish desire of the appetite, capable of influencing the will and the reason in a malign way.[61] Calvin's views on presbyterianism are, therefore, Hooker implies, the consequence of a sin of passion on the Frenchman's part, whereby he has found reasons for things he would like to be true. Given the subsequent popularity of the presbyterian discipline one can then perhaps understand Hooker's pessimistic assertion that 'there is nothing for which some colourable reason or other may not be found.'[62] Brilliant minds like that of Calvin were capable of finding arguments to support almost any position. This made it imperative that the premisses behind all arguments be carefully

[57] See ibid. 2:23.6–19 (V.2.1).

[58] See ibid. 1:3.10–12.21 (Pref.2). Calvin, in fact, did not argue that presbyterianism was the only acceptable Church discipline, and in this respect Hooker either misunderstands or misrepresents Calvin's views.

[59] See ibid. 1:10.10 (Pref.2.7).

[60] See ibid. 1:10.12–13 (Pref.2.7).

[61] See e.g. *ST* I-II.77.4 ad. 2.

[62] See *Lawes*, 3:350.12–13 (VIII.3.1).

explored, to see whether they were ultimately based on malign sensual desires.[63]

In a recent article, however, A. D. Cousins has commented on Hooker's analysis of Calvin and presbyterianism in the preface, and claimed that 'Hooker follows an unreasonable argument with a mere caricature of Calvin in action.'[64] This raises, perhaps tangentially, an interesting philosophical question: can it ever be justifiable on philosophical grounds alone to give a specific, as opposed to a general, explanation for defective belief-formation? Hooker, as we have seen, has solid scholastic reasons for accusing Calvin of having committed a sin of passion as regards church discipline, and Cousins is mistaken in describing Hooker as unreasonable in this respect. Yet it is dubious that philosophical motives alone induced Hooker to accuse Calvin, whom he never met, of the specific sin of pride, which would seem to require great familiarity with the workings of the Frenchman's mind. While Hooker's portrait may not be a 'mere caricature' it is nevertheless unquestionably rhetorical, designed to sow seeds of doubt in the reader's mind about the authority of Calvin in matters of church discipline (and perhaps in other areas as well). Hooker thus strays outside the bounds of pure philosophy of action in this passage, and it is probably true that he does so in relation to other sins of passion considered in his work as well.

To return to the subject of philosophy of action, there are a number of passages in the *Lawes* in which Hooker does not speak of the appetite influencing the reason and the will, but rather attributes influence to the imagination (or fancy) considered as a quasi-rational judicial faculty.[65] As the following passage illustrates, however, the processes are analogous for Hooker, and he here in fact virtually regards the appetite and the imagination as synonymous:

> errors have their effect many times not proportioned to that litle appearance of reason whereupon they woulde seeme built, but rather to the

[63] For other examples of false reasoning based upon the appetite, see ibid. 1:17.29–18.8 (Pref.3.10); 1:18.32–19.15 (Pref.3.13); 1:51.29–31 (Pref.9.1); 1:58.7–10 (I.1.3); 1:226.15–22 (III.8.9); 1:302.29–32 (IV.9.2); 2:27.13–28.17 (V.3.1–2); 2:291.19–292.1 (V.63.2); 2:434.7–25 (V.77.14); 3:2.1–11 (VI.1.1); Stueber, 'Richard Hooker's Place in the History of Renaissance Christian Humanism', 348–9. See also *Lawes*, 1:81.1–4 (I.7.7), where the action of the Apostles is presumably based on passion (anger?).

[64] See A. D. Cousins, 'Playing with Reason: Aspects of Hooker's Rhetoric in *Lawes* I–V', *Journal of English and Germanic Philology* 97 (1998), 180–2.

[65] See p. 65 above.

vehement affection or fancie which is cast towards them and proceedeth from other causes. For ther are divers motives drawing men to favor mightily those opinions wherein their perswasions are but weakly setled; and if the passions of the mind be strong they easily sophisticate the understanding, they mak it apt to believe upon very sclender warrant and to imagine infallible truth where scarce any probable show appeareth.[66]

Although Hooker's philosophy at this point lacks scholastic rigour, his general theory is reasonably clear. Both the appetite and the imagination are 'passions of the mind' which convey sensual desires/judgements to the reason and the will. If these are inordinate and are subsequently acted upon, a sin of passion will occur.

The above passage raises an additional question as to whether it is possible to avoid sins of passion, if the desires/judgements of the appetite and the imagination are particularly forceful. The fact that they can 'easily sophisticate the understanding' might seem to make defective action and belief-formation virtually inevitable in such instances. Yet, of course, this is to overlook the role of the will in action and belief-formation, since both forms of behaviour are by their very nature voluntary. As Hooker observes:

Men are lovers of pleasure more then lovers of God. Theire assent to his savinge truth is manie tymes withheld from it, not that the truth is too weake to perswade, but because the streame of corrupt affection carrieth them a cleane contrarie waie. That the minde therefore maie abide in the light of faith, there must abide in the will as constant a resolution to have no fellowship at all with the vanities and workes of darkenes.[67]

These remarks on faith can be applied to all aspects of human behaviour. The will, Hooker argues, can choose to reject the 'streame of corrupt affection', and direct the reason to concentrate on comprehending the truth. This does not mean that such rectitude is easy, and as will be discussed in later chapters, it may require the aid of sanctifying and/or common grace. Yet the principle remains that sins of passion are not inevitable, and can theoretically be avoided by a diligent will.

The voluntary nature of sins of passion is most clearly evident in the case of people who deliberately and maliciously reject the

[66] *Lawes*, 2:3.25–4.1 (V.Ded.5). See also 1:18.8–14 (Pref.3.11); 1:141.28–9 (I.16.7); 2:28.2–9 (V.3.1); 3:174.4–5 (VII.6.7); 3:242.1–8 (VII.15.15); Stueber, 'Richard Hooker's Place in the History of Renaissance Christian Humanism', 289–90, 340–3.

[67] *Lawes*, 2:291.24–292.1 (V.63.2).

truth as a result of passion; a rare category of sin in Hooker's work. In the circumstance where this truth concerns Christian doctrine, Hooker identifies this act with the unforgivable sin against the Holy Spirit. The example he gives concerns those Jews who converted to Christianity, but became apostates because, he argues, they could not bear to see the Gentiles treated equally with them.[68] Hooker notes that they sinned 'willfully', which means that they acted in malice, but passion would seem to be the cause of this action. Hooker compares their state with that of 'Satan and his Angells', and Satan's primordial sin was traditionally that of pride. Given the motive that Hooker gives, this would seem to imply that pride caused this act of apostasy, and the deliberate rejection of what they knew to be true. Needless to say, since the sin is committed in malice, it is theoretically in the power of the will to abstain from such actions.

There is, however, one final class of sin dealt with by Hooker which, although voluntary, cannot entirely be avoided, even by those in receipt of sanctifying and/or common grace. To understand this seeming paradox one must compare two passages from the *Lawes* together, to get to the root of Hooker's position. The first is taken from Book 5, and concerns abstinence from sin:

> They pray in vaine to have synne pardoned which seeke not also to prevent synne by prayer, even everie particular synne by prayer against all synne, except men can name some transgression wherewith wee ought to have truce. For in verie deed although wee cannot be free from all synne collectively in such sorte that no part thereof shalbe founde inherent in us, yeat distributively at least all greate and grevous actuall offences as they offer them selves one by one both may and ought to be by all meanes avoyded. So that in this sense to be preserved from all synne is not impossible.[69]

The context of this passage is explicitly Christian. Hooker is defending official Church of England prayers for deliverance 'from all adversitie', in the wake of Cartwright's criticism that such prayers are misconceived, because they ask for the impossible. The whole force of Hooker's case rests on the argument that it is lawful, and indeed right to ask for good things which we can never fully obtain. He does not suggest that Christians can be free

[68] See *Lawes*, 3:99.2–100.20 (VI.6.16). [69] Ibid. 2:200.2–11 (V.48.12).

from all adversity in this life. The above passage comes towards the end of his defence, and extends it somewhat enigmatically. The crux of the argument rests on the distinction Hooker makes between being free from all sin 'collectively', and 'distributively'. The word 'collectively' appears to be synonymous with the phrase 'no part', suggesting that it refers to a unity or whole, considered in itself.[70] 'Distributively', on the other hand, while also referring to a unity or whole, seems to consider it from the perspective of its constituent parts; or 'one by one', to use Hooker's phrase. With these definitions in mind, one can begin to make sense of Hooker's apparent paradox that it is both possible and impossible to be preserved from all sin. Considered as a whole, no one can entirely be without sin. Yet it is indubitable, Hooker argues, that any given 'greate and grevous' sin can be avoided. Since a person can avoid any individual 'greate and grevous' sin, then it seems logical that if each sin is considered separately, a person can potentially avoid all such sins.

The one truly confusing section of this passage is the final sentence. Previously Hooker states that all 'greate and grevous' sins can be avoided, although he equivocates by adding the phrase 'at least'. In conclusion, however, he makes no such distinction, arguing that 'distributively' speaking one can refrain from all sins. It is tempting to accuse Hooker of vacillation at this point. In the penultimate sentence he seems hesitant about extending his remarks beyond 'greate and grevous' sins, while in the next line he makes a completely general statement. Yet whatever the explanation for this, the final sentence would appear to be far more logical from the viewpoint of his theology as a whole. Given that he defines sin as an inherently voluntary activity, this must imply that 'distributively' speaking any given sin can be avoided, no matter how trivial it is.[71]

What Hooker means here by a 'greate and grevous' sin will be considered later, in Ch. 4.[72] For the moment one must enquire

[70] This was how Covel interpreted the term. See Covel, 'A Just and Temperate Defence', 496. Covel seems, however, to have missed Hooker's distinction between 'collectively' and 'distributively'.

[71] The author of the *Christian Letter* failed to appreciate this distinction, and as a result considered the passage to be Pelagian in its implications. See *ACL* 4:26.1–20.

[72] See pp. 205–8.

why a person should theoretically be able to avoid any particular sin, but that it should be impossible 'collectively' to avoid all sins. The answer is hinted at in this following passage, from Book I:

> while we are in the world, subject we are unto sundry imperfections, griefs of body, defectes of minde, yea the best thinges we do are painefull, and the exercise of them greevous being continued, without intermission, so as in those very actions, whereby we are especially perfected in this life, wee are not able to persist: forced we are with very wearines and that often to interrupt them[73]

Rectitude of the mind and diligence are, Hooker considers, arduous activities that cannot be continued indefinitely. A person's concentration will inevitably lapse at some point, as was commonly supposed in scholastic theory, and he or she will as a result fall into sin. Yet, with reference to the first passage, it is presumably the case that one can concentrate sufficiently so as to avoid any particular sin, though not so as to avoid all sins 'collectively'. Defective action or belief-formation which occurs through such lack of concentration will not be a sin of malice, since it is not deliberate. It would, however, be a sin of passion, if the inordinate desires/judgements of the appetite/imagination were as a consequence to go unchecked. It would alternatively be a sin of ignorance, if the reason were to cease enquiring after the truth, and the will to choose badly as a result of this. Yet such sins would still be voluntary, in that the will could theoretically have chosen to avoid them, even if it were unable to avoid them in all collective instances.[74]

In conclusion, it is important to reiterate that Hooker stresses the inherently voluntary nature of all sins, whether primarily pertaining to the reason, the will, or the appetite/imagination. People err either because they deliberately wish to, or because they in some sense lack the resolution necessary to remain in a state of rectitude. Diligence is not always sufficient, as the problem of concentration demonstrates, but even here sins are still voluntary if considered 'distributively'. This perspective on human behaviour is the result of Hooker working out in his philosophy of action the consequences of his theory of the will. His philosophy of action is

[73] *Lawes*, I:112.25–113.5 (I.11.3).

[74] On this point cf. *ST* I-II.74.3 ad. 2; I-II.109.8.

as equally opposed to both soft and hard determinism as his philosophy of mind, because it supposes that humans always have liberty of indifference to choose. This must be considered carefully in the chapters that follow, which will examine further Hooker's conception of human nature by looking at the very profound impact that divine grace, in his opinion, has upon the workings of the human mind.

Part II

Reason, Will, and Grace

In grace there is nothing of soe great difficultie as to define after what manner and measure it worketh.

DF 4:111.32–3

3

Reason, Will, and Common Grace

Part I looked at Hooker's philosophy of mind and action, examining his basic philosophical views on how the human mind is composed and operates, as a first stage in understanding his conception of human nature, and specifically of reason, will, and grace. In particular, Hooker's commitment to a strong definition of human freedom, or metaphysical libertarianism, was established, as was the fact that the mental processes involved in reasoning and in choice are, for him, identical for the human species as a whole, whether these processes are concerned with secular or with religious affairs. The manner in which Christians and non-Christians form religious beliefs is not, for instance, radically different, since all action and belief-formation involves similar interactions between the reason, the will and the lower sensitive faculties.[1] Yet Hooker did not think that an explanation of human behaviour purely in terms of these mental faculties was sufficient to account for all the things that people do, think, or believe. For example, he observes in the *Lawes* that Festus, the pagan Roman in Acts 24–6, was unable to believe in the resurrection of Jesus, even though Festus recognized that the preacher who told him this story, St Paul, was a learned man. The explanation that Hooker gives for this is not that Festus lacked diligence or was influenced by passion (though he may well have been), but rather that he lacked 'the *speciall* operation of Gods good grace and spirit'.[2] Divine aid of this particular kind was thus essential, in Hooker's opinion, for a belief in the message of St Paul's sermon. The reason and/or the will of Festus inevitably erred in some manner, without this supernatural grace. It is clear from this, therefore, that in order to appreciate fully Hooker's views on action and belief-formation, and more generally his conception of human

[1] See pp. 68–91 above. [2] See *Lawes*, 1:223.14–24 (III.8.6).

nature, careful consideration must be given to his theory of how grace interacts with the human mind.

There is a sharp dividing line for Hooker between those things that can be chosen and known or correctly believed by Christians *qua* Christians, and those which can be chosen and known or correctly believed by the rest of humanity.[3] Festus, he notes, was unable to believe in the resurrection of Jesus, since in general such matters of Christian revelation require the aid of a '*speciall*' grace to be believed and acted upon. Non-Christians can still form correct beliefs about God, he argues, but only in so far as they are based on natural law, rather than revelation. As he observes, in Book 3 of the *Lawes*:

> Howbeit for all mens playner and fuller satisfaction, first concerning the inhabilitie of reason to search out and to judge of things divine, if they be such as those properties of God and those duties of men towards him, which may be conceived by attentive consideration of heaven and earth, we know that of meere naturall men the Apostle testifieth, how they *knew both God, and the lawe of God*. Other things of God there be, which are neither so found, nor though they be shewed, can ever be approved without the *speciall* operation of Gods good grace and spirit. Of such things sometime spake the Apostle S. *Paul*, declaring how Christ had called him to be a witnes of his death and resurrection from the dead, according to that which the Prophets and *Moses* had foreshewed.[4]

Hooker distinguishes, therefore, between two types of reason, one aided and the other unaided by God's '*speciall*' grace. The latter might most fittingly be described as *mere natural reason*, since Hooker calls Festus a 'meere naturall man' because he lacks the aid of '*speciall*' grace. This term is, though, somewhat cumbersome, and could arguably be shortened to the more concise *natural reason*. Unfortunately, Hooker sometimes uses *natural reason* to denote humanity's innate reasoning ability, without regard to the absence or presence of grace. Since, therefore, Hooker can refer to *natural reason* in an explicitly Christian context, it seems preferable to use the relatively unambiguous term *mere natural reason*.[5]

[3] For Hooker's use of the term 'knowledge', see Ch. 2, n. 1.

[4] *Lawes*, 1:223.8–20 (III.8.5–6). See also 1:178.8–19 (II.7.4); 1:226.22–227.1 (III.8.9); 1:229.13–16 (III.8.11); 1:232.16–25 (III.8.15); 1:234.31–235.2 (III.8.18). Hillerdal also argues convincingly that *Lawes*, 1:231.30–232.6 (III.8.14) refers to reason with the aid of a special Christian grace. See Hillerdal, *Reason and Revelation in Richard Hooker*, 116, 118–19.

[5] See e.g. *Lawes*, 1:75.20–7 (I.6.3); 1:229.13–23 (III.8.11); 1:234.7–13 (III.8.17). *Mere natural reason* is, indeed, only relatively unambiguous. Hooker considered many non-Christians to

As regards reason aided by God's '*speciall*' grace, it would seem most appropriate to describe this as *divinely enhanced reason*. As Hillerdal has pointed out, Hooker probably employs the term 'divyne reason' in his *Answer to the Supplication* to refer, at least in part, to reason aided by grace.[6] The explicitly Christian context of this passage, and Hooker's emphasis upon arguing from Holy Scripture, give sufficient proof that he has here in mind something inaccessible to non-Christians. 'Divyne reason' is, however, a slightly confusing term, suggesting perhaps the reason of God rather than humanity. It is convenient, as a result of this, to depart from Hooker on this point, and use the more explicit term *divinely enhanced reason* instead.

Given the focal part played by the will in action and belief-formation, one must also distinguish between this faculty as it is aided and unaided by '*speciall*' grace. The two most obvious terms for these two types of will, it would follow, are *divinely enhanced will* and *mere natural will*, and it is these that will be adopted in the rest of this study. It is also convenient to have specific terms for distinguishing between people depending upon whether they lack or receive this grace. Hooker's 'meere naturall man' will be altered to the more gender-inclusive *mere natural person* for the former category, and the admittedly rather curious term *divinely enhanced person* will be adopted for the latter.

'*Speciall*' grace is, of course, a rather vague term with which to describe the divine aid that transforms the reason and the will of redeemed Christians. Hooker in fact uses this term only twice in the *Lawes*, on both occasions in Book 3. On other occasions in the *Lawes* he is content to speak simply of 'grace' aiding Christians to choose and believe in particular things.[7] He is, however, more precise in *A Learned Discourse of Justification, Workes, and How the Foundation of Faith Is Overthrowne*, in which he specifies that it is sanctifying grace that brings about a transformation in the mind of Christians that receive

be aided by a common grace, so that in a sense, there is nothing 'mere' about this reason at all. (See pp. 100–12 below.) This is still, however, the logical term to use, given Hooker's own terminology.

[6] See Hillerdal, *Reason and Revelation in Richard Hooker*, 118–19; *Answer*, 5:255.4–12. See also Hughes, 'The Theology of Richard Hooker', 11.

[7] See e.g. *Lawes*, 1:178.12–19 (II.7.4); 1:206.9–11 (III.1.14); 1:226.22–9 (III.8.9); 1:229.13–16 (III.8.11); 1:235.11–16 (III.8.16).

it, enabling them to have a true faith in Christian revelation. Since this is exactly what Hooker describes '*speciall*' grace as doing in the *Lawes*, it is clear that *in this context 'speciall'* grace and sanctifying grace are synonymous ideas.[8] This matter will, however, receive far more detailed treatment in Ch. 4, which will examine the concepts of *divinely enhanced reason, divinely enhanced will*, and sanctifying (as well as justifying) grace. This present chapter will concern itself only with *mere natural reason* and *mere natural will*, and with what *mere natural persons* are capable of choosing and knowing or correctly believing in with these two mental faculties. As was explained in the Introduction, both these chapters will deal, for the most part, only with the *Lawes* and Hooker's early tractates and sermons. Given the complexity of discussing grace in the late works, a consideration of these writings with regard to all these matter will be left until Ch. 5, except as regards a few areas such as justification and sanctification where the interpretative issues are relatively unclouded.

In the survey of philosophy of action in Ch. 2 it was argued that, in Hooker's opinion, humans can come to know and choose the good through diligence. Clearly a restriction must now be placed on the capacities of *mere natural persons*, since Hooker finds them wholly unable to act on Christian revelation without sanctifying grace: the implications of this for his views on human freedom will be examined later. Yet this would still seem to leave *mere natural persons* capable of knowing and choosing many good things, according to God's will, in both the secular and the religious realms. The situation is not, however, nearly as simple as this would suggest. In the Introduction it was noted how in his 1944 doctoral thesis Kavanagh aligns Hooker closely with Reformed theology, and above all with Calvin, on such topics as human nature, grace, merit, and natural law.[9] In particular, he stresses that, in Hooker's opinion, the human reason and will can be redeemed, for Christians, only by divine grace, and so enabled to function aright. According to this interpretation of Hooker, therefore, *mere natural persons*, who by definition lack this grace, far from being able through diligence to obey at least to some extent God's will, are subject to a state of total depravity. This approach to Hooker's views on reason and will then entered the mainstream through the work of Grislis, who went on to influence

[8] Hooker also uses the term 'special' grace in the *Dublin Fragments*, but in another sense. See pp. 297–304 below.

[9] See Introduction, p. 9.

a number of later writers in this regard, but in a manner that emphasized, for the most part, Hooker's credentials as a *via media* as opposed to a Reformed figure. The connection that Kavanagh makes between seeing Hooker as a wholeheartedly Reformed theologian, and this conception of the human reason and will, only resurfaced again recently in the important work of Kirby and Atkinson. Kirby's article entitled 'Richard Hooker's Theory of Natural Law in the Context of Reformation Theology' is especially significant in this context, as it sets out to prove that Hooker's ideas on natural law are thoroughly Reformed, and through this that Hooker advocates a Reformed conception of human nature as well as the principle of *sola scriptura.* Given that Kavanagh was working in the 1940s, it is somewhat surprising that relatively few writers have engaged with what is clearly a crucial subject for the study of Hooker; his supposed support for the idea of total depravity, and the need for a specifically Christian grace if the reason and will are to function aright. Even Lake's authoritative study *Anglicans and Puritans?* does not examine this matter, which has surely given fuel to the arguments of Atkinson and Kirby. Yet there are a number of writers, of whom W. David Neelands is probably the best example, who have argued with more or less assurance that Hooker believed in the existence of a type of grace that is available to the whole of humanity, and not just to Christians, to help it overcome the effects of the Fall.[10] It is a view that, in general, is not considered by those arguing for Hooker's support for the concept of total depravity, which is a very significant omission on the part of these critics. This grace in fact plays a pivotal role in Hooker's theology, and in his understanding of human nature. It is vital, therefore, that this concept be examined in detail, and a case will now be made for Hooker's views on this subject that is considerably more comprehensive than any that has so far been advanced. When this has been done, it will be possible to come to a fresh understanding of Hooker's views on *mere natural reason, mere natural will*, and human nature, as

[10] See Stueber, 'Richard Hooker's Place in the History of Renaissance Christian Humanism', 351, 361, 375, 388; W. Speed Hill, 'Doctrine and Polity in Hooker's Laws', *English Literary Renaissance* 2 (1972), 181–2, 188; Thornburg, 'Original Sin, Justification and Sanctification in the Thought of Two Sixteenth Century English Divines: John Jewel and Richard Hooker', 103, 148–52; David Manuszak, 'Authority in Hooker's *Polity*' (Ph.D. thesis, Univ. of Michigan, 1976), 219; Neelands, 'The Theology of Grace of Richard Hooker', 83, 123, 129–30, 132.

well as to examine closely the arguments of those writers identifying Hooker with a characteristically Reformed conception of these matters.

Common Grace

The term most frequently used to describe God's general corrective aid given to fallen humanity is 'common grace', or *gratia communis*. Part of the uncertainty surrounding Hooker's views on this subject stems from the fact that he refers to the concept just once in the entire *Lawes* and early writings, in what is a difficult and enigmatic passage. This passage, from Book 1 of the *Lawes*, needs to be considered at some length, in order to unravel its full meaning:

> For whatsoever we have hitherto taught, or shall hereafter, concerning the force of mans naturall understanding, this we always desire withall to be understood, that there is no kind of faculty or power in man or any other creature, which can rightly performe the functions alotted to it, without perpetuall aid and concurrence of that supreme cause of all things. The benefit whereof as oft as we cause God in his justice to withdraw, there can no other thing follow, then that which the Apostle noteth, even men indued with the light of reason to walk notwithstanding [Eph. 4: 17] *in the vanitie of their minde, having their cogitations darkned, and being strangers from the life of God through the ignorance which is in them, because of the hardnes of their harts*. And this cause is mentioned by the prophet *Esay*, speaking of the ignorance of idolators, who see not how the manifest law of reason condemneth their grosse iniquitie and sin. They have not in them, saith he, so much wit as to thinke, [Isa. 44: 19, 18] *shal I bow to the stock of a tree? All knowledge and understanding is taken from them. For God hath shut their eyes that they cannot see*. That which we say in this case of idolatry, serveth for all other things, wherin the like kind of generall blindnes hath prevailed against the manifest laws of reason.[11]

This passage occurs at the end of a chapter in which Hooker has discussed humanity's knowledge of natural law. In the final

[11] *Lawes*, 1:92.23–93.8 (I.8.11) (the text in square brackets is Hooker's notes). Cf. *Lawes*, 2:62.7–12 (V.17.2); *DF* 4:132.18–133.2. In addition to the other critics mentioned regarding this passage, see Kavanagh, 'Reason and Nature in Hooker's Polity', 159; Manuszak, 'Authority in Hooker's *Polity*', 219; Devine, 'Richard Hooker's Doctrine of Justification and Sanctification in the Debate with Walter Travers 1585–1586', 102–3; Neelands, 'The Theology of Grace of Richard Hooker', 83; Atkinson, *Richard Hooker and the Authority of Scripture, Tradition and Reason*, 78–9.

section he considers why some people should be ignorant of 'principall morall duties', finding the cause to be 'lewde and wicked custome'.[12] As has been argued in Ch. 2, such customs can inculcate habits in the will that impede the reasoning process.[13] Hooker takes the worship of idols, or objects created by human hands, as paradigmatic of such customs. He then attempts to go a stage further by finding a religious explanation for this whole process. It is God who makes people ignorant, out of 'his justice', for something these people have done; presumably an act or acts of sin. There is perhaps some suggestion that God does this by working through secondary causes, permitting evil customs that cloud people's minds. Yet Hooker's observation that none of the mental faculties can function correctly without help supposes a more direct type of divine intervention (or lack of intervention).

As Grislis notes, it might be possible to see in this passage 'the traditional view of the relation between primary and secondary causation'.[14] As was mentioned in Ch. 1, according to this theory of causation every act of thought requires movement, if one defines movement broadly so as to include acts of reasoning and willing.[15] Yet all movement ultimately springs from the First Mover, who is God. As Aquinas, for example, observes on this subject: 'however perfect a physical or spiritual nature is taken to be, it cannot proceed to actualize itself unless it is moved by God.'[16] Without this help, therefore, humans can neither reason nor will, nor perform any thought-act whatsoever; they will be entirely incapacitated. It is for this reason that Grislis must be correct in rejecting the help of the First Mover as a possible explanation of this passage. Hooker's reference to the 'supreme cause' perhaps encourages such a reading, since this might imply that causation plays a central part in God's aid. Yet the fact that humans, according to Hooker, can still think, albeit badly, when this aid is withdrawn, means that some other, more satisfactory explanation must be found.

An alternative reading of this text has been made by Gibbs, in the *Folger* commentary. He argues that Hooker 'is very close here to

[12] See *Lawes*, 1:91.25–30 (I.8.11). [13] See pp. 69–70.

[14] See Grislis, 'The Role of *Consensus* in Richard Hooker's Method of Theological Inquiry', 77–8. [15] See p. 36.

[16] See *ST* I-II.109.1: quantumcumque natura aliqua corporalis vel spiritualis ponatur perfecta, non potest in suum actum procedere nisi moveatur a Deo. Cf. *Lawes*, 1:87.17–20 (I.8.7).

the teaching of Aquinas about the *donum superadditum*, "the super-added gift of grace."'[17] As Aquinas observes, before the Fall humans had in addition to their natural powers a superadded grace, which allowed them to seek the highest good and to practise the infused virtues. When the Fall occurred this grace was lost, and humanity's natural powers were damaged. 'Man's restoration is possible', Gibbs notes, 'only through the free and unmerited grace of God, by which the superadded gift of grace is restored to man's nature, his sins forgiven, and power to practise the three Christian virtues infused.'[18] The problem with this interpretation is that it assumes that Hooker is here discussing the effects of something like sanctifying grace, which is a purely Christian aid. This might be suggested by his citations of Isaiah and Ephesians, which speak only of the ignorance of those who are not members of God's covenant. It is, however, quite clear from the rest of the chapter that Hooker is here discussing humanity as a whole. He mentions some pages previously, for instance, that 'meere naturall men' 'have attayned to knowe, not onely that there is a God, but also what power, force, wisedome, and other properties that God hath'.[19] Knowledge of such divine qualities is evidently obscured from the idolaters spoken of in this passage, who worship human creations. Moreover, as will be demonstrated later in this chapter, it is simply not satisfactory to read this passage, and Hooker's work in general, as if all *mere natural persons* were ignorant of natural law. In Book 4 of the *Lawes*, for example, Hooker observes how the Canaanites and Egyptians cut their hair 'as signes of immoderate and hopeles lamentation for the dead': he remarks that this is contrary to natural law, as it shows despair in the face of death.[20] Yet it is not Christians and Jews alone who understand this fact: 'The very light of nature it selfe was able to see herein a fault', Hooker notes, before describing how ancient Roman laws also forbade such practices.[21] It is fundamental to Hooker's argument within the *Lawes* that *mere natural persons* can obtain knowledge of natural law: for this reason one must conclude

[17] See Gibbs, 'Commentary: Book I', *Folger*, vi. 501.

[18] Gibbs, 'Commentary: Book I', *Folger*, vi. 501. Hooker certainly did believe that prelapsarian humans received sanctifying grace, as Neelands has convincingly demonstrated. Yet this is not what Hooker is arguing in this paragraph. See *DF* 4:102.21–3; 4:136.19–137.2; Neelands, 'The Theology of Grace of Richard Hooker', 84–6.

[19] See *Lawes*, 1:87.14–16 (I.8.7).

[20] See ibid. 1:291.10–23 (IV.6.3).

[21] See ibid. 1:291.32–292.3 (IV.6.3).

that Gibbs is mistaken in seeing a reference to (something like) sanctifying grace in the above passage.

One is left with the idea that no faculty or power in any creature can perform its functions correctly without God's continual support. The alternative, at least as regards the human reason, is ignorance of 'the manifest laws of reason'. Humans may still deliberate, for their '*cogitations*' are merely '*darkned*', not effaced, yet they will be unable through reason to come to the knowledge of the truth. As has been argued, this statement concerns all humanity; moreover, Hooker is concerned here not with supra-natural knowledge, but with knowledge of natural law. One may conclude, therefore, that God's aid is necessary for *mere natural persons*, as well as for Christians, to understand natural law. Furthermore, since this aid is only withdrawn as a punishment for sin (but not original sin), it must be available initially to the entire human race. It would seem, then, that in these lines Hooker adumbrates a theory of what is generally known as common grace, which he stipulates should be applied to all his pronouncements on the human reason. Humanity, he argues, is helped by divine grace to overcome the crippling effects of the Fall: in some people, though, this help is withdrawn as a punishment for sin, leaving them in ignorance of natural law.

The seeds of a doctrine of common grace can also be seen in the seventh chapter of Book I of the *Lawes*. Hooker does not state there that grace is necessary for the reason and the will to function correctly, but this appears to be his assumption. He argues in this chapter that 'There is in the will of man naturally that freedome, whereby it is apt to take or refuse any particular object whatsoever being presented unto it.'[22] As was noted in Ch. 1, these lines refer to liberty of indifference; the capacity of the will to accept or reject any object that is placed before it. This is, for him, part of the definition of this mental faculty, and cannot be removed from it.[23] In the marginalia of his edition of the *Christian Letter* and in the *Dublin Fragments*, Hooker comments on these lines, and distinguishes between two different capacities for choice and knowledge, which he terms 'aptnes' and 'ablenes'.[24] Aptness relates to the will's innate capacity for free choice and the reason's innate capacity for

[22] See ibid. 1:79.27–9 (I.7.6). See also Grislis, 'The Role of *Consensus* in Richard Hooker's Method of Theological Inquiry', 75.

[23] See pp. 54–5.

[24] See *DF* 4:101.10–31. See also *AN* 4:18.6–24. The subject of aptness and ableness is discussed further detail in Ch. 5, pp. 298–302.

knowledge. Ableness, on the other hand, refers to the will's capacity to actuate this choice for a particular end (such as choice of the good) and the reason's capacity to actuate this understanding for knowledge of a particular object (such as correct knowledge of the good). Hooker then remarks, concerning the Fall, that 'had wee kept our first ablenes grace should not neede, and had aptnes beene alsoe lost, it is not grace that could worke in us more then it doeth in brute creatures'.[25] Post-lapsarian humans, therefore, have in his opinion an innate capacity for knowledge and free choice, but they do not have the capacity without divine grace to actuate this potential for knowledge and free choice of the good. This distinction between aptness and ableness draws on another, Aristotelian distinction between potentiality (the capacity to perform an action) and actuality (the actualization of that capacity) that was commonly employed by scholastic theologians. Aquinas, for instance, uses this terminology in the *Summa Theologiae*, when commenting on how the aptitude for goodness cannot be destroyed by sin:

> Even in the damned the natural inclination to virtue remains; otherwise they would not experience remorse of conscience. That it remains inoperative in them, however, results from the absence of grace, according to divine justice; as also in a blind man, the aptitude to see remains in the root of the nature in so far as he is an animal naturally endowed with sight, but it is not brought into activity for lack of a cause which makes this possible by forming the organ requisite for seeing.[26]

The damned have, in Aquinas's opinion, an aptitude (*aptitudo*) for virtue, but are not able to act upon it (*non reducitur in actum*). To relate Aquinas's analogy concerning human sight to Hooker's categories of aptness and ableness, a person who is apt to choose the good is like a person without eyes who cannot actually see, despite having an innate mental capacity to do so, whereas a person who is able to choose the good is like a person with eyes who does have the

[25] See *DF* 4:101.29–31.

[26] *ST* I-II.85.2 ad. 3: etiam in damnatis manet naturalis inclinatio ad virtutem: alioquin non esset in eis remorsus conscientiae. Sed quod non reducatur in actum, contingit quia deest gratia secundum divinam justitiam: sicut etiam in caeco remanet aptitudo ad videndum in ipsa radice naturae, inquantum est animal naturaliter habens visum; sed non reducitur in actum, quia deest causa quae reducere possit, formando organum quod requiritur ad videndum. See also *ST* I.83.2 ad. 3.

capacity to see. The point Hooker is making here is, of course, to some degree essential for any orthodox theologian who would assert both the will's freedom and the necessity of grace for salvation: after the Fall, human beings without divine aid cannot be able freely to choose the good without qualification, for otherwise they could be saved through their own efforts alone, which would be Pelagianism. Sinful humans retain liberty in their choices (for Hooker this 'aptness' consists in terms of liberty of indifference and spontaneity, whereas for Aquinas it consists in terms of liberty of spontaneity alone), but this liberty must be functionally curtailed without divine grace with respect to the choice of good objects. The distinction Hooker is making between aptness and ableness is, therefore, a theologically necessary part of his theory of the will's freedom (and in his case, of the will's liberty of indifference and spontaneity), rather than a rejection of it. Precisely the same is true concerning the reason's knowledge of the good. It would seem, therefore, that when Hooker mentions the will's aptness to choose freely in Book 1 of the *Lawes*, he is concerned not with humanity's need for grace, but more generally with his philosophy of mind and action, and in particular with his theory of human freedom.[27] A similar division has been adopted in this book, between the first and second part. Hooker, at this point in Book 1 of the *Lawes*, leaves to some extent open the question of what people can actually know and choose, dealing with this matter (rather belatedly) only later in Book 1, and in Book 3. He then states explicitly that common grace is necessary for humans to be able to know and observe natural law, and sanctifying grace is necessary for humans to be able to know and observe divine law.

Common grace is discussed by Hooker not only in Book 1 of the *Lawes* but also in the *Dublin Fragments*, where he examines the subject at considerably greater length. Somewhat relectantly, however, an analysis of these important passages will be deferred until Ch. 5, which looks in detail at Hooker's late writings. The reader is, therefore, referred to this chapter for extensive further evidence of this key aspect of Hooker's theology, which he deals with so obliquely in the *Lawes* itself.[28]

[27] Hooker makes this point himself in the *Dublin Fragments* about this passage. See *DF* 4:107.18–20: 'shewing the nature of the will in itselfe, without consideration had eyther of sinne or of gods grace'.

[28] See pp. 275–91.

The doctrine of common grace is, of course, by no means original to Hooker. It has a long and varied ancestry, going back at least as far as Prosper of Aquitaine's *De Vocatione Omnium Gentium* (The Call of All Nations). This book is of particular interest since it is mentioned by Hooker in the *Dublin Fragments*, when he argues that the virtuous heathens receive grace.[29] Prosper (*c.*390–*c.*463) attempts in this book to reconcile predestinarianism, whereby God elects only certain people to salvation, with God's desire that all humanity should be saved.[30] He does this, first, by recognizing that post-lapsarian humans are naturally corrupt; their wills may choose freely, but are unable of themselves to choose the good. As he observes: 'For, although it lies in a man's power to reject what is good, yet, unless it is given him, he is unable by himself to choose this good.'[31] This is the essence of Hooker's distinction between aptness and ableness; the actual ability to perform good works is something that is only conferred by grace. Humanity is not, however, in Prosper's opinion, left in this desolate state; all receive a general grace that opens up the possibility of virtuous action.[32] In this help God's universal salvific will is manifested. Yet this grace is insufficient of itself for salvation, for it is not strong enough to bring people to Christ. Only the elect, who are given an additional special grace, through no merit of their own, will in fact be saved.[33] Prosper's view of general, or common, grace is thus very similar to Hooker's: people are helped to overcome some of the corrupting factors of the Fall, but not to the extent that they can be saved by this grace alone.

Hooker's familiarity with Prosper's *De Vocatione Omnium Gentium* is attested to by his own writings. It would not, though, have been necessary for him to have looked so far back in history to have found a writer who upholds the existence of common grace. The theory is present, for instance, in the work of Martin Bucer, who stresses that non-Christian traditions have knowledge of God from the natural

[29] See *DF* 4:111.21–6. For a consideration of this passage, see pp. 285–6, 291 below.

[30] See St Prosper of Aquitaine, *The Call of All Nations*, trans. and annotated P. De Letter, *Ancient Christian Writers: The Works of the Fathers in Translation* 14 (Westminster, Md., 1952), 89. The authorship of the work has been the subject of dispute, though there is no reason to believe that Hooker doubted it. See *The Call of All Nations*, 7–9.

[31] See Prosper, *The Call of All Nations* (*PL* 51:686), 87: Quia licet insit homini bonum nolle, tamen nisi donatum non habet bonum velle. See also ibid. 31–3.

[32] See ibid. 15, 17, 96–7, 121, 131, 209.

[33] See ibid. 15, 17, 121, 131, 144, 210.

world, as well as John Overall, who speaks of a common grace that is too weak to move humans by itself to Christian belief.[34] Yet if one wishes to compare Hooker with one of his contemporaries as regards the issue of common grace, the most obvious example must be Calvin, given that there has been so much controversy concerning the similarities and differences between the two theologians, and that Calvin does support the existence of this grace.

A considerable amount has been written on Calvin's theory of common grace in the last hundred years, perhaps most exhaustively in Herman Kuiper's book *Calvin on Common Grace*.[35] The following analysis will concentrate on just one passage from the *Institutes*, in order to illustrate Calvin's views; the reader is invited to refer to Kuiper's study for a far more detailed examination of this subject:

In every age there have been persons who, guided by nature, have striven toward virtue throughout life. I have nothing to say against them even if many lapses can be noted in their moral conduct. For they have by the very zeal of their honesty given proof that there was some purity in their nature.... These examples, accordingly, seem to warn us against adjudging man's nature wholly corrupted, because some men have by its prompting not only excelled in remarkable deeds, but conducted themselves most honourably throughout life. But here it ought to occur to us that amid this corruption of nature there is some place for God's grace; not such grace as to cleanse it, but to restrain it inwardly. For if the Lord gave loose rein to the mind of each man to run riot in his lusts, there would doubtless be no one who would not show that, in fact, every evil thing for which Paul condemns all nature is most truly to be met in himself.... Hence some are restrained by shame from breaking out into many kinds of foulness, others by the fear of the law—even though they do not, for the most part, hide their impurity. Still others, because they consider an honest manner of life

[34] See George Huntston Williams, 'Erasmus and the Reformers on Non-Christian Religions and *Salus Extra Ecclesiam*', *Action and Conviction in Early Modern Europe*, ed. Theodore K. Rabb and Jerrold E. Seigel (Princeton, 1969), 355–6; W. P. Stephens, *The Holy Spirit in the Theology of Martin Bucer* (Cambridge, 1970), 122–7; Hughes, 'The Problem of "Calvinism"', 241, 245–6.

[35] Herman Kuiper, *Calvin on Common Grace* (Goes, 1928), esp. pp. 2, 176, 182–91. See also Herman Bavinck, 'Calvin and Common Grace', *Calvin and the Reformation* (London, 1909), 103, 117–19; Abraham Kuyper, *Calvinism: Being the Six 'Stone' Lectures Given at Princeton Theological Seminary, U.S.A. A New Edition* (London, 1932), 56–7, 90, 186–90, 192, 243–5; John T. McNeill, 'Natural Law in the Teaching of the Reformers', *The Journal of Religion* 26 (1946), 180; John S. Coolidge, *The Pauline Renaissance in England: Puritanism and the Bible* (Oxford, 1970), 90; Robert Tillman Kendall, *Calvin and English Calvinism to 1649* (Oxford, 1979), 21–2; Atkinson, *Richard Hooker and the Authority of Scripture, Tradition and Reason*, 23–5.

profitable, in some measure aspire to it. Others rise above the common lot, in order by their excellence to keep the rest obedient to them. Thus God by his providence bridles perversity of nature, that it may not break forth into action; but he does not purge it within.[36]

Calvin is quite clear in this passage that humanity's natural state after the Fall is one of complete degeneracy and corruption; without God's aid we would all pursue our evil lusts, without regard to the law of God. Yet, as he notes, many unredeemed people do not behave in this manner: most obey civil laws, and some try hard to lead virtuous lives. He accounts for such behaviour by introducing the idea of a grace that 'bridles' (*refraenat*), but does not 'purge' (*purgat*) within. Recipients of this grace thus retain their natural corruption, but are restrained from enacting their evil desires, even to the extent of aspiring to lead honest lives. Actual purgation, however, whereby the individual assumes a new nature and comes to desire the things of God, must await a specifically Christian grace of renewal.

The basic structure of Hooker's arguments concerning common grace is thus similar to that of Calvin, and may possibly have been influenced by it. In both cases, this grace permits *mere natural persons* to overcome some of the effects of the Fall, and to perform some apparently virtuous deeds. The advantages of such a doctrine are readily apparent. Both theologians are as a result able to acknowledge the achievements of non-Christians, particularly in the Classical world, while at the same time giving full weight to the total depravity induced by the Fall. The necessity of grace for postlapsarian humans is emphasized precisely by the fact that even the

[36] *Inst.* II.iii.3 (*OS* 3:274–5): Omnibus enim seculis extiterunt aliqui, qui natura duce ad virtutem tota vita intenti essent. Neque moror si multi lapsus in eorum moribus notari possint: ipso tamen honestatis studio documentum ediderunt nonnihil fuisse in natura sua puritatis. . . . Exampla igitur ista monere nos videntur ne hominis naturam in totum vitiosam putemus: quod eius instinctu quidam non modo eximiis facinoribus excelluerunt, sed perpetuo tenore vitae honestissime se gesserunt. Sed hic succurrere nobis debet, inter illam naturae corruptionem esse nonnullum gratiae Deo locum, non quae illam purget, sed intus cohibeat. Nam si singulorum animos laxis habenis Dominus in libidines quaslibet exultare permitteret, nemo haud dubie esset qui non reipsa fidem faceret verissime in se competere omnia mala quibus universam naturam damnat Paulus. . . . Hinc alii pudore, alii legum metu retinentur ne in multa foeditatis genera prorumpant, utcunque suam magna ex parte impuritatem non dissimulent; alii, quia honestam vivendi rationem conducere ducant, ad eam utcunque aspirant; alii supra vulgarem sortem emergunt, quo sua maiestate alios contineant in officio. Ita sua providentia Deus naturae pervestitatem refraenat, ne in actum erumpat: sed non purgat intus. See also e.g. *Inst.* II.ii.17; III.xiv.2–3.

ancient Greeks and Romans required the aid of God in order to do anything worthy. This similarity, however, leaves many questions unresolved. It is not sufficient for establishing the unity of thought between, for instance, Hooker and Calvin on this issue, to show that they accept the same basic theory of common grace; for Hooker and Prosper do much the same. What is more important is the precise use that these theologians make of this concept. For just as writers sharing a similar basic theory of sanctifying grace may have quite different notions of its precise effect upon the human mind, so this is true of common grace as well. In order to analyse the effects that Hooker and Calvin ascribe to common grace, one must examine what these theologians say about human nature in general, and in particular what specific things *mere natural persons* can choose and know or correctly believe in. This is because common grace has by definition a common effect on the human race, so that human nature is in a qualified sense commonly human nature modified by common grace. This point is particularly evident in the *Lawes*, where although Hooker argues in Book I that humans without common grace are totally depraved and ignorant of natural law, he writes in general as if humans were commonly able at least to some degree to know and obey God's will. To the extent, therefore, that Calvin and other writers ascribe more or less to the capacities of *mere natural persons*, it would seem that they have a different conception from Hooker of the efficacy of common grace. One is thus led back to the need to analyse Hooker's views on *mere natural reason* and *mere natural will* and to establish his theory of human nature, as well as to compare these ideas with those of Reformed writers such as Calvin. In so doing, however, one must now bear in mind the general importance of common grace for Hooker, in en-abling these faculties of the human mind, without which they would be left in a state of utter depravity.

For many critics, of course, the abilities that Hooker ascribes to *mere natural persons* in the *Lawes* are those of these persons alone, without the aid of common grace; for the simple reason that these critics have not appreciated Hooker's views on this grace. This is perhaps one reason why so few writers, on the basis of the *Lawes* alone, have identified Hooker with a theory of total depravity. Before turning to examine *mere natural reason* and *mere natural will*, it is worth considering for a moment Hooker's relative obscurity on this subject. While it is now evident that this grace forms a most important part of his theological system, one is left with the fact that Hooker speaks of its existence but once in the entire *Lawes* (and only then in a difficult and enigmatic passage), and not at all in the early tractates and sermons. Perhaps the best way of illustrating this lack of clarity is to compare the *Lawes* with William Covel's 'A Just and Temperate Defence'. Covel published his work in 1603, as a response to the *Christian Letter*'s charge that the first five books of the *Lawes* contained views contrary to the Thirty-Nine Articles of the Church of England. As Hooker was unable to finish his own reply due to his death in 1600, it was left to Covel to defend the *Lawes* and the 'conformist' position.

If we are to believe some critics, Covel's work is of little interest. Vincent Mahon calls it 'a competent if uninspired effort', in which virtually every interesting phrase or sentence is culled from Hooker's work.[37] Booty expresses a similar opinion. He admits that Covel occasionally seeks 'to clarify Hooker's meaning in the light of the *Letter*'s misunderstanding', but finds that 'it adds nothing of substance to what was already available in Hooker's printed works'.[38] He too observes that 'a very large percentage' of 'A Just and Temperate Defence' is composed from Hooker's own words, and even calls Covel 'a sort of amanuensis or secretary' on this basis. Yet, as a recent article by Lake implicitly acknowledges, Covel's book is worthy of more critical note.[39] It is true that the framework of his chapters is often provided by passages and arguments taken directly from Hooker, which he is content merely to flesh out: this can clearly be seen, for instance, in articles 8, 11, and 17. Such a practice might well commend itself when he found Hooker to be lucid, and wished consequently to do little more than restate Hooker's original position. Yet Covel's work is most interesting in the few chapters in which he departs significantly from the text of the *Lawes*, and is thus obliged to provide arguments of his own. It would seem that he was forced into such behaviour by Hooker's lack of clarity on particular points, and this can be seen in his remarks on common grace.

[37] See Vincent Mahon, 'The '*Christian Letter*': Some Puritan Objections to Hooker's Work; and Hooker's "Undressed" Comments', *The Review of English Studies* 25 (1974), 306.

[38] See Booty, 'Introduction', *Folger*, iv. p. xlv.

[39] See Lake, 'Business as Usual? The Immediate Reception of Hooker's *Ecclesiastical Polity*', 462–81.

In the third part of the *Christian Letter* Hooker is condemned for purportedly making natural reason and natural law necessary supplements to Holy Scripture as regards knowledge of salvation. In view of his marginal annotations, it seems that Hooker would have replied that natural reason is indeed necessary for an understanding of Holy Scripture, and that natural law is a highly useful, though optional, additional aid.[40] Covel takes a somewhat different line. He accepts that reason and Holy Scripture are 'jointly, and not severally' necessary for salvation, quoting Hooker to this effect. He is also, however, keen to show that natural reason is vital for *mere natural persons*, since it allows them to obtain important (albeit non-saving) knowledge about God and natural law, without the aid of Holy Scripture. In order to defend himself from the possible charge of ascribing too much to humanity's natural reason, Covel then takes the highly significant step of considering how grace aids human actions. He proceeds analytically, and divides such actions into three categories:

> Natural, which are common to man with the brute beasts; as to eat, sleep, and such like, which appertain to his natural life: Secondly, Civil, which we call political, or moral, human actions; as to buy, sell, to learn any art, and to conclude any other action, which concerneth the politic, or private society of man: Thirdly, those which belong to the kingdom of God; to a perfect, happy, and true Christian life; as, to repent us of our sins, to believe in God, to call upon him, to obey his voice, to live after his precepts, and such like.[41]

Covel then asks: 'What grace and power is requisite to man, to perform any, or all these?'. Natural actions, common to all living creatures, he finds require the general participation of God as First Cause. Civil actions, expressed in the acquired virtues of justice, fortitude, temperance, and prudence, require the aid of the 'special favour of God'. This grace is available to all sections of humanity, and Covel mentions in this regard the 'gifts in the Romans and others of the heathen', and specifically those of Numa, Solon, and Lycurgus. The third class of actions, involving the supranatural virtues of faith, hope, and love which alone lead to salvation, are only performable with the aid of the 'grace of

[40] See *ACL* and *AN* 4:12.8–14.9.

[41] Covel, 'A Just and Temperate Defence', 474.

regeneration'. As one might expect, only Christians are in receipt of this third type of grace. Covel thus shows that *mere natural persons* require God's help to perform good actions, and also provides a reason why such people might be unable to comprehend Holy Scripture, and perform actions that will eventually lead to their salvation.

What is so remarkable about Covel's theory of grace is its clarity in comparison with Hooker's. He does not, like Hooker, discuss the subject in a piecemeal, and at times enigmatic fashion: he systematically categorizes the types of human action and their attendant graces, all with admirable concision. Significantly, he does not even cite Hooker as a source for this theory, merely observing that 'some men' have classified grace in this way: Hooker would appear to have left Covel feeling unable to quote the *Lawes* in defence of Hooker's own views on grace. It is, therefore, scarcely surprising that Hooker should have undertaken an analysis of grace in the *Dublin Fragments*. The *Lawes* was badly in need of such an elucidation, as the history of its critical interpretation bears eloquent witness.

Mere Natural Reason and *Mere Natural Will*

It has been shown how Hooker argues that, without common grace, 'there is no kind of faculty or power in man or any other creature, which can rightly performe the functions alotted to it'; the mental faculties reside in a state of extreme corruption, and people are unable to know or to obey natural law.[42] He gives as an example those pagans who worship the creations of their own hands; people he considers to have lost all rational sense of the absurdity of their actions. One may now turn to consider what, in Hooker's opinion, humans can achieve when they are aided by common grace, but lack the help of sanctifying grace; through the use, therefore, of *mere natural reason* and *mere natural will*. In so doing, the views of recent critics on this subject will be examined, as this is now one of the most controversial areas in Hooker studies. The ideas of Kavanagh, Grislis, Kirby, and Atkinson, in particular, will be considered, as they all argue that humans need a specifically Christian grace of renewal if the reason and the will are to function aright and are not

[42] See *Lawes*, 1:92.25–8 (I.8.11).

to be totally depraved. Kirby and Atkinson both conclude from this that Hooker is an orthodox Reformed theologian in his conception of human nature. This view will be compared with the ideas of Lake in *Anglicans and Puritans?*, who, as has been noted, in depicting Hooker as a proto-Laudian Anglican, ascribes to him a relatively benign view of original sin, and a high estimation of human capacities. It will be argued in the remainder of this chapter that a synthesis of these respective positions is the most satisfactory way of understanding Hooker's conception of human nature, though finally this synthesis will lean heavily in the direction of Lake's ideas. This will be seen as a reflection of Hooker's philosophy of mind and action which, as Part I has observed, emphasizes the freedom of the human mind through diligence (and divine grace) to avoid erroneous activity, and hence to abstain from sin.

The best way to examine Hooker's theory of *mere natural reason* and *mere natural will* in the *Lawes* is to place it in the context of the Admonitions controversy, out of which his ideas evolved.[43] The earlier tractates and sermons, where they agree with and differ from the *Lawes* in these matters, will also be analysed at the same time. In the chapters on *adiaphora* in Whitgift's 'Defence' and Cartwright's *Replye* and *Second Replie*, the key area of contention between these theologians is how humans are able to know which particular actions glorify and are obedient to the will of God. This debate arose out of the original *An Admonition to Parliament*, which argued that the Church of England should contain only a church discipline and religious ceremonies positively commanded by Holy Scripture.[44] Whitgift in the 'Defence' categorized such matters as *adiaphora*, and observed that it would be absurd if the Church were constrained to find positive scriptural warrant in such cases. It is enough, he argued, if here the Church does nothing contrary to Holy Scripture, a principle that Cartwright found to be wholly insufficient.[45] Both writers strove, therefore, over the question of how the Church can know which ceremonies, discipline, and other indifferent matters glorify and are obedient to God, and indeed how in general one can know how to obey the divine will.

[43] See Lake, *Anglicans and Puritans?*, 16, 145–53; Perrott, 'Richard Hooker and the Problem of Authority'.

[44] See 'Defence', 175.

[45] See ibid. 191–5; *Second Replie*, 56–62.

Hooker, in the *Lawes*, examines Cartwright's arguments and scrutinizes his scriptural proofs. He chooses to respond to him in a far more radical way than Whitgift, however, by looking at the question of works obedient to God in the widest possible sense, and by redefining in what such obedience consists. Rather than showing his Reformed principles by following Whitgift and Cartwright, and anchoring this question around Holy Scripture (whether interpreted by a positive or a negative construction), Hooker in the *Lawes* crucially defines all adherence to laws instituted by God as obedient works. Since these laws take diverse forms, of which divine law found in Holy Scripture is but one example, he can conclude from this that it is possible for humans to know how to obey God, in certain respects, by consulting other laws. The prime example for *mere natural persons*, who are by definition unable to comprehend Holy Scripture and divine law, is natural law, which he argues may to a considerable extent through diligence (and common grace) be known and obeyed by such persons without sanctifying grace.

In what follows, each of the above points will be established in turn. This will obviously involve a detailed consideration of the extent to which a *mere natural person* can, through the use of *mere natural reason* and *mere natural will*, know and obey natural law. In addition, reference will be made to knowledge of what may here be termed *mere natural spiritual truths*; matters such as the existence and properties of God and the immortality of the soul, which are not in themselves natural laws, but are concepts of an analogous spiritual nature that may arguably be known by *mere natural persons*, and that are intimately related to the question of works obedient to God. By no means all the views that Hooker adopts as to knowledge and obedience of natural law and related *mere natural spiritual truths* were contentious from a Reformed perspective, and no doubt Cartwright himself would have approved of some of them. This point will be explored further with respect to Calvin later in this chapter, where it will be shown that although in general Hooker ascribes considerably greater capacities to humans over such matters than is characteristic of Reformed writers such as Calvin, there are naturally numerous points on which they do agree. It is, however, still worth methodically examining Hooker's views even in such relatively uncontentious cases, in order to counter the argument of Grislis that, in Hooker's opinion, a specifically Christian grace of renewal is necessary for humans 'to draw knowledge from the hierarchical structure of reality', and to obey God's will.[46] More generally, though, the aim will be to show that Calvin, Cartwright, and Whitgift would all have disagreed with the conclusions that Hooker infers from knowledge and obedience in such matters, with respect to behaviour obedient to the will of God. For what lies at the heart of the question of obedience is the issue of religious authority; of whether Holy Scripture is alone able to reveal how the divine will should be obeyed, or whether through (amongst other things) the interpretation of natural law, reason also has authority in this area. Cartwright and Whitgift, despite their considerable differences, were both Reformed theologians, referring in their debate over this matter to the religious authority of Holy Scripture alone. Hooker, by developing the Admonitions controversy so as to consider human nature, and specifically in this context the capacities of *mere natural reason* and *mere natural will*, and the related question of the authority of reason, came to move significantly in this respect outside the fold of Reformed theology.

Before embarking upon this enquiry, by looking first at the extent to which *mere natural persons* can know and obey natural law and related *mere natural spiritual truths*, it is important to deal with some terminological problems concerning the term 'natural law'. In his initial classification of laws in Book I of the *Lawes*, Hooker makes an unusual distinction between '*natures* law' or the 'law of nature', and the 'law of *reason*'.[47] He confesses that the two former terms are commonly used to designate that law which orders the activities of 'each created thing'; it thus includes the laws that govern the movement of the planets as much as the moral codes of human conduct. Hooker rejects this usage, and restricts the term 'law of nature' so that it refers only to natural (i.e. non-rational) agents, thus excluding humanity.[48] He then introduces the term 'law of *reason*' to refer to that law which 'bindeth creatures reasonable in this world', by which he means the human race. This is in itself a simple distinction, but the issue is clouded by the fact that

[46] See Grislis, 'The Role of *Consensus* in Richard Hooker's Method of Theological Inquiry', 72, and pp. 162–3 below.

[47] See *Lawes*, 1:63.17–22 (I.3.1); 1:64.3–12 (I.3.2).

[48] Presumably, though, the operations of the human body which are not subject to rational control, such as the circulation of the blood and the processes of digestion, *are* to be considered as part of the 'law of nature'.

Hooker is not consistent in his usage; he can frequently be found using the term 'law of nature' (or occasionally '*natures* law') in a traditional manner, to refer to a body of law that binds rational *and* non-rational agents.[49] Given that this is, as he observes himself, the common usage of this term, it is the one that will be adopted in this study, modernized to 'natural law'. The only disadvantage with this approach is that Hooker in his work is concerned almost purely with those aspects of natural law that pertain to humans as rational agents; in other words, with the 'law of *reason*'. This latter term encapsulates the defining characteristic of this body of law, for Hooker, in that it can be known through the use of reason. 'Natural law', though a more familiar term, unfortunately lacks this specific reference.

Hooker is very clear in his definition of the law of reason, or those aspects of natural law that pertain to humans as rational agents. As he observes in the *Lawes*: 'the lawe of reason or humaine nature is that which men by discourse of naturall reason have rightly found out themselves to be all for ever bound unto in their actions'.[50] It is thus, by definition, something which can be known by humans through exercising their natural reason. Should anyone question the role of sanctifying grace in this process, Hooker is emphatic that *mere natural persons* can have extensive knowledge of natural law, clearly showing that common grace is alone necessary as an aid to reason in this process. As he states, referring to natural law:

> concerning the inhabilitie of reason to search out and to judge of things divine, if they be such as those properties of God and those duties of men towards him, which may be conceived by attentive consideration of heaven and earth, we know that of meere naturall men the Apostle testifieth, how they *knewe both God, and the lawe of God*.[51]

It follows, by definition, that natural law can be discovered by 'reason without the helpe of revelation supernaturall and divine', from observation of the natural world; indeed, this is one of the marks that distinguishes natural law from divine law.[52]

[49] See e.g. *Lawes*, 1:86.28 (I.8.6); 1:90.19–22 (I.8.9); 1:119.29 (I.12.1); 1:120.21–3 (I.12.2); 1:190.11 (II.8.6); 1:313.1 (IV.11.6); 1:314.8 (IV.11.7); 3.240.20 (VII.15.14).

[50] See ibid. 1:89.28–31 (I.8.8).

[51] Ibid. 1:223.9–14 (III.8.6). See also 1:63.20–2 (I.3.1); 1:84.7–16 (I.8.3); 1:86.21–3 (I.8.5); 1:87.13–17 (I.8.7).

[52] See ibid. 1:90.5–6 (I.8.9). See also 1:84.2–4 (I.8.3).

This is not in itself, however, a satisfactory definition of Hooker's view of natural law. Human laws also 'bindeth creatures reasonable in this world', and, with the exception of some of the laws of Christian societies,[53] can be framed by the use of *mere natural reason* alone. The distinction, for Hooker, lies in the degree of evidential certainty with which a person can know that a particular law is good and right. As he explains:

> Within the compasse of which [natural] laws we do not only comprehend whatsoever may be easily knowne to belong to the dutie of all men, but even whatsoever may possibly be knowne to be of that qualitie, so that the same be by *necessarie* consequence deduced out of cleere and manifest principles. For if once we descend unto probable collections what is convenient for men, we are then in the territorie where free and arbitrarie determinations, the territorie where human lawes take place.[54]

Recalling the analysis of Hooker's theory of certainty in Ch. 2, human laws correspond to the fourth degree of certainty, in that their goodness can be known with only probable assurance.[55] Natural laws, on the other hand, must correspond either to the second or third degree of certainty, in that their goodness may be definitely known. Hooker does, in fact, further refine this theory some pages later in the *Lawes*, by distinguishing between '*mixedly*' and '*meerly*' human laws.[56] Since a lawgiver might choose to codify a natural law, making it a human law in a particular country, Hooker terms such laws as '*mixedly*'. Obviously, such human laws will possess the same degree of certainty as natural laws, since their content is identical. '*Merely*' human laws, however, are not directly based on natural laws, but rather reflect what the reason of the lawgiver considers 'to be fit and convenient'; as such, they are 'but probablie' good.

This theory concerning degrees of certainty can also be applied to a distinction that Hooker makes between two classes of natural law. Citing Augustine, he explains that a division exists between 'principles' and 'conclusions':

> Wherefore as touching the law of reason, this was (it seemeth) Saint *Augustines* judgement, namely, that there are in it some things which stand as *principles* universally agreed upon: and that out of those *principles*,

[53] See ibid. 1:235.2–18 (III.8.18), concerning ecclesiastical laws.
[54] Ibid. 1:93.8–16 (I.8.11).
[55] See pp. 73–4.
[56] See *Lawes*, 1:105.6–16 (I.10.10); 1:106.1–10 (I.10.10).

which are in themselves evident, the greatest morall duties we owe towards God or man, may without any great difficultie be *concluded*.[57]

The first principles of natural law, once discerned, are immediately accepted by the mind as self-evidently true: 'as soone as they are alleaged, all men acknowledge to be good; they require no profe or furder discourse to be assured of their goodnesse.'[58] These principles correspond, therefore, to the second degree of certainty. From these principles it is then possible, by a process of 'strong and invincible demonstration', to deduce further laws of nature, which one might term 'demonstrable conclusions'. These laws correspond to the third degree of certainty, since once the process of demonstration has been understood they must be accepted by the mind, but they are not self-evidently true in their own right.[59]

This division between 'principles' and 'conclusions' can be seen in Hooker's remarks in the *Lawes* on the extent to which people can have knowledge of natural law without the aid of Holy Scripture. It is, he notes, hard to find people who are ignorant of the 'first principles', since they are 'easie' to know.[60] Regarding 'conclusions' of natural law he detects a spectrum of difficulty, although there are some apparent contradictions in his observations upon this topic. In ch. 8 of Book 1, he argues that the 'greatest morall duties . . . may without any great difficultie be concluded' from first 'principles', 'the greatest part of the law morall being so easie for all men to know'.[61] He ponders, though, on the fact that 'so many thousands of men' have nevertheless been ignorant of them, finding the root cause in the withdrawal by God of common grace.[62] Some pages later, in ch. 12, he returns to this subject in a more pessimistic strain, noting that 'in a number of thinges particular, so far hath the naturall understanding even of sundry whole nations bene darkned, that they have not discerned no not grosse iniquitie to bee sinne.'[63] In this chapter Hooker extols the merits of Holy Scripture, since it gives people access to natural laws that they

[57] *Lawes*, 1:91.20–5 (I.8.10) (my italics). Cf. 2:290.6–13 (V.63.1).

[58] See ibid. 1:86.4–9 (I.8.5). See also 1:85.6–15 (I.8.5); 1:91.20–5 (I.8.10).

[59] See ibid. 1:91.20–5 (I.8.10); 1:93.8–16 (I.8.11). For a similar scholastic approach to the question of certainty and natural law, see e.g. *ST* I-II.94.2; I-II.94.4.

[60] See *Lawes*, 1:90.5–6, 17–19 (I.8.9); 1:120.21–2 (I.12.2).

[61] See ibid. 1:91.23–93.8 (I.8.10–11).

[62] See ibid. 1:91.23–93.8 (I.8.10–11).

[63] See ibid. 1:120.22–121.2 (I.12.2).

might otherwise not know.[64] The force of this remark concerning the ignorance of 'sundry whole nations' is thus obviously directed at non-Christians, since they lack sanctifying grace, and hence the ability to comprehend Holy Scripture. It is not clear, however, whether Hooker is referring here to *mere natural persons*, or to humans who lack the aid of common as well as sanctifying grace. Yet Hooker is far from implying that all non-Christians are ignorant of these 'greatest morall duties'. To support his argument in ch. 12, Hooker quotes three authorities, all of whom remark on the ignorance of various nations concerning natural law. Yet one of these writers, Josephus, was a non-Christian Jew living in the time after the death of Christ, and presumably must, therefore, be considered a *mere natural person*. Should this example be considered too ambiguous, it is worth noting that another of Hooker's authorities, Aquinas, is quoting from Caesar's *De Bello Gallico*, on the legality of theft amongst the ancient Germans. It is true that Hooker does not mention Caesar in his footnote, but it is clear elsewhere in the *Lawes* that Hooker believed that the Romans had extensive knowledge of natural law. Thus, for instance, when Hooker gives three examples of natural law based around the theme of treating others as we would ourselves be treated, he chooses to do this by paraphrasing three passages of Roman law.[65] Overall, therefore, one may conclude that while Hooker found many non-Christians to be ignorant of the 'greatest morall duties', he also observed that many such people did in fact know these laws.

Hooker concludes the twelfth chapter of Book 1 of the *Lawes* by looking at what have been termed *mere natural spiritual truths*, and analyses the difficulty with which these can be known. As he asks regarding these *truths*, which he notes are 'not impossible to be discerned by the light of nature', 'are there not many which fewe mens naturall capacitie, and some which no mans hath beene able to finde out?'[66] Given that the subject of this chapter is nominally natural law, this change of emphasis might seem surprising. Yet what Hooker is perhaps implying here is that some natural laws

[64] As Hooker observes, one of the problems with natural law is that it is difficult for people to apply general principles to complex situations; it is possible to make mistakes. At this point Holy Scripture has a distinct advantage, as such 'conclusions' are stated there plainly for all to read. Compare *Lawes*, 1:120.15–121.2 (I.12.2) with e.g. *ST* I-II.91.4. Compare also *Lawes*, 1:121.10–2 (I.12.2) with, e.g. *ST* I-II.91.4.

[65] See *Lawes*, 1:88.18–25 (I.8.7).

[66] See ibid. 1:121.12–23 (I.12.2).

are hard to discover because the knowledge that is a prerequisite for this process is in itself very difficult to obtain. As he notes, these *truths* are 'for direction of all the partes of our life needfull', suggesting that they have a relation to law as a directive force.[67] It would seem, therefore, that the ability of a *mere natural person* to access certain natural laws is intimately linked with his or her ability to know certain *truths*. Laws concerning the soul, for instance, would seem to require some knowledge about the properties of the soul. It is important, therefore, to analyse what Hooker says about these *truths*, both to ascertain the difficulty with which they may be known, and, by way of inference, the difficulty with which natural laws associated with them may be found.

Regarding those *mere natural spiritual truths* which, as he argues, few people have found, Hooker quotes Augustine on the difficulty of discovering the immortality of the soul:

> They are, saith Saint Augustine, but a few and they indued with great ripenes of wit and judgement, free from all such affaires as might trouble their meditations, instructed in the sharpest and the subtlest poyntes of learning, who have, and that verie hardlie, beene able to finde out but onely the immortalitie of the soule.[68]

This would seem to suppose that there are many *mere natural spiritual truths* that are unknown to virtually all *mere natural persons*, since they lack the aid of Holy Scripture that would inform them clearly about such matters. Yet commenting on the powers of *mere natural reason* in Book 3 of the *Lawes*, Hooker quotes Tertullian with approval, when the latter argues that: '*there are some things even knowne by nature, as the immortalitie of the soule unto many, our God unto all*'.[69] There is no need to conclude that these two passages are contradictory, since it is easy to make a distinction that reconciles them. Few people, one might observe, can *discover* the soul's immortality, but many can *understand* this fact once it has been discovered. One may take as an analogy Copernicus's realization that the solar system is heliocentric: only in the sixteenth century was this discovered, but the fact may readily be understood by everyone today. In a similar manner, for Hooker, the work of a philosopher such as Plato can be seen as allowing the ancient

67 See *Lawes,* 1:121.13 (I.12.2).

68 See ibid. 1:121.16–21 (I.12.1).

69 See ibid. 1:225.3–6 (III.8.8). For contrast, see Kavanagh, 'Reason and Nature in Hooker's Polity', 79.

Greeks knowledge of the immortality of the soul. The difference in emphasis between the two passages in the *Lawes* is probably to be explained by referring to their respective contexts. Taking the more pessimistic passage first, one should note that previously, in chs. 8, 9, and 10 of Book 1, Hooker has discussed the laws that humans can both know and invent without requiring the help of sanctifying grace. In ch. 11, he looks at humanity's need for revelation and divine law, emphasizing that we cannot be saved alone by laws and knowledge that can be known by *mere natural reason.* Lest the reader should conclude from this that Christians, possessing revelation and divine law, do not need such natural *truths* and laws, he then observes in ch. 12 that Holy Scripture is full of them. Yet, in so doing, he must avoid giving the impression that they are superfluous to Holy Scripture, in that they might just as easily be discovered by observation of the natural world. He chooses, therefore, at this particular point, to emphasize the obscurity of some *mere natural spiritual truths* (and by extension, those natural laws that are associated with them), and the relative weakness of the human reason: this provides an explanation for the presence of such laws and *truths* in Holy Scripture. There is nothing distinctively Reformed about this attitude; it is a commonplace of scholastic theology, as can be seen by looking, for the sake of convenience, at the first article of Aquinas's *Summa Theologiae,* which similarly deals with the relationship between natural and divine law in Holy Scripture:

Hence the necessity for our welfare that divine truths surpassing reason should be signified to us through divine revelation.

We also stood in need of being instructed by divine revelation even in religious matters the human reason is able to investigate. For the rational truth about God would have appeared only to few, and even so after a long time and mixed with many mistakes[70]

In ch. 8 of Book 3, however, Hooker has returned again to the theme of reason's vitality, contrary in particular to the arguments of Cartwright and Travers. He thus needs to emphasize reason's

[70] *ST* I.1.1: Unde necessarium fuit homini ad salutem quod ei nota fierent quaedam per revelationem divinam quae rationem humanam excedunt. Ad ea etiam quae de Deo ratione humana investigari possunt necessarium fuit hominem instrui revelatione divina. Quia veritas de Deo per rationem investigata a paucis, et per longum tempus, et cum admixtione multorum errorum homini proveniret.

ability (with or without sanctifying grace) to obtain knowledge of natural law and *mere natural spiritual truths* from the natural world, and this is precisely what he does. Rhetorical demands, therefore, seem to have had a hand in the shaping of Hooker's argument in these two passages. Yet, looking beyond the requirements of rhetoric, there does not appear to be any significant contradiction between the two passages. One may, then, state, that on the basis of the available evidence, Hooker accepted that '*many*' people could, without needing sanctifying grace, have *knowledge* of the soul's immortality, even though it was very difficult for them to *discover*. As regards other *mere natural spiritual truths* that are hard to find, Hooker gives no examples, and neither does he speak about knowledge of natural laws based on such *truths*. There is, however, no reason to think that he regarded them in any very different light from the case of the immortality of the soul.

One may now look finally at that most obscure class of *mere natural spiritual truths* which, according to Hooker, 'no mans ['naturall capacitie'] hath beene able to finde out'. Just as Hooker quotes Augustine to show how some *truths* have been found by 'fewe mens naturall capacitie', so he proceeds to give an example for this particular class: 'The resurrection of the flesh what man did ever at any time dreame of, having not heard it otherwise then from the schoole of nature?'[71] The meaning here is slightly unclear, but may be understood readily enough: no one, Hooker argues, can have heard of the resurrection of the body, unless from some source *other* than the natural world. Given the illustrative function of this sentence, it would seem that Hooker is not here making a conventional remark about revealed knowledge: he is noting, rather, that the resurrection of the body is a *mere natural spiritual truth*, but one that no one has ever been able to obtain through observation of the natural world alone (even though such knowledge is theoretically obtainable in this way). It is through Holy Scripture, Hooker argues, that people come to know this *truth*, which of course provides an excellent justification for its presence there. Since, however, *mere natural persons* cannot comprehend Holy Scripture, there must be certain *mere natural spiritual truths* that such people cannot know. Yet this limitation on the powers of *mere natural reason*, while undeniable, is in fact very small. Hooker

[71] See *Lawes*, 1:121.21–3 (I.12.2).

excludes *all* humanity from obtaining knowledge of such obscure *truths* by their reason alone; he makes no distinction here between the capacities of *mere natural reason* and *divinely enhanced reason*. Not even sanctifying grace, it would seem, permits Christians to have knowledge of such truths without the aid of Holy Scripture. One might also observe that Hooker has chosen as an example of this class of *mere natural spiritual truths*, a doctrine that many theologians would have considered to be revealed knowledge.[72] Viewed from this perspective, Hooker can scarcely be described as placing a major restriction upon *mere natural reason*, if he will not give it access to something which many theologians would not have defined as merely 'natural', but rather as 'divine'. As for any limitations that this might place upon *mere natural people*'s knowledge of natural laws, these would appear to be equally limited.

The discussion has so far centred on the categories into which Hooker divides natural law and *mere natural spiritual truths*, but little has been said about their actual content. In making a list of the natural laws actually mentioned by Hooker in the *Lawes*, a distinction will again be made between 'principles' and 'conclusions', but there will be no attempt at further subdivisions. Although, as has been argued, Hooker finds some natural laws to be more obscure than others, he for the most part does not provide any such categorizations when referring to specific laws. It should suffice to say that, on the basis of the arguments that have previously been made, all the natural laws mentioned by Hooker can be known by many *mere natural persons*. The same remarks may be made regarding the *mere natural spiritual truths* discussed by Hooker, which will be dealt with later on. The only definite exception that is actually mentioned is, of course, the resurrection of the body, which has, in Hooker's opinion, proved to be beyond the reach of all *mere natural persons*, and only accessible with the aid of supernatural revelation.

Turning to discuss the 'principles' of natural law actually mentioned by Hooker in the *Lawes*, it is noteworthy that he gives few examples, presumably because they are not in themselves of particular relevance to his argument there. He divides his examples into two categories, distinguishing between 'axiomes or principles more generall', and those that are 'lesse generall': he does not,

[72] See e.g. Duns Scotus, *Ordinatio* IV, dist. xliii, q. 2, in John Duns Scotus, *Philosophical Writings. A Selection*, trans. A. Wolter (Indianapolis, 1987), 154–6. Aquinas, however, may have agreed with Hooker's position: see *ScG* IV, lxxix (but note also the end of IV, i).

however, explain the logic behind this distinction.[73] In the former category he places the principle that '*the greater good is to be chosen before the lesse*'. He also mentions, it would appear, a more expanded version of this law, which stipulates that: 'small difficulties, when exceeding great good is sure to ensue; and on the other side momentanie benefites, when the hurt which they drawe after them is unspeakable, are not at all to be respected'.[74] His 'lesse generall' class of laws seems to cover more specific areas of human action. He gives the following examples: '*God to be worshipped, Parents to be honored, Others to be used by us as we our selves would by them.*'[75] Two parts of the Decalogue, and one of Christ's two fundamental commandments ('love thy neighbour'),[76] are, therefore, according to Hooker, self-evident to the human mind: 'as soone as they are alleaged, all men acknowledge to be good; they require no profe or furder discourse to be assured of their goodnesse'.[77]

Perhaps the most basic of the 'conclusions' of natural law mentioned by Hooker concerns the relationship of the body to the soul. By a process of observation, he notes, a person can come to understand that the body is inferior to the soul, and that some parts of the soul are superior to others. On the principle that the superior should command the inferior, this produces a hierarchy in each human being: 'The soule then ought to conduct the bodie, and the spirite of our mindes the soul. This is therefore the first lawe, whereby the highest power of the minde requireth generall obedience at the handes of all the rest concurring with it unto action.'[78] The 'spirite' of the mind is the 'highest power', which

[73] See *Lawes*, 1:85.10–25 (I.8.5); 1:86.4–9 (I.8.5). See also 1:91.14–23 (I.8.10).

[74] Ibid. 1:85.22–5 (I.8.5).

[75] See ibid. 1:86.4–7 (I.8.5).

[76] See Mark 12: 28–31.

[77] See *Lawes*, 1:86.7–9 (I.8.5). It is tempting to describe the axioms given at the following line references as additional 'principles' of natural law: 1:87.21–3 (I.8.7); 1:88.21–4 (I.8.7). See also Hillerdal, *Reason and Revelation in Richard Hooker*, 97–9. These laws seem, however, to presuppose some element of reasoning before they can be accepted as true. The laws concerning God require that we know the 'relation which God hath unto us as unto children, and unto all good thinges as unto effectes, whereof himselfe is the principall cause', as Hooker notes. The laws concerning other humans require meditation on the nature of human relationships; a process of drawing conclusions by deductive reasoning. As Hooker observes: 'From which relation of equalitie betweene our selves and them that are as our selves, what severall rules and canons naturall reason hath drawne for direction of life, no man is ignorant'. See *Lawes*, 1:88.4–21 (I.8.7). See also 1:87.13–21 (I.8.7). It would seem, therefore, that Hooker does not present any of these laws as *self-evidently* true. At the last analysis, however, Hooker is vague about the categories to which these laws belong.

[78] See ibid. 1:87.5–9 (I.8.6).

the other parts of the mind are to obey. This obedience is expressed in terms of a participation in the action dictated by the 'highest power'. This recalls Hooker's philosophy of mind and action as seen in other parts of the *Lawes*. The 'highest power' is presumably the will and/or reason, which should dictate the actions of the other parts of the soul. This theory is, therefore, something that many *mere natural persons* are capable of understanding, since it is a part of natural law.

Most of the 'conclusions' of natural law that Hooker describes deal either with the individual's interaction with society, or with spiritual matters concerning God and the soul. There are one or two exceptions concerning personal rectitude, such as Hooker's stipulation that we be temperate; as he observes, natural law 'teacheth mediocritie in meates and drinkes'.[79] Even here, however, he connects this with our natural duty to be thankful to God for providing us with such things. Of the 'conclusions' dealing with social interaction, Hooker seems to place most emphasis on those which embrace the commandment to 'love thy neighbour'.[80] He quotes/paraphrases certain passages of Roman law as examples of these 'conclusions', clearly showing that *mere natural persons* can indeed have knowledge of them: '*That because we would take no harme, we must therefore doe none; That sith wee would not be in any thing extreamelie dealt with, wee must our selves avoyde all extremitie in our dealinges; That from all violence and wrong wee are utterly to abstayne.*'[81] The last of the series is the most general, since it moves away from the territory of laws that are founded purely on the selfish desire for self-preservation, towards a more universal ethical code. In more concrete terms, Hooker notes that natural law forbids, amongst other things, 'Idolatry', 'Homicide', 'rapine', and 'fornication'.[82]

As regards those parts of natural law dealing with spiritual concerns, Hooker is quite explicit that *mere natural persons* can have knowledge of them.[83] Perhaps the most important of these laws concerns love for God, which Hooker chooses to illustrate by quoting and paraphrasing Plato and Aristotle:

> these axiomes and lawes naturall concerning our dutie, have arisen, *That in all thinges we goe about his ayde, is by prayer to be craved, That he cannot have*

[79] See ibid. 1:140.31–141.5 (I.16.7).
[80] But see n. 77 above.
[81] *Lawes*, 1:88.18–24 (I.8.7), taken from the *Codex Justinianus* (1575) and the *Digest* (1576). See also 1:187.26–30 (II.8.2).
[82] See ibid. 1:313.2–19; 1:314.2–3 (IV.11.6–7).
[83] See p. 116 above, and *Lawes*, 1:223.9–14 (III.8.6).

sufficient honour done unto him, but the utmost of that we can doe to honour him we must: which is in effect the same that we read, *Thou shalt love the Lorde thy God with all thy heart, with all thy soule, and with all thy minde.* Which lawe our Saviour doth terme the *First and the great Commaundement.*[84]

The last two quotations are from Deuteronomy 6: 5 and Matthew 22: 38 respectively. *Mere natural persons* can, therefore, have knowledge of the first of Christ's two great commandments, concerning love of God, just as they can also know the second. Moreover, they can know in addition that God's help is to be asked by means of prayer.

One may now turn away from natural law in order to discuss *mere natural spiritual truths*, and those truths that are explicitly mentioned by Hooker.[85] The immortality of the soul will not be dealt with in this context, since Hooker's views on this subject have been examined already. This principally leaves the question of God's existence and His properties, which as the foundation of theology must be considered as the most important of these *truths*. On this topic, Hooker in Book 3 of the *Lawes* quotes Tertullian with approval when the latter argues that the existence of God is known to all humanity:[86] later, however, in his analysis of atheism in Book 5, Hooker takes a slightly different line, and one that is rather more nuanced:

They of whome God is alltogether unapprehended are but fewe in number, and for grosnes of witt such, that they hardlie and scarcely seeme to holde the place of humane beinge. These we should judge to be of all others most miserable but that a wretcheder sorte there are, on whome whereas nature hath bestowed riper capacitie, theire evell disposition seriouslie goeth about therewith to apprehende God as beinge not God. Whereby it commeth to passe that of these two sortes of men, both godles, the one havinge utterlie no knowledge of God, the other studie howe to perswade them selves that there is no such thinge to be knowne.[87]

The vast majority of humanity is, therefore, aware of God's existence. Hooker includes amongst this number intelligent atheists; despite their arguments to the contrary, he finds that they are

[84] *Lawes*, 1:87.17–26 (I.8.7).

[85] Although the following discussion will concentrate on '*truths*' of a spiritual nature, Hooker does of course speak highly of the secular knowledge and skills of *mere natural persons*. See e.g. ibid. 1:226.2–15 (III.8.9).

[86] See ibid. 1:225.3–5 (III.8.8). See also 2:19.22–20.7 (V.1.3).

[87] Ibid. 2:22.27–23.7 (V.2.1). See also 1:59.33–60.2 (I.2.3); 1:87.13–15 (I.8.7); 1:223.9–14 (III.8.6).

unable entirely to convince even themselves that God does not exist.[88] Hence he speaks of their '*affected Atheisme*'.[89] The only true atheists are people almost totally lacking in reason, to the extent that Hooker considers them scarcely human: presumably such people lack the aid of common grace. They are, as Hooker notes, 'but fewe in number'.

One of the most interesting arguments Hooker gives for *mere natural people*'s knowledge of God's existence is to be found not in the *Lawes*, but perhaps rather surprisingly in the early *First Sermon Upon Part of S. Judes Epistle*:

> For at the bare beholding of heaven and earth the infidels heart by and by doth give him, that there is an eternal, infinite, immortal, and everliving God; whose hands have fashioned and framed the world; hee knoweth that *every house is builded of some man*, though he see not the man which built the house, and he considereth, that it must be God which have built and created all things . . . the light of natural reason hath put this wisdome in his reines, and hath given his heart thus much understanding.[90]

This is, of course, the cosmological argument, according to which the existence of God can be inferred from the supposed fact the universe must have a Creator, or First Cause. It is also interesting to note some of the properties of God listed here, which *mere natural persons* can know; his eternal existence, infinitude, and immortality. Hooker adds to this list of known properties in the *Lawes*. He quotes Homer, Hermes Trismegistus, Anaxagoras, Plato, and Cicero (translating Zeno), to prove that *mere natural persons* can know that the First Cause is a rational agent.[91] Some pages later he observes that 'the mindes, even of meere naturall men, have attayned to knowe, not onely that there is a God, but also what power, force, wisedome, and other properties that God hath, and how all things depende on him'.[92] He also quotes from Plato's *Republic* to show that, concerning God, 'even infidels have confessed, that he can neyther erre nor deceive'.[93] This amounts to far more than a vague concept of a divine being or beings, but rather

[88] See ibid. 2:24.8–14 (V.2.2).

[89] See ibid. 2:22.26 (V.2.1).

[90] *Jude 1*, 5:23.21–7; 5:24.3–4. Cf. *Lawes*, 1:67.9–17 (I.3.4).

[91] See *Lawes*, 1:59.33–60.16 (I.2.3). I cannot agree with Kavanagh that Hooker's proclivity for citing pagan authors is mere Renaissance *copia*. Hooker wishes to make a case for the powers of *mere natural reason*, and he does this in part precisely by citing such authors. See Kavanagh, 'Reason and Nature in Hooker's Polity', 15–16, 165.

[92] See *Lawes*, 1:87.14–17 (I.8.7).

[93] See ibid. 1:132.24–5 (I.15.4).

demonstrates a quite specific knowledge of many of God's attributes. *Mere natural persons*, it would seem, can know a considerable amount about God, provided that they use their reason aright.

Mere natural persons can know more obscure information than this, however, according to Hooker. In his discussion of celestial law in Book 1 of the *Lawes*, he is quite specific that 'even the Painims' can know of the existence and behaviour of angels.[94] To prove this point, he cites Aristotle and the songs of Orpheus. Orpheus, in a passage taken from the *Carmina Orphei*, describes how the angels attend 'the fierie throne of God'. Aristotle, when discussing in the *Metaphysics* how God moves the celestial spheres, is taken by Hooker to be referring to angels. The citation of Orpheus is somewhat ambiguous as regards an illustration of the capacities of *mere natural persons*: Hooker does imply, later in Book 1, that Orpheus may have had access to Holy Scripture, and he was often associated with the supernatural in the sixteenth century.[95] No such explanation is given for Aristotle's knowledge, however, other than the presumed fact that he used his *mere natural reason*.

For further examples of *mere natural spiritual truths* which can be known by *mere natural persons*, one can also look to the first chapter of Book 5 of the *Lawes*.[96] Here Hooker talks about pagan beliefs and practices which distantly reflect divine realities. For instance, a belief in metempsychosis is said to show a perception of the soul's immortality, while divination displays a knowledge of 'the unresistable force of divine power'. This might be taken to mean that, contrary to what has been argued above, pagans have only a very partial understanding of *mere natural spiritual truths*. If the context of this argument is taken into account, however, a rather different picture emerges. Hooker's point in this chapter is that religion always helps people to behave well, no matter how corrupt it might be. As he observes, regarding corrupt religion: 'in as much as the errors of the most seduced this way have bene mixed with some truthes, wee are not to mervaile that although the one did tourne

[94] See *Lawes*, 1:70.16–22 (I.4.1). Cf. e.g. *ScG* III. cv–cix. Aquinas argues that the practices of magicians demonstrate the existence of demons, and that, since God creates nothing evil, this in turn implies the existence of angels.

[95] See *Lawes*, 1:133.27–134.6 (I.15.4). Cf. Justin Martyr, 'The Dialogue with Trypho', *Writings of Saint Justin Martyr*, trans. T. B. Falls (New York, 1948), 259, 261. Alternatively, Hooker may be implying that Orpheus had heard a primordial revelation, passed on by word of mouth from Adam.

[96] See esp. *Lawes*, 2:19.22–22.2 (V.1.3–4).

to theire endlesse woe and confusion, yeat the other had many notable effectes as touchinge thaffaires of this present life'.[97] Hooker's examples of pagan practices in this chapter are, therefore, not meant to display the height of the knowledge which *mere natural persons* have of *mere natural spiritual truths*, but to show the utility of religion even when humans err. He is not arguing that all pagans are unable fully to understand the soul's immortality, simply because some happen to believe in metempsychosis.[98] It is worth remembering at this point the following lines from Tertullian, which Hooker quotes to defend all that is good in pagan philosophy:

> *For there are some things even knowne by nature, as the immortalitie of the soule unto many, our God unto all. I will therefore my selfe also use the sentence of some such as Plato, pronouncing every soule immortall. I my selfe too will use the secret acknowledgment of the communaltie, bearing record of the God of Gods. But when I heare men alleage, That which is dead is dead; and, While thou art alive be alive; and, After death an end of all even of death it selfe: then will I call to minde both that the heart of the people with God is accompted dust, and that the very wisdome of the world is pronounced follie.*[99]

Mere natural persons can evidently, in Hooker's opinion, know many natural laws and *mere natural spiritual truths*. This is quite distinct, however, from the question of whether such knowledge pertains to behaviour that would glorify and be obedient to God. Although the degree of knowledge that Hooker ascribes to *mere natural persons* was, as will be shown, controversial in the Reformed England of his day, his observations on knowledge of obedient behaviour were even more so. Also of great theological interest are Hooker's views on the extent to which *mere natural persons* can turn their knowledge to a practical end and actually obey natural law, and therefore in addition potentially perform actions obedient to God. The preceding pages have examined Hooker's views on knowledge and *mere natural reason*, but so far nothing has been said about choice and obedience, and the capacities of *mere natural will*. Since Hooker's ideas on *mere natural will* and obedience to natural

97 See ibid. 2:20.13–17 (V.1.3). Cf. 2:21.18–27 (V.1.3), which should be read in the same way. (The *Folger* punctuation, unlike Keble's, is most helpful at this point.)

98 This last observation might also be made about the following passages: *Lawes*, 1:68.8–12 (I.3.4); 1:68.25–69.6 (I.3.4); 1:294.17–295.5 (IV.7.2).

99 Ibid. 1:225.3–12 (III.8.8). Cf. 1:223.29–224.3 (III.8.7).

law are often in the *Lawes* closely related to the question of knowledge of works obedient to God, these two topics will now be analysed concurrently. Later on the question of obedience will be explored further by itself, with regard to the topic of original sin.

The first major passage in the *Lawes* relating to knowledge of behaviour obedient to God is in Book 1, and because of its context it is somewhat negative in its wording. It is, though, useful to analyse it, before turning to look at Hooker's extended treatment of the subject in Book 2:

> The lawe of reason doth somewhat direct men how to honour God as their Creator, but how to glorifie God in such sort as is required, to the end he may be an everlasting Saviour, this we are taught by divine law, which law both ascertayneth the truth and supplyeth unto us the want of that other law. So that in morall actions, divine lawe helpeth exceedingly the lawe of reason to guide mans life, but in supernaturall it alone guideth.[100]

Hooker makes a distinction here between 'supernaturall' and 'morall' actions. The former concern redemption, and are thus directed at God in so far as He is humanity's Saviour; hence they can only be known from divine law. 'Morall' actions might more fittingly be termed 'natural moral actions', since they appear to refer to those virtuous deeds that can be known from natural law.[101] Since this law does not deal with the issue of salvation, 'morall actions' may be said to refer to God only in so far as He is humanity's Creator, not its Saviour. Hooker does emphasize, though, the utility of divine law in discovering these 'morall actions'. The point he is making here appears to be similar to that in ch. 12 of Book 1: not all natural laws are easy to know, so Holy Scripture is an excellent guide, since it is full of such laws.[102] Hooker does not state in these lines that 'morall actions' cannot be known from natural law; it is merely a question of the ease of access. Since, therefore, *mere natural persons* can have knowledge of natural law and hence of 'morall actions', they must logically have knowledge of how to honour and glorify God as their Creator. That such honorification and glorification is tantamount to obedience to God is an obvious point, and as will be seen, one that Hooker makes explicitly himself in Book 2. Such 'morall actions'

[100] *Lawes*, 1:139.3–10 (I.16.5).

[101] On the commonplace scholastic distinction between 'morall' as opposed to 'supernaturall' actions (or virtues), see e.g. *ST* I-II.62.2.

[102] See n. 64 above.

will include worship and praise of God, as well as actions that honour God only indirectly, such as personal rectitude and laudable civil behaviour. It is not clear, though, why the law of reason/natural law should only 'somewhat' direct people how to honour God as their Creator: whatever the advantages of divine law, natural law should contain all that is necessary for humanity to honour God in this manner. It is possible, though, that Hooker is thinking here of revealed knowledge of Creation, such as that to be found in Genesis. In this sense, only Christians can fully honour God as their Creator. In either case, this qualification would appear to be another example of Hooker's struggle to present the claims of natural law and divine law in a balanced light; to emphasize the powers of *mere natural reason* (and of the human reason more generally), whilst not belittling the overarching claims of Holy Scripture as one of the keys to salvation.

Hooker's most important discussion of knowledge and performance of obedient works, outside the late works, occurs in Book 2 of the *Lawes*. Here Hooker attacks what he describes as '*their first position who urge reformation in the Church of England: Namely, That Scripture is the onely rule of all things which in this life may be done by men*'.[103] His primary aim in this book is to prove that Christians may be directed by various types of law, and that Holy Scripture is not the sole source of these. Yet his arguments are sufficiently broad as to cover *mere natural persons* as well as Christians, and the rules that they should follow in their lives. The two chapters in this book of most relevance are numbers 2 and 4. In these chapters Hooker examines Cartwright's interpretations of two scriptural passages concerning glorification of and obedience to God, which Cartwright uses in the *Replye* to justify his views on these subjects. The best way to approach Hooker's arguments is first to examine the *Replye* itself, and then to look at Whitgift's response to it in the 'Defence'. In that context the significance of Hooker's observations become far more readily clear.

The first scriptural passage cited by Cartwright is 1 Corinthians 10: 31: 'Whether therefore ye eat or drinke, or whatsoever ye do, do all to the glorie of God.' Cartwright's gloss on this is as follows: 'no man can gloryfy God in any thing but by obedience, and there is no obedience but in respect of the commaundement and word

[103] *Lawes*, 1:143.2–8 (II.Title).

of God: therefore it followeth that the word of God directeth a man in all his actions'.[104] Cartwright's interpretation is that all things in life, even eating and drinking, should be directed by Holy Scripture, as this is the only way in which God can be glorified and obeyed. Whitgift criticizes this argument as a *non sequitur*, since he does not see the logic of deducing that all acts of obedience and glorification must be expressly set down in Holy Scripture. Rather, he observes, a negative construction should be adopted in all such cases of *adiaphora*, in that people should ensure that they do nothing contrary to the Word of God:

> But the true meaning of St Paul in that place is, that we seek the glory of God in all things, and do nothing that is against his word and commandment. He glorifieth God in meat and drink, which acknowledgeth God to be the giver of them, and then is thankful for them, and useth them moderately, &c.: the like is to be said of all other actions.[105]

Whitgift retains Holy Scripture as the authority to be used in discerning how to glorify and obey God, but in matters of *adiaphora* he considers a negative construction sufficient, as opposed to Cartwright's requirement of a positive commandment.

The second crucial passage is Romans 14: 23: 'whatsoever is not of faith, is sinne'. Cartwright's interpretation of this is as follows:

> But the place of S. Paul is of all other most cleare, where speaking of those things which are called indifferent, in the ende he concludeth, that whatsoever is not of fayth, is sinne: but fayth is not but in respecte of the word of God, therfore whatsoever is not done by the word of God, is sinne. And if any will say that S. Paul meaneth there a full *plerophorian* and perswasion that that which he doth is well done, I graunt it. But from whence can that spring but from fayth, and how can we perswade and assure our selves, that we do well, but whereas we have the word of God for our warrant? so that the Apostle by a metonimie *Subjecti pro adjuncto*, doth give to understand from whence the assured perswasion doth spring. Whereupon it falleth out, that forasmuch as in all our actions both publyke & private we ought to follow the direction of the word of God: in matters of the church and which concerne all, there may be nothing done but by the word of God.[106]

[104] *Replye*, 27.

[105] 'Defence', 192–3.

[106] *Replye*, 27. Cartwright gives the precise scriptural reference, Romans 14: 23, in the margin.

Whitgift again responds by observing that, as Cartwright himself accepts, St Paul is speaking here of *adiaphora*, and such indifferent matters require only a negative construction of Holy Scripture to ensure that we may obey God in our actions and avoid sin:

But the meaning of the apostle is that we should do nothing against our conscience, nothing but that which we do believe not to displease God, not to be against his word or commandment.... it is not true [regarding *adiaphora*] that whatsoever cannot be proved by the word of God is not of faith: for then to take up a straw, to observe many civil orders, and to do a number of particular actions, were against faith, and so deadly sin; because it is not found in the word of God that we should do them. Which doctrine must needs bring a great servitude and bondage to the conscience, restrain or rather utterly overthrow that part of christian liberty which consisteth in the free use of indifferent things, neither commanded nor forbidden in the word of God, and throw men headlong into desperation.[107]

Cartwright was far from being deterred by Whitgift's remarks here, and went on memorably in the *Second Replie* to argue that even in a matter as trivial as picking up a straw positive scriptural warrant should be sought.[108]

Hooker examines Cartwright's interpretation of 1 Corinthians 10: 31 in chapter 2 of the second book of the *Lawes*. He accepts Cartwright's dictum that 'no man can gloryfy God in any thing but by obedience', but then observes in turn that such obedience can refer to any law instituted by God, and not merely those to be found in Holy Scripture:

yet for any thing there is in this sentence alleaged to the contrarie, God may be glorified by obedience, and obeyed by performance of his will, and his will be performed with an actuall intelligent desire to fulfill that lawe which maketh knowne what his will is, although no speciall clause or sentence of Scripture be in every such action set before mens eyes to warrant it. For scripture is not the onely lawe whereby God hath opened his will touching all thinges that may be done, but there are other kindes of lawes which notifie the will of God, as in the former booke hath beene prooved at large: Nor is there any law of God, whereunto he doth not accompt our obedience his glorie.[109]

A person obeys and glorifies the will of God by obeying God's laws. Since natural law was instituted by God, this means that *mere*

[107] 'Defence', 193–4. [108] See *Second Replie*, 59.
[109] *Lawes*, 1:149.9–19 (II.2.2).

natural persons can know how to obey and glorify God, as Hooker then states himself, referring to 1 Peter 2: 12:

infidels themselves did discerne, in matters of life and conversation, when beleevers did well, and when otherwise; when they glorified their heavenly father, and when not: it followeth that some thinges wherein God is glorifyed, may be some other way knowne, then onely by the sacred Scripture; of which Scripture the Gentiles being utterly ignorant, did notwithstanding judge rightly of the qualitie of Christian mens actions. Most certaine it is that nothing, but onely sinne doth dishonour God.[110]

This is, of course, a wholly different argument from the one made by Whitgift, which refers all obedience and glorification to Holy Scripture. There may in fact be a veiled negative allusion to Whitgift's 'Defence' earlier in this chapter, when Hooker argues that God may be obeyed without an express intention to do so. Whitgift's own arguments concerning the consumption of food and drink, and other such actions, speak of the importance of conscious thankfulness and acknowledgement that God has given these gifts. For Hooker, God may be obeyed by adhering correctly to any of his laws, and this includes non-moral laws of nature, a point he has made earlier in Book 1:

By that which we worke naturally, as when we breath, sleepe, moove, we set forth the glory of God as naturall agents doe, albeit we have no expresse purpose to make that our end, nor any advised determination therein to follow a law, but do that we doe, (for the most part) not as much as thinking thereon.[111]

Contrary to Whitgift, even unconscious actions are capable of being obedient to the divine will. Since *mere natural persons* are obviously capable of performing as well as knowing about such actions, Hooker evidently thought that such persons could perform as well as know about works obedient to God.

Hooker deals with Cartwright's interpretation of Romans 14: 23 in the fourth chapter of Book 2, pursuing a similar line of reasoning as in the second chapter. Like Cartwright before him, he observes that the Greek word πληροφορίαν, usually translated here as 'faith', means '*a full perswasion that that which we doe is well done*'.[112] Cartwright argues that this can only refer to faith, but Hooker

110 *Lawes*, 1:150.5–13 (II.2.3).

111 Ibid. 1:138.23–7 (I.16.5). See also 1:148.26–149.19 (II.2.1–2).

112 See ibid. 1:152.15–18 (II.4.2).

observes that there are numerous ways in which we can obtain this persuasion. One of these methods, he argues, consists of an understanding of natural law, and he slyly takes Cartwright's own words from the *Second Replie* out of their original context to demonstrate the capacities of *mere natural persons* in this respect:

For as much therefore as it is graunted, that S. Paule doth meane nothing else by *Fayth*, but only *a full perswasion that that which we doe is well done*; against which kinde of fayth or perswasion as S. *Paule* doth count it sinne to enterprise any thing, so likewise some of the very Heathen have taught, as *Tullie*, ***that nothing ought to be done whereof thou doubtest whether it be right or wrong, whereby it appeareth that even those which had no knowledge of the word of God did see much of the equitie of this which the Apostle requireth of a Christian man***: I hope we shall not seeme altogether unnecessarily to doubt of the soundnesse of their opinion, who thinke simply that nothing but onely the worde of God, can give us assurance in any thing wee are to doe, and resolve us that we doe well.[113]

This is again contrary to Whitgift's interpretation, which defines obedience to God and abstinence from sin only in terms of a negative construction of Holy Scripture. What is so important about Hooker's argument here is that, like Cartwright and Whitgift before him, he naturally equates obedience to and glorification of God with abstinence from sin. Clearly in his view, therefore, *mere natural persons* may know how to abstain from sin.[114]

These ideas are summarized by Hooker in the final chapter of Book 2. It is not the substance of this chapter, however, that is so notable in this context, but rather the terminology employed. In one sentence, when speaking of humanity's knowledge of laws instituted by God, Hooker drops his references to works that glorify and obey God, and instead speaks of works that God finds 'acceptable': 'his very commandements in some kinde, as namely his preceptes comprehended in the lawe of nature, may be otherwise knowne then onely by scripture; and that to do them, howsoever we know them, must needes be acceptable in his sight'.[115] Although this passage is in complete accord with his earlier

[113] Ibid. 1:152.15–153.3 (II.4.2). I have used bold for Cartwright's own words in this quotation. See *Second Replie*, 60.

[114] For additional passages on obedience to the laws of God, see *Lawes*, 1:138.18–22 (I.16.5); 3:210.13–23 (VII.11.10).

[115] Ibid. 1:188.28–31 (II.8.5).

comments on Cartwright's work, his use of the word 'acceptable' is nonetheless highly significant. Article 10 of the Thirty-Nine Articles states that 'we have no power to do good works pleasant and acceptable to God, without the grace of God by Christ preventing us, that we may have a good will, and working with us, when we have that good will', while Article 13 states that 'Works done before the grace of Christ, and the inspiration of his Spirit, are not pleasant to God'.[116] The *Christian Letter* felt that this passage, as well as several others in the *Lawes*, was contrary to Article 13 (and also implicitly Article 10), and that it supported 'the Romish doctrine of *pura naturalia* and workes of congruitie'.[117] Hooker was in fact able to respond both forcefully and subtly to demonstrate his orthodoxy as regards Article 10 without compromising his arguments in the *Lawes*, and may well have been in a position to do the same as regards Article 13. As, however, this is a matter that concerns the late works, it will be examined in detail only later in Ch. 5.[118]

If, though, *mere natural persons* may know how to obey and glorify God, to abstain from sin and in some sense perform works acceptable to God, this raises the final and most contentious question of whether they are actually capable of choosing to do so. Hooker's approach in the *Lawes* to this matter may be divided into three categories, depending upon the class of action concerned. The first category regards non-moral, natural behaviour, such as breathing and sleeping, and it has been shown already that Hooker argues that just as *mere natural persons* are obviously capable of performing such actions, so they glorify God in so doing. The second category concerns actions or desires that are natural to humans as rational beings, but that are not usually self-conscious. Most of the examples given by Hooker here are directed at God, as the supreme source of all goodness. He finds that all humans, consciously or otherwise, wish to unite with God, and to participate in his perfection.[119] This manifests itself in quite ordinary human activities. For instance, the desire for continuance of being, expressed in this life by procreation,

[116] See Gerald Bray (ed.), *Documents of the English Reformation* (Cambridge, 1994), 290, 292: absque gratia Dei, quae per Christum est, nos praeveniente, ut velimus, et cooperante dum volumus, ad pietatis opera facienda, quae Deo grata sint et accepta, nihil valemus; Opera quae fiunt ante gratiam Christi, et Spiritus eius afflatum . . . minime Deo grata sunt.

[117] See *ACL* 4:23.11–24.8.

[118] See pp. 271–2, 292–6, 298, 313–16.

[119] See *Lawes*, 1:111.33–112.24 (I.11.2–3); 1:72.27–73.28 (I.5.1–3).

hearkens towards the eternity of God. The set routines that people follow correspond to divine immutability, while the human quest for precision reflects God's 'absolute exactnes'. Since these common human desires are directed at God, they must be considered as good, and hence as tending to God's glory.[120]

The last and obviously by far the most important category concerns self-conscious human choices and actions. Here too, in so far as people are able to obey natural law, they are capable of glorifying God and abstaining from sin. As Hooker notes, referring to Romans 1: 21: 'In reasonable and morall actions another law taketh place, a law by the observation whereof we glorifie God in such sort, as no creature els under man is able to doe.'[121] When one seeks for specific examples of such actions, concerning *mere natural persons*, there are, however, virtually none to be found in Hooker's work. Plato and Aristotle are cited, to demonstrate their *knowledge* of particular natural laws, but there are barely any case studies of pagans *acting* in a moral way. One might observe that in order to obtain such knowledge one must search diligently for it, which is a form of action in itself;[122] diligence is, moreover, the particular responsibility of the will, as has been argued in Ch. 2. In this sense Hooker does indeed give numerous examples of the moral actions of *mere natural persons*; one for each *mere natural spiritual truth*, and 'conclusion' of natural law, they are shown to know. Yet apart from this, Hooker is silent. This should not at all, though, be taken as implying that *mere natural persons* are largely incapable of moral actions. Hooker is concerned, in the *Lawes*, to show that people can know many laws and *truths* through the use of natural reason, and to explain why they should obey these laws. Specific instances of obedience are not particularly germane to his case.[123] This applies to Christians as much as to *mere natural persons*: other than mentioning the infused virtues of faith, hope, and love, Hooker gives very few specific examples of Christian obedience in

[120] For other desires that seem to fall in this category, see: ibid. 1:81.15–16 (I.7.7); 1:86.14–17 (I.8.5); *Remedie*, 5:375.7–24.

[121] See *Lawes*, 1:138.21–2, 27–32 (I.16.5).

[122] It might be noted that this is one moral action/desire that Hooker does mention, with reference to *mere natural persons*: see *Lawes*, 1:73.28–74.14 (I.5.3).

[123] Hooker's bias towards knowledge can be seen in two passages, in which he discusses *mere natural persons* and moral actions/desires, but nevertheless still places an emphasis upon knowledge of natural law: see *Lawes*, 1:73.28–74.14 (esp. 74.3–5) (I.5.3); 1:138.27–139.5 (esp. 139.3–5) (I.16.5).

his work. This raises the question, of course, of how one should establish Hooker's attitude towards *mere natural persons* and moral actions. One answer is to look at his philosophy of mind and action. This would indicate that *mere natural persons* are at best able freely through diligence (and common grace) to perform various good actions, but that they certainly cannot abstain from sin altogether. The problem of concentration, discussed in Ch. 2, means that the will cannot remain unfailingly diligent. The way in which Hooker's philosophy of action is related here to his theory of grace will be explored further in the next chapter, as regards the scholastic distinction between mortal and venial sins.[124] A second, complementary approach is to examine Hooker's statements on original sin, and the extent to which humanity was corrupted by the Fall. The more liberal Hooker's attitude to original sin, the more one would expect him to have a relatively confident view of the capacity of *mere natural persons* to glorify God and abstain from sin, and conversely the more conservative his position, the more pessimistic one would expect him to be about post-lapsarian obedience to the divine will.

Few subjects have divided Hooker's critics more than his views on original sin, and the matter is at present highly controversial. Of those critics who identify Hooker with a more liberal position, C. S. Lewis goes so far as to declare that he 'sometimes' feels that 'the doctrine of the Fall did not loom quite large enough in his universe'.[125] More recently and much more influentially, Lake in *Anglicans and Puritans?* observes that 'Hooker did not have a particularly dramatic or cataclysmic view of the effects of the fall', and that 'compared to the views of other protestants, Hooker's vision of sin as a species of ignorance, a sort of intellectual laziness, seemed almost benign'. Lake sees this as a central part of Hooker's opposition to Calvinist or Reformed orthodoxy, with its belief in the total depravity of post-lapsarian humanity: Hooker, on the contrary, emphasizes those elements in human nature that lead people towards God in spite of the Fall.[126] In marked contrast, Kavanagh, Neelands, Kirby, and Atkinson, amongst others, all find Hooker an orthodox Reformed theologian in this respect, convinced of

[124] See pp. 201–9.
[125] C. S. Lewis, *Poetry and Prose in the Sixteenth Century* (Oxford, 1954), 461.
[126] See Lake, *Anglicans and Puritans?*, 150, 182.

humanity's total depravity. Atkinson, for instance, describes Hooker's view of the Fall as 'impeccably orthodox' from a Reformed perspective, while Kirby observes that 'Hooker's formulation of the doctrine of man's total depravity is unmistakably reformed'.[127] Other critics voice virtually all shades of opinion in between these poles, in a bewildering array of perspectives.[128] What is needed here is not simply one further perspective, but a resolution to this debate that mediates between these more extreme positions, and explains why critics have so confidently adopted such diverse views. The answer is to be found in the subtlety and complexity of Hooker's theology, which to some extent encompasses both polarities, even though, as will be shown, it is ultimately hostile at this point to ideas characteristic of Reformed theology.

In one sense, as has been noted, it is right to argue that Hooker saw the Fall as having devastating consequences for the human race.[129] As he observes in Book I of the *Lawes*, without the aid of God (i.e. without common grace) 'no kind of faculty or power in

[127] See Kavanagh, 'Reason and Nature in Hooker's Polity', 95–7, 99, 144; Neelands, 'The Theology of Grace of Richard Hooker', 161–2, 170–1; Kirby, *Richard Hooker's Doctrine of the Royal Supremacy*, 46; Atkinson, *Richard Hooker and the Authority of Scripture, Tradition and Reason*, 78–9.

[128] The following is a selection of some of the more interesting and significant modern critical opinions on this subject: J. W. Allen, *A History of Political Thought in the Sixteenth Century*, 3rd edn. (London, 1951), 189; Hillerdal, *Reason and Revelation in Richard Hooker*, 50; Grislis, 'Richard Hooker's Image of Man', 75, 77; Hill, 'The Doctrinal Background of Richard Hooker's *Laws of Ecclesiastical Polity*', 131, 134; John F. H. New, *Anglican and Puritan: The Basis of their Opposition, 1558–1640* (London, 1964), 9; Grislis, 'The Role of *Consensus* in Richard Hooker's Method of Theological Inquiry', 70, 72, 74; Morrel, 'The Systematic Theology of Richard Hooker', 78–9; Hill, 'Doctrine and Polity in Hooker's Laws', 179; Leslie Croxford, 'The Originality of Hooker's Work', *Proceedings of the Leeds Philosophical and Literary Society*, 15/2 (1973), 23; Arthur S. McGrade, 'The Coherence of Hooker's *Polity*: The Books on Power', *Journal of the History of Ideas* 24 (1963), 23; Thornburg, 'Original Sin, Justification and Sanctification in the Thought of Two Sixteenth Century English Divines: John Jewel and Richard Hooker', 109–10; Manuszak, 'Authority in Hooker's *Polity*', 202; Forte, 'The Achievement of Richard Hooker', 80–1, 143, 154; Henning Graf Reventlow, *The Authority of the Bible and the Rise of the Modern World*, trans. J. Bowden (London, 1984), 118; William P. Haugaard, 'The Scriptural Hermeneutics of Richard Hooker: Historical Contextualization and Teleology', *This Sacred History: Anglican Reflections for John Booty*, ed. D. S. Armentrout (Cambridge, Mass., 1990), 166; White, *Predestination, Policy and Polemic*, 127; Gibbs, 'Introduction: Book I', *Folger*, vi. 106, 108, 110–11, 124; William P. Haugaard, 'Introduction: Books II, III & IV', *Folger*, vi. 165; William Otis Gregg, 'Richard Hooker's 'Of the Lawes of Ecclesiasticall Polity I–V': A Theology of Sacramentality' (Ph.D. thesis, Univ. of Notre Dame, 1993), 224; William J. Bouwsma, 'Hooker in the Context of European Cultural History', *RHCCC* 50; Arthur P. Monahan, 'Richard Hooker: Counter-Reformation Thinker', *RHCCC* 208.

[129] See pp. 100–9 above.

man or any other creature... can rightly performe the functions alotted to it'.[130] The human reason and will cease to function correctly, and people become, as it is stated in Ephesians 4: 17–18, '*strangers from the life of God through the ignorance which is in them*'.[131] Since common grace is a gratuitous help that we receive from God, humanity's 'natural' state after the Fall would thus appear to be one of utter depravity. Yet as has already also been observed, this passage describing humanity devoid of common grace is unique in the *Lawes* and early work, and Hooker writes in general, especially in the *Lawes*, as if humans were commonly able at least to some degree to know and obey God's will, and hence in receipt of common grace. Only those who offend God in some grievous manner have this aid withdrawn from them. In this respect, humanity's 'natural' condition after the Fall may in a qualified sense be taken to include common grace. The key point is to establish the efficacy of common grace, by looking at what in Hooker's opinion *mere natural persons* are commonly capable of achieving with this aid, and the extent to which they remain corrupted by original sin. Exactly the same is true of Calvin's theology as well, where it would be a great error to presume that Calvin thought that human behaviour as commonly encountered should be assessed without the presumption of this grace. It is thus, as will be shown, that although Hooker and Calvin both accept a doctrine of total depravity, they have profoundly different views of the common behaviour and nature of *mere natural persons*, and hence of the general effects of original sin.

Before continuing, it is worth examining a point of terminology that has perceptively been noted by Charles Thornburg.[132] When referring to the primordial sin, Article 9 of the Thirty-Nine Articles speaks of 'Original, or Birth Sin' in the English version, and *Peccatum originale* in the Latin. These were the terms commonly used in the sixteenth century to denote this sin, as reference to the index of the publications of the Parker Society goes some way to illustrate. Yet, as far as I am aware, Hooker quite extraordinarily never uses the terms 'original sin' or 'birth sin' in the *Lawes*. In the tractates and sermons he speaks once of 'sinne... *originall*' in

[130] See *Lawes*, 1:92.23–93.1 (I.8.11).
[131] See ibid. 1:92.23–93.1 (I.8.11).
[132] See Thornburg, 'Original Sin, Justification and Sanctification in the Thought of Two Sixteenth Century English Divines: John Jewel and Richard Hooker', 109–10.

The Second Sermon Upon Part of S. Judes Epistle, and three times of 'originall synne' during summaries of Roman Catholic doctrine in *A Learned Discourse of Justification* and the *Answer to the Supplication*.[133] Only in the *Dublin Fragments* does he frequently employ the term 'originall sinne', and its Latin equivalents; an excellent example of the highly distinctive nature of that work.[134] On all other occasions, he uses terms such as 'divine malediction' and 'natures obliquitie'.[135] There can be little doubt that Thornburg is correct in his assessment that this general avoidance of the term 'original sin' must be deliberate on Hooker's part. Quite why this is the case is a matter of speculation, though the implication is that Hooker felt in some way uneasy about the term, or even the idea in itself. He was, however, forced to discuss original sin explicitly in the *Dublin Fragments*, given that the writers of the *Christian Letter* had tacitly accused him of upholding the heresy of Pelagianism in the *Lawes*.

Whatever the terminology, Hooker's references to the Fall, original sin, and original corruption are remarkably few, except within the late works. In the *Lawes*, only Book 1 stands out as containing a relatively high number of references. The remaining books barely mention these subjects, and I count only six passing references in the entire extent of the enormous fifth book.[136] This is by no means to say that these topics were irrelevant to his theology. Hooker subscribed to the orthodox Christian opinion concerning the Fall, that humanity is now (to whatever extent) corrupt, and can only be redeemed by faith in Jesus Christ. The statement he made in *The Second Sermon Upon Part of S. Judes Epistle*, that 'wee are

[133] See *Jude 2*, 5:50.22; *Just.* 5:111.15; *Answer*, 5:240.2; 5:242.13–14.

[134] See *DF* 4:103.4; 4:105.d.4; 4:109.11; 4:109.g.8; 4:117.17–18; 4:138.22–5; 4:147.5–6, 15; 4:148.2; 4:151.9, 27–8. Interestingly, in the *Notes towards a Fragment on Predestination*, it looks as though Hooker was about to substitute a different term for 'originale peccatum' (he wrote 'pecc-', and then crossed it out). Two sentences later, he chose to use the term 'culpa originalis' instead. See *Pred.* 4:95.21–31.

[135] See *Lawes*, 1:66.18 (I.3.3); 1:119.22–3 (I.11.6). For other examples, see n. 136.

[136] See ibid. 1:15.20–2 (Pref.3.7); 1:66.6–26 (I.3.3); 1:81.10–20 (I.7.7); 1:96.24–32 (I.10.1); 1:100.11–15 (I.10.5); 1:108.14–17 (I.10.13); 1:115.27–116.3 (I.11.5); 1:118.11–18 (I.11.6); 1:119.18–23 (I.11.6); 1:121.29–35 (I.12.3); 1:177.8–25 (II.7.3); 1:179.27–31 (II.7.5); 1:180.32–181.4 (II.7.5); 2:99.6–9 (V.22.10); 2:104.22–5 (V.22.17); 2:199.23–200.11 (V.48.12); 2:241.21–3 (V.56.10); 2:291.19–28 (V.63.2); 2:418.15–19 (V.76.5); 3:12.18–27 (VI.3.5); 3:299.20–5 (VII.24.15); 3:301.2–302.2 (VII.24.16); *Jude 2*, 5:50.22–6; *Cert.* 5:71.16–20; 5:76.23–7; *Just.*, 5:112.26–113.4; 5:115.26–116.17; *Pride*, 5:312.19–313.1; 5:314.1–12; *Remedie*, 5:376.21–3. Generously inclusive criteria have been used in the compilation of this list of references.

full of sinne both *originall*, and *actuall*', remained true for his whole theological career. It is rather that original sin and corruption seem not to have been focal to his theological concerns.

One may now look at a variety of passages from the *Lawes*, the tractates, and the sermons, to try to exemplify his handling of the Fall and original sin on those occasions he does consider these matters. These passages need, of course, to be seen in the context of the passages that have been discussed earlier concerning the capacities of *mere natural reason* and *mere natural will*, which show Hooker ascribing very considerable abilities to *mere natural persons* who strive through diligence and grace to know and obey God's will. It is vital that the passages that deal explicitly with human corruption should not be seen in isolation, but as part of the entire web of Hooker's theology. From what has been analysed so far one would expect Hooker to have a relatively moderate view of original sin, once common grace is taken into account; the question now is whether this is also reflected in his particular remarks upon the subject.

To begin with, one may note that in the third chapter of Book 1 of the *Lawes*, Hooker takes the traditional view that the natural world was damaged in the Fall. He characteristically expresses this in legal terms: nature now sometimes departs from the laws that should govern her activities, but 'neverthelesse so constantly the lawes of nature are by naturall agents observed, that no man denieth but those things which nature worketh, are wrought either alwaies or for the most part after one and the same manner'.[137] The emphasis in this chapter is, in fact, firmly on the regularity and orderliness of the natural world, rather than the debilitating effects of original sin.

Another issue relating to the Fall that is raised in Book 1 of the *Lawes* (though not in Book 8) is that of political regiment. Hooker observes that the 'corruption of our nature' now necessitates that we have some kind of political system.[138] He also refers to this corruption when discussing the proper format for laws in a body politic, in a passage that has much exercised the minds of some critics:

> Lawes politique, ordeined for externall order and regiment amongst men, are never framed as they should be, unlesse presuming the will of man to be inwardly obstinate, rebellious, and averse from all obedience

[137] See *Lawes*, 1:66.6–26 (I.3.3).
[138] See ibid. 1:100.11–15 (I.10.5).

unto the sacred lawes of his nature; in a word, unlesse presuming man to be in regard of his depraved minde little better then a wild beast, they do accordingly provide notwithstanding so to frame his outward actions, that they be no hindrance unto the common good for which societies are instituted: unlesse they doe this, they are not perfect.[139]

The laws of human society, at least of the kind that Hooker appears to be considering, are designed to regulate the very worst aspects of humanity. They must operate under the assumption that some people will choose or desire to murder and steal, and so they must forbid these activities. Laws that take an overly optimistic view of humanity are thus, in Hooker's opinion, too feeble to deal with the consequences of the Fall. Yet this does not amount to an admission that a human is in general 'little better then a wild beast', as Hillerdal, Grislis, Forte, Atkinson, and Kirby all argue, taking these words out of their original context.[140] That would be to suppose that all citizens of political societies are bestial lawbreakers, a view that Calvin himself would have condemned, whereas Hooker is making a far more moderate observation about human corruption and the consequential necessity of political regiment.

Another passage that it is easy to interpret in too harsh a sense is taken from Book 6 of the *Lawes*. Here proper contextualization is also vital, to appreciate Hooker's argument:

Contrition doth not here import these suddayn pangs and convulsions of the mind, which cause sometymes the most forsaken of God to retracte their owne doings: it is noe naturall passion or anguish, which riseth in us against our wills, butt a deliberate aversion of the will of man from sinne which being allwayes accompanied with griefe, and greefe oftentymes partly with teares, partly with other externall signes, it hath beene thought, that in these things contrition doth cheifly consist, whereas the cheifest thing in contrition, is that alteration, whereby the will which was before delighted with sinne, doth now abhorre and shunne nothing more.[141]

[139] Ibid. 1:96.24–32 (I.10.1).

[140] See Hillerdal, *Reason and Revelation in Richard Hooker*, 50; Grislis, 'Richard Hooker's Image of Man', 77; Forte, 'The Achievement of Richard Hooker', 81; Atkinson, *Richard Hooker and the Authority of Scripture, Tradition and Reason*, 78–9; Kirby, 'Richard Hooker's Theory of Natural Law in the Context of Reformation Theology', 700.

[141] *Lawes*, 3:12.18–27 (VI.3.5). Contrition is here being opposed to the inferior act of attrition. Cf. 3:93.18–94.1 (VI.6.13).

In Book 6, Hooker defines contrition in terms of a specifically Christian act of repentance. This passage might, therefore, be taken to suggest that *mere natural persons* are totally corrupt, since the wills of the non-contrite are 'delighted with sinne'. This is, though, to impose far too rigid an interpretation upon one isolated phrase. Hooker is not here discussing *mere natural persons*, but is attempting to convince Christians that contrition requires a true change of heart. It is, therefore, to his rhetorical advantage to emphasize the depravity of the non-contrite, for only by meditating on their sinfulness will they turn their wills towards God. Moreover, theologians as diverse as Calvin and Aquinas have argued that the wills of non-Christians are corrupt and prone to sin. As Aquinas observes, for instance, 'the order of nature cannot be restored, by the submission of man's will to God, unless God draws it to himself'.[142] Where Calvin and Aquinas disagree, of course, is over the nature and extent of this corruption. In the above passage there is no more reason for detecting a Calvinist notion of total depravity, than there is for finding a Thomist judgement on the weakness of fallen humanity. The idea of original sin and corruption was, after all, the property of virtually all branches of Christianity in this period, and not solely of Calvin and Reformed theology. When one takes into account Hooker's philosophy of mind and action, and his remarks on humanity's ability to obey God in some things, a relatively moderate conception of human corruption appears to be by far the more satisfactory interpretation.

One may look now at the one passage in Hooker's writing (the late works excluded, as they are to be examined in Ch. 5) which does at least partly suggest an unqualified theory of humanity's total depravity, and is used by Atkinson to identify Hooker with this theological position.[143] It occurs in the tractate *A Learned Discourse of Justification, Workes, and How the Foundation of Faith is Overthrowne*:

I will but onely make a demaund: If god should yeld to us not as unto Abraham; if fiftye, fortie, thirtie, twentye yea or if tenne good persons could be founde in a citie, for theire sakes that citye should not be destroied: But if god should make us an offer thus large, search all the generations of men sithens the fall of your father Adam, fynde one man

[142] See *ST* I-II.109.7: ordo naturae reparari non potest, ut scilicet voluntas hominis Deo subjiciatur, nisi Deo voluntatem hominis ad se trahente. See also I-II.109.8; *Inst.* II.iii.3–5.

[143] See Atkinson, *Richard Hooker and the Authority of Scripture, Tradition and Reason*, 30.

that hath done any one action which hath paste him pure without any staine or blemishe att all, and for that one mans one only action neither man nor aungell shall feele the tormentes which are prepared for both: do youe thinck that this ransom to delyver men and aungells would be founde amonges the sonnes of men? The beste thinges we do have some what in them to be pardoned, howe then can we do any thinge meritorious and worthy to be rewarded? In deed god doth liberally promise whatsoever apperteyneth to a blessed lyfe, unto as many as syncerely kepe his lawe, though they be not able exactly to kepe it: wherfore we acknowledg a dutyfull necessitye of doinge well but the meritorious dignitye of well doinge we utterly renounce.[144]

There can be no doubt of Hooker's argument here; he observes quite plainly that the actions of humans are always at least partially sinful. This contradicts his numerous assertions in the *Lawes* that in many things *mere natural persons* can (at least to some extent) obey natural law and hence glorify God. It seems likely that about seven years passed after the preaching of these sermons until the publication of the first four books of the *Lawes*: it would not be unreasonable, therefore, to suggest that Hooker's thought developed in this time.[145] It certainly did regarding the freedom of the will, as this (very seldom mentioned) passage, also from A *Learned Discourse of Justification*, illustrates: 'The heresie of freewill was a milstone about thc pelagians neckes: shall we therefore gyve sentence of death inevitable againste all those fathers in the greek church which being misperswaded died in the errour of freewill?'[146] The freedom of the will, both in terms of liberty of spontaneity and liberty of indifference, is, as has been argued, fundamental to Hooker's philosophy of mind and action as expressed in the *Lawes* and the late works. If, therefore, Hooker's thoughts on this matter could undergo such a radical transformation, there seems no reason why his conception of original sin could not have done the same. This change of view becomes more apparent if one looks at

[144] *Just.* 5:115.26–116.11. Cf. 5:112.26–113.4.

[145] See Georges Edelen, 'Textual Introduction', *Folger*, i. pp. xvi–xix; Yeandle, 'Textual Introduction: *A Learned Discourse of Justification, Workes, and How the Foundation of Faith Is Overthrowne*', *Folger*, v. 83.

[146] *Just.* 5:143.16–19. See Ch. 1 n. 86. Hooker does not say here that the will is made free by grace; he denies its very freedom. These lines of Hooker's, and their general preoccupation with the 'foundacion of faith', are curiously similar in sentiment to the following, taken from Cartwright's *Replye*: 'For I doubt not, but dyvers of the fathers of the Greke church, which were great patrons of free wil (at lest as their wordes pretende) are saved holding the foundation of the fayth, which is Christ.' See *Replye*, 26.

one of his principal discussions of merit in the *Lawes*. In ch. 11 of Book 1, he argues that prelapsarian humans could have attained heavenly bliss through their good works. As a result of the Fall and the corruption of humanity, however, people cannot now perfectly obey natural law and by themselves merit salvation:

> Our naturall meanes therefore unto blessednes are our workes: nor is it possible that nature should ever finde any other way to salvation then onely this. But examine the workes which we doe and since the firste foundation of the world what one can say, My wayes are pure? Seing then all flesh is guiltie of that for which God hath threatned eternallie to punish, what possibilitie is there this way to be saved?[147]

This is not at all the same as arguing that *all* the works and desires of humanity are at least partially sinful. One may recall the distinction that Hooker makes in Book 5 of the *Lawes* with regard to the problem of concentration, which is perfectly applicable here: collectively speaking it is impossible that a person should be 'pure' in his or her actions, but this is not to deny the existence of distributive purity or obedience.[148] This leaves open, in a way that the previous passage does not, the idea that *mere natural persons* are capable to some extent of obeying God's will, even if this obedience is profitless as regards salvation. The distinction can be seen even more plainly in these lines, taken from *A Learned Sermon of the Nature of Pride*:

> Then seing that the heart of man is not right exactly unlesse it be found in all partes such that god examining and calling it unto accompt with all severitie of rigour be not able once to charge it with declining or swerving aside, which absolute perfection when did god ever find in the sonnes of meer mortall men? doth it not follow that all flesh must of necessity fall down and confesse, Wee are not dust and ashes but wourse, our mindes from the highest to the lowest are not right? If not right then undoubtedly not capable of that blessednes which wee naturallie seek but subject unto that which wee most abhor anguish tribulation death woe endlesse miserie.[149]

The test of humanity has been completely reversed. In *A Learned Discourse of Justification*, Hooker condemns humanity because no *single* human action has ever been without sin. Here, in *A Learned Sermon of the Nature of Pride*, he condemns humanity

[147] *Lawes*, 1:115.26–116.3 (I.11.5). See also 1:116.4–118.13 (I.11.5).
[148] See pp. 88–90 above.
[149] *Pride*, 5:312.19–28.

because everyone has committed (at least) *one* sinful act. One might, though, argue that this difference is more apparent than real. The sermons are probably contemporaneous, and it is uncertain which was written or preached first, making it difficult to argue that Hooker's view of humanity underwent a radical change between the two works.[150] What is clear, though, is that the passage from *A Learned Sermon of the Nature of Pride* fits closely with the theories Hooker expounds in the *Lawes*. *A Learned Discourse of Justification* at least appears to take a more pessimistic approach, and not one reflected in the *Lawes* nor, as will be shown, the late works. In the light of this, Atkinson's identification of the passage in *A Learned Discourse of Justification* with Hooker's general attitude to original sin is evidently mistaken in its approach.

One may look finally at one more passage on human corruption, taken from the *Lawes*. It occurs in ch. 7 of Book 2, which attempts to refute Cartwright's claim that the authority of a human '*neither affirmatively nor negatively compelleth the hearer, but only induceth him to some liking or disliking of that for which it is brought*'.[151] Hooker in response concedes that the human mind is now corrupt, but still argues that in many things it can have 'infallible' access to the truth. In terms of his theory of certainty this refers to the third order, of proof 'by strong and invincible demonstration':[152]

> Men are blinded with ignorance and error; many things may escape them, and in many thinges they may be deceived; yea, those thinges which they doe knowe, they may eyther forget, or upon sundry indirect considerations let passe; and although themselves do not erre, yet may they through malice or vanitie, even of purpose deceive others. Howbeit infinite cases there are wherin all these impediments and lets are so manifestly excluded, that there is no shewe or colour whereby any such exception may be taken, but that the testimony of man will stand as a ground of infallible assurance.[153]

These lines are in many ways representative of the attitude that Hooker takes to the question of human corruption, especially in the *Lawes*, though also in much of the early tractates and sermons.

[150] See Yeandle, 'Textual Introduction: *A Learned Discourse of Justification, Workes, and How the Foundation of Faith Is Overthrowne*', *Folger*, v. 83; 'Textual Introduction: *A Learned Sermon of the Nature of Pride*', *Folger*, v. 299.

[151] See *Lawes*, 1:174.24–175.3 (II.7.Title).

[152] As Hooker argues later in that chapter: see ibid. 1:179.8–18 (II.7.5).

[153] Ibid. 1:177.9–18 (II.7.3).

There are remarkably few references to the Fall and original sin, and the capacities of *mere natural persons* are in general viewed in a relatively optimistic light, far divorced, as will be shown, from the approach characteristic of theologians of the Reformed tradition. Hooker by no means denies post-lapsarian corruption, but it does not dominate his assessment of human behaviour, and he presents humanity as a species that through diligence and grace is capable of knowing many aspects of the divine will, and indeed in numerous ways of obeying this will, glorifying God, and abstaining from sin. Needless to say such behaviour has strict limitations for him, and as the next chapter will examine he adopts a traditional soteriological framework in which sanctifying and justifying graces are essential for salvation, and indeed for the total avoidance of mortal sin. Nevertheless, when one bears in mind the proviso that without common grace Hooker views the human mind as being wholly corrupt and without any trace of goodness, one may fairly conclude that in a qualified sense Lake has in *Anglicans and Puritans?* correctly appreciated that 'Hooker did not have a particularly dramatic or cataclysmic view of the effects of the fall', and that contrary to the characteristic Calvinist or Reformed view he rather emphasizes the aspects of human nature that lead humanity to God.[154] Such a relatively optimistic conception of human nature must be seen as a reflection of his philosophy of mind and action, and of the principles adumbrated in Chs. 1 and 2. Given that Hooker credits the human mind, through its intrinsic liberty of indifference, of being freely able through diligence (and grace) to obey the divine will in many respects, it is scarcely surprising that he came to reject the Reformed understanding of this issue, which is governed by a generally hostile attitude to the concept of human freedom. Calvin, for instance, as has been shown, does accept that humanity has a certain limited type of freedom, but in addition to arguing that there is no liberty of indifference with respect to God, he crucially has a very low view of the type of freedom that he does allow. This almost inevitably colours his perception of human nature, as his philosophy of mind emphasizes human bondage, as opposed to human freedom, and this embraces bondage to sin. The implications of this will be explored further in the next chapter in relation to the

[154] See Lake, *Anglicans and Puritans?*, 150.

doctrine of justification, where it will be argued that quite contrary to Calvin and the characteristic Reformed view more generally, Hooker's belief in human freedom led him to hold that grace must co-operate with the human will in salvation, and that humans can in a sense merit their own justification.

It remains, then, to illustrate that the argument of Kavanagh, Neelands, Kirby, Atkinson, and others—that Hooker's presentation of human nature is perfectly orthodox from a Reformed perspective—is quite mistaken, by comparing Hooker's ideas to those characteristic of the Reformed tradition. The principal Reformed writer that Kavanagh, Neelands, Kirby, and Atkinson compare with Hooker on the subject of human nature and original corruption is Calvin; a logical choice, given the influence that Calvin's ideas had in this respect on the Reformed tradition. In his recent article 'Richard Hooker's Theory of Natural Law in the Context of Reformation Theology', Kirby has extended his comparison to embrace Luther, Melanchthon, and Bullinger, but Hooker's general orientation with respect to this aspect of Reformed theology is quite clear from an examination of Calvin alone. The thirteenth of the Thirty-Nine Articles, as will be argued, appears to reflect in very general terms the conception of human nature held by Calvin, as well as that held by many other Reformed writers, and it was against this background, in a Church officially committed to ideas in various ways distinctly different from his own, that Hooker wrote the *Lawes* and his other theological works.

It is important to do justice to the relationship between Hooker and Calvin as regards original sin and human nature by pointing out their similarities on this subject, as well as their fundamental differences. Where Calvin clearly does share considerable ground with Hooker is over the question of common grace. As has been noted earlier in this chapter, Calvin like Hooker argues that 'man's nature' (*hominis naturam*) would be 'wholly corrupted' (*in totum vitiosam*) without this aid, since each person would unrestrainedly 'run riot in his lusts' (*in libidines quaslibet exultare*).[155] Yet people do not in general, he believes, behave like wild animals, and usually display some signs of rationality, indicating that the common grace of God is widely dispersed amongst the human race.

[155] See *Inst.* II.iii.3 (*OS* 3:274).

As a result of this, it is more meaningful to analyse Calvin's understanding of human nature as it is affected by common grace as opposed to when it is not, since he views human behaviour as by definition commonly modified by this aid. As with Hooker, in a qualified sense human nature is for Calvin human nature with the aid of common grace. While, though, the two theologians hold similar views on the devastating consequences of the Fall and the need for divine aid, when the question of the efficacy of common grace is considered, and the behaviour of which humans are capable who possess this grace, their radical dissimilarities become readily apparent.

In contrast to Hooker, Calvin in the *Institutes* displays great interest in the Fall, original sin, and human corruption. References to these subjects are far too numerous to be listed individually here, and are a central preoccupation of his great work. In analysing his remarks, as Kirby and Atkinson both note,[156] it is useful to observe a distinction that he makes concerning 'earthly things' (*Res terrenas*) and 'heavenly things' (*Res caelestes*):

> I call 'earthly things' those which do not pertain to God or his Kingdom, to true justice, or to the blessedness of the future life; but which have their significance and relationship with regard to the present life and are, in a sense, confined within its bounds. I call 'heavenly things' the pure knowledge of God, the nature of true righteousness, and the mysteries of the Heavenly Kingdom. The first class includes government, household management, all mechanical skills, and the liberal arts. In the second are the knowledge of God and of his will, and the rule by which we conform our lives to it.[157]

Regarding 'earthly things' (*Res terrenas*), Calvin shows considerable optimism about the ability of *mere natural persons* both to know and to perform them well: indeed he appears a good deal more optimistic than Cartwright in these matters, to judge from the latter's

[156] See Kirby, *Richard Hooker's Doctrine of the Royal Supremacy*, 41–2; Atkinson, *Richard Hooker and the Authority of Scripture, Tradition and Reason*, 21–3; Kirby, 'Richard Hooker's Theory of Natural Law in the Context of Reformation Theology', 696–9.

[157] See *Inst.* II.ii.13 (*OS* 3:256): Res terrenas voco, quae ad Deum regnumque eius, ad veram iustitiam, ad futurae vitae beatitudinem non pertingunt: sed cum vita praesenti rationem relationemque habent, et quodammodo intra eius fines continentur. Res caelestes, puram Dei notitiam, verae iustitiae rationem, ac regni caelestis mysteria. In priore genere sunt politia, oeconomia, artes omnia mechanicae, disciplinaeque liberales. In secundo, Dei ac divinae voluntatis cognitio, et vitae secundum eam formandae regula.

remarks on the human sciences in the *Second Replie*.[158] He speaks, for instance, of the social and political instincts of such people, including their understanding of the need for suitable civil laws. Some of them are able to obtain extensive knowledge of science, law, medicine, mathematics, oratory, and rhetoric, to name just some of the subjects mentioned by Calvin. 'Hardly anyone', he notes, 'is to be found who does not manifest talent in some art,' whether liberal or manual.[159] Yet, at the end of this discussion, he concludes that 'to defiled man these gifts were no longer pure, and from them he could derive no praise at all'.[160] In this he is quite unlike Hooker, who argues that whenever people obey the laws that are intrinsic to their nature, they obey and glorify God as well. For Calvin, although he finds that 'natural men' (ψυχικούς) are 'sharp and penetrating in their investigation of inferior things' (*in rerum inferiorum investigatione acutos et perspicaces*), this is nothing without those supernatural virtues which are alone the possession of the justified.[161]

When dealing with 'heavenly things' (*Res caelestes*), Calvin makes a threefold distinction between: '(1) knowing God; (2) knowing his fatherly favor in our behalf, in which our salvation consists; (3) knowing how to frame our life according to the rule of his law'.[162] Regarding knowledge of God, Calvin goes further than Hooker in arguing that absolutely no one is ignorant of his existence. Atheists, he argues, are unable entirely to convince themselves. He even states that everyone, including polytheists, know deep in their hearts of the unity of God. Yet, beyond this very basic knowledge, Calvin is deeply pessimistic about the capacities of *mere natural persons*. Even though he often emphasizes the ease with which God can be known from the design of the natural world, he concludes that people are 'so tied to confused principles as to worship an unknown God'.[163]

158 See Kuiper, *Calvin on Common Grace*, 183; Cartwright, *Second Replie*, 19.

159 See *Inst.* II.ii.14 (*OS* 3:257): nemo prope reperitur cuius in arte aliqua perspicientia non se exerat.

160 See ibid. II.ii.16 (*OS* 3:259): quia polluto homini pura esse desierunt, nequam inde laudem consequatur.

161 See ibid. II.ii.15 (*OS* 3:258).

162 See ibid. II.ii.18 (*OS* 3:260): quae tribus potissimum rebus constat, Deum nosse, paternum erga nos eius favorem, in quo salus nostra consistit: et formandae secundum legis regulam vitae rationem. See Kuiper, *Calvin on Common Grace*, 184; François Wendel, *Calvin. The Origins and Development of his Religious Thought*, trans. P. Mairet (London, 1963), 162–3; Paul Helm, *Faith and Understanding* (Edinburgh, 1997), 177–200.

163 See *Inst.* I.v.12 (*OS* 3:57): confusis tantum principiis esse affixos, ut Deum incognitum adorent.

He does sometimes accept that certain philosophers have had acute perceptions about God, particularly Cicero and Plato: here, though, he can find only a negative explanation, based upon God's desire to render people inexcusable for their sins. As he observes, referring to the three categories mentioned above:

> In the first two points—and especially in the second—the greatest geniuses are blinder than moles! Certainly I do not deny that one can read competent and apt statements about God here and there in the philosophers, but these always show a certain giddy imagination. As was stated above, the Lord indeed gave them a slight taste of his divinity that they might not hide their impiety under a cloak of ignorance.[164]

Such negative language is entirely absent from the *Lawes*, except with regard to *mere natural people*'s knowledge of matters concerning salvation; on this last point, as with all other orthodox Christian theologians, Hooker and Calvin do concur. Otherwise, however, Hooker is far more optimistic about the capacities of such people to know many of the properties of God, and on this basis in some measure to glorify Him.

Before examining the third class of 'heavenly things' (*Res caelestes*), one may deal briefly with the question of *mere natural people*'s knowledge of the human soul. Calvin is less satisfied with the judgements of the philosophers than Hooker, arguing that 'hardly one, except Plato, has rightly affirmed its immortal substance'.[165] He does accept that some other Socratics have dealt with the issue of immortality, but only in a manner which suggests that they were not fully convinced of this fact. Calvin seems, as a result, quite far from Hooker's position that many *mere natural persons* can have knowledge of the immortality of the soul.

The third category of 'heavenly things' (*Res caelestes*) concerns knowledge of natural law. Calvin seems at first sight to be much more optimistic about this matter, observing that 'There is nothing

[164] Inst. II.ii.18 (*OS* 3:260–1): Cum in primis duobus, tum vero in secundo proprie, qui sunt hominum ingeniosissimi, talpis sunt caeciores. Equidem non inficior, sparsim quaedam apud philosophos de Deo legi scite et apposite dicta: sed quae vertiginosam quandam imaginationem semper resipiant. Praebuit quidem illis Dominus, ut supra dictum est, exiguum divinitatis suae gustum, ne ignorantiam impietati obtenderent. See also *Inst.* I.iii.1; I.v.15; I.x.3; Cartwright, *The Second Replie*, 19.

[165] See *Inst.* I.xv.6 (*OS* 3:182): quorum nemo fere, excepto Platone, substantiam immortalem solide asseruit.

more common than for a man to be sufficiently instructed in a right standard of conduct by natural law'.[166] Like Hooker, and indeed like many other Reformed theologians, he argues that natural law embraces the entire Decalogue, implying that *mere natural persons* should know the basic commandments to 'Love God' and to 'Love thy neighbour'.[167] Where Calvin differs fundamentally from Hooker is in the great divide he places between the general principles of natural law, and the process by which they must be applied to particular circumstances. He gives as an example the man who condemns adultery in general, but proceeds to commit it himself. 'Herein', Calvin observes, 'is man's ignorance: when he comes to a particular case, he forgets the general principle that he has just laid down.'[168] With regard to the First Table of the Decalogue, he argues that human ignorance is so complete that people have no knowledge of how God should be worshipped. Humans are not so depraved as concerns the Second Table, since these laws deal with the preservation of civil society. Here, though, Calvin charges humanity both with ignorance of some of the human virtues, and of the fact that purely inward concupiscence is a sin. Hooker, it is true, implies that natural law 'can hardly' reach this second point, but he does not dismiss the possibility.[169] Moreover, although Hooker does accept that it is difficult for people to apply natural laws to particular circumstances, he is far from concluding that they are unable to do so.[170]

Calvin's distance from Hooker becomes clearer if one looks at the Frenchman's remarks in the *Institutes* on the threefold function

[166] See *Inst.* II.ii.22 (*OS* 3:264): Et nihil est vulgatius, quam lege naturali . . . hominem sufficienter ad rectam vitae normam institui. See also II.ii.23–4.

[167] See Atkinson, *Richard Hooker and the Authority of Scripture, Tradition and Reason*, 15–16; Kirby, 'Richard Hooker's Theory of Natural Law in the Context of Reformation Theology', 691.

[168] See *Inst.* II.ii.23 (*OS* 3:265): Haec est ignorantia, dum homo, ubi ad hypothesin ventum est, eius regulae obliviscitur quam in thesi nuper constituerat.

[169] See *Lawes*, 1:121.6–12 (I.12.2). See also Neelands, 'The Theology of Grace of Richard Hooker', 164. Hooker notes that natural law 'can hardly' deal with inward mental processes. He then proceeds to discuss 'secret concupisence', which is an inward mental process. This would imply that *mere natural persons* can, with great difficulty, discover and/or know that 'secret concupisence' is a sin. It is, of course, Hooker thinks, easiest simply to read about this matter in Holy Scripture.

[170] See *Lawes*, 1:120.21–121.2 (I.12.2) and pp. 118–23 above.

of natural law.[171] First, he observes, 'it warns, informs, convicts, and lastly condemns, every man of his own unrighteousness', since all are guilty of transgressions of the law.[172] Secondly, it acts 'by fear of punishment to restrain certain men who are untouched by any care for what is just and right unless compelled by hearing the dire threats in the law', and hence serves to maintain order in civil society.[173] Thirdly and finally, it helps Christian believers 'to learn more thoroughly each day the nature of the Lord's will to which they aspire, and to confirm them in the understanding of it', though it also serves to remind them of their sinfulness in so far as they still do not obey God's law.[174] Yet while, as Kirby notes, Calvin defines this third and most positive function as the 'principal use' and 'proper purpose' of natural law, it is a function that only pertains to a very limited category of humanity, namely justified Christians.[175] For most humans Calvin holds natural law to be a condemnatory and binding force, and thus he can state in his introduction to the subject, with reference to St Paul's observation in Romans 2: 14–16 that the Gentiles have the law engraved on their hearts, that 'The purpose of natural law, therefore, is to render man inexcusable.'[176] God has informed humanity via natural law of the actions that he considers to be sinful, and humans cannot, as a result, plead ignorance for their sinful actions. For Calvin, then, natural law is an almost negative force in the lives of *mere natural persons*, a code that exists to convict them of their depravity, and to force them into civil obedience. For Hooker, obedience to natural law is no longer the path to heavenly glory, because of the innate sinfulness of humanity. It remains, however, a basically positive rule by which people can

[171] See *Inst.* II.vii.6–12; I. John Hesselink, *Calvin's Concept of the Law* (Pennsylvania, 1992), 219–61.

[172] See *Inst.* II.vii.6 (*OS* 3:332): suae unumquenque iniustitiae admoneat, certiorem faciat, convincat denique ac condemnet.

[173] See ibid. II.vii.10 (*OS* 3:335): ut qui nulla iusti rectique cura, nisi coacti, tanguntur, dum audiunt diras in ea sanctiones, coerceantur saltem poenarum formidine.

[174] See ibid. II.vii.12 (*OS* 3:337): quo melius in dies ac certius discant qualis sit Domini voluntas, ad quam aspirant: atque in eius intelligentia confirmentur.

[175] See ibid. Tertius usus, qui et praecipuus est, et in proprium Legis finem propius spectat; Kirby, 'Richard Hooker's Theory of Natural Law in the Context of Reformation Theology', 699.

[176] See *Inst.* II.ii.22 (*OS* 3:265): Finis ergo legis naturalis est, ut reddatur homo inexcusabilis. See also William Klempa, 'John Calvin on Natural Law', *Calvin Studies* 4 (1988), 16; Hesselink, *Calvin's Concept of the Law*, 57–8.

still know how in various respects to obey and glorify the will of God, and hence to abstain from sin.

As regards the will of *mere natural persons*, Calvin appears to view it as yet more depraved than the reason. He does not agree with Hooker that natural, usually unconscious human desires can often be good and directed towards God: rather, he states that all human desires, whether those of non-Christians or Christians, are invariably sinful: 'we teach that all human desires are evil, and charge them with sin—not in that they are natural, but because they are inordinate'.[177] When discussing deliberate human actions, Calvin is careful to distinguish between non-Christians who have 'excelled in ... moral integrity' (*morum integritate praestitit*), and those who have done otherwise. This proves, he argues, that human nature 'if carefully cultivated, is not utterly devoid of goodness' (*si studio excolatur, bonitate non prorsus vacare*), and he explains this in terms of the special operation of God's common grace upon these chosen people.[178] Yet, even though such people can perform actions which appear praiseworthy, Calvin frequently repeats that all that is produced by *mere natural persons* is sinful. God, he argues, may provide such a man as Camillus with a special grace so that he will act well, perhaps to the benefit of human society: yet, when the actions of such people are examined, they will always be found to have arisen from inner sinful motives:

> all who are estranged from the religion of the one God, however admirable they may be regarded on account of their reputation for virtue, not only deserve no reward but rather punishment, because by the pollution of their hearts they defile God's good works. For even though they are God's instruments for the preservation of human society in righteousness, continence, friendship, temperance, fortitude, and prudence, yet they carry out these good works of God very badly. For they are restrained from evil-doing not by genuine zeal for good but either by mere ambition or by self-love, or some other perverse motive. Therefore, since by the very impurity of men's hearts these good works have been corrupted as from their source, they ought no more to be reckoned

[177] See *Inst.* III.iii.12 (*OS* 4:68): omnes hominum cupiditates malas esse docemus, et peccati reas peragimus: non quatenus sunt naturales, sed quia inordinatae.

[178] See ibid. II.iii.4 (*OS* 3:275–6). More generally, see II.ii.12, 26–7; II.iii.1–3, 5; II.iv.1; Kuiper, *Calvin on Common Grace*, 188.

among virtues than the vices that commonly deceive on account of their affinity and likeness to virtue.[179]

Humans are incapable, according to Calvin, of acting well, in a manner that will allow them both to obey and glorify God, and to abstain from sin. As John Hesselink has noted, for Calvin 'The correlate of the law is obedience, and the only obedience which deserves the name is that which honours God, the obedience of faith, and it is precisely this of which natural humanity is totally incapable.'[180] It is for this reason that he criticizes John T. McNeill's well-known article 'Natural Law in the Teaching of the Reformers', in which McNeill argues that 'There is no real discontinuity between the teaching of the Reformers and that of their precedessors with respect to natural law', these precedessors including the medieval scholastic theologians.[181] The problem with McNeill's approach is that it fails to take account of the emphasis that Calvin and other Reformed theologians place on human total depravity, which separates them from the medieval scholastics as regards the function of natural law.[182] While Kirby, though, also cites Hesselink's book, and is somewhat critical of McNeill's article, he himself commits a similar error. For while he succeeds in showing that Hooker shares with Reformers such as Calvin, Bullinger, and Melanchthon a number of ideas about natural law, he fails to show that their respective conceptions of human nature draw them fundamentally apart on this issue. Revealingly, the passage that Kirby most relies upon to assert Hooker's Reformed credentials in this matter is the following, taken from Book I of the *Lawes*:

The light of nature is never able to finde out any way of obtayning the reward of blisse, but by performing exactly the duties and workes of

[179] *Inst.* III.xiv.3 (*OS* 4:222): omnes a Dei unius religione alienos, utcunque ob virtutis opinionem admirabiles habeantur, non modo nulla remuneratione dignos, sed magis punitione: quod pura Dei bona cordis sui pollutione contaminant. Etsi enim Dei instrumenta sunt ad conservandam, iustitia, continentia, amicitia, temperantia, fortitudine, prudentia, hominum societatem: bona tamen haec Dei opera pessime exequuntur: quia non syncero boni studio, sed vel sola ambitione, vel amore sui, vel alio quovis obliquo affectu continentur a male agendo. Quum ergo ab ipsa cordis impuritate, velut a sua origine, corrupta sint, non magis inter virtutes ponenda erunt quam vitia quae ob affinitatem ac similitudinem virtutis imponere solent. See also Kuyper, *Calvinism*, 190.

[180] Hesselink, *Calvin's Concept of the Law*, 64.

[181] See McNeill, 'Natural Law in the Teaching of the Reformers', 168.

[182] Hesselink, *Calvin's Concept of the Law*, 69.

righteousnes. From salvation therefore and life all flesh being excluded this way, behold how the wisedome of God hath revealed a way mysticall and supernaturall...concerning that faith hope and charitie without which there can be no salvation; was there ever any mention made saving only in that lawe which God him selfe hath from heaven revealed?[183]

There is nothing distinctively Reformed about these lines on the purpose of divine as opposed to natural law, and they certainly do not as Kirby claims assert a doctrine of *sola scriptura*; a matter to be looked at in more detail later, in Ch. 4. Aquinas, for instance, makes exactly the same claim that knowledge accessible through natural reasoning alone, and hence natural law, is insufficient for salvation, when he speaks in the *Summa Theologiae* of 'the necessity for our welfare that divine truths surpassing reason should be signified to us through divine revelation'.[184] When the distinctively Reformed is distinguished from the merely commonplace, as Hesselink has done with respect to McNeill's article, then one can see that Kirby and other writers sharing his approach are mistaken in their Reformed interpretation of Hooker's views on natural law and human nature. Hooker is a good deal more optimistic about the capacities of *mere natural reason* and *mere natural will* than Calvin, and in marked opposition ascribes to *mere natural persons* the ability through grace and diligence to obey and glorify God in various ways, and thereby to abstain from sin. When one considers, for instance, the assertion of the thirteenth of the Thirty-Nine Articles, entitled 'Of Works before Justification' (*Opera ante justificationem*), that 'Works done before the grace of Christ, and the inspiration of his Spirit...have the nature of sin,' which appears close on this point to the observations of Calvin in the *Institutes* on human depravity, then one can appreciate the genuine radicalism of Hooker's thinking in the context of the late-Elizabethan English Church.[185]

Such radicalism raises the question of how Hooker was able in the *Lawes* to publish such opinions in the Reformed England of

[183] *Lawes*, 1:118.11–15; 1:119.12–15 (I.11.5, 6). See also Kirby, 'Richard Hooker's Theory of Natural Law in the Context of Reformation Theology', 685, 700.

[184] See *ST* I.1.1: necessarium fuit homini ad salutem quod ei nota fierent quaedam per revelationem divinam quae rationem humanam excedunt.

[185] See *Documents of the English Reformation*, 292: Opera quae fiunt ante gratiam Christi, et Spiritus eius afflatum...peccati rationem habere. See also Cartwright, *Replye*, 27.

his day, and also why critics have not long since identified him with this position. The answers to these questions are closely linked. The *Lawes* purports to be a critique of presbyterianism in particular, and puritanism more generally, and Hooker presents himself not as a radical but as an establishment figure, condemning dangerous minority religious beliefs and practices. He might be compared in this way to other conformist writers of the period, such as Richard Bancroft and Matthew Sutcliffe. Superficially, at least, Hooker by no means portrays the *Lawes* as an attack on aspects of Reformed theology, and given his position he could scarcely have done otherwise. By drawing on a recent excellent article by Mark Perrott, however, as well as the work of Peter Lake, one can see how in attacking Cartwright and his fellow presbyterians Hooker could covertly criticize many fundamental aspects of Reformed theology. As has been shown earlier in this chapter, in the course of the Admonitions controversy Cartwright and Whitgift argue about how Christians can know, in matters indifferent, which works glorify and are obedient to God. Cartwright requires positive scriptural warrant for all human actions, even as regards picking up a straw, whereas Whitgift asserts that Christians can reassure themselves of the obedience of such works by ensuring that there is nothing in them contrary to Holy Scripture. Both writers demonstrate their Reformed credentials by making Holy Scripture the sole authority by which the question of matters indifferent should be decided, but they differ as to whether Holy Scripture should be construed in a positive or negative sense. In the *Second Replie*, however, as Perrott has observed, Cartwright threw down a challenge to Whitgift and his fellow conformists, by alleging that if Whitgift would not rely on positive scriptural warrant alone then he should concede that his argument made use of the authority of reason, as well as that of Holy Scripture:

For albeit it can not be, but that which is not agreable unto the worde off God, is against the worde off God: and off the otherside, that which is not against the worde off God, is agreable unto it: yet he that so saithe, that certaine thi[n]ges must be doone not agai[n]st the worde, that he wil not also accorde, that they should be doone accordinge to the worde: gyvethe thereby to understand, that there is some star or light off reason, or learninge or other helpe, whereby some act may be well doone, and acceptably unto God, in which the worde off God was shut out, and not called to counsaile: as that which either coulde not, or neede not, give any direction in that behalfe.[186]

Cartwright's challenge concerning the 'star or light off reason' gains its force from the fact that he evidently felt that Whitgift, as a Reformed theologian like himself, could not take it up, and indeed Whitgift never did so. Hooker, however, in the *Lawes*, was quite ready to accept Cartwright's suggestion, and to argue that reason was an authority for establishing the nature of works that glorify and are obedient to God in civil and religious affairs, both for Christians and non-Christians. In so doing he came to attack not merely the underpinning of Cartwright's argument, but also a fundamental tenet of Reformed (and indeed Protestant) theology as well; the principle of *sola scriptura*. Moreover, in order to make such a case he needed an understanding of human nature, and specifically of the human reason and will, markedly at odds with that characteristic of the Reformed tradition, and this is precisely what he presents in the *Lawes*, as well as in much of his other work. The nature of the Admonitions controversy, therefore, allowed or encouraged Hooker to criticize fundamental aspects of Reformed theology through attacking presbyterianism and puritanism, since he had identified basic elements that were common to all three. While Perrott is right to stress that the *Lawes* is in many places concerned purely with the case against Cartwright and the presbyterians, this does not take away from the fact that as regards its theological and philosophical principles, Lake is correct in his analysis in *Anglicans and Puritans?* that 'Hooker's whole project had represented a sort of sleight of hand whereby what amounted to a full-scale attack on Calvinist piety was passed off as a simple exercise in anti-puritanism.'[187] From this one can understand why Hooker was able to publish such opinions in the England of the 1590s, and also why critics have not automatically identified him with this religious position.

The fact that the *Lawes* is not openly critical of Reformed theology has not alone, however, brought critics to fail to identify him with such theological views. As this chapter has shown, Hooker's ideas on the human reason and will are obscured by his treatment

[186] *Second Replie*, 56. See also Perrott, 'Richard Hooker and the Problem of Authority in the Elizabethan Church', 43–5.

[187] Lake, *Anglicans and Puritans?*, 239.

of common grace, which is far less clear than that of Covel in his 'Defence' of Hooker's work. It is instructive at the end of this chapter to examine the way in which a variety of critical opinions have been influenced by this lack of clarity on Hooker's part, in curiously contrary ways. For as Arthur S. McGrade has observed, Hooker 'has the unusual distinction of being severely criticized for both hypo- and hyper-rationalism',[188] just as he has been variously identified with a theology that is Reformed and anti-Reformed. Much of this extraordinary situation is attributable to his handling of grace in the *Lawes* (as well as in the late works), rather than merely to the problems that scholars face in general in the interpretation of complex works, and a number of critical controversies can be explained by looking at the way in which writers have understood Hooker's views on the relationship between reason, will, and grace.

It seems fitting to begin with the earliest published criticism of the *Lawes*; the *Christian Letter* of 1599. In Article 5, '*Of free will*', the *Letter* takes issue with Hooker's argument that the will '*is apt to take or refuse anie particular object, whatsoever being presented unto it*'.[189] This phrase is compared to Article 10 of the Thirty-Nine Articles, which the *Letter* understands as saying that we cannot will anything pleasing to God without grace. Deliberating upon the presentation of grace within the *Lawes*, the writers of the *Letter* then go on to make the following remarks:

> Shew us therefore howe your positions agree with our church and the scriptures. If you say you understande reason and will helped by the grace of God, then tell us how we may perceave it by your writing: whiche putteth difference betwixt naturall and supernaturall trueth and lawes. If you meane reason uncorrupted, not respecting how in trueth we are by Adams fall perverted, may wee not suspect that your whole discourse is subtill and cunning, because you pretend the naturall way of finding out lawes by reason to guide the will unto that which is good, pages 59. 62. 63. etc., or at least frivoulous, seeing man hath no such reason without the grace of GOD, if you meane without the grace of God, and in the state of corruption, as in deed all men naturallie nowe are?[190]

Hooker is accused here of hyper-rationalism, of ascribing too much power to the unaided natural reason and will. To put this in

[188] See McGrade, 'The Coherence of Hooker's *Polity*: The Books on Power', 166.
[189] See *ACL* 4:18.1.
[190] Ibid. 4:19.2–11.

sixteenth-century terms, he is found to be guilty of crypto-Pelagianism. Yet, of course, the theory of common grace precisely supposes that 'man hath no such reason without the grace of GOD'. Had Hooker been less obscure, it would have been far harder for the Reformed authors of the *Christian Letter* to have accused him of ignoring the role of grace in the reasoning process, even though Hooker's presentation of reason as a religious authority would still no doubt have proved unacceptable to them.

For Gunnar Hillerdal, Hooker's fault lies in another direction.[191] He finds Hooker to be a systematic theologian similar to Aquinas, who tries 'to demonstrate that a harmonic cooperation is quite possible between the laws pertaining to revelation and those set forth in the natural law or by man's reason': yet this balanced theology breaks down in his view because Hooker is confused about the operations of grace.[192] Hillerdal's principal insight concerning the *Lawes* is that grace is always necessary for reason to work aright and to comprehend the truth. Unfortunately, he does not perceive a theory of common grace in the *Lawes*, and therefore considers grace to be a purely Christian-oriented phenomenon. As a result he is forced to conclude that Hooker's theology is untenable, since it would then logically be contradictory for Hooker to argue that pagans can understand natural law, if they lack the aid of (Christian) grace.[193] It must be said to Hillerdal's credit that he comes close to seeing beyond this impasse. Towards the end of his study he analyses the *Dublin Fragments*, and discusses Hooker's remark that the virtuous pagans were aided by a special grace.[194] He even, in a footnote, cross-references between this passage and the crucial text on common grace in Book I of the *Lawes*, but he provides no commentary on this link. Ultimately, though, Hillerdal's apparent lack of background knowledge on common grace causes him to find Hooker incoherent; he does not see how someone could receive grace yet have no hope of salvation. He finishes, as a result, on an opposite note from the *Christian Letter*, by accusing Hooker of hypo-rationalism; the *Lawes*, he observes, ultimately requires that reason submit to the overarching claims of grace and revelation.[195]

[191] On this matter, see Neelands, 'The Theology of Grace of Richard Hooker', 122–32.

[192] See Hillerdal, *Reason and Revelation in Richard Hooker*, 20, 45.

[193] See ibid. 87, 118.

[194] For an analysis of this passage, see pp. 284–7 below.

[195] See Hillerdal, *Reason and Revelation in Richard Hooker*, 140–3, 147, 149.

Hillerdal has been strongly criticized for finding the *Lawes* contradictory, perhaps most notably by Grislis.[196] Yet Grislis's understanding of Hooker would appear to have much in common with that of Hillerdal. He refers to Hillerdal's study in his article 'Richard Hooker's Image of Man', and agrees that 'even reason *qua* reason must have the divine gift of grace in order to operate properly within the natural realm'. Likewise, regarding the will, he states that it 'has lost its "ableness," retaining only its "aptness," i.e. the potential to be redeemed'.[197] The two writers are also similar in not perceiving (Hillerdal's analysis of the *Dublin Fragments* aside) a theory of common grace in Hooker's work. As a result, they both argue that Christians are alone able to reason and desire aright. This is not immediately obvious from Grislis's work, since he speaks only of 'grace', rather than specifically of 'sanctifying grace', or some other explicitly Christian divine aid. His view is, however, quite apparent from the nature of his disagreement with Hillerdal. As has been shown, Hillerdal argues that Hooker fails to balance the claims of natural reason and revelation, since humans always need grace to think aright. Grislis observes in response that this does not invalidate Hooker's theology, since Hooker is addressing himself to the puritans, who as fellow Christians are in receipt of grace: natural law and revelation can only agree if seen through the eyes of *divinely enhanced reason*, yet Hooker can assume that this is precisely the grace-assisted reason that his readership will possess:

> it is only to grace-redeemed reason that Hooker ascribes the ability to draw knowledge from the hierarchical structure of reality. Such a qualification, it should be noted, does not destroy the apologetic value of Hooker's work within the setting of his age—He is after all addressing himself to Puritans whom he regards as fellow Christians albeit misguided ones.[198]

For Grislis, the puritans are in receipt of grace because they are 'fellow Christians', indicating the unity of the two states. He

[196] See Grislis, 'Richard Hooker's Image of Man', 82; 'The Role of *Consensus* in Richard Hooker's Method of Theological Inquiry', 76; 'The Hermeneutical Problem in Richard Hooker', 166.

[197] See Grislis, 'Richard Hooker's Image of Man', 75, 80–1, 84; 'The Role of *Consensus* in Richard Hooker's Method of Theological Inquiry', 70, 72–5, 77; 'The Hermeneutical Problem in Richard Hooker', 178.

[198] Grislis, 'The Role of *Consensus* in Richard Hooker's Method of Theological Inquiry', 72. Neelands has also perceived this problem in Grislis's work: see Neelands, 'The Theology of Grace of Richard Hooker', 129.

repeats this argument in another article, noting that Hooker took it for granted that he was reasoning with his fellow believers: the alternative, he argues, if Hooker had considered the puritans to be outside the domain of grace, would be naturalism.[199] Grace is thus correlated with a belief in Christianity, showing the absence of any concept of common grace in Grislis's work. It is also interesting that Grislis should wish to charge Hooker with naturalism *if* he assumed that non-Christians were capable of reasoning and desiring aright (at least as regards the acquired virtues); this mirrors the accusation of hyper-rationalism by the *Christian Letter*, and further illustrates the problems caused by Hooker's lack of clarity over common grace.

Grislis's analysis, like that of Kavanagh from whom he draws many of his ideas, falls down in many respects because it fails to consider the impact of common grace upon Hooker's view of humanity. As a result of this, both writers are led to the perhaps rather surprising conclusion that non-Christians are in Hooker's opinion largely ignorant of natural law, and unable to obey God's commandments.[200] A number of critics have been influenced by Grislis in this regard, all assuming that for Hooker Christian grace is essential for the human reason and will to function aright as regards a correct knowledge of natural law.[201] Furthermore, although Kirby and Atkinson do not present Grislis as a critic with whom they are in close agreement, perhaps because Grislis in general describes Hooker as a *via media* theologian, there is also considerable common ground between their ideas on reason, will, and grace in Hooker's work and those of both Grislis and Kavanagh. Kirby argues that Hooker's doctrine of grace follows that of the 'magisterial' Reformers, in that the fallen natural powers are alone regenerated by sanctifying grace, and that this gives to Hooker a conception of natural law similar to that of a Reformed theologian such as Calvin. As part of this Reformed interpretation of Hooker he observes that, while Hooker does argue that humanity's natural

199 See Grislis, 'Richard Hooker's Image of Man', 84.

200 See ibid. 75, 80–1, 84; 'The Role of *Consensus* in Richard Hooker's Method of Theological Inquiry', 70, 72–5, 77; 'The Hermeneutical Problem in Richard Hooker', 178; Kavanagh, 'Reason and Nature in Hooker's Polity', 101, 159, 164.

201 See e.g. Faulkner, 'Reason and Revelation in Hooker's Ethics', 681, 688, 690; Forte, 'The Achievement of Richard Hooker', 175, 177, 209, 211; Forte, 'Richard Hooker's Theory of Law', 144–5.

powers are totally depraved, he nonetheless like Calvin emphasizes the continued efficacy of humanity's natural powers as regards civil affairs.[202] This is a departure from Grislis's own analysis, but one can still see the essential link between their ideas, and those of Kavanagh as well, in that all assume that for Hooker humanity's natural powers are totally depraved without a specifically Christian grace of renewal. Atkinson's approach is much the same, as can be seen from his criticism of Hillerdal. He argues that although for Hooker humanity's natural powers are wholly depraved, reason is still efficacious naturally within the realm of civil affairs. In this regard, he observes, Hillerdal was incorrect to accuse Hooker of inconsistency, since Hooker does not suppose that grace is necessary for reason to function aright in all affairs. Yet as regards matters within the realm of religious affairs, it is only through grace that Christians are able to reason aright.[203] If both Kirby and Atkinson had appreciated Hooker's views on common grace then they would have seen that although Hooker does accept a theory of total depravity, he argues that the human reason and will are capable of achieving far more through this aid than they allow. It should also be said, though, that a more careful analysis of individual passages in Hooker's work, as well as a deeper examination of critics holding views contrary to their own (Kirby, for instance, almost totally ignores Lake's work), would have served them at least as well.

Given the apparent benefits for Hooker of a clear presentation of his views on common grace, one must ask why he was none the less so obscure about this topic? One possible explanation is that he deliberately wished to obscure his opinions in order to obtain a polemical advantage. W. Speed Hill has argued that Hooker seldom mentions grace in the *Lawes* because he is in dialogue with such men as Cartwright and Travers, who overemphasize its role: Hooker thus needs to downplay grace, in order to give reason its due.[204] Hill's argument has much merit, but is more applicable to sanctifying grace than common grace, as the next chapter will

[202] See Kirby, *Richard Hooker's Doctrine of the Royal Supremacy*, 45–53; 'Richard Hooker's Theory of Natural Law in the Context of Reformed Theology', 699–703.

[203] See Atkinson, *Richard Hooker and the Authority of Scripture, Tradition and Reason*, 28–32.

[204] See Hill, 'The Doctrinal Background of Richard Hooker's *Laws of Ecclesiastical Polity*', 199–201. See also Stueber, 'Richard Hooker's Place in the History of Renaissance Christian Humanism', 248.

show. The theological purpose of common grace, for Hooker, is that it gives humans the opportunity in many respects to think and desire aright in so far as natural law and the acquired virtues are concerned: to this end, it works to elevate the reason and the will, rather than to deny their efficacy. From a polemical perspective, it would seemingly have been to Hooker's advantage to present the theory of common grace as clearly as possible: if he wished to convince men such as Cartwright that non-Christians could have considerable knowledge of God, while avoiding an accusation of Pelagianism, it would have been very useful to have argued plainly that natural human reason is commonly supported by divine grace. The ancestry of common grace was, moreover, impeccable, being advocated by Calvin himself, even if Calvin took a quite different view as to its efficacy over the human mind. This does not, of course, entirely rule out the possibility of a polemical explanation. It will be argued in the next chapter that Hooker strengthens his case against the puritans by restricting his references to sanctifying grace in the *Lawes*, in order to emphasize the importance of the human reason. To this end, Hooker may indeed have wished to obscure his theory of common grace, fearing that it would resurrect an issue he had closed down elsewhere. If this was the case then it was arguably an unfortunate strategy, since it led in part to the *Christian Letter*'s accusation of hyper-rationalism, as well as to a good deal of other critical confusion over the years.

An alternative (and by no means exclusive) explanation is that Hooker was unsure of the veracity, catholicity, and/or acceptability of the theory of common grace, and chose to be very cautious in expressing his opinions. This is an attractive solution, but one that is difficult to prove on the basis of the *Lawes* and the early tractates and sermons. Yet, as Hillerdal has observed, if Hooker was uncertain about the nature of grace this should manifest itself in his explicit handling of the topic in the *Dublin Fragments*.[205] In the late works Hooker does indeed address the subject of grace in considerable detail, in part because the *Christian Letter* accused him of maintaining false doctrines regarding this issue, and perhaps partly as well because the *Lawes* simply required elucidation here. A further discussion of this question will, therefore, be deferred until the examination of the late works in Ch. 5. For the moment,

[205] See Hillerdal, *Reason and Revelation in Richard Hooker*, 137.

however, one may conclude that whatever the explanation for Hooker's lack of clarity, there is a problem with grace in the *Lawes*. Numerous writers have misinterpreted Hooker because they have failed to appreciate his theory of common grace, and have not distinguished between the will and reason as they are naturally depraved, and these faculties as they are commonly aided by God. For in accordance with the principles contained in his philosophy of mind and action, Hooker asserts that humans are freely able in many respects through diligence (and common grace), both in the civil and religious realms, to know and to obey God's will as revealed in natural law, and hence to abstain from sin.

4

Reason, Will, and the Graces of Sanctification and Justification

In the previous chapter Hooker's theory of common grace was examined, and what *mere natural persons* can know and desire with that divine aid. It was argued that his philosophy of mind and action forms the foundation of what is, once the presence of common grace has been considered, a relatively optimistic view of human nature, firmly distinguished from the view characteristic of the Reformed tradition as regards knowledge of and obedience to the divine will. This present chapter adopts a complementary approach by looking, not at *mere natural persons*, but at what has been termed *divinely enhanced persons*; in other words, at Christians, and what they can know and desire as Christians, with the aid of sanctifying grace. The first part of the chapter will deal with the issue of sanctifying grace, the divine aid that transforms humanity's natural mental capacities, and gives rise to what has been termed the faculties of *divinely enhanced reason* and *divinely enhanced will.*[1] Festus, it will be recalled, was in Hooker's opinion unable to comprehend the teaching of St Paul because he lacked this '*speciall*', sanctifying grace; only with this aid would he have been able to form correct beliefs about Christian revelation.[2] As is so often the case in Hooker's work, however, there is no systematic discussion of these matters, and this has led Hillerdal to argue that Hooker has no explanation for how sanctifying grace transforms the human mind.[3] It will be shown, however, that such an explanation does exist, and that Hooker does integrate his theory of sanctifying grace with his philosophy of mind and action. Hooker's views on justification will also be discussed in relation to those on sanctification, since the two

[1] For a discussion of this terminology, see p. 97.

[2] See *Lawes*, I:223.14–26 (III.8.6).

[3] See Hillerdal, *Reason and Revelation in Richard Hooker*, 148: 'he cannot define how this transformation takes place, he just speaks of gradual perfection of human nature, which makes man understand everything in a new way.' See also 68, 135, 137, 147–9.

issues are so closely linked for him that to deal with one and not the other would simply result in a loss of clarity. Moreover, as will be seen, one needs to have an understanding of his views on justification in order to appreciate fully some of his remarks on Christian behaviour, as well as his crucial change of opinion with regard to one of the central theological issues of the Reformation. The second part of this chapter will consider the question of Christian grace more generally, though still with reference to human behaviour. The aim here will be to ask how Christians receive grace, and whether this reception, and the subsequent inward operations of the Holy Spirit, are in any way detectable by the believer concerned. This is a topic at the polemical heart of the *Lawes*, concerned as it is with the relationship between reason and divine grace, and one that sets Hooker in most respects firmly against the characteristic stance of the Reformed tradition. The third and final part will look at Hooker's views on religious authority, which will involve a drawing together of many of the various conclusions that have been made thus far. With a full appreciation of Hooker's ideas on human nature, one is in a position to understand his opposition to the Reformed (and more generally Protestant) concept of *sola scriptura*, and his advocacy (in a sense that will be carefully qualified) of the religious authority of Scripture, reason, and tradition, in that order.

Divinely Enhanced Reason, Divinely Enhanced Will, Sanctification, and Justification

In the following analysis it will be argued that there was a development in Hooker's theory of justification from what one may term his early position, to that of his mature view. The former is represented by the early tractate entitled *A Learned Discourse of Justification, Workes and How the Foundation of Faith Is Overthrowne*, which contains Hooker's most extended account of the relationship between justification and sanctification. The latter is represented by Books 5 and 6 of the *Lawes* and the *Dublin Fragments*, and is in many respects a modification of the earlier position, sharing with it many core assumptions, but also revealing fundamental differences. Given the nature of his mature views on justification it is likely that his theory of sanctification underwent a similar shift, though as most of the relevant evidence for his opinions on this subject concerns the *Lawes* and the late works, it is hard to say this with complete certainty. The basic contextual reference point for an understanding of Hooker's views on these intensely controversial topics, and especially his change of opinion, is Calvin. The Frenchman had a profound impact on the Reformed conception of justification and sanctification, and he has been the theologian most widely used by Hooker critics as a comparative figure in this area. Passing reference will also be made to Roman Catholic ideas on these subjects, which provide an interesting wider background against which to appreciate Hooker's theological development. It is also vital to examine the scholastic aspects of Hooker's theory of how sanctifying grace transforms the reason and will, which because they are traditionally scholastic have close parallels with Roman Catholic thought at this point. As in previous chapters, because Hooker is so unsystematic in expressing his scholastic ideas, there is a need for a clear comparative model to elucidate his position, at least as regards commonplace scholastic concepts. Somewhat reluctantly, Aquinas will again be deployed for this purpose, in a manner that will be strictly defined in each case. Taken as a whole, Aquinas's ideas on justification (and therefore sanctification) are in no way commonplace as regards traditional scholastic theology, but certain limited aspects of them are, and he is characteristically clear and accessible in his explanations of these matters.

It will be argued that Hooker is very close to Calvin in his early position on justification (though even this statement is subject to qualification), but that his mature view represents a fundamental shift away from Calvin. The same may well be true of his theory of sanctification; certainly his mature views on sanctification are markedly different from those of Calvin, and those characteristic of Reformed theology more generally. The following discussion will begin with a general outline of Hooker's approach to justification and sanctification, covering both his early and his mature views. It will then be possible to go into greater detail, and in this process to compare his views with those of Calvin and, in certain limited respects, with the scholastic theories of Aquinas.

The very fact that Hooker considered justification to be distinct from sanctification shows the essentially Protestant nature of his approach to this subject.[4] Roman Catholic theologians accepted no such division, and spoke purely of justification, and of its sanctifying effect upon the individual.[5] Hooker treated these processes as wholly separate, even while insisting that they were closely related in a variety of ways. Justification, as he describes it in characteristically Protestant terms in both his early and mature theories, is not a process by which the believer *becomes* just, but rather by which he or she is *regarded* as just by God. A transformation thus occurs in God's perception, rather than in the intrinsic nature of the believer. Justification does not in itself cause people to become inherently righteous, Hooker argues, but merely leads God to regard them as if they were.[6] This is the so-called forensic theory of justification, since it supposes that the sinner is declared publicly to be righteous in the *forum* of heaven, even though no inner change has taken place.[7]

Hooker's reasons for holding this position are perhaps best understood by looking at his criticism of the Roman Catholic view of justification. In so doing, though, one must distinguish between Hooker's own presentation of the Roman Catholic view, and what modern scholarship believes the Roman Catholic view historically to have been in Hooker's day and before. In *A Learned Discourse of Justification* Hooker cites the Roman Catholic

[4] See *Just.* 5:109.6–8: 'There is a glorifyinge righteousnes of men in the Worlde to comme, and there is a justefying and a sanctefyinge righteousnes here'; *Just.* 5:113.16–19: 'Nowe concerninge the rightuousnes of sanctification ... we distinguishe it as a thinge in nature differente from the rightuousnes of justification'; *DF* 4:117.10–14: 'To be justifyed, is to be made righteous. Because therefore, righteousnes doth imply first remission of sinnes, and secondlie a sanctifyed life, the name is sometyme applyed severally to the former, sometymes joyntlie it comprehendeth both.' See also *Certain Sermons or Homilies*, ed. Ronald B. Bond (Toronto, 1987), 81.

[5] See McGrath, *Iustitia Dei*, 189, 259.

[6] See *Just.* 5:112.22–4: 'the rightuousnes wherein we muste be found if we wilbe justefied, is not our owne, therefore we cannott be justefied by any inherente qualitie'; *Just.* 5:112.28–113.2: 'him beinge found in Christe through faith ... hym god *beholdeth with a gratious eye*, putteth awaie his syn by not ymputing it ... and accepteth him in Jesus Christe as perfectly rightuous'; *DF* 4:117.22–6: 'our Saviours death and obedience performed in their behalfe doth redound to them, by beleeving it, they make the benefitt thereof to become their owne. Soe that this only thing *is imputed unto them for righteousnes*, because to remission of sinnes, there is nothing else required' (my italics).

[7] On this subject, see Stueber, 'Richard Hooker's Place in the History of Renaissance Christian Humanism', 380–1; Hillerdal, *Reason and Revelation in Richard Hooker*, 34; C. F. Allison, *The Rise of Moralism*, 3; Lee W. Gibbs, 'Richard Hooker's *Via Media* Doctrine of Justification', *Harvard Theological Review* 74 (1981), 216; Neelands, 'The Theology of Grace of Richard Hooker', 31; McGrath, *Iustitia Dei*, 291.

Augustinian, Gaspar Casal (1510–84), and paraphrases from the decrees of the Council of Trent, to show that there is general agreement between Roman Catholic and Reformed theologians concerning four of the five scholastic causes of justification.[8] The reverse is true, however, he argues, as regards the vital formal cause, which as he notes concerns the 'essence' or definition of a thing. In order to summarize the Roman Catholic view on this matter he paraphrases from Aquinas's *Summa Theologiae*,[9] and expounds a highly simplified version of Aquinas's theory that the formal cause is an infused habit within the believer:

> When they are required to shewe, what the rightuousnes is whereby a christian man is justefied, they aunswere, that it is a devyne spirituall qualitie, which qualitye receyved into the soule, doth firste make it to be one of them who are borne of god, and secondly endue it with power to bringe forth suche workes as they do that are borne of him.[10]

The Roman Catholic position is, therefore, according to Hooker, that justification not only involves an inward change or growth in righteousness, but is formally caused by that change. In other words, God infuses righteousness into a person, and then proceeds to justify him or her *because of* this inherent quality. In his defence of the sermons that make up *A Learned Discourse of Justification*, in *Master Hookers Answer to the Supplication that Master Travers made to the Counsell*, Hooker paraphrases the Council of Trent regarding agreement on the other four scholastic causes, but he is curiously imprecise concerning the formal cause, merely noting that the Council defined justification in terms of 'inherent righteousnes'.[11] His understanding in these early works of the Roman Catholic position as regards the formal cause, and the role of inherent righteousness, would thus appear to be strongly based on the work of Aquinas. In the *Dublin Fragments*, though, he is less ready to identify the views of Aquinas, and those of his followers, with that of the Roman Catholic Church more generally. He observes only that 'The Schoolemen which follow *Thomas*' believe that justification comprises in part a 'formall habite, or inherent qualitie which

[8] See *Just.* 5:109.20–110.6. See also Grislis, 'Commentary', *Folger*, v. 711–13; McGrath, *Iustitia Dei*, 269.

[9] He paraphrases parts of *ST* I-II.110, and cites more generally I-II.113. See *Just.* 5:110.g.

[10] *Just.* 5:110.11–16.

[11] See *Answer*, 5:242.24–245.1.

maketh the person of man acceptable, perfecteth the substance of his minde, and causeth the vertuous actions thereof to be meritorious'.[12] This qualification is significant, as in fact the views of Aquinas, and the early Dominican school of theology that was heavily influenced by him, constituted only part of a diverse range of views on justification that were present in the medieval Church.[13] Roman Catholic theologians in general agreed that justification involved an inward growth in righteousness, in contrast to the later Protestant distinction between purely external justification and inward sanctification. Yet the late Franciscan school of theology, for instance, influenced by Duns Scotus, argued that the formal cause of justification was the external acceptance of a person by God.[14] Although the point has been controversial, McGrath has argued at length that while the Council of Trent limited the framework of legitimate Roman Catholic discussion about justification, it made no judgement between the medieval schools as to whether the formal cause was internal or external.[15] Like many of his Protestant contemporaries, therefore, Hooker at least in his early writings condemns the Roman Catholic Church in a simplified and distorted manner when he associates it as a whole with the view that justification is formally caused by internal, infused grace. The fact that some Roman Catholic writers believed in an external formal cause is most significant, and needs to be borne in mind later when looking at Hooker's mature theory of justification and sanctification, which has considerable parallels with some of the less Thomist theories of justification held by such theologians as Duns Scotus.

Nonetheless, one can now state clearly that Hooker's view of justification is formulated in part as a criticism of what he perceives to be, at least in his early writing, the official Roman Catholic theory that humans are justified *because of* an inherent quality that God infuses into them. Fundamentally, he cannot accept this position because for him this assumes that someone could be righteous enough to merit justification. Humanity is, he observes, too sinful for this ever to be possible, with the consequence that we must rely totally upon the merits of the one

[12] See *DF* 4:118.22–9.
[13] See McGrath, *Iustitia Dei*, 158–60.
[14] See ibid. 163–6. See also 166–72.
[15] See ibid. 268–9.

righteous human, Jesus Christ.[16] According to Hooker's theory, then, God imputes the merits of Christ to the believer, and declares that from henceforth He will regard that person as if he or she were inherently perfect in righteousness. Yet this transfer of merit is purely notional, and the believer remains as much a sinner as before. As Hooker expresses this forensic theory of justification himself:

> the rightuousnes wherein we muste be found if we wilbe justefied, is not our owne, therefore we cannott be justefied by any inherente qualitie. Christe hath merited rightuousnes for asmany as are *found in hym.* In him god findeth us if we be faithfull for by faith we are incorporated into hym. Then although in ourselves we be altogether synfull and unrightuous, yett even the man which in him self is ympious, full of inequity, full of synne, him beinge found in Christe through faith, and having his synne in hatred through repentaunce, hym god beholdeth with a gratious eye, putteth awaie his syn by not ymputing it, taketh quite awaie the ponishemente due therunto by pardoninge it, and accepteth him in Jesus Christe as perfectly rightuous as if he had fullfilled all that is comaunded hym in the lawe[17]

In this passage Hooker speaks of 'beinge found in Christe through faith', and some lines later notes that we are 'justefied by faith'.[18] This inevitably raises the important question of the role that faith plays in the process of justification. Such phrases have an obvious affinity with the Reformation concept of justification by faith alone (*sola fide*), which would further demonstrate his Protestant credentials. This matter is, however, of some complexity, since it is possible to speak of faith 'justifying' in more than one sense. A discussion of this matter will, therefore, be deferred until somewhat later in this chapter, when Hooker's views on justification will be dealt with in greater detail.

Although Hooker's theories of justification are forensic, he does not of course thereby suppose that someone can be saved without an inner, spiritual transformation having taken place. As with many Protestant theologians, he deals with this inward change under the quite separate heading of 'sanctification'. Like Luther and Calvin,

[16] See *Just.* 5:112.22–113.3. See also 110.6–112.21; 5:115.24–116.17; *DF* 4:117.20–30; 4:118.9–12.

[17] *Just.* 5:112.22–113.3. Cf. *DF* 4:117.22–6.

[18] See *Just.* 5:114.6. Cf. *DF* 4:118.9–10.

he views this change in terms of a mystical incorporation into the body of Christ, whereby through the influence of the Holy Spirit we come to participate in the supernatural endowments that Christ possessed as a human.[19] These endowments are for him chiefly expressed in the three theological, or infused virtues, of faith, hope, and love (or charity).[20] Such virtues are to be found only in sanctified Christians, and have a transformative effect upon the workings of the human mind, creating by definition what has been termed the faculties of *divinely enhanced reason* and *divinely enhanced will*. This is something that will be discussed in considerable detail later in this chapter. First, however, it is important to look at Hooker's views on how justification and sanctification are related to one another, beginning with reference to his early position on justification, as espoused in *A Learned Discourse of Justification*.

Early Theory of Justification

As has been stated above, Roman Catholics did not in general recognize any distinction between justification and sanctification, seeing both as part of the one process called 'justification'. Not perceiving this distinction in the writings of Protestant theologians, they often tended to condemn such forensic theories of justification for suggesting that one could be saved without the existence of an inward, redemptive transformation.[21] Hooker, like Calvin, appears to have been sensitive to this accusation, and to have shaped his views partially in response;[22] certainly his theory of justification, as found in *A Learned Discourse of Justification*, seems designed to emphasize that an inward transformation always accompanies an outward justification. The key to this theory lies in his division of sanctification

[19] See McGrath, *Iustitia Dei*, 224; *Lawes*, 2:240.13–243.9 (V.56.8–11): 'the participation of Christ importeth, besides the presence of Christes person, and besides the mysticall copulation thereof with the partes and members of his whole Church, a true actuall influence of grace whereby the life which wee live accordinge to godlines is his, and from him wee receave those perfections wherein our eternall happines consisteth'; *Lawes*, 2:223.14–225.7 (V.54.5–6).

[20] See e.g. *Just.* 5:129.2–130.12: 'we have alredy shewed, that there are two kindes of christian rightuousnes the one without us which we have by imputacion, the other in us which consisteth of faith hope charitie and other christian virtues'; *Lawes*, 1:118.27–119.23 (I.11.6).

[21] See McGrath, *Iustitia Dei*, 259.

[22] See *Inst.* III. Calvin discusses sanctification in great depth before dealing with justification.

into two different categories: habitual and actual. As he states himself in this tractate, concerning sanctification:

The proper and moste ymediate efficiente cawse in us of this latter is the *spirite of adoption* which we have receyved into our hartes: that whereof it consisteth whereof it is really and formally made are those infused virtues proper and particuler unto saintes, which the spirite in that very momente when firste it is gyven of god bringeth with it. The effectes thereof are suche accions, as the apostle doth call *the fruites the workes the operacions* of the spirit: the difference of which operacions from the roote whereof they springe maketh it nedfull to putt ii kindes likewise of sanctifying rightuousnes *habituall and actuall. Habituall* that holynes wherewith our soules are inwardly indued the same instante when firste we begyn to be the temples of the holy goste: *Actuall* that holynes which afterward bewtefieth all the partes and actions of our life, the holynes for which *Enoch Job Zachery Elizabeth* and other saintes are in scriptures so highly comended.[23]

Habitual sanctification thus refers to the inherent condition of a believer, and in particular to the possession of 'those infused virtues' or habits of faith, hope, and love 'proper and particuler unto saintes'. Actual sanctification, on the other hand, relates to specific actions performed by the sanctified, such as the holiness of Job in refusing the temptations of Satan. Having made this distinction, Hooker goes on to present part of an *ordo salutis*, or an order in which sanctification and justification occur in the life of a Christian:

If here it be demaunded which of theis we do firste receyve? I aunswere that the spirite, the virtues of the spirite, the habituall justice which is ingrafted, the externall justice of Christe Jesus which is ymputed, theis we receyve all att one and the same tyme. Whensoever we have any of theis we have all, they goe together. Yett sith no man is justefied excepte he beleeve and no man beleeveth except he hath faith and no man hath faith unles hee *have receyved the spirit of adoption* for asmuche as theis do necessarily inferre justification, but justification doth of necessity presuppose them, we muste nedes holde that ymputed rightuousnes in dignitye being the chefeste is notwithstandinge in order the laste of all theis, but actuall rightuousnes which is the rightuousnes of good workes succedeth all followeth after all both in order and in tyme[24]

Perhaps the most important phrase in this difficult passage is the final one: 'in order and in tyme'. By separating these two ideas

[23] *Just.* 5:129.10–24. See also Stueber, 'Richard Hooker's Place in the History of Renaissance Christian Humanism', 384; Gibbs, 'Richard Hooker's *Via Media* Doctrine of Justification', 217; McGrath, *Iustitia Dei*, 291.

[24] *Just.* 5:129.24–130.5.

Hooker indicates that they are not synonymous, and that it is therefore possible to distinguish between the order of events on a non-temporal basis. This would appear to be the case as regards habitual sanctification and justification, where Hooker is emphatic that both sets of events occur simultaneously. Imputed righteousness, or justification, he argues, occurs 'in order' after the various processes associated with sanctification, so that Hooker is here making a logical, as opposed to a temporal distinction. Actual sanctification, however, follows at a later point in time from both habitual sanctification and justification; presumably because a person has the opportunity to perform charitable actions only after the infused virtues have been received. Justification and habitual sanctification are to all appearances both one-off procedures, albeit with lasting results, whereas actual sanctification is a process that will presumably last the rest of the believer's life.

It is worth spending some time pondering the implications of such a theory. Since habitual sanctification is logically prior to justification, all those who are forensically justified are in one sense already inherently righteous. This removes any possibility of a person being justified yet remaining inwardly untransformed, thus addressing Roman Catholic concerns. Yet in solving this problem, Hooker may potentially have raised another difficulty. Since, by a logical distinction, all who are justified are already inherently righteous, one might enquire whether inherent righteousness is not in fact for him the formal cause of justification? This would, of course, commit him to a tacit acceptance of the Roman Catholic position on justification associated, amongst many others, with Aquinas, plainly contrary to his apparent espousal of forensic theory. This would appear to be the implication of Gibbs's article 'Richard Hooker's *Via Media* Doctrine of Justification', since Gibbs concludes that 'Hooker has identified the internal formal cause of the extrinsic imputation of Christ's righteousness . . . as the *inherent* righteousness of sanctification.'[25] This seems to me, though, an unfortunate reading of Hooker's work, since it identifies him with a viewpoint that he expressly opposes. As has been shown above, Hooker observes that the only genuine difference between Roman Catholic and Reformed theologians exists over the formal cause; in all other areas

[25] See Gibbs, 'Richard Hooker's *Via Media* Doctrine of Justification', 220. See also Neelands, 'The Theology of Grace of Richard Hooker', 45.

they are agreed: yet the formal cause is also the most important, since it is concerned with the 'essence' or definition of justification. When, in *A Learned Discourse of Justification*, Hooker discusses what he in that work takes to be the general Roman Catholic view that the formal cause is an inherent quality in the soul, he goes on to consider whether people who uphold such a belief can still be saved. Evidently, then, Hooker thought of the formal cause as something external, rather than as an inherent quality. It is true that he calls faith 'a parte of sanctification... unto justificacion necessary', but he does not thereby suggest that faith or sanctification are causes of justification.[26] It might, perhaps, be more appropriate to speak of faith and sanctification as logical prerequisites for justification, and also to describe faith as a type of passive instrument that God uses in the act of justification (in the sense of 'justification by faith alone'), yet with neither faith nor sanctification having a causal influence on justification. In the absence, therefore, of an inherent formal cause, it is clear that Hooker did indeed uphold a forensic theory of justification, as the previous analysis of his writing has plainly shown. This would imply, to use Hooker's own words, that he considered the formal cause to be 'the externall justice of Christe Jesus which is ymputed' to humanity, even though he does not state this explicitly himself.[27] Humanity is in Hooker's opinion, therefore, justified *per fidem propter Christum*, as McGrath has argued, and it is in this sense that Hooker can be said to subscribe to the Protestant concept of *sola fide*.[28]

Before continuing, it is worth looking briefly at Hooker's views on the other four scholastic causes of justification. Citing Gaspar Casal, he states quite clearly in *A Learned Discourse of Justification* that 'Christe as god be the efficiente, as man the meritorious cawse'.[29] Neither the instrumental nor the final causes are mentioned in this tractate, but he does observe that he disagrees with the Roman Catholic Church only as regards the *formal* cause of

[26] See *Just.* 5:130.7–8. For further evidence, see Hooker's remarks in *AN* 4:21.33–4: 'Is faith ⟨alone⟩ then the formall cause of justification? And faith alone a cause in this kind. Who hath taught you this doctrine?' This passage will be discussed in more detail later in the chapter.

[27] See *Just.* 5:129.25–8. See also Booty, 'Commentary', *Folger*, iv. 196.

[28] See McGrath, *Iustitia Dei*, 292, 486. His citation of *Just.* 5:159.29–160.2 is particularly useful.

[29] See *Just.* 5:109.24–6.

justification.[30] Since he remarks, in the *Answer to the Supplication*, that the Council of Trent held the final cause to be '*godes glory and our felycitie*' (not in any case a controversial statement), this was presumably his view as well.[31] It would also follow from this that he considered the instrumental cause to be baptism, in line with the Council of Trent.[32] These five causes may now be tabulated for the sake of clarity, as representative of his early view on justification:

Final cause:	The glory of God and the felicity of mankind
Efficient cause:	Christ as God
Meritorious cause:	Christ as man
Instrumental cause:	Baptism
Formal cause:	The righteousness of Christ, which is imputed to us

This detailed analysis of Hooker's early theory of justification leaves unresolved, however, what is potentially the key question of all: did Hooker believe faith to be a work in which a person co-operates freely with grace, or is it a divine work alone? The theory of justification outlined so far is, as will be shown, very similar to that of Calvin, yet at the heart of Calvin's theory is the notion that the faith through which a person is justified is a purely divine work. To take the opposite view would be, for reasons that will shortly be examined, a major departure from the Reformed tradition. McGrath suggests, especially by comparing Hooker's views on the role of faith in justification to those of Luther, that faith is a divine work alone for Hooker, but the evidence he gives from *A Learned Discourse of Justification* is unpersuasive.[33] He cites the passage in which Hooker observes that 'It is the spirite of adoption which worketh faith in us,' but

[30] See *Just.* 5:109.15–110.11; *Answer*, 5:241.21–245.1. [31] See *Answer*, 5:242.11.

[32] To be precise, the Council of Trent asserted that baptism was the instrumental cause of the first justification; sinners may subsequently restore their justification through the instrument of penance. Since Hooker's early view is, to all appearances, that justification is a one-off procedure, this would presumably mean that he agreed with Trent concerning baptism as the instrumental cause. See McGrath, *Iustitia Dei*, 269–70. Hooker was certainly prepared to argue that baptism was an instrumental cause of justification in the *Lawes*: see *Lawes*, 2:255.1–13 (V.60.2): 'baptisme... also as an instrument or meane whereby wee receive grace ...and so through his most pretious merit obteine as well that savinge grace of imputation which taketh away all former guiltines, as also that infused divine vertue of the holie Ghost'.

[33] See McGrath, *Iustitia Dei*, 292, 313, 486.

this in no way precludes the Spirit from co-operating with the human will.[34] He also quotes from the following passage, which he takes to refer to 'man's passivity in his justification': yet Hooker is in fact at this point not speaking of justification, through which a person's sins are remitted, but of the predestinating act of election, by which God from eternity chose those humans who would be saved:

> [Eph. 1: 4] In him we were elected to be heires of life. Thus farre god through Christe hath wroughte in suche sorte alone that our selves are mere patientes working no more then dead and senceles matter, wood or stone or Iron doth in the artificers hand, no more then the claye when the potter appointeth it to be framed for an honorable use, naie not so muche, for the matter wherupon the craftes man worketh he chooseth being moved with the fitnes which is in it to serve his turne: in us no such thing.[35]

Hooker himself cites Ephesians 1: 4 in this context, and Grislis also detects references to 2 Timothy 2: 20 and Daniel 5: 23, but the primary scriptural reference is to Romans 9: 19–24, which is capable of being interpreted in a variety of different senses.[36] Even, though, if the view expressed in this passage were consonant with the position that Hooker takes in his late work that 'God knows by reason that Peter having been chosen should have to be saved before He knew that he would have the merits through which he was to be saved,' it does not advance McGrath's case. As has been observed in Ch. 1, it is not a necessary consequence that since Hooker accepted that a person is wholly passive in the act of election, he also believed that humans lack liberty of indifference with respect to God and divine grace.[37] Certainly Hooker holds that in the actual act of justification the person being justified is wholly passive, because the action is external, but this has no implications in itself for whether faith is a work in which a person co-operates freely with grace. In fact, there is no explicit evidence in the early work to indicate Hooker's view on this matter. It is true that in *A Learned Discourse of Justification* he is for once negative about the freedom of the will, and this could be taken to support the view that at this time he considered the human will to be passive as regards the act of faith. Yet this argument is inconclusive, and it is

[34] See *Just.* 5:137.3–4.
[35] Ibid. 5:152.27–153.6.
[36] See Egil Grislis, 'Index of Scriptural References', *Folger*, v. 881.
[37] See Ch. 1, n. 98.

therefore not possible to say with certainty whether Hooker changed his mind when, in the *Lawes* and late work, he implicitly adopted the position that faith is a work in which humans co-operate freely with grace.

Mature Theory of Justification

Hooker does not give a systematic account of his mature views on justification in the *Lawes* and the *Dublin Fragments*, and thus does not discuss some of the issues that he deals with carefully in *A Learned Discourse of Justification.* Given that his mature theory is basically a modification of his earlier position, it is reasonable to think that he did not change his mind on such issues unless there is a conflict between them and his new opinions. This applies to the final, efficient, meritorious, and formal causes of justification:[38] it is also true of the relation between justification and habitual and actual sanctification, in so far as the former two of these three occur at the moment of baptism. None of these matters are discussed in the *Lawes* and the *Dublin Fragments*, but his earlier remarks on these subjects are fully in harmony with his mature theory of justification. One of the areas in which he does differ, however, is as regards his conception of which sins are remitted in justification. In his earlier theory, justification is to all appearances a one-off procedure that covers the believer's entire life; God declares that He will from henceforth regard the believer as if he or she were perfectly righteous. Hooker's mature position puts much more emphasis upon the importance of repentance, and comes to regard justification as an act that purely pertains to the believer's past sins. As such, it is in his opinion possible for a justified person to sin and fall from a state of grace, lose his or her justification, and require that he or she be justified again. Precisely which sins are sufficient, in his view, to cause such a fall from grace will be examined later, in the discussion of sanctification. For the moment, it is important to look at the evidence for Hooker's modification of his earlier theory of justification, beginning with this passage from the *Dublin Fragments*:

To the imputation of Christs death for remission of sinnes, wee teach faith alone necessarie; wherein it is not our meaning, to separate thereby

[38] For Hooker's remarks on the formal cause of justification in his marginal notes to the *Christian Letter*, though, see p. 187.

faith from any other qualitie or dutie, which God requireth to be matched therewith, butt from faith to seclude in justification the fellowship of worth through precedent workes as the Apostle St. *Paul* doeth. For in *Children* God exacteth butt baptisme unto remission of sinne; in converts from infidelitie both faith and penitencie before baptisme; and for remission of sinnes actuall after baptisme, penitencie in all men as well as faith; Nor doeth any faith justifye, butt that wherewith there is joyned both hope and love. Yet justifyed wee are by faith alone, because there is neyther *Jewe* nor *Gentile*, neyther *Martyr*, nor *Sainct*, noe man whose workes in whole or in part cleere can make him righteous in Gods sight.[39]

Hooker is very clear in this passage that since no one is perfectly inherently righteous, no one can be justified in God's sight on the basis of their own works. Justification is by faith alone, in the sense that in the act of justification faith is not a work, but a passive instrument which God uses when imputing the external righteousness of Christ to the believer (*per fidem propter Christum*). Yet Hooker is also careful to note that there are other qualities or duties that God requires be matched with faith if justification is to take place, even though these prerequisite works are not part of the act of justification itself. Children and adult converts are both, Hooker states, justified (i.e. have their sins remitted) initially during baptism, but the latter require faith and repentance as prerequisites for this act. For the sins of Christians to be remitted after baptism, faith and repentance are again seen as necessary prerequisites: a most significant point, as it plainly indicates that the Christians referred to have lost their justification, which they now need to regain.[40] As Hooker observes in Book 6 of the *Lawes*, again speaking in the context of repentance of those of whom God 'remitteth sinne':

If God be satisfyed, and doe pardon sinne, our justification restored, is as perfect, as it was att the first bestowed. For the Prophet *Esaiah* wittnesseth, *Though your sinnes were as crimosin, they shall bee made as whyte as snow, though they were all scarlett, they shall be as whyte as wool.* And can wee doubt concerning the punishment of revenge, which was due to sinne, but that if God be satisfyed, and have forgotten his wrath, it must bee even as St. *Augustin* reasoneth, *What God hath covered hee will not observe, and what he observeth not he will nott punish.*[41]

[39] *DF* 4:117.33–118.10.

[40] Hooker, of course, accepts that all Christians are sinners: he is, therefore, thinking here specifically of those Christians who have lost their justification through mortal sin, as will be shown below. See pp. 208–9.

[41] See *Lawes*, 3:57.5–23 (VI.5.5).

It should be noted that Hooker has not changed his position, as expressed in *A Learned Discourse of Justification* and his other early tractates, that the justified believer will inevitably be saved. As Neelands has pointed out, Hooker argues in the *Dublin Fragments* that all those who are truly justified are elect, and are therefore granted the grace of final perseverance.[42] If Seán F. Hughes is correct in his analysis that the notion that 'regeneration, saving faith, justification, sanctification, and final perseverance are all part of an unbreakable golden chain which only applies to the elect' is 'a genuinely distinctive Reformed position', Hooker was as regards his acceptance of this view unquestionably Reformed.[43] Yet rather than seeing repentance as having implications purely for the believer's sanctification,[44] this act is now viewed by Hooker as vital for the believer's justification as well. It is true that he is at pains in *A Learned Discourse of Justification* to stress that people will be damned if they do not repent their sins.[45] Indeed, he affirms in general that sanctification, of which repentance is a part, is necessary for salvation.[46] Yet if justification is a one-off procedure, by which the believer's sins are remitted for his or her entire life, then the importance of repentance is logically downgraded. It is no wonder that many Reformed theologians observed that a Christian who produces no good works is probably not justified; in a Reformed theology where a one-off justification is connected with final perseverance, it would be disastrous for those who believe that they are justified to conclude that good

[42] See *DF* 4:165.32–167.1; Neelands, 'The Theology of Grace of Richard Hooker', 176–85. For Hooker's view in *A Learned Discourse of Justification*, see *Just.* 5:138.19–139.2. It is interesting in this context to compare article 5 of the *Lambeth Articles* with Hooker's own version of this article. Article 5 of the *Lambeth Articles* states that 'A true, living and justifying faith, which the Holy Spirit sanctifies, cannot be extinguished, nor can it fall away or disappear in the elect, either finally or totally' (Vera, viva et iustificans fides, et Spiritus Dei sanctificans non extinguitur, non excidit, non evanescit in electis, aut finaliter aut totaliter), whereas Hooker's version states 'That to Gods foreknowne elect, finall continuance of grace is given.' Hooker's version, unlike the official document itself, leaves open the possibility that an elect individual with the grace of final perseverance could none the less for a time cease to be both justified and sanctified. See *Documents of the English Reformation*, 399–400; *DF* 4:167.6–7. See also White, *Predestination, Policy and Polemic*, 137.

[43] See Hughes, 'The Problem of "Calvinism"', 245, 249.

[44] See *Just.* 5:154.9–11: 'As for workes they are a thing subordynate, no otherwise necessary then becawse our sanctificacion cannott be accomplished without them.'

[45] See ibid. 5:146.16–19.

[46] See ibid. 5:151.12–16.

works are irrelevant for their salvation.[47] By making justification a state from which one can lapse, Hooker gives real emotional as well as logical force to the call for repentance. He still considers that those who have been justified are also elect, but he argues alongside this that they will only be saved, should they fall from grace, by repentance and the renewal of their initial justification. This is a most interesting combination of Reformed theology with views that are, as will become increasingly apparent, quite alien to the Reformed tradition.

If repentance has such efficacy as regards justification, this raises the question of whether there is a direct causal relation between the two. Hooker is quite clear that this is not the case, observing that grace is alone necessary for the remission of sins, and that repentance is simply 'a dutie or condition required in us'.[48] Hooker makes no concessions to his forensic theory of justification, and will not allow that an inherent quality can be a cause of a declaration of perfect righteousness. Yet he argues, nevertheless, that repentance, alongside faith, is a necessary prerequisite for the process of justification among converts from infidelity and among sinful Christians: as such, God will not declare anyone perfectly righteous on the basis of his or her own repentance, but he may declare a person to be perfectly righteous on the basis of the merits of Jesus Christ, *because* they have repented. Repentance can be a cause of God initiating the procedure of justification, but not a cause of justification itself.

Since repentance can initiate justification, one can then ask whether it is legitimate in any sense to speak of humans meriting justification? Obviously Hooker here excludes any notion of direct merit, since he believes that no one can be justified on the basis of an inherent quality. More generally, he consistently throughout his writings condemns the notion that Christians can be saved through their own meritorious acts.[49] Merit can, however, be defined in a number of different ways, and it is important at

[47] See e.g. *Certain Sermons or Homilies*, 96: 'every man must examine himself diligently, to know whether he have the same true lively faythe in hys harte unfaynedly or not, whiche he shall know by the fruictes therof'.

[48] See *Lawes*, 3:74.10–13 (VI.6.5). See also *DF* 4:118.9–12.

[49] See e.g. *Jude 2*, 5:49.9–19; *Just.* 5:161.12–15; *Lawes*, 1:118.8–14 (I.11.5–6); *DF* 4:117.17–21.

this point to consider the traditional scholastic distinction between condign and congruous merit. The former is merit in an unqualified sense, pertaining to an act that in itself deserves a reward. The latter is merit in a qualified sense, pertaining to an act that, although imperfect and not strictly deserving of a reward, is still accepted to a degree by God and is rewarded. There are strong grounds for believing that Hooker's condemnations of merit, at least in the *Lawes* and the late works, regard the former and not the latter.[50] Hooker does state that '*Repentance* is a name which noteth the habitt and operation of a certayne Grace or vertue in us,' which could be read as meaning that humans are wholly passive in this divine work.[51] This would, however, be quite contrary to his affirmations of liberty of indifference, and also to his clear statements in the *Dublin Fragments* that grace is resistible.[52] This means that, as Lake has argued, repentance is for Hooker a work in which a person must co-operate freely with grace, and that that person will be partially responsible for its successful completion.[53] It is thus legitimate to speak of a person meriting justification congruously, in that he or she has co-operated with grace and met God's requirements for justification, and God proceeds to remit his or her sins accordingly. As Hooker expresses this himself in Book 6 of the *Lawes* (curiously citing Bonaventure's commentary on the *Sentences*):

> Wherefore all sinne is remitted in the only faith of Christs passion, and noe man, without beleefe thereof justifyed. Faith alone maketh Christs satisfaction ours: howbeit that faith alone which after sinne, maketh us by conversion his.
>
> 3. For in as much as God will have the benefitt of Christs satisfaction both thanckfully acknowledged, and duely esteemed of all such as enjoy the same he therefore imparteth soe high a treasure unto noe man, whose faith hath not made him willing by repentance to doe even that which of itselfe how unavaylable soever, yet being required and accepted with God, wee are in Christ made thereby capable, and fitt vessells to receive the fruit of his satisfaction, yea wee soe farre please and content God, that because when wee have offended, he looketh but for repentance att our hands: our repentance and the workes thereof, are therefore termed

[50] In the early tractate *A Learned Discourse of Justification* Hooker condemns the concept of congruous merit, at least with respect to Christian vocation, and of condign merit with respect to final salvation. See *Just.* 5:154.17–26.

[51] See *Lawes*, 3:54.29–30 (VI.5.4).

[52] See pp. 54–9.

[53] Lake argues that, for Hooker, repentance is a work that is necessary to claim the merits of Christ. See Lake, *Anglicans and Puritans?*, 185–6.

satisfactorie, not for that soe much is therby done as the justice of God can exact, butt because such actions of greefe and humility in man after sinne, are *illices divinae misericordiae* (as *Tertullian* speaketh of them:) they drawe that pitty of Gods towards us, wherein he is for Christs sake contented upon our submission, to pardon our rebellion against him; and when that little which his law appointeth is faithfully executed, it pleaseth him in tender compassion and mercie to require noe more.[54]

Hooker does not speak here explicitly of congruous merit, but this is the logic of his position. No one can, in his opinion, condignly merit justification, since no one is perfectly inherently righteous. Yet a person can, through God's mercy, deserve the initiation of justification, which is a form of congruous merit. It is little wonder, then, as John Henry Newman noted, that in Book 5 of the *Lawes* Hooker will not go so far as to condemn Ambrose for holding that repentance can bring about the forgiveness of sins, since it would seem that this was the position he had reached himself:[55]

whether trulie it may not be said that poenitent both weeping and fasting are meanes to blot out sinne, meanes whereby through Gods unspeakable and undeserved mercie wee obteine or procure to our selves pardon, which attainment unto anie gracious benefit by him bestowed the phrase of antiquitie useth to expresse by the name of merit[56]

Exactly the same argument which has just been made with reference to repentance can also be made with respect to faith in the *Lawes* and late works. Faith is a habit that requires the help of grace, but since in Hooker's opinion grace is resistible and humans have liberty of indifference, faith must also, contrary to the view that McGrath seems to detect in Hooker's early tractates, be a work in which humans co-operate freely with grace. Since, as

[54] *Lawes*, 3:54.7–28 (VI.5.2–3).

[55] See John Henry Newman, *Lectures on Justification* (London, 1838), 421, 443. Newman argues more generally that Hooker's mature views on justification should be distinguished from those to be found in *A Learned Discourse of Justification.*

[56] *Lawes*, 2:391.30–392.2 (V.72.9). Covel discusses this passage, and observes that 'Aquinas himself understandeth by the name of Merit, not a Work not due, which should deserve a reward; but a Work which mercifully, and by the goodness of God, a reward followeth.' See 'A Just and Temperate Defence', 487–8. See also *ACL* 4:21.2–9. Richard Montague would appear to have had this passage from the *Lawes* in mind when he defended the concept of merit in *A New Gagg*, the opinions in which he was eventually pressured into renouncing by Parliament. See Richard Montagu, *A Gagg for the New Gospell? No: A New Gagg for an Old Goose* (London, 1624; facsimile edn. Amsterdam, 1975), 156: 'Which procuring of reward at Gods hand, both for things Temporall and Eternall, the phrase of Antiquity hath called *merit.*'

Hooker argues with regard both to the justification of converts from infidelity and penitent Christians, 'The condition required in us for our personall qualification heereunto, is faith,'[57] it would seem that humans can in his opinion through faith congruously merit justification. It should be noted that this does not conflict with his belief that justification is by faith alone as opposed to by works, for he regards faith in the act of justification itself as a passive instrument used by God, rather than an inherent quality or work that formally causes justification.

This leaves the question of what, in Hooker's mature view, is the instrumental cause of justification. Evidently, as regards a person's initial justification, baptism must still be viewed as the instrumental cause, and Hooker indeed identifies baptism as an instrumental cause of justification in Book 5 of the *Lawes*.[58] The problem rather concerns the subsequent justifications of repentant sinful Christians. One obvious possibility is repentance itself, with regard to one of the three traditional stages into which Hooker divides it: contrition, confession, and satisfaction. The difficulty with this is that Hooker, as will be noted in the next part of this chapter, tends to associate the conferral of grace with outward ceremonies, and one would certainly expect him to do so with such an important grace as justifying grace. This might suggest ministerial absolution as a likely instrumental cause, though it would bring him very close to regarding penance as a sacrament. Yet Hooker is clear in Book 6 of the *Lawes* that absolution by a minister is unnecessary for repentance and divine forgiveness.[59] This leaves Holy Communion as the probable instrumental cause of post-baptismal justifications in Hooker's mature theory, and he does seem to hint at this in two passages. First, in Book 5 of the *Lawes* he notes concerning Christ that 'what *merit force or vertue soever there is in his sacrificed bodie and blood*, wee freely fullie and whollie have it by this sacrament', which would include the notion of justification.[60] Secondly, in the *Dublin Fragments* he observes that the sacraments are signs of the bestowal of justifying grace and the remission of sins, seemingly referring to both Holy Communion and baptism.[61] If this was the case, then

[57] See *DF* 4:117.16–17. See also *DF* 4:118.5–8.

[58] See *Lawes*, 2:255.1–13 (V.60.2).

[59] See ibid. 3:82.11–14 (VI.6.8).

[60] See ibid. 2:336.5–7 (V.67.7). See also Neelands, 'The Theology of Grace of Richard Hooker', 255.

[61] See *DF* 4:117.2–10.

he presumably thought that Christian sinners who repented would then receive Holy Communion, and simultaneously be justified again.

Having examined in detail Hooker's theological development between his early and mature theories of justification, it is now appropriate to contextualize this development against the dominant background of Reformed theology. Calvin, given his profound impact on the Reformed understanding of justification and sanctification, is an excellent comparative figure for this purpose, as a number of Hooker critics have appreciated in the past. A good starting point for this analysis is Gibbs's remarks on this subject, since he has argued that Hooker is critical of Calvin's teaching on justification, particularly as regards the vital formal cause.[62] It will be seen, however, that although superficially they may seem to differ with respect to the formal cause, they are basically in substantive agreement on this issue, and share a similar forensic theory of justification. It is rather the modifications that Hooker made to his early theory that are the principal cause of their division, although the role that Hooker ascribes to faith in his early theory must also be considered.

The problem with Gibbs's argument is that it is based purely on a marginal note, made by Hooker in his copy of the *Christian Letter*: 'Is faith ⟨alone⟩ then the formall cause of justification? And faith alone a cause in this kind. Who hath taught you this doctrine? Have you bene tampering so long with Pastors Doctors Elders Deacons that the first principles of your religion are now to learn?'[63] The reason that Hooker is so upset with the writers of the *Christian Letter* is that, since faith is an inherent quality of the soul, it cannot according to forensic theory be a formal cause of justification. That would be to assume, in Hooker's opinion, that the faith of the believer is so pure that God declares that person to be inherently perfectly righteous, whereas justification can only occur on the basis of the merits of Jesus Christ.[64] Hooker accuses the writers of ignorance rather than heresy, and it is clear that he does not consider the implicit rejection of forensic doctrine to be

[62] See Gibbs, 'Richard Hooker's *Via Media* Doctrine of Justification', 214–15. For the views of other critics on this subject, see especially Bauckham, 'Richard Hooker and John Calvin: a Comment', 30–1, 33; McGrath, *Iustitia Dei*, 292.

[63] *AN* 4:21.33–22.2.

[64] See *Just.* 5:112.17–113.15.

deliberate. Yet his question, concerning the source of this error, should serve to provoke suspicion of Gibbs's argument. Were Calvin commonly to be identified with such a position it seems unlikely that Hooker would have been so puzzled. Since, however, Calvin was a well-known proponent of a forensic theory of justification, Hooker had no particular reason to look to him for an answer. Yet what is so curious is that, as Gibbs points out, Calvin is actually a potential source for the remark in the *Christian Letter*, since the French theologian does indeed argue that faith is the formal cause of justification. Such an apparent contradiction in Calvin's position obviously requires an explanation.

Calvin's remarks on the causes of justification are certainly peculiar. In both his Romans commentary, and in the Latin editions of the *Institutes* from 1539 onwards, he states that faith is the 'instrument' or 'instrumental cause' of justification, and then some pages later in both works observes that faith is the 'formal or instrumental' cause.[65] According to the standard scholastic definitions of these terms, the instrumental cause is a type of proximate efficient cause, and cannot thus be identical to the formal cause. I am unable to explain why Calvin should have used these terms in the way he did, other than to say that his attention must have wandered at this point.[66] It is perhaps not insignificant that the 1560 French edition of the *Institutes*, which is later than all of Calvin's Latin editions and was probably prepared by Calvin himself, speaks only of faith as an instrumental, not as a formal cause of justification.[67] This would suggest that Calvin revised his Latin text at this point to make it philosophically more consistent. What

[65] See *Calvin's Commentaries. The Epistles of Paul The Apostle to the Romans and to the Thessalonians*, ed. D. W. Torrance and T. F. Torrance, trans. R. Mackenzie (Edinburgh, 1960), 73, 75 (*OC* 49:60): Ut ergo iustificemur, causa efficiens est misericordia Dei: Christus, materia: verbum cum fide, instrumentum; (*OC* 49:61): formalem, seu instrumentalem, esse fidem e verbo conceptam; *Inst.* III.xi.7 (*OS* 4:189): fidem . . . quae instrumentum est duntaxat percipiendae iustitiae; III.xiv.17 (*OS* 4:235): formalem quoque vel instrumentalem quam esse dicemus nisi fidem?

[66] One possible explanation concerns Calvin's comparison of faith to a vessel that passively receives grace. Faith could here be described as the 'form' that receives the 'material' of grace. Yet such a model still defines justification in terms of an inherent quality, even if it is passively received, and as such seems inappropriate given Calvin's clear espousal of forensic justification. See *Inst.* III.xi.7.

[67] With regard to the passage in the Latin editions in which Calvin speaks of the 'formal or instrumental cause', see John Calvin, *Institution de la Religion Chrestienne*, ed. Jean-Daniel Benoit (Paris, 1960), III.xiv.17: De la cause qu'on appelle instrumentale, quelle dirons-nous qu'elle est, sinon la foy? Cf. n. 65 above.

does seem apparent, as a result of this, is that it is advisable to set aside Calvin's discussion of formal causation when considering his views on justification. Once this has been done, the nature of Calvin's opinions is clear, as the following refutation of Osiander in the *Institutes* demonstrates:

Osiander laughs at those men who teach that 'to be justified' is a legal term; because we must actually be righteous. Also, he despises nothing more than that we are justified by free imputation.... Osiander objects that it would be insulting to God and contrary to his nature that he should justify those who actually remain wicked. Yet we must bear in mind what I have already said, that the grace of justification is not separated from regeneration, although they are things distinct. But because it is very well known by experience that the traces of sin always remain in the righteous, their justification must be very different from reformation into newness of life.[68]

Hooker and Calvin, therefore, share a similar conception of the forensic nature of justification. More generally, as regards Hooker's early theory, there are few differences that can in any way be detected. Hooker makes a logical distinction between the order of justification and habitual sanctification, which is not present in Calvin. Hooker also almost certainly considers baptism to be the instrumental cause of justification, whereas as we have seen, Calvin observes, in this case quite coherently, that the instrumental cause is 'faith conceived by the Word' (*fidem e verbo conceptam*). Even here, however, this difference is less real than apparent, for although Calvin does not use a scholastic terminology of causation with regard to baptism, he is relatively content in the later editions of the *Institutes* to speak of sacraments as instruments used by God.[69] The one fundamental exception would be if Hooker in his early tractates did regard faith as a work in which

[68] *Inst.* III.xi.11 (*OS* 4:193): Ridet eos Osiander qui iustificari docent esse verbum forense: quia oporteat nos re ipsa esse iustos; nihil etiam magis respuit quam nos iustificari gratuita imputatione.... Excipit Osiander, contumeliosum hoc fore Deo, et naturae eius contrarium, si iustificet qui re ipsa impii manent. Atqui tenendum memoria est quod iam dixi, non separari iustificandi gratiam a regeneratione, licet res sint distinctae. Sed quia experientia plus satis notum est, manere semper in iustis reliquias peccati, necesse est longe aliter iustificari quam reformantur in vitae novitatem. See also Paul van Buren, *Christ in Our Place: The Substitutionary Character of Calvin's Doctrine of Reconciliation* (London, 1957), 122–3; McGrath, *Iustitia Dei*, 223.

[69] See e.g. *Inst.* IV.xiv.12. See also B. A. Gerrish, *Grace and Gratitude: The Eucharistic Theology of John Calvin* (Edinburgh, 1993), 9–12; Neelands, 'The Theology of Grace of Richard Hooker', 263–71.

humans co-operate freely with God, since Calvin regarded faith as a work of God alone.[70] Given, though, Hooker's negative attitude to free will and congruous merit in *A Learned Discourse of Justification*, it seems fair to state that, on the available evidence, Hooker's early theory of justification is probably Calvinist in its essentials, in the sense that it appears close to the views of Calvin himself.

One may now examine how far Hooker departed from Calvin as a result of the modifications he made in his mature theory. One of the most obvious differences concerns the fact that Calvin considers justification (i.e. the remission of sins) to be a one-off process, linked to baptism. In the act of justification God remits not only an individual's past sins but also all future sins as well. Baptized Christians who have subsequently sinned and then repented need only, in Calvin's opinion, consider their baptism to know that their sins have already been remitted. The justification of baptism is thus a 'sole and perpetual cleansing' (*unicae ac perpetuae ablutionis*) from which it is impossible to lapse:

> But we are not to think that baptism was conferred upon us only for past time, so that for newly committed sins into which we fall after baptism we must seek new remedies of expiation in some other sacraments, as if the force of the former one were spent.... But we must realise that at whatever time we are baptized, we are once for all washed and purged for our whole life. Therefore, as often as we fall away, we ought to recall the memory of our baptism and fortify our mind with it, that we may always be sure and confident of the forgiveness of sins.[71]

[70] See *Inst.* III.i.4 (*OS* 4:5): 'faith is the principal work of the Holy Spirit' (fides praecipuum est eius opus); III.ii.35 (*OS* 4:46): 'Here Paul calls faith "the work of God," and instead of distinguishing it by an adjective, appropriately calls it "good pleasure." Thus he denies that man himself initiates faith, and not satisfied with this, he adds that it is a manifestation of God's power' (Ubi fidem vocans opus Dei, et loco epitheti insigniens, appositive vocans beneplacitum, negat esse ex proprio hominis motu: neque eo contentus, adiungit, specimen esse virtutis divinae); III.ii.34 (*OS* 4:45): 'the support of the Holy Spirit is necessary, or rather, his power alone thrives here' (necessariae ergo sunt Spiritus sancti suppetiae, vel potius vis eius sola hic viget). Cf. *Certain Sermons or Homilies*, 80: 'true and lively faithe in the merites of Jesu Christe, whiche yet is not oures, but by Gods workyng in us'.

[71] *Inst.* IV.xv.3 (*OS* 5:286–7): Neque vero existimandum est, Baptisma in praeteritum duntaxat tempus conferri, ut novis lapsibus, in quos a Baptismate recidimus, quaerenda sint alia nova expiationis remedia in aliis nescio quibus sacramentis, perinde acsi illius vis obsoleta esset.... Sic autem cogitandum est, quocunque baptizemur tempore, nos semel in omnem vitam ablui et purgari. Itaque quoties lapsi fuerimus, repetenda erit Baptismi memoria, et hac armandus animus, ut de peccatorum remissione semper certus securusque sit.

As if baptism itself were not the sacrament of penance! But if penance is commended to us throughout life, the power of baptism too ought to be extended to the very same limits. Therefore, there is no doubt that all pious folk throughout life, whenever they are troubled by a consciousness of their faults, may venture to remind themselves of their baptism, that from it they may be confirmed in assurance of that sole and perpetual cleansing which we have in Christ's blood.[72]

Calvin is, of course, chiefly criticizing in these lines the doctrine of sacramental penance of the Roman Catholic Church. Yet it is clear that Hooker's conception that justification can be lost, and regained through repentance, is also effectively covered by these remarks. Calvin's objection does not centre around repentance itself, which he considers to be a vital part of sanctification, and something that will always be present in a justified person.[73] It is rather that he cannot accept that repentance, as a human and therefore sinful work like any other, can in any way bring about a declaration of perfect righteousness. In part he is attacking a view that Hooker does not hold; namely that with the help of grace people can condignly merit justification after baptism, and that penance can be a direct cause of the remission of sins. Yet even Hooker's notion of congruous merit, linked as it is to a strict forensic theory of justification, allows that human actions can despite their unworthiness be accepted by God, and thus initiate the procedure of justification. As Calvin observes, alluding to the traditional scholastic axiom that he who does what is in himself can dispose himself towards the reception of the gift of grace (*facienti quod in se est Deus non denegat gratiam*):[74] 'If they say that we must do what is in us, we are always brought back to the same point.

[72] *Inst.* IV.xv.4 (*OS* 5:288): Quasi vero Baptismus ipse non esset poenitentiae sacramentum. Quod si haec in totam vitam nobis commendatur, vis quoque Baptismi ad eosdem usque fines extendi debet. Quare nec dubium quin pii omnes toto vitae curriculo, quoties vitiorum suorum conscientia vexantur, sese ad Baptismi memoriam revocare audeant, ut se inde confirment in illius unicae ac perpetuae ablutionis fiducia quam habemus in Christi sanguine. See also *Inst.* IV.xix.17. Cf. *The Westminster Confession of Faith*, 11.5, in *Documents of the English Reformation*, 496: 'God doth continue to forgive the sins of those who are justified... they can never fall from the state of justification.'

[73] See *Inst.* III.iii.20; III.iv.3. Calvin does, however, condemn a number of ideas concerning repentance that are held by Hooker. Calvin criticizes those who divide repentance into contrition, confession, and satisfaction, and also the traditional scholastic distinction between contrition and attrition. See *Inst.* III.iv.1; *Lawes*, 3:12.18–27 (VI.3.5); 3:93.18–94.1 (VI.6.13).

[74] On this axiom, see McGrath, *Iustitia Dei*, 83–91.

For when will anyone dare assure himself that he has applied all of his powers to lament his sins?'[75] What lies at the heart of the division between Hooker and Calvin is again, of course, their respective views on human behaviour, and their conception of the human will. Hooker believes that God can be satisfied by repentance, even if justification occurs because of the merits of Jesus Christ, whereas Calvin cannot see how sinful human efforts can have any effect on justification, even in the congruous sense of fulfilling a limited condition or pact laid down by God. As concerns faith, Hooker implicitly regards it as a work in which humans co-operate freely with grace, whereas for Calvin humans have no such liberty of indifference with respect to grace, with the consequence that he regards faith as a divine work in which the believer is wholly passive. It is thus possible for Hooker to conceive of a person congruously meriting justification through faith, whereas this notion is inadmissible for Calvin. Hooker's mature theory of justification is thus distinctly different from that of Calvin, and indeed from theories characteristic of Reformed theology more generally. Although justification is defined by Hooker in a forensic sense, he allies this to the idea that only past sins are remitted during justification, that justification can be lost, and also that human works can with the help of grace congruously merit justification; all of which taken together results in a stance that is anathema to the view of justification characteristic of the Reformed tradition. The nearest parallels to this hybrid theory of Hooker are probably to be found in the Roman Catholic Church, among such theologians as those of the late Franciscan school of theology, who argued that although faith could be congruously merited, the formal cause was external to the person being justified. Hooker of course differs from such writers in his Protestant distinction between justification and sanctification, whereas they would recognize no such divide. Yet given, as will now be shown, the strongly traditional scholastic nature of Hooker's mature theory of sanctification, and the fact that the late Franciscan school did not make the infused virtues a formal cause of justification,[76]

[75] *Inst.* III.iv.2 (*OS* 4:88): Si dixerint faciendum quod in nobis est, eodem semper revolvimur; quando enim audebit sibi promittere quispiam, omnes se vires contulisse ad lugenda peccata? Cf. in particular *Lawes*, 3:54.11–28 (VI.5.3). See also Gerrish, *Grace and Gratitude*, 96–9.

[76] See pp. 171–2 above.

this is perhaps not so essential a difference as it may initially appear. Whether Hooker was aware of such a similarity, or was influenced by Roman Catholic writers in this regard, is a question that may repay future study, especially given the other possible links to Franciscan theology that have been noted earlier in this study.[77]

Turning now to examine Hooker's views on sanctification, it is most convenient to deal with them in a somewhat different manner. Hooker outlines the basics of his theory in *A Learned Discourse of Justification*, but unlike his theory of justification he leaves many questions unanswered in that work, particularly relating to his philosophy of mind and action. There is therefore insufficient evidence from the tractates and sermons to compile a detailed picture of Hooker's early theory of sanctification. Much more evidence can be assembled in a fragmentary fashion from the *Lawes* and the late work, which reveals his complex scholastic approach to the subject. It may be, though, that like his theory of justification, the theory of sanctification revealed in these works represents a significant theological development from his early views: indeed the general harmony between these two sets of theories in these works does suggest such a conclusion. The following analysis will, therefore, look at the evidence from Hooker's work as a whole, but as the more controversial material stems from after the early tractates and sermons, it is not unreasonable to regard it as portraying only his mature theory of sanctification.

Due to the complexity of the issues, and the fact that Hooker's mature theory of sanctification is traditionally scholastic in nature, Aquinas will again be used initially for the purposes of convenience to illustrate certain commonplace scholastic ideas. In this instance, given that Aquinas's views on justification (and hence sanctification, since he made no distinction) are in many respects far from merely commonplace, it is important to appreciate that he is only being referred to here as regards the commonly held view of the way in which the infused virtues transform the human

[77] It is also worth noting on this score that Richard Tuck has detected Scotist elements in Hooker's theory of natural law. He observes in this context that logic was the one course in Oxford in which Duns Scotus was still taken seriously in the late sixteenth century, and that Daniel Featley recalled that Hooker had a reputation in Oxford as a star lecturer in logic. Cf. Richard Tuck, 'Hooker's Political Thought', Richard Hooker 400th Anniversary Lectures (Examination Schools, Oxford, 17 November 2000).

mental faculties. Calvin will again be used as a measure of Hooker's relation to the Reformed tradition, and his ideas will also briefly be discussed before the analysis of Hooker's own views. It will be seen that the differences between his and Hooker's mature positions on justification are also reflected in their respective opinions on sanctification.

Beginning with Calvin's theory of sanctification, it is noteworthy that it is in some of its most basic aspects very similar to that of Hooker.[78] Calvin gives a classic statement of the Protestant distinction between sanctification and justification, and defines sanctification in terms of the inward transformation of the believer, whereby he or she is reborn in Christ through a mystical incorporation into Christ's body. In this way, through the power of the Holy Spirit, the image of God is restored within humanity. This involves the reception of the three theological virtues of faith, hope, and love (or charity), which cause an abhorrence of sin, repentance, and then 'the desire to live in a holy and devoted manner'.[79] Calvin stresses, though, that this sanctification is a gradual process and one that never reaches perfection in this life; all Christians are sinners, and desire on a continual basis to commit sin.[80] What is lacking from Calvin's account, however, is any serious integration of this theory into his philosophy of mind and action; a matter which presumably did not interest the practically oriented French theologian. He does not, like Hooker, attempt to give a theoretical explanation of how exactly, in terms of the various faculties of the mind, humans are changed by this process.[81] Such an account is, however, to be found in the writing of many traditional scholastic theologians, including of course Thomas Aquinas.

Aquinas's account of the inner transformation that justification (*justificatio*) (and hence sanctification) brings about in the believer also deals with the three theological virtues of faith (*fides*), hope (*spes*), and love (*caritas*). A virtue, as Aquinas defines it, is a habit that inclines us towards our own perfection.[82] Virtues can be located in the intellect, in the will, or in the sensitive

[78] See especially *Inst.* III.ii.35, 41–2; III.iii.1–12.

[79] See ibid. III.iii.3 (*OS* 3:58): sancte pieque vivendi studium.

[80] See Wilhelm Niesel, *The Theology of Calvin*, trans. H. Knight (London, 1956), 126; Wendel, *Calvin: The Origins and Development of his Religious Thought*, 259.

[81] He does, though, go so far as to define faith as a cognitive act. See *Inst.* III.ii.7; Gerrish, *Grace and Gratitude*, 63.

[82] See *ST* I-II.55.1.

appetite.[83] Humanity is directed by the so-called moral virtues (temperance, justice, prudence, and fortitude) and intellectual virtues (wisdom, science, and understanding) towards the end of natural happiness.[84] Yet, as Aquinas argues, humanity does not naturally have any virtues to direct it to supernatural happiness, but requires that God infuse such virtues into the mind in the process of justification:

> A person is perfected by virtue towards those actions by which he is directed towards happiness, as was explained above. Yet man's happiness or felicity is twofold, as was also stated above. One is proportionate to human nature, and this he can reach through his own resources. The other, a happiness surpassing his nature, he can attain only by the power of God, by a kind of participation of the Godhead... Because such happiness goes beyond the reach of human nature, the inborn resources by which a man is able to act well according to his capacity are not adequate to direct him to it. And so, to be sent to this supernatural happiness, he must needs be divinely endowed with some additional sources of activity... Such sources of action are called theological virtues.
>
> They are called so both because God is their object, inasmuch as they direct us rightly to him, and because they are infused in us by God alone; and because they are made known to us by divine Revelation contained in Sacred Scripture.[85]

Faith is a habit of the intellect that brings about an awareness of the articles of faith, which are the principles of divine theology. Hope and love are both habits of the will, although in different ways: hope brings the will to seek God as something attainable; love causes the will to desire friendship with God, and consequently to desire those things that are also loved by Him.[86] The result is a sophisticated

[83] See ibid. I-II.56.3, 4, 6.

[84] See ibid. I-II.57.1–2.

[85] Ibid. I-II.62.1: virtutem perficitur homo ad actus quibus in beatitudinem ordinatur, ut ex supra dictis patet. Est autem duplex hominis beatitudo sive felicitas, ut supra dictum est. Una quidem proportionata humanae naturae, ad quam scilicet homo pervenire potest per principia suae naturae. Alia autem est beatitudo naturam hominis excedens, ad quam homo sola divina virtute pervenire potest, secundum quamdam Divinatis participationem... Et quia hujusmodi beatitudo proportionem humanae naturae excedit, principia naturalia hominis, ex quibus procedit ad bene agendum secundum suam proportionem, non sufficiunt ad ordinandum hominem in beatitudinem praedictam. Unde oportet quod superaddantur homini divinitus aliqua principia per quae ita ordinetur ad beatitudinem supernaturalem.... Et hujusmodi principia, virtutes dicuntur theologicae. Tum quia habent Deum pro objecto, inquantum per eas recte ordinantur in Deum; tum quia a solo Deo nobis infunduntur; tum quia sola divina revelatione in sacra Scriptura hujusmodi virtutes traduntur. See also I-II.109.1; I-II.113.1.

[86] See ibid. I-II.62.3; II-II.23.1.

picture of the mind, showing how habits are formed in two of the mental faculties: a much more philosophically precise approach than that attempted, and perhaps desired, by Calvin.[87]

Hooker's theory of how sanctification affects the human mind is somewhat harder to piece together. It is perhaps best to start with *A Learned Discourse of Justification*, since this tract does at least deal with sanctification in detail. Here he observes that the formal cause of sanctification 'are those infused virtues proper and particuler unto saintes', and indicates that these 'consisteth of faith hope charitie and other christian virtues.'[88] He does not state what these other 'christian virtues' might be, however, and when discussing sanctification some lines later refers only to the three theological virtues.[89]

Some further details of Hooker's theory are provided by a passage in Book I of the *Lawes*.[90] Coming in the book in which he expounds much of his philosophy of mind and action, one would hope for a clear explanation of how sanctifying grace transforms the human mind. Unfortunately, Hooker does not mention sanctification at this point, and merely provides glimpses of his overall position. He argues that, with the frustration of humanity's natural path to heaven by the Fall, God through his mercy provided humanity with a 'way of supernaturall dutie'. This path involves what he terms the 'divine virtues' of faith, hope, and love. He explains that these virtues are imperfect in this life, but that 'there can be no salvation' without them. Furthermore, since he states that there is 'not in nature any cause from which they flow', they can only be received directly from God. Their supernatural status

[87] Aquinas also argues that the theological virtues are unable by themselves to direct the intellect and the will correctly on all occasions, and that Christians therefore require the aid of seven gifts (*dona*) infused by the Holy Spirit. These form special habits in the reason and will, to guide these faculties when the theological virtues fail. This aspect of scholastic theory need not concern us, however, as Hooker does not appear to refer to it in his work. See ibid. I-II.68.1–4.

[88] See *Just.* 5:129.2–15. As regards the other causes of sanctification, Hooker's does not describe them all. He does indicate, though, that the efficient cause is 'the *spirite of adoption*', and the instrumental cause is baptism, and almost certainly Holy Communion as well. This would obviously make baptism and Holy Communion double instrumental causes, of justification and sanctification. See *Just.* 5:129.10–11; *Lawes*, 2:331.5–11 (V.67.1); 2:336.5–7 (V.67.7); 2:255.1–13 (V.60.2); *DF* 4:117.2–9; Booty, 'Introduction: Book V', *Folger*, vi. 225.

[89] See *Just.* 5:130.6–12. It is just possible that these other virtues refer to the gifts of the Spirit enumerated by Aquinas. See n. 87 above.

[90] See *Lawes*, 1:118.4–119.23 (I.11.5–6).

is further emphasized by the fact that knowledge of them is denied to *mere natural reason*; they are, Hooker argues, only mentioned 'in that lawe which God him selfe hath from heaven revealed'. Their function, as he puts it rather obliquely, is 'to rectifie natures obliquitie', demonstrating that they transform, in some as yet unspecified manner, humanity's natural mental capacities.

As regards the precise functions of these three virtues, the only one that Hooker defines in any detail is 'faith', although his observations on the subject are somewhat problematic. The following lines are taken from Book 5 of the *Lawes*, from a passage in which Hooker argues that Christian doctrine consists, like natural knowledge, of first principles and demonstrative conclusions: 'That which is true and neither can be discerned by sense, nor concluded by meere naturall principles, must have principles of revealed truth whereupon to build it selfe, and an habit of faith in us wherewith principles of that kinde are apprehended.'[91] In a previous passage in Book 5 Hooker connects the knowledge of first principles with the intellectual act of apprehension, and knowledge based on conclusions deducted from these principles with the intellectual act of assent.[92] He now goes on to identify faith as a habit which apprehends first principles. This connection of apprehension with first principles is, however, illogical, given Hooker's general philosophy of mind and action.[93] First principles are propositions, and not simple essences that are perceived in a non-complex manner by the mind. The concept of a cat is an example of such an essence, whereas the first principle that '*the greater good is to be chosen before the lesse*' is a proposition that requires a mental act of assent. As has been observed, according to Aquinas the human mind always does assent to such propositions, because it has a habit of first principles in the intellect that induces it to do so.[94] Hooker recognizes in part that knowledge of first principles is connected with the action of a habit, because this is how he defines the operation of faith. Yet the reason does not need habits to make it apprehend objects in a particular manner, for since apprehension is concerned with simple essences, it can

[91] Ibid. 2:290.20–4 (V.63.1). See also 1:229.33–230.2 (III.8.11). On the scholastic view that theology is a science involving first principles and demonstrative conclusions, cf. e.g. *ST* I.1.2; I.1.8.

[92] See *Lawes*, 2:84.31–85.24 (V.21.3) and pp. 30–1 above.

[93] See p. 30–1.

[94] See p. 29.

only perceive them in a non-complex way. It is rather in the case of propositions, such as that '*the greater good is to be chosen before the lesse*', that a habit is required to induce a particular act of assent. The same is presumably true as regards faith. A supernatural first principle, such as, for instance, that Jesus was resurrected from the dead, can either be assented to or rejected. Someone with a habit of faith will of course assent to this proposition. Thus Hooker should have connected the habit of faith with the act of assent. In fact, he does so himself some lines earlier, when he argues that we must 'assent' to first principles found in Holy Scripture, and he again associates faith with assent to principles in Book 6 of the *Lawes*, clearly showing his confusion over this matter.[95]

Not surprisingly, Hooker's own confusion has resulted in some quite variant readings among the critics. Neelands, for instance, argues that faith is characterized by both apprehension and assent, and like Devine, sees assent as an act of the will.[96] In fact, both acts pertain to the reason,[97] but faith itself should only be identified with assent. Devine has also argued on the basis of this that the dead faith of the devils and the unjustified, which Hooker describes in *A Learned Discourse of Justification*, is constituted by apprehension, but not assent. The following is what Hooker remarks upon this subject:[98] 'Devills know the same thinges which wee beleeve, and the mindes of the most ungodly maie be fully perswaded of the truth, which knowledge in the one and perswasion in the other is sometymes termed faith but equivocally, being indede no suche faith as that whereby a christian man is justified.'[99] Yet if the devils and the unjustified do not assent to supernatural truth, it is hard to see how they can possibly believe in it. Hooker is rather making a different distinction, and one that is vital to grasp given Shuger's claim that he gives faith 'an emotional and also sensuous dimension' not present in Aquinas.[100] Hooker is in fact identical to Aquinas in observing (if for apprehension one here

[95] See *Lawes*, 2:290.13–18 (V.63.1); 3:8.4–8 (VI.3.2). See also 2:291.19–25 (V.63.2). Cf. *ST* I.1.8; II-II.1.2; II-II.4.5; II-II.5.2.

[96] See Devine, 'Richard Hooker's Doctrine of Justification and Sanctification in the Debate with Walter Travers 1585–1586', 275; Neelands, 'The Theology of Grace of Richard Hooker', 36–7.

[97] See pp. 30–1 above.

[98] See Devine, 'Richard Hooker's Doctrine of Justification and Sanctification in the Debate with Walter Travers 1585–1586', 275–6.

[99] *Just.* 5:136.30–137.3.

[100] See Shuger, *Habits of Thought in the English Renaissance*, 43–4, 81, 83.

reads assent), in his tractate entitled *A Learned and Comfortable Sermon of the Certaintie and Perpetuitie of Faith in the Elect*, that 'the fayth of a christian man doth apprehend the wordes of the law, the promisses of god, not only as true but also as good'.[101] It is this difference that distinguishes the faith of the demons from that of true Christians according to Aquinas.[102] The demons are compelled by the evidence to believe in Christian doctrine, and thus consider it as something true, although not as something good. The will of a demon directs its intellect to assent to the truth purely because of the evidence. A similar motion of the will prior to the act of assent is also characteristic of true faith, but here the will does not only regard the evidence, but also the supreme goodness of the object of faith, God. The will comes to love God, in the sense of the theological virtue of love (*caritas*), and desires to assent to Christian doctrine. The intellect does not assent purely on the basis of this act of desire, since humans cannot directly choose what they believe: rather, evidence and love work together to induce assent.[103] Thus, as Hooker observes, true faith apprehends (or rather, assents to) Christian doctrine 'not only as true but also as good', and it is the lack of this second quality that condemns the dead 'faith' of the devils and the unjustified. Faith is, therefore, formed by love (*fides formata caritate*); a traditional definition that long predates Aquinas.[104] It is from this perspective that Hooker can speak in the *Lawes* of 'thaffection of faith', noting that 'hir love to Godward [is] above the comprehension which she hath of God'.[105] This does not prevent him from observing some lines later that 'faith be an intellectual habit of the minde and have hir seate in the understandinge';[106] it is rather that the intellectual act of assent is partly motivated by the love for God present in the will. Hooker's conception of faith is thus not a manifestation of a particular Renaissance habit of thought, as Shuger suggests, but rather a traditional scholastic formulation phrased in slightly confused terms.[107]

[101] See *Cert.* 5:71.2–4.

[102] See *ST* II-II.5.2.

[103] See Thomas Aquinas, *De Veritate*, XIV, 1, cited in T. C. O'Brien, 'Appendix 4', *ST*, xxxi. 210; T. C. O'Brien, commentary, *ST*, xxxi. 64–5; Westberg, *Right Practical Reason*, 254. See also p. 84 above.

[104] See Galatians 5: 6.

[105] See *Lawes*, 2:290.28–31 (V.63.1).

[106] See ibid. 2:291.20–1 (V.63.2).

[107] As such, it lacks the Lutheran notion of faith as *fiducia*, or trust, as found for instance in Cranmer's Homily of Faith. See *Certain Sermons or Homilies*, 92–3; Neelands, 'The

Compared with his remarks on faith, Hooker has very little to say about the other theological virtues of hope and love. In Book I of the *Lawes* he notes that love 'beginning here with a weake inclynation of heart towardes him unto whome wee are not able to aproch, endeth with endlesse union'.[108] Its role as regards the habit of faith has been mentioned above. With respect to hope, Hooker also observes in Book I of the *Lawes* that 'beginning here with a trembling expectation of thinges far removed and as yet but onely heard of, [it] endeth with reall and actuall fruition of that which no tongue can expresse'.[109]

From the above analysis it may be seen how Hooker's theory of sanctification is related to his philosophy of mind and action. He defines faith in a traditionally scholastic manner as a habit of the reason, which inclines the reason to assent to certain supernatural truths.[110] As regards the virtues of hope and love, it is evident that Hooker also considers these to be habits, since he terms the process of which they are the formal cause '*habituall*' sanctification.[111] These virtues are, therefore, according to Hooker, habits that reside in particular mental faculties, inclining them in ways that are in accordance with humanity's 'supernaturall dutie'. It would appear, therefore, in the light of this evidence, that Hillerdal is mistaken in arguing that Hooker has no explanation for how the mental capacities of the sanctified are transformed by grace. It is the action of the three theological virtues on the human mind that produce what has been defined as the faculties of *divinely enhanced reason* and *divinely enhanced will*.

Having described the nature of *divinely enhanced reason* and *divinely enhanced will*, it is important to examine what sort of actions these faculties are capable of performing, that go beyond the capacities of *mere natural reason* and *mere natural will*. To some extent this question has already been answered as regards the reason, in that faith makes accessible the supernatural principles that open up the field of divine

Theology of Grace of Richard Hooker', 35. Hooker's definition of faith, as well as Shuger's remarks upon this subject, will be analysed from a somewhat different angle later in this chapter. See pp. 244–6.

[108] See *Lawes*, 1:119.9–11 (I.11.6).

[109] See ibid. 1:119.6–9 (I.11.6). For other passing references to virtues/properties that are infused by God, see 1:206.9–11 (III.1.14); 2:224.23–225.4 (V.54.6); 2:241.18–244.25 (V.56.10–13); 2:255.1–13 (V.60.2); 3:7.29–31 (VI.3.2).

[110] See Kavanagh, 'Reason and Nature in Hooker's Polity', 84; Hillerdal, *Reason and Revelation in Richard Hooker*, 60.

[111] See *Just.* 5:129.2–21.

theology. Festus, in Hooker's example, is unable to comprehend the words of St Paul because he lacks faith, and hence the principles that would allow him to understand the Apostle. This is, however, purely a question of theoretical knowledge, and one that does not in itself cover moral actions and thought-processes. In these areas as well, one would certainly expect Hooker to distinguish between sanctified Christians and *mere natural persons*, ascribing to the former a greater capacity for upright behaviour. Hooker does, in fact, make such a distinction, and one that rests on theoretical grounds. Yet, once again, he does not discuss this subject systematically, and his views must be reconstructed from a comparison of various passages in his work. This question is, however, of considerable interest, as it deals with the division he makes between mortal and venial sins. This distinction is, though, to be found only in the *Lawes* and the late work, and appears to relate closely to his mature, as opposed to his early, theory of justification. There are thus strong grounds for supposing that it represents a development in Hooker's theology, again towards a more traditional scholastic position.

As has been done previously in this chapter, Hooker's views on this subject will be placed in the context of those of Calvin and Aquinas. The traditional scholastic nature of Hooker's opinions on mortal and venial sins again merits an appeal back to Aquinas, who articulates what are, for the purposes of this study, commonplace traditional scholastic ideas on these subjects in characteristically clear language.[112] Calvin, on the other hand, like the Reformed tradition more generally, is sharply at odds with Hooker over this matter, and it is illuminating to consider precisely why this is so. On this occasion it is most convenient to begin with Aquinas, and only consider Calvin's reaction against such views after Hooker's own theories have been discussed.

At its most basic, of course, mortal sin is traditionally defined by the fact that, unless repented of, it is punished eternally in hell. The traditional Roman Catholic view as regards venial sins which are not repented of is that they are punished for a finite period in purgatory. There is no evidence to suggest that Hooker ever believed in purgatory; quite what his views were on the question of venial

[112] On the topic of Aquinas and the Roman Catholic understanding of mortal and venial sins more generally, see O'Neil, 'Sin', 4–11; I. McGuiness, 'Sin (Theology of)', *New Catholic Encyclopedia*, xiii. 241–5.

sins and punishment will be considered later in this chapter. For the moment, though, one may concentrate on examining what sorts of actions fall into each of these two categories of sin. On this subject Aquinas is quite precise, but his theory is somewhat complex and best represented initially in his own words:

The difference between venial and mortal sin follows upon a diversity of disorder inherent in the concept of sin itself. This disorder is twofold: one involves the abandonment of the very source of order, the other only involves departure from secondary elements in that order... Now the principle of the whole moral order is the ultimate goal... Hence, when the soul is so disordered by sin that it turns away from its ultimate goal, God, to whom it is united by charity, then we speak of mortal sin. However, when this disorder stops short of turning away from God, then the sin is venial.[113]

This, as is so often the case, resolves itself into a question of philosophy of action. Sin, according to Aquinas, is action contrary to the law of God, and can be the result of the motions of the intellect, the will and/or the sensitive appetite. Crucially, however, only the intellect (and through it, the will) is capable of ordering actions to an end (in this case God), and can be said to be responsible for mortal sin. As Aquinas observes: 'Reason alone and not man's sensual part orders him to his ultimate goal. Disorder relative to the goal can only happen in the faculty which should provide that order. Accordingly, mortal sin can be found only in reason, and never in the sensual part of man.'[114] Inordinate motions of the sensitive appetite are thus never mortal, unless they are consented to by the intellect (which of course involves an act of the will): such inordinate motions will, however, be venial, unless they are consciously repressed by the intellect (and the will).[115] As regards sinful

[113] *ST* I-II.72.5: Differentia autem peccati venialis et mortalis consequitur diversitatem inordinationis, quae complet rationem peccati. Duplex enim est inordinatio: una per subtractionem principii ordinis; alia qua, salvato principio ordinis, fit inordinatio circa ea quae sunt post principium... Principium autem totius ordinis in moralibus est finis ultimus... Unde quando anima deordinatur per peccatum usque ad aversionem ab ultimo fine, scilicet Deo, cui unimur per caritatem, tunc est peccatum mortale: quando vero fit deordinatio citra aversionem a Deo, tunc est peccatum veniale.

[114] *ST* I-II.74.4: Ordinare autem aliquid in finem non est sensualitatis, sed solum rationis. Inordinatio autem a fine non est nisi ejus cujus est ordinare in finem. Unde peccatum mortale non potest esse in sensualitate, sed solum in ratione. Such remarks do not exclude the will from mortal sin, because of its intimate relationship with the intellect: as Aquinas notes, the will moves the intellect to its act, yet the intellect is the formal cause of the will's motion. See I-II.74.5 ad. 2.

[115] See ibid. I-II.74.3.

acts of consent by the intellect, not all pertain to mortal sin; the key issue is whether the sin involves a turning away from humanity's ultimate goal, God. Aquinas gives as an example a man who momentarily thinks the resurrection of the dead is impossible, since it is contrary to natural law, but then goes on to reconsider when he consults divine law.[116] The man is guilty of venial sin for denying this Christian doctrine, but he is not guilty of a mortal sin since he does not directly doubt divine law. Had he deliberated upon the matter and still rejected the resurrection of the dead, then this would have constituted a turning away from God, and hence a mortal sin. Clearly, therefore, the act of deliberation, as well as the nature of the thought or act itself, is crucial to the existence of a mortal sin.

Mortal sin occurs because the intellect fails to refer all its deliberations to its last end, namely God. In humanity's natural state after the Fall, Aquinas argues, it is possible for people to avoid many such sins, but not all of them, since the intellect and the will are not entirely subject to God as their last end. Avoidance of mortal sin is only possible when the corruption of these faculties has been rectified by justifying grace, and the theological virtues and gifts of the Holy Spirit have been infused:

> even before man's reason, which is the subject of mortal sin, is restored by justifying grace, he can avoid individual mortal sins, any one for a certain space of time, because he does not have to be committing acts of sin all the time. But it is not possible for him to remain without mortal sin for long... And this is because just as the lower instincts ought to be subject to the reason, so too the reason should be subject to God, and make him the end of its will... For when a man does not have his heart firmly established in God, in such a way that he does not wish to be separated from him for the sake of obtaining any good or avoiding any evil, many things arise to obtain or to avoid which man departs from God, rejecting his precepts, and so sins mortally.[117]

[116] See ibid. I-II.74.10, and I-II.74.3–9 more generally.

[117] Ibid. I-II.109.8: etiam antequam hominis ratio, in qua est peccatum mortale, reparetur per gratiam justificantem, potest singula peccata mortalia vitare, et secundum alioquod tempus; quia non est necesse quod continuo peccet in actu. Sed quod diu maneat absque peccato mortali, esse non potest.... Et hujus ratio est, quia, sicut rationi subdi debet inferior appetitus, ita etiam ratio subdi debet Deo, et in ipso constituere finem suae voluntatis.... Cum enim homo non habet cor suum firmatum in Deo, ut pro nullo bono consequendo vel malo vitando ab eo separari vellet, occurrunt multa propter quae consequenda vel vitanda homo recedit a Deo, contemnendo praecepta ipsius; et ita peccat mortaliter.

Yet, although justification rectifies the intellect and the will, it does not alter the sensitive appetite, which remains just as corrupt as it was before. This means that inordinate desires can still arise from the sensitive appetite, which must be held in check by the intellect. Due, however, to the problem of concentration, which has been mentioned in Ch. 2, the intellect cannot resist every motion of the sensitive appetite.[118] As a result of this, inordinate desires will inevitably be given expression, and although they can subsequently be rejected by a deliberation of the intellect, a venial sin will nevertheless have been committed. As Aquinas observes:

> In this state man can refrain from mortal sin, which is the affair of the reason, as was maintained above. But he cannot refrain from every venial sin, owing to the spoiling of his lower sensual instinct; the reason can indeed restrain individual movements of its desire (and this is why they have the character of sinfulness and voluntariness), but not all of them: while he tries to resist one, perhaps another makes its attack, nor again can the reason always be on guard to avoid these movements[119]

He gives as an example a man who, in order to avoid thoughts about concupiscence, starts to consider natural knowledge or science, and is unable as a result to suppress an unpremeditated feeling of vainglory.[120] Diligence can reduce the number of occasions on which such events occur, but it cannot stop them from happening completely.

To conclude, Aquinas argues that the justified have the capacity to abstain from all mortal but not all venial sins, whereas *mere natural persons* cannot totally abstain from either. He thus explains how in general the moral behaviour of justified Christians differs from those who are not justified, and integrates this theory completely into his philosophy of mind and action. No such systematic

[118] See pp. 88–90.

[119] *ST* I-II.109.8: In quo quidem statu potest homo abstinere ab omni peccato mortali, quod in ratione consistit, ut supra habitum est. Non autem potest homo abstinere ab omni peccato veniali, propter corruptionem inferioris appetitus sensualitatis; cujus motus singulos quidem ratio reprimere potest, et ex hoc habent rationem peccati et voluntarii, non autem omnes; quia dum uni resistere nititur, fortassis alius insurgit, et etiam quia ratio non semper potest esse pervigil ad hujusmodi motus vitandos. See also I-II.63.2 and William A. Van Roo, *Grace and Original Justice According to St. Thomas* (*Analecta Gregoriana*, 75; Rome, 1955), 80–3.

[120] See *ST* I-II.74.3.

account is to be found in Hooker, who never discusses these matters in any detail. In the following pages, however, it will be argued that by looking at several passages in his work the fragments of such a traditional scholastic theory do indeed emerge.

There are two key passages that demonstrate that Hooker did make a distinction between mortal and venial sins, and they need close comparison with each other. The first has already been discussed in Ch. 2, regarding the problem of concentration. It is a difficult text, and worth quoting again:

They pray in vaine to have synne pardoned which seeke not also to prevent synne by prayer, even everie particular synne by prayer against all synne, except men can name some transgression wherewith wee ought to have truce. For in verie deed although wee cannot be free from all synne collectively in such sorte that no part thereof shalbe founde inherent in us, yeat distributively at least all greate and grevous actuall offences as they offer them selves one by one both may and ought to be by all meanes avoyded. So that in this sense to be preserved from all synne is not impossible.[121]

It will be recalled that Hooker is here making a distinction between the collective and the distributive avoidance of sin, and that he is speaking of Christians as opposed to *mere natural persons*. Despite his seeming vacillation on the point, the logic of this passage, and of his theology as a whole, points to the fact that all sins can be avoided if considered separately, or 'distributively' speaking, but that no one can 'collectively' avoid all sins.[122] The reason for this is the problem of concentration, just as it is in Aquinas's explanation of sin. The one remaining question concerns the phrase 'greate and grevous'.

[121] *Lawes* 2:200.2–10 (V.48.12). See pp. 88–90 above and Neelands, 'The Theology of Grace of Richard Hooker', 56.

[122] A similar point is made by Richard Montague in 1624, who distinguishes between what is possible in the course of nature, and what is ordinarily impossible but is theoretically possible with the grace of God. He concludes from this both that a person with God's grace could theoretically keep all God's commandments, and that in the normal course of events no one will ever do so. Yet he by no means infers from this that all the works of humans are ordinarily sinful. As he observes: 'No man in the state of Grace regenerate, by any ordinary course or assistance of Grace, ever did or can observe all the Commandements of God, in every part; no, not in that degree which God hath fitted him unto, and requireth of him, at all times: At some time he may, in some particulars; or peradventure in all particulars in some time, or some particulars in all time.' See Montagu, *A New Gagg*, 118–22.

If this passage existed by itself one might suspect that this referred to mortal sin, but there would not be any definite proof for this. Yet, by a turn of events, this is not the case. The writers of the *Christian Letter* evidently failed to appreciate Hooker's distinction between 'collectively' and 'distributively' avoiding sin, and thought that Hooker was implying that complete sinlessness was humanly possible. Hooker was thus brought, as a result, to defend his initial remarks, and the marginalia in his edition of the *Christian Letter* are most interesting at this point:

> Vide August. de civ. Dei. lib. 14. ca. 9. Apostolus ordinandos praecipit non qui sine peccato sunt sed qui sine crimine. Nam alias nemo ordinari posset teste Johanne epist. prima. Having bent your self before against the necessity of all vertue, you are now an enemie to the invocation of Gods aid against all vice.
> Vide August. Enchir. c. 64. de discrimine criminis et peccati.[123]

In the chapter of *De Civitate Dei* to which Hooker refers, Augustine argues against the Stoic principle of *apatheia* (impassibility), on the basis that certain emotions inevitably 'occur in defiance of reason and which disturb the thoughts'.[124] This accords with Hooker's observation in the *Lawes* that, 'collectively' speaking, it is impossible to be free from all sin in this life. As regards his subsequent remarks in Latin, Hooker notes how St Paul (the Apostle or *Apostolus*) requests that only those of upstanding character should be ordained, but argues that this does not imply that such persons should be sinless. Hooker cites 1 John 1: 8 in evidence, where the epistle writer observes that 'If we say that we have no sinne, we deceive our selves, and trueth is not in us.' Clearly, then, Hooker believes that certain sins can be avoided, but not others. To refer to these two categories of sin Hooker uses the words *peccatum* and *crimen*, which look remarkably similar in meaning to the scholastic terms *peccatum veniale* and *peccatum mortale*. Rather than simply assuming that this is the case, one may examine further evidence in favour of this argument.

[123] *AN* 4:26.21–6.

[124] See Augustine, *Concerning the City of God Against the Pagans*, trans. H. Bettenson (Harmondsworth, 1972), 564; *Aurelii Augustini Opera* (*Corpus Christianorum*, Series Latina, 27–57; Turnhout, Belgium, 1954–). xlviii. 428: quae contra rationem accidunt mentemque perturbant.

Hooker's final note in this section of marginalia is a reference to Augustine's *Enchiridion*. In the sixty-fourth section of this work Augustine argues that there are two categories of sin, one from which devout Christians may abstain, but another to which they will inevitably fall prey:

their response to the promptings of the Spirit of God and their advance as sons of God towards God is conditioned by the fact that as the sons of men they are also moved by their own spirit, weighed down as it is by a corruptible body, and under the influence of certain human passions fall away to their own selves, and thus commit sin. But a distinction must be made according to the gravity of the case: it does not hold that because every crime is a sin, therefore every sin is a crime. We can say, then, that the life of holy men, as long as they remain in this mortal life, can be found to be without crime; but says the great Apostle, *if we say that we have no sin, we deceive ourselves, and the truth is not in us.*[125]

Augustine does not use a specific term to refer to those sins that are not crimes (*crimina*), but Hooker in his gloss simply uses the word *peccata*. This again looks remarkably similar to the kind of scholastic theory to be found in Aquinas, but it is still perhaps inconclusive, since Hooker here provides no definition of the term *crimina*. He comes very close to doing this, however, in a passage in the *Lawes*, in which he notes that 'heresie and *manie other crimes* which *whollie sever from God* do sever from the Church of God in *part onlie*'.[126] 'Crime' is obviously derived etymologically from the Latin *crimen*, and, given the context, this may suggest that it is used here in the technical sense of the Latin term. If this is the case then *crimina* are synonymous with *peccata mortalia*, since one of the effects of mortal sin according to Aquinas is that it severs the believer from God, through a loss of the theological virtues.[127]

[125] See Augustine, *Faith, Hope, and Charity*, trans. Louis A. Arand. Ancient Christian Writers, The Works of the Fathers in Translation, vol. 3 (Westminster, Md., 1947), 65–6; *Augustins Enchiridion*, ed. O. Scheel (Tübingen, 1903), 41: sic tamen spiritu dei excitantur, et tamquam filii dei proficiunt ad deum, ut etiam spirtu suo, maxime aggravante corruptibili corpore, tamquam filii hominum quibusdam humanis motibus deficiant ad se ipsos, et ideo peccent. Interest quidem quantum; neque enim quia peccatum est omne crimen, ideo crimen est etiam omne peccatum. Itaque sanctorum hominum vitam, quamdiu in hac mortali vivitur, inveniri posse dicimus sine crimine: *Peccatum* autem *si dixerimus quia non habemus*, ait tantus apostolus, *nos ipsos seducimus, et veritas in nobis non est.*

[126] See *Lawes*, 2:351.13–14 (V.68.6).

[127] See *ST* I-II.63.2: 'Mortal sin is incompatible with divinely infused virtue' (*virtus divinitus infusa... non compatitur secum aliquod peccatum mortale*). See also II-II.4.4; II-II.24.10, 12; O'Neil, 'Sin', 9.

One final piece of evidence can be gathered from *A Learned Discourse of Justification*, in which, when speaking of Roman Catholic doctrine, Hooker equates 'mortall syn' with 'heynous cryme'.[128] *Peccata*, as distinguished by Hooker from *crimina*, is then logically synonymous with *peccata venialia*; actions which, although sinful, do not completely sever one from God.[129] Hooker does appear, therefore, to have a theory of mortal and venial sin, although he does not use these actual terms.

His application of these concepts would appear, though, to be more radical in his notes on the *Christian Letter* than in the *Lawes*. In ch. 48 of the *Lawes* he argues cautiously that it is at least possible for Christians to abstain 'distributively' from all mortal sins or 'greate and grevous actuall offences', but he does not say that it is possible for them to avoid all these sins 'collectively'. In his marginal notes, however, he observes that St Paul commanded that only those without mortal sin or crime (*sine crimine*) should be ordained, and he then cites a section of the *Enchiridion* where Augustine remarks that holy men can remain in this life without crime (*sine crimine*). This is strongly suggestive that Hooker's private view, which he did not choose to publish in the *Lawes*, was that Christians through diligence and grace could and should abstain not only 'distributively' from all mortal sins, but also 'collectively' as well. He had thus, by the time at least of the late works, apparently adopted the traditional scholastic position, found for instance in Aquinas, that Christians could and should abstain 'collectively' from all mortal sins, although they are not able to abstain 'collectively' from all venial sins. Since only mortal sins sever a person from God, one can infer from this that *mere natural persons* must in Hooker's view, unlike Christians, be incapable of abstaining 'collectively' from all cases of either class of sin. This leads to the conclusion that Hooker did indeed believe that sanctification has a qualitative effect upon human behaviour, in that sanctifying grace makes it possible for humans to abstain 'collectively' from all mortal sins.

Two further inferences may now be drawn. First, Hooker's mature theory of justification supposes that it is possible for a

[128] See *Just.* 5:160.10–11.

[129] Hooker does once speak of 'veniall' actions in the *Lawes*, but it is doubtful that he there uses the word in its technical sense: see 2:380.16–381.1 (V.71.8).

person to lose his or her justification through a fall from grace. Since the sins of the justified are remitted, and the sins of the unjustified retained, Hooker must logically have thought that justification is lost, at least temporarily, by mortal sin. Secondly, this would also imply that the venial sins of justified Christians will not be punished by God in any way, since God regards the justified as if they were perfectly inherently righteous. This would follow logically from the fact that Hooker rejects the concept of purgatory, but holds a forensic theory of justification, although there is no positive proof that this was in fact his view.

This still leaves the question of how Hooker relates his theory of mortal and venial sins to his philosophy of mind and action. He certainly does not discuss this matter himself, but it is perhaps possible to infer his overall position. As has been argued in Ch. 2, Hooker holds the problem of concentration responsible for cases of sin amongst even the most diligent persons. This can be used to explain how a person could avoid mortal, but not all venial sins. Hooker observes in the *Lawes* that the theological virtues 'rectifie natures obliquitie', healing the human mind in some sense: presumably they do so in a manner that still leaves the mind unable to concentrate in certain situations, and hence still subject to venial sin.[130] It would seem reasonable to suggest that, as for instance in Aquinas, these virtues operate by rectifying the reason and the will, but not the sensitive appetite, with the result that inordinate sensitive desires continue to arise: as the reason is unable to concentrate on these desires in all circumstances, venial sins will inevitably occur. Since Hooker shares so much common ground with a traditional scholastic theologian such as Aquinas over this matter, it seems likely that this is the missing link in Hooker's theory of defective behaviour. This explanation is, moreover, fully in harmony with the rest of his theology. It is not, though, possible to state definitely that this was how he viewed the activity of sin in relation to the human mind, yet it does seem the most reasonable interpretation on the basis of the available evidence.

Since, in Hooker's opinion, humans have liberty of indifference and grace is resistible, this would suggest that the avoidance in particular cases of both mortal and venial sin is in itself condignly meritorious. Given that, in Hooker's mature opinion, justification

[130] See ibid. 1:119.22–3 (V.11.6).

can be congruously merited, this raises the question of whether Christians who co-operate with grace can in some sense merit not only their salvation, but also their specific eternal reward. Hooker's early position on this matter, as illustrated by *A Learned Discourse of Justification*, *A Learned Sermon of the Nature of Pride*, and *A Sermon Fragment on Proverbs 3.9–10*, is that no Christian works can merit a reward, but that God does reward some works 'through his mere mercie'.[131] By the time of the *Lawes*, however, his position appears to have changed, as the following lines from Book 2 demonstrate:

> Finally some thinges although not so required of necessitie that to leave them undone excludeth from salvation, are not withstanding of so great dignitie and acceptation with God, that most ample reward in heaven is laid up for them. Hereof wee have no commandement either in nature or scripture which doth exact them at our handes: yet those motives there are in both which drawe most effectually our mindes unto them. In this kinde there is not the least action but it doth some what make to the accessory augmentation of our blisse. For which cause our Saviour doth plainely witnesse that there shall not bee as much as a cup of colde water bestowed for his sake without rewarde. Hereupon dependeth whatsoever difference there is betweene the states of Saincts in glory: hither we referre what soever belongeth unto the highest perfection of man by way of service towardes God: hereunto that fervor and first love of Christians did bend it selfe causing them to sell their possessions, and lay downe the price at the blessed Apostles feete: hereat Saint Paule undoubtedly did aime in so far abridging his owne libertie, and exceeding that which the bond of necessarie and enjoyned dutie tyed him unto.[132]

By doing more than the minimum required for salvation, people can augment their bliss in heaven, Hooker observes. Haugaard argues on the basis of this that Hooker 'comes close to affirming works of supererogation', and 'approaches a doctrine of merit'.[133] If one defines works of supererogation as works performed beyond the minimum required, for which one receives an additional

[131] See *Just.* 5:116.5–17; 5:130.12–23; 5:153.16–154.26; 5:159.4–160.21; 5:161.2–15; *Pride*, 5:346.5–11; *SFP* 5:416.2–11. See also Devine, 'Richard Hooker's Doctrine of Justification and Sanctification in the Debate with Walter Travers 1585–1586', 292–4; Neelands, 'The Theology of Grace of Richard Hooker', 51–3.

[132] *Lawes*, 1:188.2–25 (II.8.4). On the subject of merit more generally in the *Lawes* see: 1:89.19–26 (I.8.8); 1:115.26–7 (I.11.5); 2:242.14–17 (V.56.10); 3:276.12–28 (VII.22.6–7).

[133] See Haugaard, 'Commentary: Book II', *Folger*, vi. 550.

reward, then there seems little need for such qualifications, given Hooker's belief in liberty of indifference and the resistibility of grace. On such a definition one may indeed affirm with Lake that Hooker upholds a theory of works of supererogation.[134] Haugaard also notes wisely that Hooker here 'approaches the medieval distinction between evangelical precepts, binding on all Christians, and counsels, available for those seeking perfection (without identifying these with monastic vows)'.[135]

The writers of the *Christian Letter* were highly displeased by these lines, and contrasted them with the fourteenth of the Thirty-Nine Articles, 'Of Works of Supererogation' (*Opera supererogationis*). The article reads as follows:

> Voluntary works besides, over and above God's commandments, which they call works of supererogation, cannot be taught without arrogance and impiety. For by them men do declare that they do not only render unto God as much as they are bound to do, but that they do more for his sake than of bounden duty is required; whereas Christ saith plainly: 'When ye have done all that are commanded to you, say: We be unprofitable servants'.[136]

Hooker's unusually lengthy marginal notes in his edition of the *Christian Letter* regarding this accusation of heresy are most interesting. He clearly feels that the accusation is unfair, and goes on to defend his initial distinction between good works that are commanded, and good works that are not commanded. He gives several examples of the latter type of action, including Paul's decision not to marry, and evidently feels that the concept of counsels of perfection does not fall within the condemnation of Article 14. He then ends with these remarks: 'But as for supererogation in poperie it belongeth unto satisfactory actions and not unto meritorious. Whereas therfore with them workes not commaunded are chiefly meritorious, and in merit no supererogation held, you do ill to say that he which maketh any thing not commaunded allowable

[134] See Lake, *Anglicans and Puritans?*, 185–6.

[135] See Haugaard, 'Commentary: Book II', *Folger*, vi. 549–50. The distinction is brought out even more clearly by Covel, who speaks explicitly of the three counsels of perfection. See Covel 'A Just and Temperate Defence', 492–5.

[136] See *Documents of the English Reformation*, 292: Opera quae supererogationis appellant, non possunt sine arrogantia et impietate praedicari, nam illis declarant homines non tantum se Deo reddere quae tenentur, sed plus in eius gratiam facere quam deberent; cum aperte Christus dicat: 'Cum feceritis omnia quaecunque praecepta sunt vobis, dicite: Servi inutiles sumus'; *ACL* 4:24.10–21.

establisheth workes of supererogation.'[137] Hooker demonstrates here his knowledge of Roman Catholic doctrine, by observing that 'in poperie' there is a fundamental distinction between meritorious and satisfactory works. Satisfactory works are acts of penitence carried out to atone for past sins, after they have been forgiven. If they are not atoned for in this life then they must be atoned for in purgatory. They are thus characterized by the fact that the penitent is paying off a debt for sin, whereas in meritorious works the believer is building up a reward that will be paid in heaven. As Hooker appreciates, in strict Roman Catholic doctrine works of supererogation are the superabundant works of satisfaction carried out by saints, who having more than paid off their own debt for past sins, have an excess that can be used to pay off the debts of other persons. Supererogation in this sense has nothing to do with meritorious works, since through acts of merit a person can build up the attendant rewards only for himself or herself.[138] As Hooker phrases it: 'in merit no supererogation held'. By heeding the counsels of perfection, however, such as those concerning chastity and poverty, people can meritoriously increase the extent of their own heavenly reward. When people commonly refer to works of supererogation, it is often this latter definition that they have in mind. Hooker, though, adopts the strict Roman Catholic definition, and in so doing places himself in an excellent (if not uncontentious) position to demonstrate his agreement with Article 14: after all, he did not agree with Roman Catholic doctrine concerning works of satisfaction. Yet in defending counsels of perfection he associates them intimately with meritorious works, and shows his belief that such works receive an additional reward in heaven. In the vulgar sense of the term, therefore, one may state that he here defends works of supererogation.[139] From this it follows logically that since, in his mature opinion, Christians can congruously merit justification, it is also possible for Christians, with the help of grace at every step of the way, to merit congruously their specific eternal reward.

[137] *AN* 4:25.19–24. For further summaries by Hooker of the Roman Catholic view on this matter, see *Just.* 5:160.9–15; *Lawes*, 3:68.15–28 (VI.5.9).

[138] See Joseph Pohle, 'Merit', *Catholic Encyclopedia*. x. 203; Pelikan, *Reformation of Church and Dogma (1300–1700)*, 135–6.

[139] It is interesting to note that Montague in *A New Gagg* distinguishes between two definitions of supererogation: works performed according to counsels of perfection, and the Roman Catholic view concerning superabundant actions that can be transferred to other persons. He takes only the Roman Catholic view to be contrary to Article 14. See *A New Gagg*, 103–5.

It should be quite obvious by now that Hooker's mature views on Christian behaviour are far removed from those of Calvin, and those characteristic of the Reformed tradition more generally. Calvin's position may be swiftly summarized, since he does not attempt to provide an explanation for sanctification in terms of philosophy of mind and action. Thus while he speaks of the infusion of the three theological virtues, he does not describe them as habits, or explain how exactly they operate upon the faculties of the human mind.[140] He does, of course, believe that sanctified Christians are capable of behaviour unattainable by the unsanctified: this primarily consists, as has been noted above, of faith, hope, love, abhorrence of sin, repentance, and 'the desire to live in a holy and devoted manner' (*sancte pieque vivendi studium*). These virtues and desires will then, as a result, express themselves in good works. Yet Calvin does not distinguish the actions of the sanctified from those of the unsanctified on the basis of the avoidance of mortal sin, for he totally rejects any distinction between sins of a mortal and of a venial type.[141] All sin is mortal, he argues, because all sin involves disobedience to God's law, and transgression of this law is always worthy of death. Moreover, since Calvin finds all human desires to be sinful in that they are inordinate, it follows that sanctified Christians are continually guilty of mortal sin.[142] Thus while Calvin expects Christians to behave morally and grow in holiness, he finds them just as guilty of mortal sin as the most lawless of the unsanctified. Salvation, therefore, is not a process whereby the believer is justified, infused with the theological virtues, and then merits an eternal reward through abstaining from mortal sin. Rather, the focus is placed exclusively upon God's forgiveness, which alone makes the sins of Christians 'venial' (*venialis*) by not punishing them with death. The notion that Christians can, in whatever sense, merit an eternal reward is anathema to Calvin, and he sternly condemns both the concepts of works of supererogation and the counsels of perfection.[143] Salvation and heavenly rewards are ascribed purely to divine action, and anything less would be, for him, to deprive God of part of his glory, and deify the capacities of the human mind.[144] Thus despite his advocation of a strict theory of forensic justification, Hooker was sharply at odds with Calvin and other

[140] See *Inst.* III.ii.

[141] See ibid. II.viii.58–9; III.iv.28.

[142] See p. 155. Cf. *The Westminster Confession of Faith*, 6.5.

[143] See *Inst.* III.xiv.12–21; IV.xiii.12.

[144] See ibid. III.xiv.17; III.xviii.2–4.

Reformed theologians on a wide variety of theological doctrines concerning mortal and venial sins, works of supererogation, the counsels of perfection, and of course congruous merit (and the linked topic of the freedom of the human will). He was, as has been shown, in conflict with a Reformed interpretation of Article 14 of the Thirty-Nine Articles regarding works of supererogation, and also, as Ch. 5 will examine, potentially with a Reformed interpretation of Article 12 in its statement that the good works of justified Christians 'cannot put away our sins, and endure the severity of God's judgement'.[145] One can, therefore, again appreciate the genuine radicalism of Hooker's thinking in the Reformed England of the 1590s, and why the Reformed authors of the *Christian Letter* should have accused him of heresy in these matters, and of traducing '*Calvin and the reformed churches*'.[146]

The fact that Hooker has no systematic account of sanctification and of the faculties of *divinely enhanced reason* and *divinely enhanced will* has made it difficult to reconstruct his views. This is particularly true of such matters as 'habits' and venial and mortal sins, which he refers to in only a few brief passages scattered throughout his writings. This is perhaps why Hooker was able to publish some of these controversial opinions within the *Lawes*, as unlike his ideas on the relationship between reason and Holy Scripture they are far from being a prominent feature of that work. Yet even the foundation of his theory of sanctification, that the reason and the will are transformed by sanctifying grace, is not expressed with the type of clarity to be found, for instance, in Covel's 'A Just and Temperate Defence'.[147] This has again resulted in the misinterpretation of Hooker's views by a variety of different critics, in a similar way to what is surely his more obscure handling of common grace. For the final part of this section, as in the previous chapter, it will be useful to look at the views of some of these critics, and ask why Hooker failed to be more perspicuous as regards the subject of divine grace.

The most obvious failure to comprehend Hooker's views on *divinely enhanced reason* and *divinely enhanced will* can be found in Peter

[145] See *Documents of the English Reformation*, 291: peccata nostra expiari et divini iudicii severitatem ferre non possunt.

[146] See *ACL* 4:55.1–64.24.

[147] See Covel, 'A Just and Temperate Defence', 474–5, 481–4.

Munz's book *The Place of Hooker in the History of Thought*.[148] Not perceiving Hooker's argument that sanctifying grace transforms the human mind, Munz appears to assume that Hooker's statements on the mental capacities of sanctified Christians relate to *mere natural reason* and *mere natural will*. This leads Munz to what would then be the logical conclusion that Hooker is guilty of 'naturalism or rationalism'.[149] Had Hooker been more lucid about the role of sanctifying grace, in the same manner as Covel, such a charge would probably never have been made.

A more prevalent misapprehension has resulted in part from a relatively simple omission on Hooker's part. As regards those natural actions that can be performed by both Christians and non-Christians, he never states clearly that sanctifying grace aids the reason and the will only by making them more diligent: these two faculties are healed, and as a result possess the capacity of abstaining from all cases of mortal sin. As has been observed in the previous chapter, a number of critics have assumed that sanctifying grace has a much more wide-ranging effect upon the human mind, and that without it the reason and will are totally depraved. Hooker's failure to explain his views on common grace is equally responsible for this problem, since both omissions veil the precise distinction he makes between nature and supernature. As it is, Kavanagh, Kirby, Atkinson, and others all identify Hooker with the view that humanity's powers are totally depraved without an explicitly Christian grace of renewal, while Grislis observes that Hooker denies *mere natural persons* 'the ability to draw knowledge from the hierarchical structure of reality'. Of course, if Hooker had in addition been much clearer about his overall mature position as to the nature and effects of sanctifying and justifying grace, it would have been much harder for critics to consider him, at least in the *Lawes* and the late works, as a generally 'orthodox' Reformed theologian.

This naturally raises the question again of why Hooker was not clearer in explaining his views on sanctifying grace, in a way that would presumably have helped prevent such contradictory evaluations. The range of possible explanations is very similar to that

[148] See Munz, *The Place of Hooker in the History of Thought*, 60–2. On this subject, see Neelands, 'The Theology of Grace of Richard Hooker', 120–1.

[149] See Munz, *The Place of Hooker in the History of Thought*, 62.

discussed in the previous chapter regarding common grace. First, Hooker may have obscured his opinions by deliberately downplaying the role of grace within the *Lawes*. In so doing, he may have hoped to have gained a polemical advantage over Cartwright and Travers, who place considerable emphasis upon grace in contrast to reason. This argument, made by W. Speed Hill, is more credible in relation to sanctifying grace than it is to common grace, since it was sanctifying grace that the presbyterian theologians were themselves concerned with.[150] This matter will be discussed in some detail in the next part of this chapter, looking at the ways in which the role of grace is minimized within the *Lawes*, and how this appears related to Hooker's polemical objectives. Yet even if Hooker did have such an aim in mind, it is not necessarily an exclusive explanation for his treatment of sanctifying grace in that work. It is also quite possible that he was unsure about the veracity, catholicity, and/or (most particularly) the acceptability of his opinions, especially where he owed his deepest debts to traditional scholasticism. There was nothing controversial in arguing that sanctifying grace transformed the human mind, but his mature views on justification, congruous merit, works of supererogation (vulgarly defined), the counsels of perfection, and the distinction between mortal and venial sins, related as they are to his controversial philosophy of mind and action, were of a wholly different nature. Calvin's attitude towards the latter is no doubt indicative of the reaction Hooker could have expected in the English Church, had he been more vocal. He clearly had good reason to be cautious. He was also, moreover, not writing a *summa*, and did not always have cause to give a systematic account of his views. All these factors would seem to account for his general lack of clarity on these issues, and hence for the manifold interpretations by the critics that surround his work.

The Operations of the Holy Spirit

The first section of this chapter has dealt with Hooker's views on justifying and sanctifying grace, and with his mature development away from the Reformed tradition in these matters. This next

[150] See Hill, 'The Doctrinal Background of Richard Hooker's *Laws of Ecclesiastical Polity*', 199–201.

section will continue this analysis by looking at what Hooker has to say about grace, still with regard to Christians, in a more general and less abstract manner. This is one of the most interesting and important aspects of his writing, as it reveals so much about the nature of his mature theological position. This section is split into two parts. In the first, Hooker's views on when and in what circumstances grace is given to Christians will be examined, as this illustrates the way in which he circumscribes the operations of the Holy Spirit within certain carefully defined boundaries. This analysis will then be extended in the second part to a consideration of how the Holy Spirit manifests himself with regard to the human mind. This question has, of course, already been considered from the perspective of philosophy of mind and action in the previous section, but the aim will now be to take a less theoretical psychological approach, and to look at whether, in Hooker's opinion, Christians can be aware of the operations of the Holy Spirit within them, and what this says in general about his views on how grace interacts with the human reason. Particular emphasis will be placed upon the *Lawes* in this study, as this is the work in which he develops most of these ideas, though his other writings will be referred to occasionally where relevant. It will again be seen, as in the previous section, that Hooker was in the *Lawes* articulating ideas on grace and the human mind that were anathema to Calvin, in areas where the Frenchman has been taken to be a model of Reformed theology. As with the case of his forensic theory of justification, however, Hooker appears to have remained deeply committed to certain distinctively Reformed doctrines throughout his life, and it will be argued that this is also true in certain respects of one aspect of his handling of the relationship between reason and grace, even though for the most part he is firmly opposed to the Reformed tradition in this matter.

The Reception of Christian Grace

In the previous section it was argued that baptism and Holy Communion are, at least in the *Lawes* and late works, instrumental causes of both justifying and sanctifying grace, and it is certainly with these sacraments that Hooker is principally concerned when he discusses the reception of Christian grace in his writings. It is clear, though, that he believes that grace is given in other ways as well, and it is useful to examine briefly his remarks on this subject. This will help to establish the general principle that, in a Christian context, the reception of grace is almost always for Hooker accompanied with an outward sign of that reception, and this will be of use in the next part of this chapter on the way that Christian grace interacts with human reason.

Having said that Hooker in a Christian context almost always relates the reception of grace to an outward sign, it is convenient to deal first with one of the cases in which he does not insist on this connection, by looking at the following passage from Book 5 of the *Lawes*:

> The true necessitie of baptisme a fewe propositions considered will soone decide. All thinges which either are knowne *causes* or sett *meanes*, whereby anie greate good is usually procured, or men delivered from greivous evell, the same wee must needes confesse necessarie.... unless as the Spirit is a necessarie inward cause, so *water* were a necessarie outward meane to our regeneration, what construction should wee give unto those wordes wherein wee are said to be nue borne, and that ἐξ ὕδατος, even of *water*?...What purpose had they in givinge men advise to receive outward baptisme, and in perswadinge them it did availe to remission of synnes? If outward baptisme were a cause in it selfe possessed of that power either naturall or supernaturall, without the present operation whereof no such effect could possiblie growe, it must then followe, that seinge effectes doe never prevent the necessarie causes out of which they springe, no man could ever receive grace before baptisme: which beinge apparentlie both knowne and also confest to be otherwise in many particulars, although in the rest wee make not baptisme a cause of grace, yeat the grace which is given them with theire baptisme doth so farre forth depende on the verie outward sacrament that God will have it imbraced not only as a signe or token what wee receive, but also as an instrument or meane whereby wee receive grace.[151]

'Outward baptisme' refers to the administration of water during the baptismal ceremony; the outward and visible sign of the reception of an inward and invisible grace. Inward baptism is thus the action of the Holy Spirit within the believer; 'a necessarie inward cause' of regeneration, presumably through the infusion of grace. Outward baptism is not a 'cause' of regeneration; it is rather an 'instrument or meane' of regeneration. In the key

[151] *Lawes*, 2:254.4–255.6 (V.60.1–2).

sentence, Hooker postulates that if outward baptism were itself to be a cause of regeneration, without which regeneration could not occur, then no one could receive grace before baptism; a conclusion he cannot accept is true. Thus while the grace given in baptism is firmly linked by Hooker to the outward ceremony of baptism, he observes that the receipt of grace is not inextricably linked to outward ceremonies, because it is not caused by them. One may think in this context of common grace, which is not linked to any outward ceremony. As regards regeneration, Hooker notes here that people can receive grace which makes them 'growe' towards regeneration before they have been baptized: indeed this idea is most important if he is to account for why people should be drawn to have faith in Christ, and to be baptized. Hooker does not explain how exactly this process occurs, though it would be reasonable to suggest a traditional scholastic explanation that the Holy Spirit induces acts of faith in a person, as opposed to an enduring habit of faith (which requires the sanctification of baptism). What is clear, though, is that Hooker believes that grace can be received before baptism, and, moreover, that grace can be given without the existence of an outward ritual, or 'signe' of this reception.

This analysis is important, for there are several passages in Book 5 of the *Lawes* that can be read as suggesting that grace is given only through the sacraments.[152] For instance, Hooker describes grace as 'a consequent of Sacramentes', and notes that 'Neither is it *ordinarilie* his [God's] will to bestowe the grace of sacramentes on anie, but by the sacramentes.'[153] This seems to run counter to the remarks on pre-baptismal grace, which would imply that Hooker is here contradicting himself. Yet it is perfectly possible to bring all these passages into harmony with one another. By speaking of grace as 'a consequent of Sacramentes', Hooker would simply appear to mean that the sacraments are signs, or instrumental causes of the reception of grace. This does not imply that grace can *only* be received in this manner. Similarly, by observing that 'the grace of sacramentes' can '*ordinarilie*' (i.e. in the course of God's usual working) be received only in the sacraments, Hooker

[152] An accusation in fact made by the *Christian Letter*. See *ACL* 4:40.28–30.

[153] See *Lawes*, 2:246.20–33 (V.57.4).

is merely speaking about sacramental graces.[154] The particular grace given in baptism, for instance, can only '*ordinarilie*' be received in baptism, although Hooker is prepared to concede that in extraordinary cases this may not be necessary, as when a person is martyred before baptism, or an infant dies before the ceremony can be performed.[155] Other graces can presumably be received in other ways, as must logically happen with pre-baptismal grace. Thus when Hooker observes that the sacraments are 'meanes conditionall which God requireth in them unto whome he imparteth grace', it would seem that he is here also thinking only of sacramental graces.[156] As the following examples will show, Hooker certainly associates the reception of grace with rituals other than the sacraments of baptism and Holy Communion.

One such ritual is Confirmation, which involves the laying on of hands, and prayers for the individuals concerned. Hooker calls prayers 'our meanes to obteine the graces which God doth bestowe', and observes that we can of course pray for others as much as for ourselves.[157] In Confirmation, a bishop prays that those persons before him may receive grace, and lays his hands on their heads as the outward sign of the reception of an inner grace. Hooker insists that there is nothing sacramental about this process; he rather describes Confirmation as a 'sacramentall complement'.[158] The particular grace involved does not initiate the Christian life, but rather augments the grace received in baptism, to the further benefit of the individuals concerned. Its particular efficacy is, as Hooker describes it, that it 'assisteth us in all vertue, armeth us against temptation and synne', and is thus presumably a form of sanctifying grace.[159]

As regards the ability of prayer to procure grace, Hooker's remarks appear to be quite general, extending to circumstances other than just Confirmation. This might be taken as implying that grace can be received at any point in time, whenever prayer has requested it. As will be shown, however, Hooker does place considerable emphasis upon the idea of the reception of grace being signified by the performance of an outward ritual. This

[154] For this usage of the term '*ordinarilie*', see *Lawes*, 1:17.15–19 (Pref.3.10); 2:90.4–5 (V.22.3).

[155] See Appendix, pp. 326–7.

[156] See *Lawes*, 2:246.1–2 (V.57.3).

[157] See ibid. 2:321.3–5 (V.66.1).

[158] See ibid. 2:326.19 (V.66.6).

[159] See ibid. 2:323.28–9 (V.66.4).

may well suggest that the other circumstances in which prayer can procure grace are also ritually based, such as baptism and Holy Communion. Yet his remarks about pre-baptismal grace demonstrate that ritual is not always a necessary accompaniment for Hooker, and that a person might pray for a grace which is subsequently infused without the presence of a ceremony.

The other ritual mentioned by Hooker in this context is ordination. He is concerned here to explain the meaning of the words spoken by the bishop in the ordination service: '*Receive the holie Ghost.*'[160] Hooker at first explains this in terms of the reception of 'an holie and a Ghostlie authoritie, authoritie over the soules of men, authoritie a parte whereof consisteth in power to remitt and reteine sinnes', where '*holie Ghost*' is a metonym for these gifts of the Spirit.[161] Subsequently, however, Hooker goes on to claim that the rite also involves a very real infusion of the Spirit into the ordinand, whereby he is strengthened for his vocation, and receives authority by the existence of this indwelling presence: 'when wee take ordination wee also receive the presence of the holy Ghost partlie to guide direct and strengthen us in all our waies, and partlie to assume unto it selfe for the more authoritie those actions that apperteine to our place and calling.'[162]

There is one final context in which Hooker speaks of the reception of grace. The outward ritual with which it is connected, the laying on of hands, has already been mentioned before, but here the grace is quite different, for it confers the ability to perform miracles.[163] Hooker observes that this ability was initially conferred upon people by the Apostles, and subsequently by their successors, the bishops, purely through the use of prayer and the laying on of hands. He is quite specific about some of the miraculous powers that could be received, referring here to the gospel of Mark, the book of Acts, and to Irenaeus; they include: exorcism, speaking in tongues, foreknowledge, visions, prophecy, the ability to cure diseases, neutralize poisons, drive away snakes, and resurrect the dead. Hooker accepts, though, with St Augustine, that such gifts are no longer 'vulgar' in the Church, and implies that bishops are now unable to bestow these miraculous powers.

[160] See ibid. 2:427.17–20 (V.77.5).
[161] See ibid. 2:427.26–7 (V.77.5); 2:429.3–10 (V.77.7).
[162] Ibid. 2:430.36 (V.77.8).
[163] See ibid. 2:322.8–323.21 (V.66.2–3).

He is, however, quite clear that such powers do remain in the Church, speaking of 'the like extraordinarie graces more rarely observed in some . . . of later daies'.[164] Exactly how such graces are received, and whether it is through the use of a particular ritual, he does not say.

Hooker, then, evidently believed that grace could be received by Christians in many different ways, but that the Holy Spirit in general chose to manifest his invisible operations by connecting them to outward ceremonies. In this the strongly ritualistic nature of Hooker's theology can be seen. Perhaps the clearest statement of this position is to be found in the following passage. Although Hooker is here referring to the sacraments, his remarks are applicable to all the methods for receiving grace that have been described above, except in the case of grace received before baptism:

> sith God in him selfe is invisible and cannot by us be discerned workinge, therefore when it seemeth good in the eyes of his heavenly wisdome, that men for some speciall intente and purpose should take notize of his glorious presence, he giveth them some plaine and sensible token whereby to knowe what they cannot see. For Moses to see God and live was impossible. Yeat Moses by fire knewe where the glorie of God extraordinarilie was present. The Angell, by whome God indued the waters of the poole cald *Bethesda* with supernaturall vertue to heale, was not seen of anie, yeat the tyme of the Angels presence knowne by the troubled motions of the waters them selves. Thapostles, by fierie tongues which they saw, were admonished when the spirit, which they could not behold, was upon them. In like manner it is with us. Christ and his holie Spirit with all theire blessed effectes, though enteringe into the soule of man wee are not able to apprehend or expresse how, doe notwithstandinge give notize of the tymes when they use to make theire accesse, because it pleaseth almightie God to communicate by sensible meanes those blessinges which are incomprehensible.[165]

The Manifestations of the Holy Spirit

One may now turn to the second topic of this section; the manner in which the Holy Spirit manifests himself in individual Christians. As has already been observed, this subject has been discussed earlier in this chapter as regards sanctification, and the way this brings

[164] See *Lawes*, 2:322.8–323.21 (V.66.2–3).

[165] Ibid. 2:246.2–20 (V.57.3).

about what has been termed as the mental faculties of *divinely enhanced will* and *divinely enhanced reason*. This topic may now be approached from another angle, by asking whether the presence and operations of the Holy Spirit, and his concomitant graces, can be perceived by those in whom this Spirit dwells? This was a question of great concern to Hooker, since he saw himself as confronted with opponents who justified their false beliefs on the basis of their inner experience of the Holy Spirit. As regards Hooker's understanding of what this inner experience comprised, he does not appear to have thought in terms of direct sensory apprehension: he nowhere refers to people claiming that they have directly heard or felt the Spirit within them. The single exception he appears to make is in the case of a miraculous awareness of the Holy Spirit,[166] but such manifestations he argues can only be verified by demonstrative arguments, or the performance of miracles.[167] Hooker never assumes in his work that he is dealing with people who have experienced such an awareness, whether genuine or otherwise. He rather talks in terms of people experiencing strong emotions or feelings: they think that these sensations have been caused by the work of the Spirit within them, and then form certain beliefs on this basis. Hooker's explanation for these phenomena seems to relate to the activities of the sensitive faculties of the soul; in particular, to the imagination or fancy, and to the fancy considered as an inferior judicial power of the soul.[168] He sees the desires/judgements of these sensitive faculties as corrupting the reasoning process, in the manner described in Ch. 2, resulting in defective belief-formation and a sin of passion.[169] The reason works to justify the delusions of these inferior sensitive faculties; a process that can only result in error. Interestingly enough, Hooker is in this context sometimes prepared to follow the chain of causation back one stage further, by blaming demonic spirits for these motions of the sensitive

[166] By far Hooker's clearest discussion of the process of divine revelation occurs in *The First Sermon Upon Part of S. Judes Epistle*. There he describes how God uses dreams and visions to communicate with people, sometimes talking with them 'as a man would talke with his neighbour in the way'. Hooker is much more guarded about such matters in his subsequent writings, but he does at one point in the *Lawes* hint that divine revelation may involve direct sensory awareness. See *Jude 1*, 5:15.8–25; 5:17.3–24; and n. 183 below.

[167] See *Lawes*, 2:46.7–47.9 (V.10.1).

[168] See e.g. ibid. 1:17.29–18.14 (Pref.3.10–11); 1:19.13–22 (Pref.3.13); 1:44.24–8 (Pref.8.7); 1:164.3–12 (II.5.7); 2:3.22–4.23 (V.Ded.5–6); 2:46.7–47.9 (V.10.1).

[169] See pp. 84–8.

faculties.[170] This does not conflict with his belief in liberty of spontaneity and indifference, since it is the will, and not these other faculties, to which he ascribes the power of free choice. His solution to this problem should come as no surprise, in that he sought to overcome the danger of such defective behaviour by stressing the primacy of reason. Only by subordinating the inferior faculties of the soul to the reason, in his opinion, could one hope to discover the truth. As a result of this, one can see why Hooker should have stressed, as the following analysis will attempt to demonstrate, that the Holy Spirit manifests himself only by using reason as his instrument (with the sole exception of miracles). In this way Hooker can continue to argue that the Holy Spirit guides humanity to the truth, while avoiding the danger of basing his beliefs on possibly defective foundations. It is people with strong arguments for their beliefs, ideally from first principles, who in his opinion truly manifest the work of the Spirit in matters of religious doctrine.

In the light of this, it of course becomes of prime importance to establish whose theology it was that Hooker was opposing in this matter. The answer would at first appear to be simple, for as has been noted in Ch. 3, the *Lawes* purports to be a critique of presbyterianism in particular, and of puritanism more generally, with special emphasis on the writings of Cartwright and Travers. Yet although Hooker cites the works of both these authors frequently in the *Lawes*, they are not cited as regards this subject, and interestingly, neither are the works of any other author; Hooker in general merely refers broadly to presbyterian opinion in these matters. When one comes to examine the works of Cartwright and Travers that contribute towards the Admonitions controversy, and that are as a consequence generally cited by Hooker, it appears somewhat less remarkable that Hooker should not have mentioned them in this context: they are in fact a poor source for the kind of position that Hooker was here opposing. With regard to Cartwright this is probably in part because conformist writers such as Bancroft and Sutcliffe had accused him of encouraging fanatics like Edmund Copinger, who believed that God had called him personally to crown the unfortunate William Hacket as the

[170] See e.g. *Lawes*, 1:17.10–15 (Pref.3.10); 1:18.4–8 (Pref.3.10); 1:232.29–33 (III.8.15); 2:4.2–27 (V.Ded.6).

new Messiah.[171] Cartwright was, in the light of this, wary in the Admonitions controversy of making any remarks about the inward manifestations of the Holy Spirit. This does not, of course, mean that Cartwright and Travers were not advocates of the kind of view that Hooker was here opposing, whether verbally or in other writings, and indeed if one looks at one of Cartwright's non-Admonitions writings then one can in places find him espousing such ideas. Revealingly, one such work is *A Confutation of the Rhemists Translation*, an exhaustive critique of the well-known Roman Catholic Reims translation of the Bible complete with extensive glosses and annotations. When one looks at the wider context of the views that Hooker was attacking as regards inner manifestations of the Holy Spirit then one can appreciate more generally why such ideas should have appeared in this work, but not in those related to the Admonitions controversy, for these ideas are in fact archetypally Reformed. Cartwright did not need to raise them in the Admonitions controversy, for he was dealing with Reformed opponents who shared many of his basic theological principles, whereas with Roman Catholic writers these points were highly controversial.[172] A much plainer discussion of the full range of views that Hooker was attacking as regards inward manifestations of the Holy Spirit can, however, be found in Calvin's *Institutes* and biblical commentaries, in an area where Calvin has been considered to be a classical exponent of Reformed doctrine.[173] Hooker was, therefore, as will now be shown, again opposing characteristically Reformed doctrine under the cover of an attack on puritanism and presbyterianism, a 'sleight of hand' that was directed at theological principles that were common to both. This is presumably why Hooker was able to publish such opinions in late Elizabethan England, and why he has not automatically been associated with a critique of Reformed theology in this regard.

Due to the polemical context in which Hooker expressed his thinking on the Holy Spirit, his ideas on this subject are

[171] See Patrick Collinson, *The Elizabethan Puritan Movement* (Oxford, 1967), 419–20, 424–5. See also Thomas Cartwright, *A Brief Apologie* (Middelburg, 1596; facsimile edn., Amsterdam, 1970), B2v–C2v.

[172] I am indebted to Peter Lake for this observation.

[173] On this subject, see in general Richard H. Wilmer Jr., 'Hooker on Authority', *Anglican Theological Review* 33 (1951), 103, 107; Gibbs, 'Commentary: Book I', *Folger*, vi. 516.

best explored through specific cases in which he considered his opponents to have gone awry. The first two examples that have been chosen both demonstrate Hooker's belief that the Holy Spirit never ordinarily manifests himself apart from through the human reason, but they do so in ways that help to build up a picture of his overall position. The chapter will conclude with an examination of a third, more enigmatic example of Hooker's attitude to the Holy Spirit, on which his opinions appear to have fluctuated over the course of time.

The first of these examples concerns Holy Scripture, and the manner in which a person can know that it is the Word of God, or divine revelation. As Lake and Shuger have argued (and Atkinson has strongly denied), the basic position that is unacceptable to Hooker is that Holy Scripture is self-authenticating, on the basis of the direct internal testimony of the Holy Spirit within the believer.[174] The corollary of this position is that reason can have no part in the authenticating process, as its religious judgement is of little or no value compared to that of the Holy Spirit.[175] Hooker clearly feels that this approach is nothing other than a turn towards irrationalism, in a manner that ignores the rational nature of faith.[176] As he observes in Book 3 of the *Lawes*, broadly summarizing in the first sentence the views of his opponents:

> If I believe the Gospell, there needeth no reasoning about it to perswade me: If I doe not believe, it must be the spirit of God and not the reason of man that shall convert my hart unto him. By these and the like disputes an opinion hath spread it selfe verie farre in the world, as if the waye to be ripe in faith, were to be rawe in wit and judgement; as if reason were an enimie unto religion, childish simplicitie the mother of ghostlie and divine wisedome.[177]

Hooker returns to this subject again some pages later in Book 3, where he discusses it in more detail.[178] There he begins by denying that it is self-evident that the Holy Scriptures are the Word of

[174] See Lake, *Anglicans and Puritans?*, 155; Shuger, *Habits of Thought in the English Renaissance*, 28, 41; Atkinson, *Richard Hooker and the Authority of Scripture, Tradition and Reason*, 93, 108.

[175] It might also be considered that reason would be made superior to revelation if it was used to authenticate the latter. Interestingly, when Atkinson incorrectly identifies Hooker with the (Reformed) view that Holy Scripture is self-authenticating on the internal witness of the Holy Spirit, he makes precisely this claim about reason and revelation. See Atkinson, *Richard Hooker and the Authority of Scripture, Tradition and Reason*, 93.

[176] See pp. 197–9.

[177] *Lawes*, 1:222.22–8 (III.8.4). See also 1:221.25–9 (III.8.4).

[178] See ibid. 1:230.25–235.18 (III.8.13–8).

God, though he does not mention the Holy Spirit at this point. From there he moves on to admit the force of tradition and the authority of the Church as regards the authentication of Holy Scripture, but emphasizes that a mature person will seek to confirm his or her beliefs by the use of reason. His ensuing remarks then demonstrate his great confidence in the powers of human reason (aided of course by grace):

the ancient fathers being often constreined to shew, what warrant they had so much to relie upon the scriptures, endevored still to maintein the autority of the books of God by arguments such as unbeleevers them selves must needs thinke reasonable, if they judged therof as they should. Neither is it a thing impossible or greatly hard, even by such kind of proofes so to manifest and cleere that point, that no man living shalbe able to deny it, without denying some apparent principle such as al men acknowledge to be true.[179]

Hooker notes, first, that the Church Fathers defended Holy Scripture by arguments that unbelievers would be compelled to 'thinke reasonable' if they judged the matter correctly. He does not as yet explain what may have prevented these people from reasoning aright, but his later remarks about the necessity of (sanctifying) grace as regards reasoning in divine matters would seem to provide the likely explanation.[180] He then goes a step further, and claims that the status of Holy Scripture can be established by demonstrative arguments, although he does not actually attempt such a proof himself. Exactly the same point has also been made earlier in this passage, taken from Book 2 of the *Lawes*:

we all beleeve that the Scriptures of God are sacred, and that they have proceeded from God; our selves we assure that wee doe right well in so beleeving. We have for this point a demonstration sound and infallible.[181]

Having made these observations, Hooker then comes to the most important part of his discussion, which is worth quoting at length:

Neither can I thinke that when grave and learned men do sometime hold, that of this principle there is no proofe but by the testimony of the spirit, which assureth our harts therin, it is their meaning to exclude utterly all force which any kind of reason may have in that behalfe; but

179 Ibid. 1:232.2–10 (III.8.14).

180 See ibid. 1:234.31–235.2 (III.8.18).

181 Ibid. 1:153.16–17 (II.4.2). Shuger observes that this is contrary to the views of both Calvin and Augustine. See Shuger, *Habits of Thought in the English Renaissance*, 42.

I rather incline to interpret such their speeches, as if they had more expresly set downe, that other motives and inducements, be they never so strong and consonant unto reason, are notwithstanding uneffectual of them selves to worke faith concerning this principle, if the special grace of the holy ghost concur not to the inlightening of our minds.[182]

Reason in other words requires (sanctifying) grace in order to understand the Gospel and accept that Holy Scripture is divine revelation; a principle that has been outlined earlier in this and the previous chapter. What Hooker here effectively denies is that the testimony of the Holy Spirit concerning Holy Scripture is received apart from the use of reason as his instrument. He does not name the 'grave and learned men' that he is referring to, but if he is thinking of Calvin and other major Reformed theologians of a like mind then his interpretation is very free, if not disingenuous. As will shortly be illustrated, Calvin believed that the Holy Spirit worked directly to assure the believer of the nature of Holy Scripture, and did not use reason as his instrument for this purpose. Hooker's interpretation, though apparently an attempt to find agreement between two divergent theological positions, appears merely to distort his opponents' point of view.

Hooker does more, though, than suggest that the Holy Spirit manifests himself through the human reason; he questions the genuineness of all other ways in which the Spirit might appear to manifest himself. He seems to assume, on this subject, that there is one point of agreement between him and his opponents, in that 'as we know' the Holy Spirit can never be directly sensed. This is, as Hooker again states, because of his non-material nature; his operations are 'of another and an higher kind then that they can be by us perceived in this life'.[183] Logically, then, the Holy Spirit can only be perceived through his secondary effects upon the human mind. At this point Hooker warns that great care must be taken in this process, 'lest men thinke that the spirit of god doth testifie those things which the spirit of error suggesteth'.[184] Apparent spiritual

[182] *Lawes*, 1:232.16–25 (III.8.15).

[183] See ibid. 1:232.33–233.3 (III.8.15). Hooker may make an exception with regard to a miraculous awareness of the Holy Spirit. He observes that 'The operations of the spirit, *especially these ordinary which be common* unto all true christian men, are as we know, things secret and undiscernable' (my italics), which may imply that extraordinary operations can sometimes be directly felt. The matter is, however, somewhat unclear.

[184] See ibid. 1:232.32–3 (III.8.15).

manifestations may be the work of demonic forces. Hooker suggests, therefore, an inversion of the practices of his opponents. Rather than basing their beliefs and actions upon their spiritual experiences, they should base their awareness of the operations of the Spirit upon 'the qualitie of things beleeved or done'.[185] The quality to which Hooker refers here is presumably reason; the more an action or belief is justified by sound reasoning, especially from first principles, the more likely it is that the Holy Spirit has been at work in forming it. Such an approach effectively denies the validity of all other methods of discerning the work of the Spirit, as subject to error and infernal influence, even if it be in something so traditional as believing that the Holy Scriptures are the Word of God.

To turn now to the views of those theologians whom Hooker is opposing, it is evident from some of the passages in *A Confutation of the Rhemists Translation* that Cartwright believes that Holy Scripture is self-authenticating on the internal witness of the Holy Spirit. This can be seen, for instance, in his response to the Reims annotation on Galatians 2: 4, where the Reims Bible adopts the traditional Roman Catholic position that Holy Scripture is authenticated by the Church. Cartwright remarks that 'Iudges of the Scriptures we neither make our selves, nor will admit you, which proudly lift up your selves into that judgement seat', and argues instead 'that as one iron whetteth another, so one Scripture is the touchstone of another, and is tryed by another'.[186] He thus regards neither the Church nor individual Christians as able to authenticate Holy Scripture; it is rather authenticated on its own internal evidence.

A much fuller statement of the position that Hooker is opposing, that makes clearer the role of the Holy Spirit in the process of authentication, can be found in Calvin's works. Calvin does not deny that the authority of the Church is useful in bringing people to revere Holy Scripture, though of course he strongly denounces the view that Holy Scripture receives its authentication from this source.[187] He also spends the entire eighth chapter of Book I of

[185] See ibid. I:233.3–9 (III.8.15).

[186] See Thomas Cartwright, *A Confutation of the Rhemists Translation* (Leiden, 1618; facsimile edn. Amsterdam, 1971), 466–7.

[187] See *Inst.* I.vii.1–3; H. Jackson Forstman, *Word and Spirit: Calvin's Doctrine of Biblical Authority* (Stanford, Calif., 1962), 71; George S. Hendry, *The Holy Spirit in Christian Theology* (London, rev. edn. 1965), 77.

the *Institutes* making out a rational case for the revealed nature of Holy Scripture. For him, however, such arguments can result only in opinions, and not the certainty that is required by faith: they are useful aids for believers, but they will never convince anyone who does not already believe.[188] The only way in which the Word will truly be accepted as divinely inspired, he argues, is through the direct inward manifestation of the Holy Spirit:

If we desire to provide in the best way for our consciences—that they may not be perpetually beset by the instability of doubt or vacillation, and that they may not also boggle at the smallest quibbles—we ought to seek our conviction in a higher place than human reasons, judgments, or conjectures, that is, the secret testimony of the Spirit. . . . The testimony of the Spirit is more excellent than all reason. For as God alone is a fit witness of himself in his Word, so also the Word will not find acceptance in men's hearts before it is sealed by the inward testimony of the Spirit. The same Spirit, therefore, who has spoken through the mouths of the prophets must penetrate into our hearts to persuade us that they faithfully proclaimed what has been divinely commanded.[189]

Calvin makes this point yet more forcefully in the next chapter of the *Institutes*, when he argues that Holy Scripture is self-authenticating to those taught by the Holy Spirit:

those whom the Holy Spirit has inwardly taught rest upon Scripture, and that Scripture indeed is self-authenticated; hence, it is not right to subject it to proof and reasoning. And the certainty it deserves with us, it attains by the testimony of the Spirit. For even if it wins reverence for itself by its own majesty, it seriously affects us only when it is sealed upon our hearts through the Spirit. Therefore, illumined by his power, we believe neither by our own nor by anyone else's judgment that Scripture is from

[188] See *Inst.* I.vii.4–5; I.viii.1–13.

[189] *Inst.* I.vii.4 (*OS* 3:69–70): Iam si conscientiis optime consultum volumus, ne instabili dubitatione perpetuo circunferantur, aut vacillent, ne etiam haesitent ad minimos quosque scrupulos, altius quam ab humanis vel rationibus, vel iudiciis, vel coniecturis petenda est haec persuasio, nempe ab arcano testimonio Spiritus. . . . Atqui testimonium Spiritus omni ratione praestantius esse respondeo. Nam sicuti Deus solus de se idoneus est testis in suo sermone: ita etiam non ante fidem reperiet sermo in hominum cordibus quam interiore Spiritus testimonio obsignetur. Idem ergo Spiritus qui per os Prophetarum loquutus est, in corda nostra penetret necesse est, ut persuadeat fideliter protulisse quod divinitus erat mandatum. See also Niesel, *The Theology of Calvin*, 30; Edward A. Dowey Jr., *The Knowledge of God in Calvin's Theology* (New York, 1952), 108, 110, 118, 120, 123–4; Forstman, *Word and Spirit*, 71; Wendel, *Calvin: The Origins and Development of his Religious Thought*, 157; Hendry, *The Holy Spirit in Christian Theology*, 75.

God; but above human judgment we affirm with utter certainty (just as if we were gazing upon the majesty of God himself) that it has flowed to us from the very mouth of God by the ministry of men.[190]

The theory that Hooker espouses, that the Holy Spirit uses reason as his instrument in authenticating Holy Scripture, is evidently anathema to Calvin: indeed in Book 4 of the *Institutes* Calvin describes subjecting the validity of Holy Scripture to the judgement of men as 'a blasphemy unfit to be mentioned'.[191] Hooker thus cannot legitimately interpret Calvin in a way conducive to his own theological position. Yet Calvin's views on this subject have been described by George S. Hendry as the classical formulation of the Reformed doctrine of '"the inner witness of the Holy Spirit"... one of the best known elements in the Reformed theological tradition'.[192] It is little wonder, then, that Hooker chose not to cite Calvin, or any other major Reformed theologians, to demonstrate his orthodoxy in this matter. To do so would merely have been to emphasize the extent to which he had departed from the views of these 'grave and learned men' in his thinking over the relation of reason to the Holy Spirit.

Before progressing, it is worth making one further point about the theology of Calvin and Cartwright concerning the Holy Spirit. Like Hooker, Calvin was obviously concerned about people who claimed the Holy Spirit as the source for opinions of, as he perceived it, an irreligious or unchristian nature. To establish a

[190] *Inst.* I.vii.5 (*OS* 3:70): quos Spiritus sanctus intus docuit, solide acquiescere in Scriptura, et hanc quidem esse αὐτόπιστον, neque demonstrationi et rationibus subiici eam fas esse: quam tamen meretur apud nos certitudinem, Spiritus testimonio consequi. Etsi enim reverentiam sua sibi ultro maiestate conciliat, tunc tamen demum serio nos afficit quum per Spiritum obsignata est cordibus nostris. Illius ergo virtute illuminati, iam non aut nostro, aut aliorum iudicio credimus, a Deo esse Scripturam: sed supra humanum iudicium, certo certius constituimus (non secus acsi ipsius Dei numen illic intueremur) hominum ministerio, ab ipsissimo Deo ore ad nos fluxisse. See also *Calvin's Commentaries: The Second Epistle of Paul The Apostle to the Corinthians and the Epistles to Timothy, Titus and Philemon*, ed. D. W. Torrance and T. F. Torrance, trans. T. A. Smail (Edinburgh, 1964), commentary on 2 Timothy 3: 16, pp. 329–30.

[191] See *Inst.* IV.9.14 (*OS* 5:163): Subiicere enim in eum modum Dei oracula hominum censurae, ut ideo rata sint quia placuerint hominibus, blasphemia indigna est quae commemoretur.

[192] See Hendry, *The Holy Spirit in Christian Theology*, 72, 76. See also *The Westminster Confession of Faith*, 1.5, in *Documents of the English Reformation*, 488: 'our full persuasion and assurance of the infallible truth and divine authority thereof [of Holy Scripture] is from the inward work of the Holy Spirit bearing witness by and with the Word in our hearts'.

bulwark of orthodoxy, therefore, he argues that the Holy Spirit would never teach anything contrary to, or indeed apart from, what he had already revealed in Holy Scripture.[193] In a similar manner, Cartwright in his *Christian Religion* notes that the Holy Spirit 'doth not ordinarily suggest any thing to us, but that which it teacheth us out of the word'.[194] It is presumably with this principle in mind that Cartwright, in the *Replye*, warns those who believe that they have an 'extraordinary' inner calling from God, outside the normal lines of Church authority, to examine themselves diligently 'lest under pretence of the spirite of God whome they make author of their calling, it fall out that it be but their own headlong affection that hath thrust them in'.[195] Hooker, Calvin, and Cartwright, therefore, all seek to guard against 'false' revelations of the Spirit, of the kind represented for the Englishmen by figures such as Edmund Copinger, and what was often broadly characterized as 'Anabaptist' beliefs. Nonetheless, both Calvin and (as will become plainer below) Cartwright were prepared to accept a wide range of direct inward manifestations of the Spirit as wholly genuine, whereas Hooker will have nothing to do with any of them.

The second of the examples concerning Hooker's views on manifestations of the Holy Spirit deals with the interpretation of Holy Scripture. As Lake and Shuger have again argued, the basic position that is unacceptable to him, in this instance, is that the Holy Spirit inwardly guides people in their exegesis of the Word without using reason as his instrument.[196] As Ch. 2 has shown, Hooker argues in the *Lawes* that Christian doctrines necessary for salvation are either mentioned expressly in Holy Scripture, or may be interpreted from it by a process of demonstrative reasoning. Other beliefs and practices grounded on Holy Scripture are gathered by probable reasoning.[197] The principal passages where Hooker considers the opposing view that the Holy Spirit does not use reason as his instrument in this process occur in the preface to

[193] See *Inst.* I.ix.1–2; Forstman, *Word and Spirit*, 75–6.

[194] See Thomas Cartwright, *Christian Religion: Substantially, Methodicallie, Plainlie, and Profitablie Treatised* (London, 1611), 169–71. See also 285.

[195] See *Replye*, 71.

[196] See Lake, *Anglicans and Puritans?*, 155, 158; Shuger, *Habits of Thought in the English Renaissance*, 28, 37, 41.

[197] See pp. 76–7.

the *Lawes*, where Hooker expounds upon the dangers of the presbyterian movement. One may start with ch. 3, in which Hooker discusses the methods used to convince the '*common*' or '*ordinarie sort of men*' that Holy Scripture commands the institution of a presbyterian church discipline.

The one method that Hooker does not allow in this chapter is that the '*common*' people have been convinced of presbyterian beliefs by reasoning from first principles.[198] They are, he feels, simply not in a position to understand all the '*particular reasons*' that the learned presbyterians give for their beliefs, and so be totally convinced by them. As such, other '*generall inducements*' must have been used to convince the '*common*' people, and Hooker finds these to be inconsonant with reason. Five such inducements are listed by him, only the last of which is relevant in this context.[199] In this case, he argues that people '*credulous and over capable of such pleasing errors*' are persuaded that '*it is the speciall illumination of the holy Ghost, whereby they discerne those things in the word, which others reading yet discerne them not*'. This scarcely suggests that he considered this process of interpretation to be rational, or in any way orthodox. To underline the dangers of such a belief he cites 1 John 3: 4, which warns that not every spirit comes from God. Hooker again implies, therefore, that beliefs that appear to come from a direct inward manifestation of the Holy Spirit may in fact have an infernal origin. He then makes almost precisely the same point concerning reason and the Holy Spirit as he does later, in Book 3 of the *Lawes*, as regards the authentication of Holy Scripture:

> *There are but two waies whereby the spirit leadeth men into all truth: the one extraordinarie, the other common; the one belonging but unto some few, the other extending it selfe unto all that are of God; the one that which we call by a speciall divine excellency* Revelation, *the other* Reason. *If the Spirite by such revelation have discovered unto them the secrets of that discipline out of Scripture, they must professe themselves to be all (even men, women, and children) Prophets.*[200]

Only in '*extraordinarie*' or miraculous cases, quite out of the way of God's usual manner of working, will the Holy Spirit not use reason as his instrument.[201] As has been shown above, Hooker did believe that prophecy was a fairly common gift in the early Church, but that

[198] See *Lawes*, 1:15.6–12 (Pref.3.5).

[199] See ibid. 1:17.10–18.8 (Pref.3.10).

[200] *Lawes*, 1:17.15–22 (Pref.3.10). See in this context n. 183 above.

[201] For this usage of the term '*extraordinarie*', see *Lawes*, 2:90.4–5 (V.22.3).

this had ceased to be the case by the time of Augustine.[202] Clearly he feels the title of 'prophet' is grossly inappropriate when applied to the entire presbyterian movement, something he emphasizes by his use of syntax. By placing '*children*' next to '*Prophets*' he attempts to show the foolishness of their beliefs, if even their youngest members are supposed to be the recipients of divine revelation. Reason, he argues, is alone the instrument through which the Holy Spirit ordinarily works, and his operations can be seen from the strength of the arguments that people give for their views. The more strongly reasoned is a person's belief, the more likely it is that the Holy Spirit has been at work within him or her. As Hooker observes, citing 2 Thessalonians 2: 11: '*It is not therefore the fervent earnestnes of their perswasion, but the soundnes of those reasons whereupon the same is built, which must declare their opinions in these things to have bene wrought by the holie Ghost, and not by the* fraud *of that evill Spirit which is even in his illusions strong.*'[203] An infernal origin is yet again implied for beliefs founded on the apparent direct inward manifestations of the Holy Spirit.

Although Hooker says no more at this point about the interpretation of Holy Scripture, he does make one further remark of considerable interest. It appears designed to illustrate the poor regard that the leaders of the presbyterian movement have for reason, but it does so in a most striking and acerbic manner.[204] Hooker complains that the presbyterians spend most of their labour attempting to convince women, which militates against them since women are '*commonlie*' weaker in their judgements than men (a conventional evaluation of women at this time). Referring to 2 Timothy 3: 6 ('For of this sorte are they which crepe into houses, and lead captive simple women laden with sinnes, and led by divers lustes'), Hooker then makes the following, somewhat contorted observations:

> *And although not* women loden with sinnes, *as the Apostle S. Paule speaketh, but (as we verelie esteeme of them for the most part) women propense and inclinable to holines be otherwise edified in good things, rather then carried away as captives into any kinde of sinne and evill by such as enter into their houses, with purpose to plant there a zeale and a love towards this kind of discipline: yet some occasion is hereby ministred for men to thinke, that if the cause which is thus furthered did gaine by the soundnes of proofe, whereupon it doth build it selfe, it would not most busilie endevor to prevaile where least habilitie of judgement is.*[205]

[202] See p. 221.

[203] *Lawes*, 1:18.4–8 (Pref.3.10).

[204] See ibid. 1:18.32–19.22 (Pref.3.13).

[205] See ibid. 1:19.1–10 (Pref.3.13).

I would agree with Haugaard at this point that Hooker's interpretation of 2 Timothy 3: 6 is in line with Chrysostom, rather than Calvin, seeing in these sinful women specifically sexual desires.[206] Haugaard does not explain his reasons for this interpretation, but his rationale seems evident from Hooker's ensuing remarks about the presbyterian women. Hooker raises the text from 2 Timothy, but then emphasizes that these presbyterian women will not behave in this sinful way. Yet by subsequently describing what these women will not do, he can only insinuate that some of them will indeed behave in this manner. The word '*plant*' seems central to Hooker's meaning. Its sexual implications seem clear enough with regard to the intentions of the ministers who enter these women's houses, especially given the existence of a tradition of reading 2 Timothy 3: 6 in a sexual sense. Perhaps there is even a suggestion, however faint, that the spirit planted during such encounters may be seminal in origin. This would certainly demonstrate Hooker's stern suspicion of the operations of the Spirit aside from the human reason. It would also display an image of Hooker very different from the mild and sober cleric of Walton's *Life*.

Although Hooker moves away from the question of scriptural interpretation after these remarks, he does return to it once more in the preface in ch. 8, during his discussion of Anabaptism.[207] W. D. J. Cargill Thompson has described this chapter as a final smear against the presbyterians, in which Hooker resurrects the sixteenth-century bogey of Anabaptism to illustrate the dangers of private judgements being left unrestrained.[208] There is much justice in this assessment, since Hooker effectively compares by association the peaceful presbyterians with the radical fringe-group of Anabaptists responsible for the violent events in Münster in 1534–5. Looking beyond this, however, it is possible to see a certain logic in Hooker's analysis, even if he extends it further than is warranted. The Anabaptists, as Hooker observes, emphasize

[206] See William P. Haugaard, 'Commentary: The Preface', *Folger*, vi. 429.

[207] See in particular *Lawes*, 1:44.7–45.11 (Pref.8.7).

[208] See W. D. J. Cargill Thompson, 'The Philosopher of the "Politic Society": Richard Hooker as a Political Thinker', *Studies in Richard Hooker: Essays Preliminary to an Edition of his Work*, ed. W. S. Hill (Cleveland, 1972), 15. This argument is enhanced by the fact that ch. 8 appears to be a last-minute addition, the result of suggestions for revision made by George Cranmer to enhance the polemical strength of the *Lawes* against the presbyterians. See Haugaard, 'Introduction: The Preface', *Folger*, vi. 40, 46, 50.

the importance of direct inward manifestations of the Spirit, especially as regards scriptural interpretation. Cartwright's critique of Anabaptist belief, based on the supposition that those who believe they have an 'extraordinary' calling ignore Holy Scripture in their emphasis upon the Spirit, does not apply in this case. Hooker has chosen an example of supposed Anabaptist practice that is designed to have a direct parallel with the behaviour he observes amongst the presbyterians. If Hooker is correct in arguing that both groups interpret scripture by this same method, then whatever the divergences, there is a considerable substantive similarity between them here.

The Anabaptists, according to Hooker, place less emphasis upon the saving power of preaching than do the presbyterians. Both parties are alike, however, in believing that Holy Scripture can be properly understood only by the aid of the Spirit. As Hooker observes, speaking of the Anabaptists:

> *the truth was, that when the word is said to engender faith in the hart, and to convert the soule of man, or to worke any such spirituall divine effect, these speeches are not therunto appliable as it is read or preached, but as it is ingrafted in us by the power of the holy Ghost opening the eies of our understanding, and so revealing the mysteries of God.*[209]

It might be objected at this point that Hooker says no less, regarding the work of the Holy Spirit in the human reason. He makes clear, however, that he is referring to supposed direct inward manifestations of the Spirit, when he complains about the vivid imaginations of the Anabaptists: '*When they and their Bibles were alone together, what strange phantasticall opinion soever at any time entred into their heads, their use was to thinke the Spirit taught it them.*'[210] Hooker cites his source, Guy de Brès, on how this led to an enormous variety of theological opinions: '*so that scarcely was there found any one of them, the forge of whose brayne was not possest with some speciall mysterie*'.[211] The point here is not that this is an equally suitable description of the presbyterian movement: the respect amongst its members for authority in itself guaranteed that this was not the case. Hooker is rather warning of the dangers latent in such a method of

[209] *Lawes*, 1:44.10–15 (Pref.8.7).
[210] See ibid. 1:44.24–6 (Pref.8.7).
[211] See ibid. 1:45.3–5 (Pref.8.7).

scriptural interpretation, which he sees as encouraging people to place a divine seal upon the products of their imagination. Only an approach that emphasizes the primacy of reason could, in his opinion, overcome this tendency to individual self-expression. From this attitude to reason one can see how Hooker could legitimately identify the presbyterians at least in part with the Anabaptists.

In *A Confutation of the Rhemists Translation* Cartwright can quite plainly be seen espousing the view that the Holy Spirit inwardly guides people in the interpretation of Holy Scripture, and that this principally occurs directly, without the use of reason as the Spirit's instrument. As he observes: 'for that the understanding of the Scriptures dependeth not principally of the sharpnes of mens wits or of their learning, but of the spirit of God which is given to the simple that humbly seek for it by prayer'.[212] The fact that Hooker's net was cast much wider than Cartwright and the English presbyterians can, however, be seen again by looking at the much fuller discussion of this matter to be found in Calvin's work. Forstman, in his book *Word and Spirit: Calvin's Doctrine of Biblical Authority*, cites a string of references from Calvin's biblical commentaries to illustrate Calvin's views, on a subject where he has again been taken as a classical exponent of the Reformed position on the relation between the Holy Spirit and Holy Scripture. Of these references by Forstman, the commentaries on 1 Corinthians 2: 14 and Acts 17: 11 provide perhaps the best examples:

> the Spirit of God, from whom the teaching of the Gospel comes, is the only true interpreter for opening it up to us.[213]

> For Scripture is the true touchstone by which all doctrines must be tested. If anyone objects that this kind of examination will be ambiguous, since Scripture is often obscure, and twisted to yield different meanings, I say that we must at the same time bring in the judgment of the Spirit, who is not called the Spirit of discernment without good reason. But with the

[212] Cartwright, *A Confutation of the Rhemists Translation*, 685. See also 144, 466–7.

[213] *Calvin's Commentaries. The First Epistle of Paul The Apostle to the Corinthians*, ed. D. W. Torrance and T. F. Torrance, trans. J. W. Fraser (Edinburgh, 1960) (*OC* 49:344), 62: Hoc est spiritus Dei, a quo procedit evangelii doctrina, solus est verus eius interpres, qui eam nobis patefaciat.

Spirit as leader and director, believers will form a judgment about any doctrine at all from no other source than the Scriptures.[214]

Neither of these passages can be interpreted in a manner conducive to Hooker, which is anathema to Calvin. The human reason is, in Calvin's opinion, wholly incapable of acting as a mediating force between the Word and the believer, due to its innate corruption. Only the Spirit acting alone can offer him the degree of certainty he looked for in the interpretation of Holy Scripture.[215] For Hooker, this view is intrinsically dangerous, and puts Calvin together with Cartwright, and other Reformed theologians of this opinion, in the same camp as the Anabaptists as regards their fundamental principles of scriptural interpretation. This is not to say that Hooker failed to distinguish between fanatics such as Copinger and theologians of a far more orthodox complexion. It is rather to say that Hooker believed that he had identified principles that were common to both, and that were innately conducive to a false understanding of theological questions. Whether these principles manifested themselves, for instance, in a presbyterian exegesis of the Bible concerning Church discipline, or in the type of fanaticism seen in Copinger and some of the militant Anabaptists, was for Hooker only a difference in degree, rather than in kind.

Before continuing, it is worth making some general remarks about the two examples discussed so far concerning the manifestations of the Holy Spirit. By making reason the prime instrument of the Holy Spirit, Hooker creates a kind of barrier, or filter, between the Spirit and the believer. This is most clearly seen in his statement that the work of the Spirit should be discerned from 'the qualitie of things beleeved or done', as opposed to basing one's beliefs upon the supposed direct work of the Spirit. The believer is inevitably distanced from the Spirit in this process, no longer expecting to detect his operations in moments of intense

[214] *Calvin's Commentaries: The Acts of The Apostles*, ed. D. W. Torrance and T. F. Torrance, trans. J. W. Fraser (Edinburgh, 1966) (*OC* 48:400–1), 101: Scriptura enim vere lydius est lapis, ad quem examinandae sunt omnes doctrinae. Si quis excipiat, hoc genus examinis fore ambiguum, quum saepe obscura sit scriptura et in varios sensus flectatur: dico simul adhibendum esse iudicium spiritus, qui non abs re vocatur spiritus discretionis. Caeterum duce ac directore spiritu, non aliunde quam ex scripturis iudicium facient fideles de qualibet doctrina. See Forstman, *Word and Spirit*, 77–85; Hendry, *The Holy Spirit in Christian Theology*, 72–8; Presbyterian Church (USA), 'The Nature of Revelation in the Christian Tradition from a Reformed Perspective', in D. K. McKim (ed.), *Major Themes in the Reformed Tradition* (Grand Rapids, Mich., 1992), 47–9.

[215] See Forstman, *Word and Spirit*, 83–5.

feeling or emotion. This emphatically does not mean that Hooker disregarded the Holy Spirit, or felt no personal relationship with him: the Spirit guaranteed for him the veracity of sound reasoning in the Church, as well as providing the graces he meditates upon so deeply in parts of Books 5 and 6 of the *Lawes*, and in the *Dublin Fragments*. Yet the logic of his position would seem to militate against the degree of intense closeness supposed in Calvin's work, and in the work of many other Reformed writers. If this does not always seem to describe the reality of Hooker's beliefs, then this may possibly be ascribed to certain inconsistencies upon his part; a matter that will be dealt with later in this chapter. Yet one can appreciate the immense benefits that this stance gave to Hooker's theology as a whole. From a polemical perspective, it was clearly to his advantage if his dialogue with the presbyterian movement (and indeed with Reformed theology more generally) took place on the ground of his own choosing. As such, he needed to persuade his opponents to cease appealing directly for their views to the Holy Spirit, and to engage with him on purely rational grounds. If Hooker could win this debate, they would logically be compelled to agree with him, having no higher source of authority for their beliefs. As Hill has argued, it was thus in certain respects to Hooker's advantage to minimize the role of grace and the Holy Spirit in the *Lawes*, and to concentrate on rational argumentation.[216] This is precisely what his theory of reason and the Spirit achieves, placing rational debate in the foreground, and leaving the 'victor' of this debate to conclude that his arguments had been shaped by the Spirit. Whether Hooker adopted this theological stance purely as a result of his polemical encounter with the presbyterians, or as a result of other factors, is perhaps impossible to know, although a combination of factors would not seem unlikely. His polemical context might well have persuaded him of the value of amplifying previously held views. This stance is, though, a striking feature of the *Lawes*, and perhaps accounts for some of the problems with grace in that work. It was seemingly to his benefit to limit his references to the Holy Spirit, and this may have resulted in some of the ambiguities that have caused so much critical debate.

[216] See Hill, 'The Doctrinal Background of Richard Hooker's *Laws of Ecclesiastical Polity*', 199–201.

The way in which the Holy Spirit is so often thrust into the background in Hooker's theology can be illustrated quite usefully by looking briefly at one additional case of the manifestations of the Holy Spirit, prior to the more detailed study of the third example of this subject, concerning knowledge of election. The case in question concerns preaching, and Cartwright's opinion that the Holy Spirit will only 'ordinarily' ensure that Holy Scripture is efficacious for salvation when it is preached, as opposed to being read.[217] It is noteworthy that this view was also held by Calvin, yet again suggesting that the Frenchman and Reformed theologians sharing his opinions were a principal target of the *Lawes*.[218] One of Hooker's prime objections to this position springs from the belief that the Holy Spirit will never subvert the natural order, rendering one lawful Church practice ineffectual, while favouring another. The Spirit, in his opinion, will always aid the Church in all its lawful pursuits, according to their intrinsic nature. As he observes, in Book 5 of the *Lawes*:

> as we know that God doth aide with his grace, and by his speciall providence evermore blesse with happie successe those thinges which him selfe appointeth, so his Church we perswade our selves he hath not in such sorte given over to a reprobate sense, that whatsoever it deviseth for the good of the soules of men, the same he doth still accurse and make frustrate.[219]

This is very significant, as it means that Hooker can ignore the operations of the Holy Spirit in assessing the relative merits of preaching and reading. He observes that sermons, for instance, have the advantage of being able to deal with current affairs, and that a preacher may use inflection and gesture to influence his audience: homilies and lessons, he notes, have their own particular benefits.[220] Both are assessed by Hooker on empirical grounds, since he believes that the Spirit aids them equally. This inevitably places less emphasis upon the work of the Spirit than the views of Calvin and Cartwright, who argue that particular activities such as

[217] See *Replye*, 159–60; *Second Replie*, 374–5, 378, 380–1, 383–4, 396; *Christian Religion*, 172.

[218] See *Inst.* IV.i.5–6; Niesel, *The Theology of Calvin*, 213; Forstman, *Word and Spirit*, 78. One may also make the subsidiary point that Calvin and Cartwright were both agreed, *contra* Hooker, that the sacraments are only efficacious when a sermon is preached to the congregation. See *Lawes*, 2:288.22–289.4 (V.62.22); Lake, *Anglicans and Puritans?*, 176; *Inst.* IV.xiv.4–5; Niesel, *The Theology of Calvin*, 212–13, 216; Cartwright, *The Second Replie*, 364.

[219] See *Lawes*, 2:101.7–102.19 (V.22.13). More generally, see 2:87.18–110.5 (V.22).

[220] See ibid. 2:100.18–101.2 (V.22.12).

preaching manifest his operations far more clearly than others—this might even impinge itself upon the consciousness of the preacher and congregation, as regards the special status of sermons. As has been declared above, this emphatically does not mean that Hooker ignored the Spirit in his theology: a preacher, in his view, might well reflect that the Spirit had aided him in the scripting and preaching of a sermon. Yet the work of the Spirit is of less immediate importance in Hooker's theology than it is in that of Calvin and Cartwright, emphasis rather being placed on reason, and observable phenomena. As Hooker remarks, concerning the difference between reading and preaching, one should examine the 'substance of matter, evidence of thinges, strength and validitie of argumentes and proofes... [and] anie other vertue els which wordes and sentences maie conteine'.[221] Only in his discussions of election does Hooker sometimes relax this emphasis upon reason in relation to the Spirit and adopt a more Reformed perspective, and it is to this subject that one may finally turn now.

The final example regarding the operations of the Holy Spirit, and how they can be detected by individual Christians, concerns whether a person can know that he or she is elect, and will with certainty avoid damnation. Hooker again deals with this subject in the preface to the *Lawes*, in his condemnation of the practices of the '*common sort*' amongst the presbyterian movement. His remarks seem perfectly in keeping with his general argument, that the Holy Spirit only ever ordinarily manifests himself through the human reason:

> *After that the phancie of the common sort hath once throughlie apprehended the Spirit to be author of their perswasion concerning discipline, then is instilled into their hearts, that the same Spirit leading men into this opinion, doth thereby seale them to be Gods children, and that as the state of the times now standeth, the most speciall token to know them that are Gods owne from others, is an earnest affection that waie.*[222]

The '*phancie*', or imagination of these people presumably leads them to believe that the Spirit is working within them, indicating to them that they are amongst the elect. This process is clearly, in Hooker's eyes, divorced from reason, the product of an erring '*affection*' for God. Thus one might conclude that, in Hooker's opinion, no one can truly know that they are elect, unless the Holy Spirit can somehow work purely through the human reason to convince them of this fact.

[221] See ibid. 2:107.14–108.12 (V.22.19).
[222] Ibid. 1:18.8–14 (Pref.3.11).

What is so interesting about this condemnation of presbyterian 'practice' is that it does not necessarily tally with Hooker's own approach to the subject of election. This is certainly true of two of Hooker's earliest surviving works, *The First Sermon Upon Part of S. Judes Epistle* and his Latin letter to John Rainolds, both written well before the publication of the *Lawes*. John Keble has argued, though, that by the time of the tractate *A Learned and Comfortable Sermon of the Certaintie and Perpetuitie of Faith in the Elect*, Hooker had taken up his mature stance on this issue, denying that humans can be infallibly sure of their election in this life.[223] The problem with this argument is that although Keble's evidence is strong, and can be supported by other passages from the *Lawes* and the *Dublin Fragments*, there are also grounds for believing that Hooker may not entirely have changed his mind. Hooker's early approach to knowledge of election, which, as will be shown, was thoroughly Reformed in its nature, may have proved more enduring than has previously been thought, despite the contradictions this led him into as regards the operations of the Holy Spirit.

One may start with what is probably Hooker's earliest extant work, *The First Sermon Upon Part of S. Judes Epistle*, where Hooker expresses his views with penetrating clarity:

> It behoveth you therefore greatly every man to examine his owne estate, and to try whether you be bond or free, children or no children... Judge thy selfe. God hath left us infallible evidence, whereby we may at any time give true and righteous sentence upon our selves. We cannot examine the harts of other men, we may our owne... *I trust, beloved, wee knowe that wee are not reprobates*, because the spirit doth bear us record, that the faith of our Lord Jesus Christ is in us.
>
> 14. It is as easie a matter for the spirit within you to tell whose yee are, as for the eies of your body to judge where you sit, or in what place you stand ... If wee can make this account with our selves; I was *in times past dead in trespasses and sinnes, I walked after the prince that ruleth in the aire, and after the spirit that worketh in the children of disobedience; but God, who is rich in mercy, through his great love, wherewith he loved me, even when I was dead hath quickned me in Christ.* I was fierce, heady, proud, high minded; but God hath made me like the child that is newly wained... Surely if the spirit have been thus effectuall in the secret worke of our regeneration unto newnesse of life; if wee endeavour thus to frame our selves anew, then we may say boldly with the blessed Apostle in the 10. to the *Hebrewes, We are not of them which withdraw our selves to perdition, but which follow faith to the conservation of the soule.*[224]

[223] See Keble, 'Editor's Preface', i. pp. lv–lvi.

[224] See *Jude 1*, 5:28.1–30.9. See also *Jude 2*, 5:56.4–6; Keble, 'Editor's Preface', i. pp. lv–lvi; Neelands, 'The Theology of Grace of Richard Hooker', 31, 185–204.

The Spirit works to convince people that they are elect, beyond any possible doubt. The way It does so, according to Hooker, is not through any process of direct sensory awareness, or even through intense emotions. Rather, we are asked to examine our behaviour, to see whether the Spirit has been at work inside us. Those who have behaved virtuously, and evince a true faith in Christ, demonstrably have the Spirit, and are therefore elect. Such thinking is definitely at odds with the passage quoted earlier from the preface to the *Lawes*. Whether the '*common sort*' of presbyterians to whom Hooker there refers supposedly examined their behaviour, or felt strong emotions inclining them to believe that they were elect, is immaterial. As will be shown with regard to William Perkins, these two different methods are perfectly compatible with one another. What matters, as regards the passage on *Jude*, is that the work of the Spirit is not here found by a posterior analysis of the activities of the reason, but in some other way. Hooker does not ask believers to consider the soundness of their reasoning, and thereby to deduce the operations of the Holy Spirit, but rather to look at whether they have behaved in a virtuous manner. Of course the reason is involved in analysing past behaviour, but the same might be said regarding intense emotions or feelings: to detect the work of the Spirit in anything other than the reason is, according to Hooker's previously stated principles, to risk defective belief-formation. This places Hooker's opinions, as expressed in this early sermon, in substantively the same category as those of the presbyterians he condemns in the *Lawes*.

Hooker also raises the question of election in his early Latin letter to the famous Reformed theologian John Rainolds. Rainolds was Hooker's tutor at Corpus Christi College, Oxford, and the two men seem to have remained friends. This passage is taken from Craig R. Thompson's translation, in the *Folger* edition: 'I could enlarge on this topic and confirm by God's holy Word that greater steadfastness in afflictions than is ever seen at other times gives proofs of our election in Christ Jesus, more exalted exercises of faith and righteousness, more numerous effects of the Spirit's active power.'[225] Hooker again argues that certain forms of behaviour manifest the work of the Spirit, and give positive proof of election. His basic position here is, therefore, exactly the same as that in *The First Sermon Upon Part of S. Judes Epistle*.

[225] *LL* 5:424.28–31; 5:431.1–4: Addere hoc loco possem, idque e sacro dei verbo confirmare, firmiora in afflictionibus quam usquam alias conspici electionis nostrae in Christo Jesu argumenta; praestantiora fidei et pietatis exercitia; plura spiritus potenter operantis effecta.

Hooker's approach to this subject in the tractate *A Learned and Comfortable Sermon of the Certaintie and Perpetuitie of Faith in the Elect* is far more traditionally scholastic. He makes a triple distinction between intrinsic certainty, certainty of evidence, and certainty of adherence, which by implication denies that people can infallibly know of their election in this life. The first two types of certainty have been discussed in Ch. 2, but the relevant passage is worth quoting again at length in order now to analyse what he understands by certainty of adherence:

> Certainty of evidence wee call that, when the mind doth assent unto this or that; not because it is true in it selfe, but because the truth therof is cleere, because it is manifest unto us. Of thinges in them selves most certain, except they be also most evident, our persuasion is not so assured as it is of thinges more evident although in themselves they be lesse certayn. It is as sure if not surer that there be sprites as that there be men: but wee are more assured of these then of them because these are more evident... The other which wee call the certaintie of adherence is when the hart doth cleave and stick unto that which it doth beleeve. This certaintie is greater in us then the other. The reason is this: the fayth of a christian man doth apprehend the wordes of the law, the promisses of god, not only as true but also as good, and therefore even then when the evidence which he hath of the trueth is so small that it greaveth him to feele his weaknes in assenting thereunto, yeat is there in him such a sure adharence unto that which he doth but faintly and fearfully beleeve that his spirit *having once truly tasted the heavenly sweetnes* thereof all the world is not able quite and cleane to remove him from it.[226]

It will be recalled that Hooker is in part distinguishing here between metaphysical intrinsic certainty, whereby the existence of spirits may be said to be more certain than that of human beings,

[226] *Cert.* 5:70.1–71.10. See also *Answer*, 5:236.20–237.7; Neelands, 'The Theology of Grace of Richard Hooker', 185–204; Grislis, 'The Assurance of Faith According to Richard Hooker', 244. Shuger makes much of the fact that Hooker speaks about the 'hart', rather than the 'will', cleaving to God, arguing that it is evidence of a 'traditional mystic epistemology'. This usage does give a certain emotive force to the argument, making it somewhat less abstract than it might otherwise be; something not inappropriate in a tractate based upon Hooker's original sermons. Yet as has been noted earlier in this chapter, the scholastic foundation of the argument is quite apparent, and 'hart' would appear to be synonymous with 'will' as regards the explanation that Hooker gives for a believer's adherence to faith. Hooker's theory of habits and the theological virtues has been too well documented for one to consider that he disregards it at this point. See Shuger, *Habits of Thought in the English Renaissance*, 43–4. See also Bouwsma, 'Hooker in the Context of European Cultural History', 48. For another example of 'hart' being used as an emotive synonym for 'will', see pp. 70–1.

and evidential certainty or proof-worthiness, whereby the existence of humans is to us more certain than that of spirits.[227] He then goes on to observe that the certainty of faith is different from both of these other types of certainty, and he employs a common scholastic distinction which can be found, for instance, in Aquinas's *Summa Theologiae.* As Aquinas observes, regarding different degrees of knowledge:

> Other mental acts are marked by a pondering that is inconclusive, lacking firm assent, either because the act leans towards neither of the alternatives—the case with doubt; or because it leans to one alternative, but only tentatively—the case with suspicion; or because it decides for the one side but with fear of the opposite—the case with opinion. The act of believing, however, is firmly attached to one alternative and in this respect the believer is in the same state of mind as one who has science or understanding. Yet the believer's knowledge is not completed by a clear vision, and in this respect he is like one having a doubt, a suspicion, or an opinion.[228]

Aquinas argues here that the nature of faith is twofold. In one respect it partakes of the certainty of science (*scientia*), which is knowledge attained by demonstrative reasoning from first principles. Both are completely certain, in that a person gives wholehearted assent to the veracity of the knowledge concerned. Yet despite this wholehearted assent faith is still prone to doubt, and so is similar to the less perfect types of knowledge that Aquinas enumerates. Hooker's point would appear to be identical. Faith assents to Christian doctrine as wholly true, and yet because it presupposes the lack of complete evidential certainty from first principles, it will always do so in an imperfect, and in at times a weak and faltering manner.

Underlying this theory of certainty is Hooker's scholastic conception of faith, which has been examined earlier in this chapter.[229] The will desires God as something perfectly good, and persuades

[227] See pp. 74–5.

[228] *ST* II-II.2.1: Quidam vero actus intellectus habent quidem cogitationem informem absque firma assensione, sive in neutram partem declinent, sicut accidit dubitanti; sive in unam partem magis declinent sed tenentur aliquo levi signo, sicut accidit suspicanti; sive uni parti adhaereant, tamen cum formidine alterius, quod accidit opinanti. Sed actus iste qui est credere habet firmam adhaesionem ad unam partem, in quo convenit credens cum sciente et intelligente; et tamen ejus cognitio non est perfecta per maniestam visionem, in quo convenit cum dubitante, suspicante et opinante.

[229] See pp. 197–9.

the reason to assent to Christian doctrine: the will is moved to desire by the habit of love, and the reason to assent by the habit of faith. Clearly Hooker believes that this intellectual act of assent (or apprehension as he sometimes mistakenly calls it) is imperfect, since the evidence is not here sufficiently forceful to compel assent, as in the case of an argument that a person perceives to be logically deduced from first principles. This must mean that it is the habit of love, inherent in the will, that ensures the 'certaintie of adherence'. Where Hooker departs from Aquinas, and many other medieval scholastic theologians, is in arguing that this 'certainty of adherence' is such that it ensures that faith is perpetual in those who possess it. Any person who has once experienced true faith, he observes, will never entirely lose it, which is an assertion of the perseverance of saints amongst the justified. The implications of this passage for Hooker's views on election should, though, now be clear. If faith is defined by the fact that it is a form of imperfect knowledge, not based on complete evidential certainty, then it is hard to see here how the evidence for election, from a person's study of his or her own behaviour, can be sufficiently demonstrative as to result in an infallible proof. As Aquinas, for instance, observes, humans can know of their election conjecturally, through signs, but such knowledge cannot be certain.[230] Hooker thus appears to reject by implication, in this tractate, his earlier view that Christians can know with certainty of their election.

Such a rejection can also be seen in several passages in the *Lawes* and the *Dublin Fragments*. His remarks in the preface to the *Lawes* on knowledge of election and the presbyterians have already been quoted, where he condemns them for their emphasis upon direct inward manifestations of the Spirit. He also mentions election, in a discussion on the necessity of outward baptism for salvation, in Book 5 of the *Lawes*. Here he is anxious to show that even the elect require baptism if they are to be saved, since God has decreed that this be so:

> So that by sacramentes and other sensible tokens of grace wee may boldly gather that he, whose mercie vouchafeth now to bestowe the meanes, hath also longe sithence intended us that whereunto they leade... In which respect wee justlie hold it [baptism] to be the doore of our actuall enterance into Gods howse, the first apparent beginninge of life, a seale

[230] See *ST* I-II.112.5.

perhapes to the grace of *election* before received, but to our sanctification heere a step that hath not anie before it.[231]

Hooker's wording here is cautious, and he goes no further than Aquinas in allowing that knowledge of election can be gathered from visible signs. Baptism is only 'perhapes' a sign of this grace, from which one can 'boldly gather', but not actually prove. This is far from his statement in *The First Sermon Upon Part Of S. Judes Epistle* that Christians have 'infallible evidence' in this matter. Such reservation can further be seen in the *Dublin Fragments*, where Hooker gives his own version of the *Lambeth Articles*. As Neelands, Shuger, and White all observe, Hooker completely omits Article 6 on the assurance of faith, which argues that justified Christians can be certain (*certus*) of their eternal salvation.[232]

The one passage that questions the notion that, from the time of *A Learned and Comfortable Sermon of the Certaintie and Perpetuitie of Faith in the Elect* onwards, Hooker wholly rejected his early position on knowledge of election, is to be found in Book 5 of the *Lawes*, in his consideration of Holy Communion:

> Whereas therefore in oure infancie we ar incorporated into Christ, and by baptisme receyve the grace of his sprite without any sense or feelinge of the guift whiche God bestowethe, in the Eucharist, we so receyve the guifte of God, that wee knowe by grace what the grace is which God givethe us, the degrees of oure owne increase in holines and vertue wee see and can judge of them, wee understande that the strengthe of oure life begun in Christe is Christe, that his fleshe is meate, and his blood drinke, not by surmised imagination but trulye, even so trulie that throughe faithe wee perceive in the bodie and bloode sacramentallye presented the verye taste of eternall life, the grace of the sacramente is heere as the foode which wee eate and drinke.[233]

The argument in this passage is perhaps rather unclear, and requires careful interpretation. Much of the problem stems from Hooker's use of the words 'sense' and 'feelinge' with regard to baptism, which might be taken as meaning that grace/the Spirit can actually be felt in the reception of the elements. This would certainly be a most unusual admission on Hooker's part, since on

[231] *Lawes*, 2:256.10–26 (V.60.3).

[232] See *DF* 4:167.1–12; Neelands, 'The Theology of Grace of Richard Hooker', 201; Shuger, *Habits of Thought in the English Renaissance*, 79; White, *Predestination, Policy and Polemic*, 137.

[233] *Lawes*, 2:331.5–16 (V.67.1).

no other occasion, except with regard to miracles, does he accept that the operations of the Spirit can be sensed tangibly. Yet Hooker's remarks on Holy Communion are most probably concerned with the process of rational understanding, rather than sensory perception. As he observes, we 'knowe' about the grace that God gives to us, and 'understande' that his flesh and body are the food of eternal life. Likewise, in the final lines, do we 'perceive', presumably through a similar process of rational understanding, that grace is present in Holy Communion. To interpret 'perceive' as referring to sensory perception would be to alter this emphasis upon understanding, and to produce a reading of Hooker widely at variance from anything else in his work.

Hooker thus argues in this passage that those who receive grace in Holy Communion are able to understand that they have done so, through the aid of this grace within them. They are then, as a result of this, presumably able to conclude that they are elect, metaphorically tasting 'eternall life' in the elements of bread and wine. Furthermore, Hooker indicates that 'holines and vertue' are themselves 'sensible tokens of grace', since by their increase people can know that the Spirit works within them, and presumably, therefore, that they are elect. This process is not simply one in which a person conjectures on the basis of the evidence; knowledge of grace and election is not gained through 'surmised imagination', but is real. In precisely the same manner, then, as in *The First Sermon Upon Part of S. Judes Epistle* and the Latin letter to Rainolds, albeit with somewhat less clarity, Hooker here observes that virtuous behaviour manifests the operations of the Holy Spirit. Similarly, the action of partaking in Holy Communion becomes a sign to the sanctified that the Spirit is working within them. Thus although Hooker's theology underwent considerable changes between his earliest writings and the *Lawes*, and despite the fact that he had already implicitly rejected the notion that infallible knowledge of election is possible, he still implicitly argues in this passage that there is a recognizable link for the individual between the Holy Spirit and certain types of human behaviour. He does this, moreover, even though by the time of his writing the *Lawes* he had adopted the general position that the Spirit only 'ordinarily' manifests himself in the operations of the human reason. This results in the contradiction that he can berate the presbyterians in the preface for believing that the Spirit will inform them that they are elect, and yet can imply in the fifth book that, by examining our actions, we can know that the Spirit works within us, and that the Spirit can, therefore, presumably inform us that we are elect.

As has been observed earlier, Hooker's general position in the *Lawes* regarding reason and the Spirit was highly effective in his critique of the presbyterians, and through them of views characteristic of Reformed theology more generally. He criticizes them for supposedly identifying the impulses of their inferior sensitive powers with the motions of the Spirit, and for falling as a result of this into error. By adopting this position, as has been argued, he moved away from the characteristically Reformed position regarding the perception of the Holy Spirit. Yet he continued to uphold the view, at least in this one powerfully emotive passage, that certain actions manifest the operations of the Spirit; an idea which was, as will now be illustrated, typical of the thinking of many Reformed writers in this period.[234] Why he should have done this is, of course, a matter of conjecture. It is possible, though, that the notion of the elect being sure of their salvation was of great importance to him, and that he was reluctant to dispense with the notion. Thus even when his theology of reason, faith, and the Holy Spirit, as well as the polemic of the *Lawes*, demanded a rejection of the idea, it still lingered on in his thought, especially as regards the personal communion with God that he found in Holy Communion.

Although Calvin has served as an excellent example for many of the Reformed positions that have been examined so far in this book, he is not representative of the Reformed view on knowledge of election to be found in the Latin Letter, *The First Sermon Upon Part of S. Judes Epistle*, and the passage in the *Lawes* on Holy Communion. Human beings were, in Calvin's eyes, too sinful for their behaviour ever to be an adequate sign of election, no matter how virtuous or holy they might be. He rather points people to Holy Scripture, and to the crucifixion of Jesus Christ, which he considers enough, through the inward testimony of the Spirit, to assure them that they are saved.[235] Many later Reformed writers,

[234] See Kendall, *Calvin and English Calvinism to 1649*, 29–66.

[235] See Niesel, *The Theology of Calvin*, 164–5, 170–80; Wendel, *Calvin: The Origins and Development of his Religious Thought*, 244–5, 266, 274–7; Dowey, *The Knowledge of God in Calvin's Theology*, 187–8; Kendall, *Calvin and English Calvinism to 1649*, 13–28. One possible point of common ground between Hooker and Calvin is Calvin's idea that, to the sanctified, participation in Holy Communion can act as a sign of election. See Niesel, *The Theology of Calvin*, 180.

however, including self-professed followers of Calvin, took a different approach to this matter, though not necessarily realizing that they differed from Calvin here.[236] William Perkins is one of the classic exemplars of such writers, and as he gives a far clearer treatment of the topic than Cartwright, will be used to illustrate the doctrine that Hooker sometimes adopts, and sometimes strongly opposes, in his various works.[237] The treatise of Perkins that contains his most systematic account of this subject is *A Golden Chaine*. The relevant chapter is the fifty-seventh, where he observes that there are 'especially two' methods by which a person can discern his or her election: 'The testimonie of Gods Spirite, and the workes of Sanctification'.[238] It is fascinating to find both methods discussed here side by side. Hooker in the preface to the *Lawes* vehemently rejects the former method, in his condemnation of the '*common sort*' amongst the presbyterians whose '*earnest affection*' informs them that they are saved. Yet in the passage in the *Lawes* on Holy Communion Hooker does indeed appear to accept implicitly that reflection on the works of sanctification can, through grace, lead a person to have knowledge of his or her personal election. As Perkins comments, on the second method of knowledge, through reflection on 'the workes of Sanctification':

If the testimonie of Gods Spirit, be not so powerful in the elect, then may they iudge of their election, by that other effect of the holy Ghost: namely, sanctification: like as we use to iudge by heat that there is fire, when we cannot see the flame it selfe... And of all the effects of sanctification, these are most notable... To strive against the flesh, that is, to resist, & hate the ungodly motions thereof, & with griefe to thinke them burthenous & troublesome... To cal upon God earnestly, & with teares... To flie al occasions of sin, and seriously to endevour to come to newnes of life... Now, if so be al the effects of the spirit are very feeble in the godly, they must know this, that God trieth them, yet so, as they must not therewith be dismayed, because it is most sure, that if they have faith, but as much as a grane of mustard seed, and as weake as a young infant is, it is sufficient to ingraffe them into Christ, & therefore we must not doubt

236 On the Reformed doctrine of assurance, see *The Second Helvitic Confession*, ch. 10, in *Reformed Confessions of the 16th Century*, 241–2; *The Westminster Confession of Faith*, 18.1–2, in *Documents of the English Reformation*, 500.

237 See, though, Cartwright, *A Confutation of the Rhemists Translation*, 352.

238 See William Perkins, *A Golden Chaine*, trans. [R. Hill] (London, 1591), ch. 57. See also ch. 36; William Perkins, *A Case of Conscience* (London, 1592), 16–17, 30; Kendall, *Calvin and English Calvinism to 1649*, 51–66.

of their election, because they see their faith feeble, & the effects of the holy Ghost faint within them.[239]

Holy and virtuous behaviour is taken to be a clear sign of the presence of the Holy Spirit, and the election of the individual concerned.[240] Thus although Perkins's appeal to the 'testimonie of Gods Spirite' would appear to place him in the same category as the Anabaptists and presbyterians of the preface to the *Lawes*, Hooker himself states something quite similar in Book 5 regarding knowledge of election and Christian behaviour. This reveals the complexity of Hooker's mature theological position, critical as it is of the Reformed understanding of how the operations of the Holy Spirit can be detected, even though Hooker had earlier held some of these views himself. It is not entirely surprising that traces of this earlier position should survive on into the *Lawes*, indicating the difficulty of the path that Hooker had taken in so many ways away from the Reformed tradition. He had strong theological and polemical reasons for denying that the Holy Spirit could be detected in anything other than a posterior analysis of the workings of the reason, but perhaps also strong personal reasons for wishing to find proof of election in holy and virtuous Christian behaviour. Having been brought up in the then predominant Reformed tradition in his youth, particularly under the tutelage of John Rainolds, Hooker evidently remained Reformed in various important respects throughout his life, despite his manifold and fundamental developments away from Reformed theology in his later years.

Religious Authority

From Ch. 2 onwards there has been an implicit theme running throughout much of this book: the nature of religious authority. It is probably fair to state that this is the one subject on which Hooker is still regularly cited, even by authors who have little or no familiarity with his writings. The traditional view is that Hooker articulated, and was possibly the originator of the idea that there exists a triple source of religious authority: scripture, reason, and tradition, in that order. On the vexed topic of

[239] Perkins, *A Golden Chaine*, ch. 57.

[240] For a discussion of the problem of temporary faith, with regard to knowledge of election in Perkins's work, see Kendall, *Calvin and English Calvinism to 1649*, 67–76.

Anglican identity numerous writers have seen this theory of authority as central to Anglican self-understanding, and naturally in this context one recalls Lake's observation in *Anglicans and Puritans?* that Hooker to some extent invented Anglicanism.[241] This is, therefore, a subject at the very heart of Hooker studies, not least because of its wider theological import. This traditional understanding of Hooker's conception of religious authority, stated with considerable clarity by Haugaard in the 1993 *Folger* commentary, has been subjected to repeated criticism in recent years, not least by Kirby and Atkinson.[242] With regard to reason, their argument is essentially that it is authoritative for Hooker in secular but not in religious affairs, and in this he basically followed the views of mainstream Protestant theologians such as Luther and Calvin. Similarly, with regard to tradition, Atkinson argues that Hooker joined mainstream Protestant theologians such as Calvin and Luther in valuing it as one source of authority as concerns *adiaphora*, such as church government, ceremonies, and orders. Yet as regards Christian doctrine, defined as those dogmas which must be believed in in order to attain salvation, both critics argue that Hooker considered that Holy Scripture is the sole authority. In this respect, they observe, Hooker embraced the Reformed, and more generally Protestant, concept of *sola scriptura*, even though he has been repeatedly misinterpreted on this matter since the time of the Oxford Movement.

Chapter 3 concluded with the observation that, contrary to the concept of *sola scriptura*, Hooker argues that reason is authoritatively able to inform *mere natural persons* how to glorify and obey God as humanity's Creator, and hence how to abstain from sin. After the consideration of Hooker's ideas on the operations of the Holy Spirit, which is the source of religious authority, it is now opportune to extend this examination, and look at Hooker's theory of religious authority as it pertains to divine law and knowledge unattainable by *mere natural reason*: in other words, as concerns Christian doctrines, beliefs, and practices. The groundwork for this discussion has been laid earlier in this chapter, and also in Ch. 2, and

[241] See Lake, *Anglicans and Puritans?*, 227.

[242] See Haugaard, 'Introduction: Books II, III & IV', *Folger*, vi. 161–9; Kirby, 'Richard Hooker as an Apologist of the Magisterial Reformation', 227, 230; Kirby, 'Richard Hooker's Theory of Natural Law in the Context of Reformation Theology', 702–3; Atkinson, *Richard Hooker and the Authority of Scripture, Tradition and Reason*, 30, 52, 60, 93, 108–9.

these threads may now be drawn together regarding the relationship between Holy Scripture and reason. It will also be necessary to look at one topic that has not been treated in detail so far: the religious authority of tradition. The aim will be to resolve the critical controversy over this subject, and to show that, in a carefully qualified sense, Hooker did indeed accept the religious authority of scripture, reason, and tradition, in that order, as has historically been claimed.

Kirby and Atkinson are wholly correct in arguing that Hooker thought that Holy Scripture is alone the source of the revealed knowledge that Christians must believe in order to be saved. Hooker is impeccably Protestant in his rejection of the Roman Catholic notion that Holy Scripture must be supplemented by Apostolic traditions in this regard. As Hooker, for instance, observes in Book 2 of the *Lawes*:

> And even hereby it commeth to passe, that first such as imagine the generall and maine drift of the body of sacred scripture not to bee so large as it is, nor that God did thereby intend to deliver, as in truth he doth, a full instruction in all things unto salvation necessary, the knowledge wherof man by nature could not otherwise in this life attaine unto: they are by this very meane induced, either still to looke for newe revelations from heaven, or els daungerously to ad to the word of God uncertaine tradition, that so the doctrine of mans salvation may be compleate; which doctrine we constantly holde in all respectes without any such thing added to be so compleate, that we utterly refuse as much as once to acquaint our selves with any thing further.[243]

As well as disallowing the authority of tradition concerning such 'necessary' revealed beliefs Hooker also, of course, here rejects the view that reason can discover such truths independently of Holy Scripture. This by itself, however, in no way constitutes a theory of *sola scriptura*, as it is far from denying the authority of reason as it relates to Holy Scripture. Earlier in this chapter it was shown how Hooker considers reason essential for both authenticating and interpreting Holy Scripture.[244] The authoritative guidance of the Holy Spirit comes in his opinion not directly, but through the use of reason as his instrument.[245] Further back, in Ch. 2, the philosophical basis for this position was examined. Doctrines necessary

[243] *Lawes*, 1:189.11–22 (II.8.5). See also *Just.* 5:119.12–26; *Lawes*, 1:123.3–18 (I.13.2); 1:129.3–130.4 (I.14.5); 1:147c (II.1.4); 1:191.14–20 (II.8.7).

[244] See pp. 226–41.

[245] See pp. 228–9, 233–4.

for salvation are defined for Hooker by the fact that they are either expressly stated in Holy Scripture, or can be deduced from Holy Scripture by demonstrative reasoning, rather than the mere probability that pertains to non-mandatory Christian beliefs and practices.[246] In an analogous manner, Holy Scripture is itself authenticated by demonstrative reasoning.[247] Moreover, since Holy Scripture is not self-authenticating, Hooker, while observing that it contains all revealed knowledge necessary for salvation, denies that it contains all knowledge that is necessary for salvation *in toto*:

> In like sort, albeit scripture do professe to conteyne in it all things which are necessarye unto salvation; yet the meaning cannot be simplye of all things that are necessarye, but all things that are necessarye in some certaine kinde or forme; as all things that are necessarye, and eyther could not at all, or could not easily be knowne by the light of naturall discourse; all things which are necessarye to be knowne that we may be saved, but knowne with presupposall of knowledge concerning certaine principles whereof it receaveth us already perswaded, and then instructeth us in all the residue that are necessarie. In the number of these principles one is the sacred authoritie of scripture.[248]

Atkinson would seem to have perceived the importance for his argument in severing the link between Holy Scripture and reason, since he argues (incorrectly, as has been shown) that Holy Scripture is self-authenticating for Hooker on the basis of the direct inward manifestation of the Holy Spirit.[249] It is because Hooker opposes the characteristically Reformed concept that the Holy Spirit works directly to authenticate and interpret Holy Scripture that he can argue for a theory of religious authority so contrary to the Reformed, and more generally Protestant, notion of *sola scriptura*. For Hooker, Holy Scripture and reason are both religious authorities as regards doctrines that are necessary for salvation.

This is not, however, to state that Hooker considered them of equal authority. Chapter 2 has examined Hooker's view that Holy Scripture is intrinsically more certain than demonstrative reasoning, and even than human sense data, as it reveals God's very Word. As he observes: 'the strongest proofe of all, and the

[246] See pp. 75–8.
[247] See pp. 226–7.
[248] *Lawes*, 1:125.32–126.10 (I.14.1).
[249] See p. 226.

most necessaryly assented unto by us (which do thus receive the scripture) is the scripture'.[250] Presumably its primacy as a source of authority also stems from the fact that it is the sole source of revealed doctrines necessary for salvation. Yet Holy Scripture is less evidentially certain than sense data for Hooker, as its revealed status cannot be intuitively known by human beings. On the basis of Hooker's maxim that 'We must be surer of the profe then of the thinge proved, otherwise it is no profe,'[251] Holy Scripture is for him at best only as evidentially certain as the demonstrative arguments to be made in its favour, and the same is true of the dogmas necessary for salvation that it contains. Even dogmas expressly mentioned in Holy Scripture rely indirectly on the demonstrative evidence that Holy Scripture is the Word of God. The authority of reason (backed of course, as has been shown, by divine grace) is thus essential if the authority of Holy Scripture is to be proved. Thus when Hooker argues for the primacy of Holy Scripture as a source of religious authority in matters necessary for salvation, he is far indeed from denying the authority of reason in this area as well. His theory of religious authority in such matters may thus not unjustly be summarized as Holy Scripture and reason, in that order. The importance of this binary pairing is more generally underlined by Hooker in this passage from Book I of the *Lawes*, and it may serve as a general illustration of his fundamental opposition to the concept of *sola scriptura*:

> There is in scripture therefore no defect, but that any man what place or calling soever hee holde in the Church of God, may have thereby the light of his naturall understanding so perfected, that the one being relieved by the other, there can want no part of needfull instruction unto any good worke which God himselfe requireth, be it naturall or supernaturall, belonging simplie unto men as men, or unto men as they are united in whatsoever kinde of societie. It sufficeth therefore that nature and scripture doe serve in such full sort, that they both joyntly and not severallye eyther of them be so complete, that unto everlasting felicitie wee neede not the knowledge of any thing more then these two, may easily furnish our mindes with on all sides, and therefore they which adde traditions as a part of supernaturall necessarye truth, have not the truth, but are in error.[252]

[250] See *Lawes*, 1:179.23–5 (II.7.5).
[251] See *Answer*, 5:236.28–30.
[252] *Lawes*, 1:129.3–16 (I.14.5).

Holy Scripture and reason 'both joyntly and not severallye' serve to give humans knowledge of all that is necessary for salvation, and this is of the very essence of which Hooker's *magnum opus*, the *Lawes*, is built.[253]

In the realm of *adiaphora*, concerning Christian beliefs and practices which are not necessary for salvation, Hooker, as one would expect, has a wider conception of religious authority. The binary pairing of Holy Scripture and reason remains important for him, though of course by definition their authority in such matters is not infallibly certain. As Hooker argues, reason can in matters of *adiaphora* at best make out only a probable case that Holy Scripture should be interpreted in a particular way. One of the examples he gives, as noted in Ch. 2, is that of the perpetual virginity of the Virgin Mary after the birth of Christ.[254] He considers her perpetual virginity to be probable, but the lack of a demonstrative argument means for him that people are free to decide whether to believe that this is true or not. This would seem to be the case for him more generally as regards all indifferent Christian beliefs; he considers them ultimately matters for the individual Christian conscience. In this respect inner beliefs are to be distinguished from Church discipline, ceremonies, and orders, and other indifferent matters of an outward nature, where he is careful to make a distinction between public authority and private probable reasoning. One of the central arguments of the *Lawes* is that although, rationally considered, a given thing may be indifferent in itself, a Church is free to prescribe a particular practice or form of behaviour for its members which it considers fit. As he notes, God ordained certain beliefs and practices as mandatory in Holy Scripture, and left the Church free to ordain, and if necessary over the course of time alter, other practices in themselves indifferent.[255] Christians are obliged to submit their private judgements to that of the Church in which they live for the sake of societal order, and as a result these matters cease to be indifferent for the individuals concerned. Whatever they may privately think, they must publicly conform. The authority of the Church, like that of any other society with respect to its members, is thus for

[253] See W. David Neelands, 'Hooker on Scripture, Reason and "Tradition"', *RHCCC* 89.

[254] See pp. 73–4.

[255] See *Lawes*, 1:236.3–5 (III.9.1).

Hooker superior to the judgement of its private citizens. As he observes in Book 3 of the *Lawes*, quoting Proverbs 6: 20:

Unto lawes thus made and received by a whole Church, they which live within the bosome of that Church, must not thinke it a matter indifferent either to yeeld or not to yeeld obedience. Is it a smal offence to despise the Church of God? *My sonne keepe thy fathers commandement*, saith Salomon, *and forget not thy mothers instruction, bind them both alwaies about thine hart.* It doth not stand with the duty which we owe to our heavenly father, that to the ordinances of our mother the Church we should shew our selves disobedient. Let us not say we keepe the commandements of the one, when we breake the law of the other: For unlesse we observe both, we obey neither.[256]

Taken by itself, this would seem to suggest, as Grislis notes, that Hooker has the following triple model of religious authority: Scripture, reason, and the Church, in that order.[257] Indeed this is what Hooker would appear to be arguing in this passage from Book 5 of the *Lawes*, in what is probably Hooker's most well-known statement on religious authority:

what scripture doth plainelie deliver, to that the first place both of creditt and obedience is due; the next whereunto is whatsoever anie man can necessarelie conclude by force of reason; after these the voice of the Church succeedeth. That which the Church by her ecclesiasticall authoritie shall probablie thinke and define to be true or good, must in congruitie of reason overrule all other inferior judgmentes whatsoever.[258]

One must, therefore, consider carefully in the light of this precisely what Hooker understands by the authority of the Church.

As the above passage illustrates, the authority of the Church is principally defined for Hooker in terms of probable certainty. Doctrines expressly mentioned in Holy Scripture, Holy Scripture interpreted by demonstrative reasoning, and demonstrative reasoning more generally, are superior to Church authority. It is for this reason that Hooker argues, with regard to the authentication of Holy Scripture, that although 'the first outward motive leading men so to esteeme of the scripture is the authority of Gods Church', total authoritative certainty can only come through some other means.[259] In this respect Hooker demonstrates his Protestant

[256] Ibid. 1:237.29–238.7 (III.9.3). See also 1:141.28–9 (I.16.7).
[257] See Grislis, 'Commentary', *Folger*, v. 800.
[258] *Lawes*, 2:39.8–14 (V.8.2).
[259] See ibid. 1:231.15–232.10 (III.8.14).

credentials in opposing the Roman Catholic argument that Holy Scripture is authenticated by the Church; Calvin says much the same in the *Institutes*.[260] Where, though, Calvin believes that Holy Scripture is self-authenticating based on the inner witness of the Holy Spirit, Hooker argues that it is demonstrative reasoning that infallibly authenticates Holy Scripture. His overall approach regarding the fallibility of the Church is captured very well in his remarks on the authority of general Church Councils: 'although ten thousand generall Councels would set downe one and the same definitive sentence concerning any point of religion whatsoever; yet one demonstrative reason alleaged... could not choose but overweigh them all; in as much as for them to have beene deceived it is not impossible, it is that demonstrative reason... should deceive'.[261] It follows from this that the authority of a Church with regard to its ecclesiastical laws is abrogated if a person can offer a demonstrative argument either from natural or divine law which proves them to be wrong: 'The publique power of all societies is above every soule contayned in the same societies. And the principall use of that power is to give lawes unto all that are under it, which lawes in such case we must obey, unlesse there be reason shewed which may necessarily enforce that the lawe of reason or of God, doth enjoyne the contrarie.'[262] This presumably forms for Hooker a legitimization of the Reformation, in which the Reformers refused to show obedience to the Church in matters that they considered contrary to the Gospel. The Church is thus only superior to private probable reasoning, and not to Holy Scripture or demonstrative reasoning, in matters of *adiaphora*.

Not all ecclesiastical laws need be based on probable reasoning, for as Hooker notes the Church is free to legislate on the basis of divine laws obtained from Holy Scripture, just as civil societies can frame laws based on natural law.[263] Yet the distinctive authority of such laws will come primarily from Holy Scripture and reason, and only secondarily from the Church. Such laws will be infallibly certain not because they have been issued by the Church, but because the Church has used Holy Scripture and demonstrative reasoning in arriving at them. This is an important point, because it shows that the religious authority of the Church is derivative for Hooker.

260 See *Inst.* I.7.3; I.8.12.

261 *Lawes*, 1:180.23–9 (II.7.5).

262 Ibid. 1:139.18–23 (I.16.5).

263 See ibid. 1:106.20–3 (I.10.11) and p. 117.

The same is logically true as regards *adiaphora*: a Church's religious authority in such matters is derived from the probable reasoning that is used when framing ecclesiastical laws. Hooker repeatedly stresses the rational nature of law throughout his work, and denies that authority can legitimately ignore reason or make laws that are contrary to it.[264] Although he writes in Book 7 of the *Lawes* that both a prince and the Church should be presumed to have a reason for their actions even if it is not expressed, he evidently expects that a reason will exist.[265] Thus when, in his famous threefold description of religious authority in Book 5, Hooker speaks of 'That which the Church by her ecclesiasticall authoritie shall probablie thinke and define to be true or good', he would seem to be referring to probable reasoning.[266] This would suggest that behind the triple authority of scripture, reason, and the Church there lies a more fundamental source of authority for Hooker: that of scripture, demonstrative reasoning, and probable reasoning.

Yet the religious authority of the Church is not based only on the authority of reasoning for Hooker, but also on the authority of tradition. In his fine discussion of Hooker's views on religious tradition, Neelands makes a careful distinction between Hooker's handling of the term 'tradition' and the concept itself.[267] As Neelands shows, the term itself usually has negative connotations for Hooker, but only because it is usually identified by him with the Roman Catholic position that tradition must supplement Holy Scripture as regards knowledge of doctrines necessary for salvation. Neelands cites as evidence, for instance, *The First Sermon Upon Part of S. Judes Epistle*, where Hooker starkly contrasts 'religion and superstition, Ministers and Massingpriests, light and darknesse, truth and errour, traditions and Scriptures', and *A Learned Discourse of Justification*, where Hooker condemns the Roman Catholic Church for giving equal credit to 'unwrytten verities' alongside Holy Scripture.[268] Neelands also cites a number of similar, if more

[264] See *Pride*, 5:309.11–19; 5:341.18–26; *Lawes*, 1:58.26–32 (I.2.1); 1:61.18–23 (I.2.5); 1:63.6–14 (I.3.1); 1:181.4–182.2 (II.7.6); 2:45.2–4 (V.9.3); *DF* 4:131.14–133.22; 4:161.30–162.11; Voak, 'Reason, Will and Grace in the Works of Richard Hooker', 51–83.

[265] See *Lawes*, 3:241.22–242.8 (VII.16.3).

[266] See ibid. 2:39.11–13 (V.8.2). See also 1:181.4–182.2 (II.7.6).

[267] See Neelands, 'Hooker on Scripture, Reason and "Tradition"', 89–94. See also Lee W. Gibbs, 'Richard Hooker's *Via Media* Doctrine of Scripture and Tradition', *Harvard Theological Review* 95 (2002), 232–3.

[268] See *Jude 1*, 5:21.3–5; *Just.* 5:119.18–26.

moderately expressed, passages from the *Lawes*, of which this, which forms part of a discussion of erroneous views of religious authority, is a representative example: 'The schooles of Rome teach scripture to be so unsufficient, as if, except traditions were added, it did not conteine all revealed and supernaturall truth, which absolutely is necessarie for the children of man in this life to know that they may in the next be saved.'[269] As Neelands argues, however, when tradition is defined in terms of *adiaphora* the concept is entirely amenable to Hooker, though he often shows a preference for less controversial synonyms such as 'custom', 'long usage', and 'long experience'.[270] This caution over the direct use of the term can be seen particularly clearly in Hooker's defence of the tradition of signing with the cross during baptism, in Book 5 of the *Lawes*. In a passage from this chapter he provides a redefinition of the term that is normative for his practice in the *Lawes*, where in fact the value of tradition or custom is valued very highly:

> What reason there is to justifie tradition use or custome in this behalfe, *either thou maist of thy selfe perceyve, or els learne of some other that doth.* Least therefore the name of tradition should be offensive to any, consideringe how farre by some it hath bene and is abused, wee meane by traditions ordinances made in the prime of Christian religion, established with that authoritie which Christ hath left to his Church for matters indifferent, and in that consideration requisite to be observed till like authoritie see just and reasonable cause to alter them. So that traditions Ecclesiasticall are not rudlie and in grosse to be shaken of, because the inventors of them were men.[271]

Hooker begins, quoting from Tertullian's *De Corona Militis*, by speaking synonymously of 'tradition use or custome', before justifying his use of the term 'tradition' in terms of *adiaphora* or 'matters indifferent'. He defines traditions as ordinances laid down by the early Church which are binding on Christians, until such time as the Church sees fit to change them. Such traditions are, therefore, like the probable reasoning of the Church, superior in authority to the probable reasoning of private individuals, and both together form a part of the Church's derivative religious authority.

269 See *Lawes*, 1:191.16–20 (II.8.7).

270 For Hooker's use of synonymns for tradition, see e.g. *Lawes*, 1:165.14–166.4 (II.5.7); 1:288.11–26 (IV.5.1); 1:337.15–19 (IV.14.1); 3:147.14–148.16 (VII.1.4).

271 Ibid. 2:302.1–11 (V.65.2).

The basis of Hooker's theory of tradition can be seen in a passage from Book 1 of the *Lawes*, in which he makes a commonly quoted distinction between knowledge of truth through 'signs and tokens' and through 'causes':

And of discerning goodnes there are but these two wayes; the one the knowledge of the causes whereby it is made such, the other the observation of those signes and tokens, which being annexed alwaies unto goodnes, argue that where they are found, there also goodnes is, although we know not the cause by force whereof it is there.

Signes and tokens to know good by, are of sundry kinds: some more certaine and some lesse. The most certaine token of evident goodnes is, if the generall perswasion of all men do so account it. And therefore a common received error is never utterly overthrowne, till such time as we goe from signes unto causes, and shew some manifest root or fountaine thereof common unto all, whereby it may cleerely appeare how it hath come to passe that so many have beene overseene.[272]

The strongest sign and token of the truth is the general agreement of humanity, which is analogous to a tradition or custom of universal consent. The more widely held the custom, both as regards time and the number of persons concerned, the more likely it is to reflect divine truth. Hooker even goes so far as to add that 'The generall and perpetuall voyce of men is as the sentence of God him selfe.'[273] This would seem, though, to be an exaggeration on his part, for as he notes in the above passage, commonly held errors can be overthrown only through an enquiry into the causes of truth. One might recall in this context Hooker's later observation that demonstrative reasoning is more certain than the judgements of ten thousand general councils of the Church. Tradition remains for him, therefore, only a probable testimony to the truth, which lacks the certainty that can be gained by a fundamental, reasoned enquiry into causes. As he remarks in Book 4, regarding 'a lawe which the custome and continuall practise of many ages or yeares hath confirmed in the mindes of men', such laws can legitimately be removed 'when they are unnaturall, or impious, or otherwise hurtefull unto the publique communitie of men, and against that good for which humaine societies were instituted'.[274] Since such laws are by their very nature indifferent,

[272] Ibid. 1:82.27–83.1 (I.8.2); 1:83.16–23 (I.8.3).

[273] See ibid. 1:83.33–84.2 (I.8.3).

[274] See ibid. 1:337.8–338.20 (IV.14.1–2).

a Church has authority to remove them and institute new and more suitable laws. There will, however, need to be strong probable reasons to justify a Church getting rid of long traditions, and in the case of some traditions, like those of pagan religions in the time of Christ, perhaps even an infallible evidential proof:

> If we have neither voice from heaven that so pronounceth of them, neither sentence of men grounded uppon such manifest and cleare proofe, that they in whose handes it is to alter them may likewise infallibly even in hart and conscience judge them so; upon necessitie to urge alteration is to trouble and disturbe without necessitie.[275]

The 'voice from heaven' is divine revelation, which in terms of the Christians of Hooker's day means in practice Holy Scripture. Thus only Holy Scripture (whether through its express meaning or through infallible interpretation by demonstrative reasoning) or demonstrative reasoning by itself (from natural first principles) can compel a Church to remove a long-held tradition. Otherwise the weight of the tradition must be balanced by the Church against the probable arguments for and against the tradition's continued observance. To phrase this more generally, tradition is for Hooker of inferior authority to Holy Scripture and demonstrative reasoning, while its authority in relation to probable reasoning is variable, depending upon the antiquity and universality of the tradition concerned. Tradition and probable reasoning are, therefore, simply two different kinds of probable proof, one from the 'signs and tokens' of truth and one from an enquiry into its 'causes'.

All the arguments made so far concerning religious authority may be summarized as follows. The highest source of religious authority for Hooker is doctrines present in Holy Scripture 'by expresse literall mention', since they do not need to be proved, and would seem metaphorically to partake of the certainty of humanity's knowledge of natural first principles.[276] As he observes in Book 5 of the *Lawes*, 'what scripture doth plainelie deliver, to that the first place both of creditt and obedience is due'.[277] None the less, these doctrines are still not as evidentially certain as natural first principles, because they rely on the evidential proof (whether through demonstrative reasoning or the probable

[275] *Lawes*, 1:338.10–15 (IV.14.2).
[276] See p. 77.
[277] See *Lawes*, 2:39.8–9 (V.8.2).

authority of the Church) that Holy Scripture is the Word of God. The second degree of authority is demonstrative reasoning, whether through the interpretation of Holy Scripture or as regards natural laws and *mere natural spiritual facts* deduced from natural first principles. It could perhaps be argued that as Holy Scripture is for Hooker intrinsically more certain than natural first principles, the former of these two classes is in a sense the more certain of the two. The third source of authority is probable reasoning and tradition licensed by a society such as a Church. Finally, the fourth source of religious authority is private probable reasoning. If traditions are defined not merely as ordinances of a Church, but more generally as long-standing indifferent beliefs and customs, then tradition can also be considered a part of this fourth level of authority. Traditions imposed by a Church will not be indifferent for the persons concerned, but traditions concerning indifferent religious beliefs such as the perpetual virginity of the Virgin Mary were for Hooker a matter for the individual conscience. It will be seen that this hierarchy of authority in general follows the philosophical distinctions between different degrees of evidential certainty discussed in Ch. 2.

These four levels of authority can now be tabulated, in descending order of authority (only levels (1) and (2a) refer directly, of course, to revealed doctrines necessary for salvation):

1. Doctrines found in Holy Scripture 'by expresse literall mention'.
2. (a) Doctrines deduced from Holy Scripture by demonstrative reasoning; and
   (b) Natural laws and *mere natural spiritual facts* deduced by demonstrative reasoning.
3. Probable reasoning and tradition licensed by a society such as a Church.
4. Private probable reasoning and tradition.

Given the superiority of demonstrative reasoning to tradition, these four classes may not unfairly be condensed into the traditional triple classification of Scripture, reason, and tradition, in that order. One must, however, immediately qualify this triple classification. Different writers have understood different things by these categories, and it is misleading to cite Hooker as a source for this doctrine without appreciating the exact nature of his views.

Demonstrative reasoning plays a vital role in his theory of religious authority; in the deduction of natural laws and *mere natural spritual facts*, and above all in the authentication and interpretation of Holy Scripture. Wanting to ground Christian doctrine on a completely certain basis, but unable to accept that either the Church or the direct internal witness of the Holy Spirit could offer this, he turned instead to the authority of demonstrative reasoning. Modern theologians who accept the authority of Scripture, reason, and tradition may very well feel uncomfortable in speaking about demonstrative reasoning in religious matters, and may place much more emphasis upon probable reasoning. Such an approach is distinctly different from that of Hooker. None the less, when this qualification is borne in mind, Church of England theologians who accept the authority of Scripture, reason, and tradition, in that order, may not unjustly look back to Hooker as a theological predecessor, for he mounts in the *Lawes* a classic defence of these three sources of religious authority. When one also considers the radicalism of his opposition to the Reformed, and more generally Protestant, concept of *sola scriptura*, then dominant in the Church of England of his day, then one can also see him as, at the very least, one of the originators of this theory within the English Church.

As a final reflection on the distance of Hooker's concept of religious authority from that characteristic of Reformed theology, it is worth looking briefly at what would appear to be a logical consequence of his view that Holy Scripture can be authenticated by demonstrative reasoning. This is not to say that Hooker adopted or was even aware of this consequence, as he never mentions it himself and always in his writings associates assent to Christian doctrine with the imperfection of faith,[278] but it is highly interesting none the less. Hooker observes, as has been shown, that people first accept that Holy Scripture is the Word of God on the authority of the Church. The Christian doctrines contained within Holy Scripture that are necessary for salvation are thus first accepted on the basis of a probable proof, and hence by definition as a matter of faith. Yet Hooker argues that Christian theologians (unlike of course the great majority of Christians) can subsequently through labour demonstrably prove that Holy Scripture is the Word of God, and this presumably embraces its perfect inerrancy, in

[278] See e.g. *Cert.* 5:70.19–30; *Lawes*, 2:290.6–291.2 (V.63.1).

which, as one would expect of a sixteenth-century theologian, he believed.[279] Christian doctrines necessary for salvation can then simply be read in Holy Scripture, or can demonstrably be deduced from it. The consequence of this viewpoint can be expressed as a syllogism:

Holy Scripture is demonstrably the inerrant Word of God;
Christian doctrines necessary for salvation are either expressly mentioned in Holy Scripture or can demonstrably be deduced from it;
Therefore (with sanctifying grace) a theologian with the aid of Holy Scripture can demonstrably prove Christian doctrines necessary for salvation.

This recalls indirectly the old scholastic argument that philosophers who (unlike most theists) can prove the existence of God, believe in God not through faith but through certain knowledge.[280] Hooker would appear to be logically committed to the radical view that a Christian theologian can rise from having faith in the articles of Christian doctrine necessary for salvation, to knowing them to be true with demonstrative certainty.[281] This is a very long way indeed from the Reformed position that the sole source of infallible religious authority is Holy Scripture authenticated and interpreted by the direct internal witness of the Holy Spirit.

[279] See *Jude 1*, 5:15.8–17.24. Nothing in his later writings contradicts this sermon in this matter.

[280] See e.g. *ST* II-II.2.4.

[281] In the light of this it may appear that Hooker had an overly cerebral attitude to religion. An excellent corrective to this picture is provided by Shuger, who rightly emphasizes the role that emotions have in the act of worship for Hooker. See Shuger, '"Society Supernatural": The Imagined Community of Hooker's *Lawes*', 130–6. See also, for instance, his famous consideration in the *Lawes* of the power of music: *Lawes*, 2:151.4–154.4 (V.38). Hooker probably considered, at least with regard to the common people, that it was his puritan opponents, with their intense concern for preaching and Bible study, who had the overly cerebral approach.

5

Reason, Will, and Grace in the Late Works

In 1599 the tract entitled *A Christian Letter of Certaine English Protestantes . . . Unto That Reverend And Learned Man Maister R. Hoo[ker]* was published anonymously, accusing Hooker of holding, in the first five books of the *Lawes*, a variety of positions contrary to the Thirty-Nine Articles of the Church of England. Hooker, as was described in the Introduction, read this work, and made notes in the margin of his edition. He then began assembling a reply for publication, but was unable to complete this task due to his death in November 1600, at the age of 46. What remains of this reply survives in manuscript form in Trinity College Dublin, and has come to be known as the *Dublin Fragments*. There are also various pages of notes surviving in Trinity College that relate to the subject of predestination, and that Hooker would appear to have written up in the third essay of the *Dublin Fragments*. All these writings, published in the fourth volume of the *Folger* edition, have been designated in this study as Hooker's 'late' works. Hooker's responses to the *Christian Letter* were directed at showing how the first five books of the *Lawes* were in fact in agreement with the Thirty-Nine Articles. In order to do this, he often needed to expand upon certain of his remarks in the *Lawes*, to make his position clear. In my opinion, there are no major substantive disagreements between the theology of the *Lawes* and the late works; in this respect, he did not alter his views in a dramatic way when answering the *Christian Letter*. There is, however, a tremendous difference in emphasis. As regards the points Hooker was accused of, most of those he chose to reply to at length in the *Dublin Fragments* deal with grace. Given the problems in his presentation of grace within the *Lawes* that have been discussed in the previous two chapters, this would scarcely seem surprising; there were many outstanding issues that Hooker needed to clarify. Yet it does mean that subjects dealt with often only sketchily in the *Lawes*—such as the nature of grace, and the effects of original sin—now receive in-depth treatment in their own right. This obviously makes this body of writing of great interest and importance to anyone concerned with Hooker's thought.

The principal point of interest in the late works, as regards this study of Hooker's thought, is, of course, the issue of human nature. His discussions of predestination and the sacraments, as fascinating as they are in themselves, will, therefore, be dealt with only in so far as they relate to this central topic. The late works have, of course, been mentioned in earlier chapters, for instance as regards the distinction between mortal and venial sins and Hooker's mature views on justification and sanctification; these subjects will not be raised again now. In these cases the issues were relatively simple, and there was little danger of obscuring Hooker's meaning by looking at them apart from the rest of the late work. The same cannot, however, be said of his attitude to human nature in these works in general. Many passages can read as characteristically Reformed in their attitude to the reason, the will, and grace, quite contrary to the views that have been outlined in the rest of this book. For instance, in the *Dublin Fragments* Hooker explicitly describes how the Fall has had a devastating impact upon humanity, crippling the reason and will, and leaving humanity of itself able to perform only evil deeds. One can see in the light of this why Atkinson should have observed that 'Hooker's most careful treatment of Reformed orthodoxy is to be found in the *Dublin Fragments*', and Kirby that 'In the *Dublin Fragments* Hooker constructed his most extensive statement of his commitment to the orthodox reformed theology of grace.'[1] It might seem as if either the *Lawes* should dramatically be reinterpreted, or that Hooker inexplicably became convinced by the very opinions he so forcefully opposes in his earlier work. Only when the late works are considered as a whole, and the highly subtle distinctions in them investigated, does it become apparent that they have only the superficial appearance of being characteristically Reformed in these matters. One must bear in mind that it was in Hooker's interest to sound Reformed at this time, given that he had just been accused of crypto-papistry, and with holding positions contrary to the Thirty-Nine Articles. In reality, his relation to the

[1] See Atkinson, *Richard Hooker and the Authority of Scripture, Tradition and Reason*, 28; Kirby, *Richard Hooker's Doctrine of the Royal Supremacy*, 34.

Reformed tradition in these writings is no different than in the *Lawes* itself, as the previous analysis of his observations on such subjects as justification and free will, and the distinction between mortal and venial sins, has already eloquently testified.

To turn to the views of Hooker's critics, many have simply ignored the late works. Yet those who have looked at them in detail have not been slow to realize their import. Some critics, when discussing Hooker's conception of human nature, seem to accord them almost more weight than the *Lawes* itself, presumably on the grounds that Hooker is giving in these writings his final and expanded views on this subject.[2] The problem, though, is that the late works are highly complex, and have seldom received the systematic treatment they deserve. All too often critics have quoted brief passages which, stripped from their original context, do little to aid an understanding of Hooker's overall position. One of the difficulties is that the *Dublin Fragments* are indeed fragments, made up of three distinct essays: the third of them lacks an ending and, more pertinently, the first of them lacks a beginning. Another difficulty is that Hooker's autograph notes in the margin of his edition of the *Christian Letter* are sometimes cryptic, and hard to interpret with complete surety. Most importantly of all, although Hooker discusses the nature of grace at considerable length in the *Dublin Fragments*, he does so in a manner that can scarcely be described as lucid and plain. The ingenuity of the critics in elucidating Hooker's terminology is surpassed only by Hooker himself, who in categorizing the different forms of grace on various occasions never duplicates exactly the same sets of terms. Moreover, terms such as 'inward grace' and 'speciall grace' are used without any comprehensive definitions of what they actually mean. If one assumes that these are specifically Christian graces then it is easy to see, in Hooker's condemnations of those who lack them, a theory of total depravity very similar to that of Calvin, at least with regard to *mere natural persons*. Only by a very careful analysis does it emerge what a vital role the concept of

[2] See e.g. Grislis, 'Richard Hooker's Image of Man', 75, 81, 83; Thornburg, 'Original Sin, Justification and Sanctification in the Thought of Two Sixteenth Century English Divines: John Jewel and Richard Hooker', 137–8, 145–69; Kirby, *Richard Hooker's Doctrine of the Royal Supremacy*, 15, 34, 46, 51, 53; Atkinson, *Richard Hooker and the Authority of Scripture, Tradition and Reason*, 28–31.

common grace has to play in the late works, and how complex, and indeed opaque, is Hooker's terminology of grace.

The only way to deal satisfactorily with the late works, as regards the subject of human nature, is to analyse them systematically. In order to do this it is important to start by looking at the *Christian Letter*, and the accusations this tract makes concerning Hooker's views on reason, the will, and grace. The relevant chapters in the *Christian Letter* are numbers 5 and 7. In both cases the following discussion will examine the specific charges levelled against Hooker, and which of the Thirty-Nine Articles he was being accused of contradicting.

To begin with ch. 5, entitled '*Of free will*', the accusation is based on Hooker's crucial discussion of the reason and the will in the seventh chapter of Book 1 of the *Lawes*. It will be recalled that Hooker argues there that 'There is in the will of man naturally that freedome, whereby it is apt to take or refuse any particular object whatsoever being presented unto it,' and also that 'There is not that good which concerneth us, but it hath evidence enough for it selfe, if reason were diligent to search it out.'[3] The first passage is an assertion of the will's liberty of indifference, the second of the reason's freedom through effort to comprehend truth. Regarding these two passages, the *Christian Letter* makes these remarks:

> Heere we pray your helpe to teach us: how will is apt (as you say) freelie to take or refuse anie particular object what soever, and that reason by diligence is able to find out anie good concerning us: If it bee true that the Church of England professeth, that without the preventing and helping grace of God, we can, will, and doe nothing pleasing to God.[4]

The Article being cited in opposition to Hooker is number 10, 'Of Free Will' (*De libero arbitrio*). Quoting the article in full demonstrates the extent to which the authors of the *Letter* were working with the Thirty-Nine Articles by their side, as a bastion of Protestant orthodoxy against Hooker's supposed heresies:

> The condition of man after the fall of Adam is such that he cannot turn and prepare himself by his own natural strength and good works to faith and calling upon God; wherefore we have no power to do good works

[3] See *Lawes*, 1:79.27–9; 1:80.29–31. See also pp. 55, 80–1.

[4] *ACL* 4:18.13–27.

pleasant and acceptable to God, without the grace of God by Christ preventing us, that we may have a good will, and working with us, when we have that good will.[5]

The *Christian Letter*'s accusation is based on an equation of Hooker's statements on liberty of indifference, and the capacity of reason through diligence to comprehend the truth, with the ability to perform works 'pleasant and acceptable to God' (*Deo grata sint et accepta*) referred to in Article 10. This is tantamount to a charge of Pelagianism, since the *Christian Letter* evidently sees Hooker as affirming that people do not of necessity require God's help in order to perform good deeds which are pleasing to him; they naturally have the freedom to do this themselves. As the title of ch. 5 indicates, it is this freedom of the will, apart from grace, which here disturbs the authors of the *Christian Letter*: they consider this to be quite impossible, given the Fall, and humanity's inherent depravity.

Chapter 5 ends with a request that Hooker explain how these two remarks on the reason and will agree with Romans 8: 7: '*The wisedome of the flesh is ennimitie against God, for it is not subject unto the law of God, neither in deed can be.*' This would appear to be a reference not to Article 10 but rather to Article 9, entitled 'Of Original, or Birth Sin' (*Peccatum originale*). The relevant part of this article observes the following of original sin, alluding itself to Romans 8: 7:

And this infection of nature doth remain, yea in them that are regenerated, whereby the lust of the flesh, called in Greek *phronema sarkos*, which some do expound the wisdom, some sensuality, some the affection, and some the desire of the flesh, is not subject to the Law of God.[6]

The *Christian Letter* was, therefore, questioning the soundness of Hooker's views on original sin, and in particular asking him to demonstrate how they were consonant with Paul's observations on the wisdom of the flesh in Romans.

[5] See *Documents of the English Reformation*, 290: Ea est hominis post lapsum Adae conditio, ut sese naturalibus suis viribus et bonis operibus ad fidem et invocationem Dei convertere ac praeparare non possit, quare absque gratia Dei, quae per Christum est, nos praeveniente, ut velimus, et cooperante dum volumus, ad pietatis opera facienda, quae Deo grata sint et accepta, nihil valemus.

[6] See ibid. Manet etiam in renatis haec naturae depravatio, qua fit ut affectus carnis, Graece *phronema sarkos*, quod alii sapientiam, alii sensum, alii affectum, alii studium interpretantur, legi Dei non subiiciatur.

Chapter 7 of the *Christian Letter*, entitled '*The virtue of workes*', approaches the same subject from a different angle. Of the passages from the *Lawes* singled out for criticism by the *Letter*, two are of particular interest. In the first of these Hooker argues that it is through obedience to the laws of its nature that an agent acts righteously, as opposed to acting sinfully:

Good doth followe unto all things, by observing the course of their nature, and on the contrary side evill by not observing it: but not unto naturall agents that good which wee call *Reward*, not that evill which wee properly tearme *Punishment*. The reason whereof is, because amongst creatures in this world, only mans observation of the lawe of his nature is *Righteousnes*, only mans transgression *Sinne*.[7]

The *Letter* could equally well have quoted from Book 2 of the *Lawes*, and especially Hooker's commentary on Romans 14: 23.[8] It will be recalled that in this book Hooker argues, contrary to Cartwright, and also implicitly contrary to other Reformed theologians such as Calvin, that *mere natural persons* are capable to some extent of performing works that glorify and are obedient to God, and hence of abstaining from sin. The key issue for Hooker is whether a person obeys God's will, which is revealed in natural and divine law. In his summary at the end of this book, however, Hooker briefly changes his terminology, and rather than speaking in terms of obedience and glorification refers to works that are 'acceptable' to God. It is from this passage that the *Christian Letter* found the substance for another of its attacks on Hooker's supposed unorthodoxy: 'his very commandements in some kinde, as namely his preceptes comprehended in the lawe of nature, may be otherwise knowne then onely by scripture; and that to do them, howsoever we know them, must needes be acceptable in his sight'.[9] The principal article cited against Hooker by the *Christian Letter* on this occasion is number 13, entitled 'Of Works before Justification' (*Opera ante justificationem*). It reads:

Works done before the grace of Christ, and the inspiration of his Spirit, are not pleasant to God, forasmuch as they spring not of faith in Jesu Christ, neither do they make men meet to receive grace, or as the School authors say, deserve grace of congruity; yet rather for that they are not

[7] *Lawes*, 1:93.30–94.4 (I.9.1). [8] See pp. 134–5.
[9] *Lawes*, 1:188.28–31 (II.8.5). See also pp. 135–6.

done as God hath willed and commanded them to be done, we doubt not but they have the nature of sin.[10]

There are three distinct elements in this article, and although the *Christian Letter* conflates them it is important to keep them apart. First, there is the observation that works performed 'before the grace of Christ, and the inspiration of his Spirit' are not 'pleasant to God' (*Deo grata sunt*). The *Christian Letter* contrasts this with Hooker's understanding that *mere natural persons* can to some extent glorify and obey God, and hence abstain from sin.[11] Hooker himself seems to encourage this contrast when he talks in the above passage of these works being 'acceptable' in God's sight, since Article 10 speaks of works 'pleasant and acceptable to God' (*Deo grata sint et accepta*) as if these two ideas were synonymous. Secondly, there is the observation that these works not 'pleasant to God' do not 'deserve grace of congruity' (*Neque gratiam ... de congruo merentur*). The *Christian Letter* takes Hooker's remarks on 'acceptable' works to be suggestive of the 'Romish doctrine of *pura naturalia* and workes of congruitie'. Thirdly, the article observes that works performed 'before the grace of Christ, and the inspiration of his Spirit' have the 'nature of sin' (*peccati rationem habere*). Here the *Christian Letter* enquires of Hooker, with regard to his comments on abstinence from sin, 'in what sence can you call that righteousnes in man, which our Church calleth sinne?' The *Christian Letter*'s charge is thus again that of Pelagianism, but viewed now from the perspective of human sinfulness, rather than human freedom. Hooker is accused of teaching, contrary to the Church of England, that the unjustified are capable without God's aid of performing good works that are pleasing and acceptable to God. The *Christian Letter* plainly sides with the characteristically Reformed argument, discussed in Ch. 3, that works that glorify and obey God are the sole preserve of justified Christians.

Chapter 7 also contains one other possible accusation against Hooker. In addition to citing Article 13, the authors of the *Letter* also quote part of Article 12, 'Of Good Works' (*De bonis operibus*).

[10] See *Documents of the English Reformation*, 292: Opera quae fiunt ante gratiam Christi, et Spiritus eius afflatum, cum ex fide Iesu Christi non prodeant, minime Deo grata sunt. Neque gratiam, ut multa vocant, de congruo merentur; imo cum non sint facta ut Deus illa fieri voluit et praecepit, peccati rationem habere non dubitamus.

[11] See *ACL* 4:23.10–24.8.

This article stresses that the good works of the justified cannot 'endure the severity of God's judgement', even though these works are 'pleasing and acceptable' (*grata sunt et accepta*) in His sight. The *Christian Letter* does not pursue this point further, and it is possible that this article is quoted only to lend emphasis to the above accusation. It is also possible, however, that the authors of the *Letter* wished to imply that Hooker had unsound views regarding the meritorious nature of Christian good works. Since this question is of some interest, and Hooker chose to respond (briefly) to this quotation from Article 12, one may regard the matter as if the *Letter* had in fact accused Hooker of unorthodoxy on this point. Quoted in full, Article 12 reads:

> Albeit that good works, which are the fruits of faith, and follow after justification, cannot put away our sins, and endure the severity of God's judgement; yet are they pleasing and acceptable to God in Christ, and do spring out necessarily of a true and lively faith, in so much that by them a lively faith may be as evidently known, as a tree discerned by the fruit.[12]

Three other chapters of the *Christian Letter* are also concerned in some manner with the will, reason, and divine grace. Chapter 3, entitled '*The holy scripture containe all thinges necessarie to salvation*', deals, as its name suggests, largely with other issues.[13] It takes as its focus Article 6 of the Thirty-Nine Articles, which asserts that Holy Scripture contains all things necessary to salvation. Yet part of this chapter does discuss Hooker's views on reason and the relationship of natural law to Holy Scripture. In so far as the authors of the *Letter* believe that Hooker claims too much here for the unaided capacities of the human reason (and will), they are implicitly accusing him of contradicting Articles 10 and 13, a charge they make explicit in their later chapters. Chapter 9, entitled '*None free from all sinne*', is also concerned with such questions, since it accuses Hooker of holding that humans have the capacity to abstain from all sin.[14] This charge, the result of a definite misunderstanding, concentrates on one specific text in Book 5 of the

[12] See *Documents of the English Reformation*, 291–2: Bona opera quae sunt fructus fidei et iustificatos sequuntur, quamquam peccata nostra expiari et divini iudicii severitatem ferre non possunt, Deo tamen grata sunt et accepta in Christo, atque ex vera et viva fide necessario profluunt, ut plane ex illis, aeque fides viva cognosci possit, atque arbor ex fructu iudicari.

[13] See *ACL* 4:11.8–14.9.

[14] See ibid. 4:26.1–26.

Lawes. This matter has already been discussed at length in Chs. 2 and 4, and since Hooker chose not to deal with it in the *Dublin Fragments*, it will not be raised again now.[15] Finally, ch. 8, entitled '*Workes of supererogation*', accuses Hooker of holding views contrary to Article 14, which condemns belief in such works. Since the *Christian Letter*'s remarks on this subject, and Hooker's response to them, have been discussed in Ch. 4, they will also not be mentioned again now.[16]

Hooker, then, in order to defend himself from these accusations, needed to be clear on five particular points. First, he had to show whether, and in what sense, justified Christians and *mere natural persons* have the freedom to know and choose the good. Secondly, he had to address the question of whether all the works of *mere natural persons* are sinful, and whether these works can ever be 'pleasant and acceptable' (*grata*... *et accepta*) to God (and what this means). Thirdly, he had to look at whether the works of *mere natural persons* can in any sense congruously merit grace. Fourthly, he had to demonstrate his general belief in original sin, even amongst justified Christians, and specifically his agreement with Romans 8: 7. Finally, he needed to consider in what sense the good works of justified Christians deserve the appellation 'good'. In so doing he had to ensure, if at all possible, that his arguments were in full accord with Articles 9, 10, 12, and 13 of the Thirty-Nine Articles, and to answer any related queries raised by the authors of the *Christian Letter*. In the light of Philip B. Secor's claim that 'the theology of the *Articles* is entirely congenial with his own moderate brand of Calvinism', the question must then be whether Hooker was able (and in what sense) to demonstrate his agreement with these articles which, as an ordained minister, he had subscribed to by oath, or whether his opposition to aspects of the Reformed tradition brought him into substantive conflict with them.[17]

The next logical step, having surveyed the accusations against Hooker, might appear to be an analysis of Hooker's autograph notes in his edition of the *Letter*. The problem with this is that these notes are usually very brief, and as regards the subjects now under discussion, often either cryptic or easy to misinterpret. Since Hooker often expands upon these notes in the *Dublin*

[15] See pp. 88–9, 205–6. [16] See pp. 210–12. [17] See Secor, *Richard Hooker*, 249.

Fragments, it is most appropriate to consider the autograph notes alongside the analysis of the latter work. This is probably the best way of elucidating Hooker's position as a whole.

The key to the *Dublin Fragments*, at least as regards the subject of human nature, is the concept of common grace. Without it the *Fragments* do indeed appear to be characteristically Reformed in their approach to reason, the will, and divine grace, albeit in a highly confused and contradictory manner. Once the crucial role of common grace is recognized, it becomes possible to disentangle many of the complex arguments in the *Fragments*, and to see the harmony between them and the *Lawes*. Unfortunately, Hooker never uses the term 'common grace' in the late works, or indeed any other analogous term. It will be necessary, therefore, to begin by showing the central importance of common grace within the *Dublin Fragments*, and the terminology that he uses to discuss this idea. In order to do this, one may now reverse Hooker's strategy within the *Lawes*.[18] Rather than looking first at the beginning of the *Dublin Fragments* and working through to the end, seeing how the argument builds logically upon itself, one may start with the very end of these writings. The *Fragments* are comprised of three essays: a substantial account of Hooker's philosophy of mind and action in relation to divine grace; a short discussion of the sacraments; finally, an extended account of Hooker's views on predestination.[19] The first and third essays deal explicitly with accusations made by the *Christian Letter*, while the second is in its present form more tangential. The first essay is obviously the one of central relevance to this chapter, but it is necessary to approach it extremely carefully; its initial section is missing and, perhaps because of this, it invites misinterpretation. One may begin, therefore, by examining a series of pages that falls towards the end of the third essay, which deal with common grace. Once the importance of this concept has been established, and the terminology Hooker uses to discuss it, one may return to the first essay and analyse it in detail.

The passages of interest in the third essay centre mostly around the biblical Pharaoh of Exodus.[20] Hooker discusses Pharaoh in

[18] See *Lawes*, 1:57.24–33 (I.1.2).

[19] To give some idea of the relative lengths of these essays, within the *Folger* edition the first essay occupies nearly 13 pages, the second essay nearly 6½ pages and the third essay 43½ pages.

[20] See *DF* 4:157.13–163.14.

the context of predestination, like many other theologians, because of God's promise in Exodus 7: 3 and elsewhere that He 'wil harden Pharaohs heart'. Due to this act of 'hardening' Pharaoh refuses to do as Moses asks of him, despite the miracles that Moses performs, and consequently brings great suffering upon himself and his people. This raises the question of whether God had an active or a passive part in this process and, if active, how precisely God 'hardened' his heart. Since Pharaoh is taken as a paradigm for all those who obstinately oppose God's will, this matter is obviously of great importance in any consideration of predestination.

Hooker analyses Pharaoh's actions in the precise context of a discussion of how '*inward grace*' relates to predestination. Having previously examined external or 'outward grace', he begins this discussion with these remarks:

> The inward meane whereby his will is to bring men to eternall life, is that grace of his holy Spiritt, which hath beene spoaken of allreadie att large, in the article that concerneth free will. *Now from whome this inward grace, is eyther withheld altogether, or withdrawne*, such being left to themselves, waxe hard and obdurate in sinne. Touching the manner of their obduration, it hath beene ever on all sides confest, that the malice of mans owne heart doeth harden him, and nothing else.[21]

Several points should be noted here. First, Hooker speaks of '*inward grace*', rather than using any more specific term. This is a crucial point, and one that will be returned to later in this chapter. Secondly, Hooker connects his present remarks on inward grace with those he has made in the first essay of the *Dublin Fragments*, 'in the article that concerneth free will'; in both instances, then, he is talking about the same phenomenon. Thirdly, inward grace works by ameliorating in some manner the natural, innate hardness of people's hearts. From this one may conclude that everyone is inherently full of malice, except when this grace is present within them.

Turning to look at Pharaoh, Hooker observes:

> And concerning himselfe thus farre to *Moses* alsoe God did reveale... That the grace of his holy Spiritt, which softneth inwardly the hearts of men, and whereby they are driven to obedience, should not in this action

[21] *DF* 4:157.17–23.

be given, eyther to *Pharaoh*, or, to any of his servants, *I will harden them*, soe that to *Pharaohs* obduration, it plainly appeareth there did concurre, not only on his part malice, butt alsoe from God himselfe a *Prohibition* or *restraint* of grace, which restraint generally being an Act, not of policie, butt of severitie in God, there is noe doubt butt *Pharaoh* did otherwise deserve the same, even as they all doe to whome divine grace is denyed. This of the *Gentiles St Paul* witnesseth, *Knowing God they glorifyed him not as God, neyther were thanckfull: Therefore God alsoe gave them up to their owne hearts lusts*... For seeing the naturall will of God desireth to impart unto all creatures all goodnes soe farre as they are by the lawes of his providence capable thereof; it cannot be chosen butt in that respect, as his desier is, that all men were capable of inward grace because without grace there is noe salvation. Now there are that have made themselves incapable of both; thousands there have beene, and are in all ages, to whose charge it may truely be laid, that they have resisted the Holy Ghost, that the grace which is offered they thrust from them, and doe thereby, if not in word, yet in effect pronounce themselves unworthy of everlasting life, and of all effectuall helps thereunto belonging.[22]

Inward grace is spoken of as being denied to Pharaoh and his servants 'in this action', not in general throughout their lives. The clear implication is that Pharaoh was given inward grace prior to this 'hardening' process, but that it was then withdrawn from him. Hooker notes that this '*Prohibition*' of grace is not part of God's general policy towards humanity, but is rather a special punishment for human sinfulness; it is ordinarily God's will that all people receive inward grace. The sinfulness referred to is evidently not merely that of original sin, but relates to specific human actions. The Gentiles mentioned by St Paul are punished because of their rejection of God, and not for any inherent sinful condition. It follows that these Gentiles received inward grace prior to this punishment, when it was then withdrawn from them. Like Pharaoh, once this restraining force is removed, they devote themselves entirely to the evil desires of their hearts, which are natural to humans unaided by God's inward grace. In conclusion, one may state that, in Hooker's opinion, God desires that all humans receive inward grace, which alone can restrain evil desires, but as a punishment for certain acts of sinfulness this grace is withdrawn, and human depravity goes unchecked. This is precisely what Hooker argues in the crucial 'supreme cause'

[22] *DF* 4:158.19–159.16.

text in Book I of the *Lawes*, which was examined at the beginning of Ch. 3.[23] The only type of grace broad enough to cover all these instances is common grace; an aid given to all human beings, unless they merit its withdrawal. This does not mean, though, that the term 'inward grace' should here be taken as wholly synonymous with 'common grace'. As will be demonstrated, Hooker uses 'inward grace' as an umbrella term to cover all inward graces, of which common grace is merely one example. Yet in the above passage concerning Pharaoh and the Gentiles, it is inward grace considered as a common aid offered to all humanity that Hooker would appear specifically to have in mind.

This broad use of the term 'inward grace' can be seen right at the end of the third essay, where Hooker gives his own modified version of the *Lambeth Articles*. These *Articles* arose from the heated debates in Cambridge between Peter Baro and William Whitaker on predestination, and were drawn up under Whitgift's supervision to produce a Reformed consensus in the Church that would help constrain future controversy on this issue. The seventh of the *Lambeth Articles* reads as follows: 'Saving grace is not granted, communicated or given to all men, so that they might be saved by it if they wished to be.'[24] Hooker's version is somewhat shorter: 'That inward grace whereby to be saved, is deservedly not given unto all men.'[25] As Peter White has noted, Hooker carefully leaves open the question of inward graces that do not save, and in so doing illustrates his use of 'inward grace' as an umbrella term, which can cover common as well as sanctifying grace.[26]

Clearly then, as has also been shown with respect to the *Lawes*, the concept of common grace plays an important part in the *Dublin Fragments*. To illustrate this point further, one may now turn to the first essay of the *Fragments*, and to one footnote in particular. This footnote is one of the longest in Hooker's entire corpus, which should certainly be taken as an indication that it deserves the closest scrutiny. It appears at first to be a passage from Aquinas's *Summa Theologiae*, but is actually a loose paraphrase

[23] See *Lawes*, 1:92.23–93.8 (I.8.11) and pp. 100–3.

[24] See *Documents of the English Reformation*, 400: Gratis salutaris non tribuitur, non communicatur, non conceditur universis hominibus, qua servari possint, si voluerint.

[25] *DF* 4:167.7–8. Since Hooker omits the article on assurance, the equivalent article is no. 6 in his ordering.

[26] See White, *Predestination, Policy and Polemic*, 137.

taken from an unknown commentator on the *Summa*.[27] This point is particularly significant as there is a major substantive difference between the commentary and Aquinas's original text. One may begin by analysing the commentary, and then look briefly at what Aquinas actually wrote. Here is an English translation of the Latin by Ronald Bayne:

See Thomas: 1. 2. q. 109. ar. 2°. concerning grace. To elicit a good act from the free will God may pour in a threefold aid. 1. A general aid as a first cause flows into a second cause, which influx is modified in the second cause according to the matter of the second cause. For it is received in one way in a natural cause, in another way in a free cause. In a natural cause it flows in as co-operating determinately to one thing: but for a free cause it cooperates for opposite things according as the cause determines itself; this aid therefore is necessary in every act, good or bad, of the free will. 2. A special aid flows into an act morally good, and is necessary in time of fallen nature on account of the declension caused in the strength of the soul from original sin; but it was not necessary in an unfallen nature, on account of the tranquillity which was in the strength of the soul from original righteousness, whence at that time a general aid was enough to elicit acts morally good. In the case of the whole man and of the sick, acts are the results of the Power that moves. 3. A special supernatural aid is necessary to elicit an act meritorious and worthy of bliss, or, if we are to express ourselves more completely,—to an act acceptable and pleasing to God, of which acts the chief is to believe; faith is necessary, but not faith by itself as a mere quality, but by reason of its object, Christ. For so it is itself made acceptable and makes all other acts acceptable. For Christ alone has deserved bliss which we obtain in Him by God's free favour, and not on account of the worthiness of our works. The works receive a reward, but by grace, not by their own worthiness. For since there are in us two sources of action, God's grace and our nature, even our best acts savour of both sources.[28]

[27] Although Hooker used Thomas de Vio Cajetan's heavily annotated edition, the commentator is not Cajetan.

[28] See *DF* 4:109.g.1–19; Booty, 'Commentary', *Folger*, iv. 244: Vide Thom: 1. 2. q. 109. ar. 2°. *de gratia. Deus respectu boni actus eliciendi a libero arbitrio potest infundere triplex auxilium. 1. Auxil. universale, sicut causa prima influit in secundam, qui influxus modificatur in* 2da*. causa, secundam materiam causae secundae. Aliter enim recipitur in causa naturali, aliter in causa libera. In causa naturali sic influit, quod cooperatur ei determinate ad unum; causae. m. liberae cooperatur ad opposita secundum quod ea sese determinat, quare hoc auxilium est necessarium in omni actu liberi arbitrii tam bono quam malo. 2. Auxilium speciale influit ad actum moraliter bonum, et est necessarium tempore corruptae naturae, propter declinationem causatam in viribus animae, ex culpa originali, non autem erat necessarium in natura integra propter tranquillitatem quae erat in viribus animae ex justitia originali, unde tempore illo sufficiebat universale auxilium ad eliciendos bonos actus moraliter: Potentiae motivae actus in sano et infirmo. 3. Auxilium speciale supernaturale necessarium est ad eliciendum meritorium et condignum faelicitate, vel*

With admirable precision, the commentator distinguishes between three different kinds of grace. The first (*Auxil. universale*) is evidently the help of the First Cause required by all secondary agents: as mentioned previously, it is necessary in all actions, whether those of inanimate objects or those of rational beings.[29] The third grace (*Auxilium speciale supernaturale*) encompasses the theological virtue of faith (in Christ), and the notion of a merited heavenly reward; it thus presumably refers to justifying/sanctifying grace.[30] This leaves the second grace (*Auxilium speciale*) as a divine aid for morally good actions performed by rational agents, which do not deserve a heavenly reward. Given that the theological virtues are the result of the third grace, it would follow that these moral actions stem from the acquired virtues, which do not need justifying/sanctifying grace. The grace is clearly received internally, as it is described as flowing into (*influit*) an action. Furthermore, the grace cannot be natural and external (e.g. natural law) since such graces existed before the Fall, and the commentator describes this one as being introduced as a result of it. Supernatural external graces (e.g. Holy Scripture) are also excluded, since they pertain to salvation, and hence those matters dealt with by the third grace. This would all suggest that the second grace is common grace; an inward help given to humans for performing morally good actions that do not pertain to salvation.

It is especially interesting that the commentator should speak here of common grace, given that no such grace is to be found in Aquinas's *Summa Theologiae*. In the article the commentator is discussing, Aquinas actually distinguishes between only two types of grace: the help of God as 'primary mover' 'in order to do or to will any good at all',[31] and a justifying (or in Hooker's sense a

potius si fuse loqui volumus ad actum Deo acceptabilem et gratiosum inter quos principalis actus, est, credere, fides autem non per se tanquam qualitas, sed ratione objecti Christi. s. et ipsa redditur acceptabilis, et reddit alios actus omnes. Solus enim Christus meruit faelicitatem quam nos in ipso obtinemus ex gratuito favore Dei, non propter operum dignitatem. Remunerantur quidem opera sed gratiose non propter ipsorum dignitatem. Cum sint enim in nobis dua principia agendi, Dei gratia et natura nostra, sapiunt actus nostri etiam optimi utrumque principium.

[29] See p. 36. Note how in this commentary, contrary to Aquinas himself, the help of the First Mover allows the agent to determine its own act: the help is extrinsically efficacious. This looks, therefore, like a Scotist reading of Aquinas. See pp. 37–8, 41–2.

[30] Aquinas himself would certainly have thought in terms of justification, but the commentator's description of this grace would correspond to Hooker's conception of sanctification.

[31] See *ST* I-II.109.2: natura humana indiget auxilio divino ad faciendum vel volendum quodcumque bonum, sicut primo movente.

sanctifying) grace 'in order to be healed, and further that he may perform the good proper to supernatural capacity, which is meritorious.'[32] The commentator splits up the process of healing and the conferral of supernatural virtue, attributing each to a separate grace. In so doing he makes an assumption not present in Aquinas; namely, that humans are unable to perform morally good actions without a special (common) grace. Aquinas does accept that morally good actions, pertaining to the acquired virtues, cannot be performed perfectly without a special (justifying/sanctifying) grace; but he nevertheless argues that such actions can still be imperfectly performed. As a result, he does not require a concept of common grace to account for the morally good actions of *mere natural persons*. Hooker, of course, has chosen to quote the commentator, and not Aquinas directly, showing a preference for the description of common grace not in the original text. Given the role this grace has to play in the Pharaoh passage examined above, as well as in the *Lawes*, this preference should not appear particularly surprising.

This preoccupation with common grace can in fact be traced throughout the first essay of the *Dublin Fragments*. In order to show this as clearly as possible, one may now divide this first essay into two parts. Hooker begins the essay by making some remarks about his philosophy of mind and action, responding to the criticisms of the *Christian Letter*, and then proceeds to give a series of definitions of the nature of grace. It is this latter discussion, of which Hooker's quotation from the commentary on Aquinas forms an opening part, that one may analyse now.[33] This should result in a detailed understanding of Hooker's conception of grace in this work, prior to an examination of the difficult first part, which lacks its initial paragraphs or pages.

[32] See ibid. I-II.109.2: scilicet ut sanetur, et ulterius ut bonum supernaturalis virtutis operetur, quod est meritorium.

[33] See *DF* 4:109.4–113.26. For an analysis of this latter discussion, and other related passages on grace in the *Dublin Fragments*, see the following critics: Stueber, 'Richard Hooker's Place in the History of Renaissance Christian Humanism', 377–8; Hillerdal, *Reason and Revelation in Richard Hooker*, 141–7; Hill, 'The Doctrinal Background of Richard Hooker's *Laws of Ecclesiastical Polity*', 147–8; Thornburg, 'Original Sin, Justification and Sanctification in the Thought of Two Sixteenth Century English Divines: John Jewel and Richard Hooker', 148, 153–69; Devine, 'Richard Hooker's Doctrine of Justification and Sanctification in the Debate with Walter Travers 1585–1586', 251–2, 256–62; Neelands, 'The Theology of Grace of Richard Hooker', 134–85; White, *Predestination, Policy and Polemic*, 136–7.

Hooker begins his discussion of the nature of grace in the first essay by providing three different definitions, and quoting the passage from the commentator on Aquinas. One would expect the definitions of the commentator and Hooker to match, but curiously they do not: 'the grace of Almighty God signifyeth eyther his undeserved love and favour, or his offerd meanes of outward instruction and doctrine, or thirdly that grace which worketh inwardlie in mens hearts'.[34]

Nothing in the commentary on Aquinas relates to the notion of 'outward instruction and doctrine', meaning that Hooker's definitions need to be assessed in their own right. This does not mean that Hooker quotes the commentary only to ignore it; in fact he makes extensive use of it, but this is a point that becomes clear only somewhat later in the *Dublin Fragments*.

Turning to look at Hooker's definitions of grace, the first ('his undeserved love and favour') presents perhaps the greatest problem. It is tempting to relate it to the first grace mentioned by the commentator—the help of the First Cause given to all secondary agents—but there is really nothing to justify this move. Given that, for Hooker, grace is something that by its nature can never be condignly merited, it seems likely that he is here simply giving a general definition of grace as God's 'undeserved love and favour'.[35] Since all types of grace can be described in such terms, there seems little warrant for referring these words to any specific type.

The second and third definitions of grace need to be seen in the context of the paragraphs that immediately follow, where Hooker attempts to rebut the charge implicit in the *Christian Letter* that the *Lawes* is a Pelagian work, and prove that his views on grace are perfectly orthodox. In a manner characteristic of his writing, Hooker places the Pelagian heresy in its original historical setting, and shows his allegiance to the orthodox party represented by Augustine. He starts by observing that the Pelagians came to accept that grace was necessary for salvation, but that they meant by this only 'externall' or 'outward' graces, and not those which are received inwardly in the heart/soul.[36] This obviously relates to Hooker's second definition of grace as God's 'offerd meanes of outward instruction and doctrine'. 'Externall' or 'outward' in this

[34] *DF* 4:109.7–10.
[35] Cf. *Just.* 5:160.22–161.15; *DF* 4:117.4–5.
[36] See *DF* 4:109.7–110.8.

context means external to the human mind, and Hooker gives as examples 'the Lawe, the Prophets, the Ministers, the workes of God'. All these are 'externall incitements unto faith and godlines' in that they direct humans towards God/the good, but leave them entirely at the disposal of their own natural powers as to whether or not they will respond. Hooker's list of external graces appears to be purely Judaeo-Christian; 'Lawe' probably refers here to the Law of Moses. This is not surprising, given that he is at this point discussing the question of salvation with regard to the Pelagian heresy. This should not of course, though, be taken as suggesting that Hooker believes that the only external graces are those that pertain directly to salvation; as the *Lawes* itself makes clear, Hooker also considers natural law to be an external grace.[37] From this one may say that Hooker's second definition of grace refers to any aid external to the human mind, whether of natural or supernatural origin, that instructs human beings about the nature of God and the divine will.

Hooker's third definition of grace, as that 'which worketh inwardlie in mens hearts', plainly refers to a divine aid that has a direct effect upon the human mind ('hearts' here being an emotive synonym for either the will, or the mind in general).[38] This was the form of grace, he notes, that was unacceptable to the Pelagians, since they argued that humans could respond to external graces and attain salvation without any additional help. It is highly significant that Hooker speaks only of 'inward' grace, not using any more specific terms. Certainly, in a discussion of Pelagianism and salvation, one would expect this category to embrace sanctifying grace, which is an inwardly received divine aid. Yet, as the Pharaoh passage demonstrates, Hooker also speaks of common grace as an 'inward' grace. The commentary on Aquinas is also indicative, as all three of the graces the commentator describes could be subsumed under Hooker's category of 'inward' grace, including the second, common grace. This all suggests that Hooker defines this third grace in a very general sense, as any divine aid acting inwardly on the human mind.

Having discussed Pelagianism, Hooker then proceeds to look at the subsequent historical development of Semi-Pelagianism, with

[37] See also ibid. 4:111.21–6, and the ensuing discussion of these lines.

[38] See pp. 70–1 and Ch. 4, n. 226.

reference to inward grace. As he observes, this heresy was fostered by those theologians who believed that Augustine's emphasis upon the necessity of inward grace undermined the role of choice in human salvation. Consequently, although they accepted that no one could be saved without this grace, they nevertheless argued that people could naturally merit its initial bestowal by desiring that this grace be given to them. Hooker joins Augustine and the other orthodox theologians in condemning this move, and also implicitly stresses his own agreement with the Thirty-Nine Articles. Inward grace, he observes, is necessary not only to choose/perform the good, but also to desire to choose/perform it, and the latter grace he terms prevenient ('*preventing*').[39] In this way he demonstrates his accordance with Article 10 of the Thirty-Nine Articles, which states that prevenient and subsequent grace are both requisite if we are to will the good.

Hooker's next remarks are difficult, and best quoted in full:

> unlesse wee everie where diligentlie marke, there is noe man butt may be abused by the words whereby *Pelagians* and *Demi Pelagians* seeme to magnifye the grace of God, the one meaning only *externall grace*, the other *internall*, butt only to perfect that which our owne good desiers without grace have begunne. The diviner sorte of the Heathens themselves, sawe, that their owne more eminent perfections in knowledge, wisdome, valour and other the like qualities, for which sundrie of them were had in singular admiration, did growe from more then the ordinarie influence, which that supreme cause instilleth into things beneath. Noe merveile then in the Schoole of Christ to heare from the mouth of a principall instructer, *not I, butt the grace of God which is with mee.*[40]

The question that must asked is what *special* type of grace did the 'diviner sorte of the Heathens' receive? It cannot be the aid given by the First Cause to all secondary agents; Hooker excludes that himself when he refers to the 'ordinarie influence' of the 'supreme cause'. This means that Hooker is speaking here either of an external grace, or an internal grace other than the help of the First Cause. There are two strong reasons for preferring the latter of these options. First, Hooker has just stated in his consideration of Semi-Pelagianism that no one can choose/perform the good without inward grace. The perfections of the heathens must,

[39] See *DF* 4:111.8–9. See also 4:101.4; 4:107.26–8; *ST* I-II.111.3.
[40] *DF* 4:111.10–21.

therefore, stem from such an inward aid, and not merely from external stimuli such as natural law. Secondly, the whole thrust of Hooker's argument depends upon the idea that heathens receive inward grace. He moves from an analysis of the errors of Pelagianism and Semi-Pelagianism to an observation on the need for inward grace amongst virtuous heathens; he can then state that it is 'Noe merveile' that Christians acknowledge this inward aid, since even heathens themselves do. If the heathens received only external graces, there would be no logical progression between these three sentences. He would also have failed to stress the importance of inward grace, contrary to the two heresies he is opposing at this point. One may conclude, therefore, that in the above lines Hooker asserts that both heathens and Christians need inward grace to choose/perform the good, and indeed to desire to do these actions.

Hooker further pursues this comparison between heathens and Christians some lines later, and these observations are also worth quoting in full:

> Now amongst the Heathens which had noe bookes wherby to know God besides the volumes of heaven and earth, that small *vitall odor* which (as Prosper noteth:) breathed upon them to the end they might live, became notwithstanding the *odor* of death soe that even by those visable testimonies, it might be plainly perceived, *how the letter killeth where the Spiritt quickneth not*; But of heathens what should wee speake, sith the first grace saveth not the Church itselfe by vertue of the second without the third. Saving grace is the guift of the Holy Ghost which lighteneth inwardly the mindes, and inflameth inwardlie the hearts of men, working in them that knowledge approbation and love of things divine, the fruite wherof is aeternall life.[41]

The remarks on heathens are based on a passage from Prosper of Aquitaine's *De Vocatione Omnium Gentium*. Since one cannot hope to grasp Hooker's meaning unless one understands Prosper's, one may quote the relevant lines from his work:

> the greater number of men who were left to walk in the ways of their own choice, did not understand nor follow this Law. The vivifying fragrance that breathed life became for them *a deadly odour unto death*, so that we learned also of those testimonies of the visible world that *the letter killeth, but the spirit quickeneth*. Thus, what the promulgation of the Law

[41] Ibid. 4:111.21–32. See also Hillerdal, *Reason and Revelation in Richard Hooker*, 143.

and the preaching of the Prophets did for Israel, that the testimony of the whole creation with all the wonders of God's goodness wrought at all times for all nations.[42]

The natural world, Prosper notes just prior to this, offers humanity knowledge of natural law; the whole universe preaches the majesty of the Creator. Yet, as he then adds, most people either fail to follow or to understand this law. The metaphor of 'fragrance' (*odor*) he then uses is taken from 2 Corinthians 2: 14–16, where Paul compares the knowledge of Christ to a fragrance spread before humanity: for some people this fragrance leads them to life, while others are condemned to death. In applying this metaphor to the heathens, Prosper makes natural law the fragrance that is spread before all nations: some people react to it positively, while others do not. He then refers to 2 Corinthians 3: 6, where Paul famously argues that 'the letter killeth, but the Spirit giveth life': Mosaic Law brings only condemnation, but the Holy Spirit rather gives life. By extending this metaphor, Prosper observes that natural law (the 'letter' (*littera*), or written code of the heathens) serves only to condemn people to death, unless they are vivified by the inward Spirit. He then goes on to look briefly at this inward common grace in the following chapter.

Returning to the passage from the *Dublin Fragments*, one can now see that the '*vitall odor*' referred to by Hooker is not an inward grace, despite its ethereal connotations, but rather the external grace of natural law. This is particularly evident from his observation that 'those visable testimonies' show '*how the letter killeth where the Spiritt quickneth not*'. As a comparison with the Prosper passage illustrates, these testimonies are not those of the heathens themselves, but rather of the 'volumes of heaven and earth', or the natural world. These testimonies, offering knowledge of natural law, function as a 'killing letter' unless inward grace illuminates people's minds. Hooker is arguing, therefore, that inward grace is essential if non-Christians are to profit from external graces, such as natural law.

[42] Prosper, *The Call of All Nations* (*PL* 51:691), 97: maximus numerus hominum, qui vias voluntatis suae ambulare permissus est, non intellexit, nec secutus hanc legem est, et odor vitae, qui spirabat ad vitam, factus est ei odor mortis ad mortem... ut etiam in illis visibilibus testimoniis disceretur quod littera occideret, spiritus autem vivificaret... Quod ergo in Israel per constitutionem legis et prophetica eloquia gerebatur, hoc in universis nationibus totius creaturae testimonia et bonitatis Dei miracula semper egerunt. See also *The Call of All Nations*, 31–3, 95, 97, 197.

Hooker then proceeds in this passage to note that all three categories of grace he has mentioned previously are necessary if Christians are to find salvation. This raises several problems, in that it is unclear why Hooker suddenly introduces the term 'saving grace', and what he understands by the 'first grace'. To deal with the former matter initially, if one presumes that Hooker is, in this one long paragraph, consistent in his definitions of the second and third graces, then he is observing here that Christians cannot be saved by external grace without inward grace. This would accord with his critique of Pelagianism, and also with his remarks on heathens. Just as he previously argued that it is 'Noe merveile' that what is true for heathens regarding inward grace must also be true for Christians, so he now repeats this idea, introducing it with the phrase 'But of heathens what should wee speake'. Neither are able to profit from external graces without inward grace. On this occasion, however, Hooker introduces the idea of salvation with regard to Christians, which must signal an element of discontinuity between them and the heathens. After all, the inward (common) grace that heathens receive may help them profit from natural law, but this will not in itself ultimately save them. Hooker must, therefore, specify which inward grace separates Christians from heathens, and this is what he does, speaking now of 'saving grace'. Unfortunately, he does not signal clearly that this is what he is doing, and it would be easy to take 'saving grace' as wholly synonymous with the third grace. As the Pharaoh passage, his version of the *Lambeth Articles*, and the above discussion of the heathens illustrate, however, Hooker uses 'inward grace' as an umbrella term to include the notion of common grace as well as that of saving/sanctifying grace. It is merely on this occasion, when Hooker's subject matter demands that he be more explicit or be accused of ignoring the role of justification and sanctification, that he specifies which inward grace he is describing, and talks explicitly of 'saving grace'. One might compare this with his remarks on the sacraments in the second essay of the *Dublin Fragments*, where his context also requires him to speak specifically of 'tokens of... saving grace'.[43]

This leaves the question of what Hooker understands here by the 'first' type of grace. His list of the three graces, in reference to

[43] See *DF* 4:115.11.

Christians, suggests that they are mentioned in order of ascending spiritual utility, with the third being the most crucial of all to salvation. Given the general nature of the categories of 'external' and 'inward' grace, this would suggest that the first grace is probably the help of the First Cause given to all secondary agents. It has previously been observed that Hooker might have classified this help as an inward, or 'third' grace, but there now seem reasons for believing that this is not the case.[44] The help of the First Cause is certainly quite different from other inward graces, in that it merely permits secondary agents to have their own motions, rather than ameliorating the thought-patterns of the human mind in some manner. It is also possible that Hooker's previous description of the first grace as God's 'undeserved love and favour' is not merely a general definition of grace, but a reference to the help of the First Cause, though one could be excused for thinking otherwise.[45] For further evidence concerning the nature of this first grace one needs to look, though, at Hooker's final discussion of the threefold nature of grace in this essay of the *Dublin Fragments*. It occurs several lines later in the text, and it is to this passage that one may now turn:

> Thus of the three kinds of Grace; the Grace whereby God doth incline towards men, the grace of outward instruction, and the grace of inward sanctification, which twoe worke mans inclination towards God, as the first is the well spring of all good, and the second the instrument thereof to our good, soe that which giveth effect to both in us, whoe have noe cause att all to thinck ourselves worthy of eyther, is the gratious and blessed guift of his Holy Spiritt: This is that baptisme with heavenlie fyer, which both illuminateth and inflameth.[46]

Hooker's initial description of the first grace ('the Grace whereby God doth incline towards men') in this passage is so broad that it could again be taken as a definition of the concept of grace in general. The word 'kinds', however, indicates that it is in fact a specific category of grace. If these lines appeared in isolation one might be tempted to identify it either with the help of the First Cause given to all secondary agents, or with common grace. The latter would be quite feasible, since common grace does incline people towards God, and could be described as the 'well spring of

[44] See p. 282.

[45] For evidence to the contrary, though, see the remarks concerning grace and the sacraments on p. 290.

[46] *DF* 4:112.2–9.

all good'. The previous analysis suggests, however, that this is not the case, and that the first grace must be defined in some other way. Some light can perhaps be gleaned from a fine distinction that Hooker makes between the first and second grace. The second grace must be external grace, since it is indeed 'outward', and is a source of 'instruction': this would also correspond with Hooker's previous definitions of this grace in the preceding pages. He notes that this grace allows us to use the potency given by the first grace to 'our' good, while the first grace itself is merely the source of 'all' good. Hooker has previously argued that nothing good can be performed or desired by a person without inward grace, of which common grace forms a part, as his remarks on the heathens illustrate. Common grace thus allows people to perform actions that are to their personal benefit (or 'own' good), since they are in accordance with the natural laws founded by God. The help of the First Cause can, however, be described in a more impersonal sense as the source of 'all' good, since it makes possible the very basic good that is human action. It would not, in any case, be logical for common grace to be listed here prior to external grace: the three graces are placed in an ascending hierarchy of spiritual utility, the most important being placed last, and common grace utilizes external grace, and not vice versa. It would seem, then, after all, that Hooker does define the first grace as the help of the First Cause in these lines, in a manner consistent with the arguments in the preceding few pages.

Hooker also, of course, identifies the third grace with sanctifying grace in this passage, which serves as an additional source of confusion. One can merely restate the remarks made in relation to 'saving grace'; that Hooker is now preoccupied with issues of salvation, and needs to be specific about the form of inward grace involved. The documentation relating common grace to inward grace is too great for this point to be in real doubt. One might observe, though, that although Hooker's discussion of the threefold nature of grace in this essay of the *Dublin Fragments* is logical and sequential, it can scarcely be called clear or perspicuous. Much of the problem stems from Hooker's apparent unwillingness to speak plainly about common grace, and to define it as a type of inward grace. As a result of this, it is all too easy for the reader to assume erroneously that 'inward grace' is an exclusively Christian idea. Why Hooker should have dealt with common grace in this way is, of course, an important issue, and one that will be examined at the end of this chapter.

There are two other discussions of the manifold nature of grace in the other essays of the *Dublin Fragments*, and it is worth taking the opportunity to look briefly at these. The first occurs in the second essay during Hooker's analysis of the sacraments, and needs to be seen in this context. His concerns are different here, and he has adapted his categorization of grace accordingly:

> Touching *Sacraments* whether many or few in number, their doctrine is, that *ours both signifye and cause grace*; butt what grace and in what manner? By grace wee allwayes understand as the word of God teacheth, first, his favour and undeserved mercie towards us; Secondlie, the bestowing of his holy spiritt which inwardlie worketh; thirdlie, the effects of that Spiritt whatsoever butt especiallie saving vertues, such as are, *faith, charitie*, and *hope*, lastly the free and full remission of all our sinnes. This is the grace which *Sacraments* yeeld, and whereby wee are all justifyed.[47]

These appear to be definitions of the word 'grace', rather than classifications of particular types of grace. The first seems to be a definition of grace in general, recalling Hooker's description of the 'undeserved love and favour' of God in the first essay of the *Fragments*. Hooker then speaks of the reception of the Holy Spirit, an act that is presumably synonymous with the receipt of inward grace. Hooker's third definition looks at the effects of the Holy Spirit's presence, and most especially at the infusion of the theological virtues. His description leaves room, however, for the workings of common grace, as the effects of the Holy Spirit in a non-sacramental context. The fourth definition evidently deals with justification, since grace is here described in terms of the 'free and full remission of all our sinnes'. No reference is made in this passage to the help of the First Cause given to secondary agents, since this is not connected with the reception of the sacraments.

The final discussion of the manifold nature of grace occurs late in the third essay, shortly before the Pharaoh passage with which it is connected. Hooker's particular concern in this essay is with predestination, and this is the context in which these lines must be seen:

> It remaineth therefore that wee come now unto those things about ourselves, which by Gods owne appointment are meanes of bringing his desier and our Saviours meritt finally to that effect which they both covet.... There are meanes which God hath appointed towards us,

[47] *DF* 4:117.2–10. See also 4:118.22–6.

meanes to be in us, and meanes which are to proceede from us. The meane toward us, is that grace, wherby wee are outwardly called, and chose into the fellowship of Gods people.[48]

Once again leaving aside any reference to the general aid of the First Cause, Hooker proceeds after this passage to give a particularly full account of the first of these three graces, which is the 'meane toward us' or external grace.[49] He describes it as encompassing the 'grace of externall vocation', by which people are brought within the Christian Church, or the elect race of Israel.[50] Such people can subsequently benefit from the external grace that is divine revelation, whether in Jewish or Christian scriptures, or in the form of oral communications.[51] Hooker does not, though, leave aside the question of heathen peoples, and again quotes from Prosper's *De Vocatione Omnium Gentium* on the universal testimony that is natural law.[52] External grace thus extends to all nations, although it is clearly concentrated in great richness amongst Christians, and to a lesser extent, Jews.

Some pages later Hooker then describes the second grace: 'The inward meane whereby his will is to bring men to eternall life, is that grace of his holy Spiritt, which hath beene spoaken of allreadie att large, in the article that concerneth free will.'[53] This is evidently inward grace, and given the context, this must encompass the grace of sanctification necessary for salvation. Yet, as has been noted above, Hooker goes on to discuss this grace in connection with Pharaoh, plainly demonstrating that it includes the notion of common grace as well.[54]

The third grace ('meanes which are to proceede from us') is more enigmatic, since Hooker never returns to discuss it in detail, and it has no parallel elsewhere in the *Dublin Fragments*. The most likely candidate, though, is gratuitous grace, a divine aid given to individuals so that they can bring other people nearer to God.[55] This accords with Hooker's observation that, through this grace, people are brought nearer to God and salvation through means which proceed 'from us'.

[48] Ibid. 4:153.6–18.
[49] For a definition of external grace, see pp. 282–3.
[50] See *DF* 4:153.25–8.
[51] See ibid. 4:155.15–27: 'those outward meanes of conversion'.
[52] See ibid. 4:155.8–15.
[53] See ibid. 4:157.17–19.
[54] See p. 276.
[55] See e.g. *ST* I-II.111.1; Devine, 'Richard Hooker's Doctrine of Justification and Sanctification in the Debate with Walter Travers 1585–1586', 251–3. Devine actually applies Aquinas's description of gratuitous grace to another grace described in the *Dublin Fragments*, but I am indebted to him in general for the notion of this grace.

Having dealt with this material, there is still one other subject that needs to be discussed, prior to an analysis of the opening part of the first essay of the *Dublin Fragments*. In this opening part, Hooker attempts to demonstrate his orthodoxy as regards Article 10 of the Thirty-Nine Articles, which states that 'we have no power to do good works pleasant and acceptable to God, without the grace of God by Christ preventing us, that we may have a good will, and working with us, when we have that good will'.[56] Hooker does indeed talk about these good works (*pietatis opera*) pleasing and acceptable to God (*Deo grata sint et accepta*), but, perhaps because the introduction to the *Fragments* is missing, he never defines what he understands by them. As will become apparent, this is an important issue, since it is a source of certain of the misunderstandings surrounding Hooker's views on *mere natural persons* in this work. Fortunately, there are three passages in other areas of his late writings which do deal with this subject, and it is these that we may examine now.[57]

The first of these passages comes from the commentary on Aquinas's *Summa Theologiae*, and the description of the third aid, sanctifying grace. The commentator observes that this grace is necessary 'to elicit an act meritorious and worthy of bliss, or, if we are to express ourselves more completely,—to an act acceptable and pleasing to God, of which acts the chief is to believe'.[58] These works acceptable and pleasing to God (*actum Deo acceptabilem et gratiosum*) are subsequently rewarded, presumably in the afterlife. It is stressed that such works are acceptable to God because Christ has made them so, rather than because of any condign merit upon the part of the believer. Crucially, the commentator also notes that faith in Christ 'makes all other acts acceptable'.[59] It would seem, therefore, in this long passage quoted by Hooker, that works 'pleasing and acceptable to God' are defined as the good deeds of justified and sanctified Christians, which stem from faith in Christ. This accords with Article 12 of the Thirty-Nine Articles, which observes that such works 'are the fruits of faith, and follow after justification'.[60]

[56] See *Documents of the English Reformation*, 290: absque gratia Dei, quae per Christum est, nos praeveniente, ut velimus, et cooperante dum volumus, ad pietatis opera facienda, quae Deo grata sint et accepta, nihil valemus.

[57] In addition to these two texts, see also *Just.* 5:154.17–26.

[58] See *DF* 4:109.g.12–14 and pp. 279–80 above: *ad eliciendum meritorium et condignum faelicitate, vel potius si fuse loqui volumus ad actum Deo acceptabilem et gratiosum inter quos principalis actus, est, credere.*

[59] *ipsa redditur acceptabilis, et reddit alios actus omnes.*

[60] See *Documents of the English Reformation*, 291: sunt fructus fidei et iustificatos sequuntur.

Hooker's basic agreement with the commentator and Article 12 on this point can be seen from two of his autograph notes in the margin of his edition of the *Christian Letter*. There are considerable textual difficulties surrounding the first note, as the original text is damaged, and the two early copies disagree with one another. To make this situation clear, one may quote all three sources side by side:

The workes of heathen men not acceptable propter praemium . . . principium. [C^1: Hooker's autograph notes in Corpus Christi College, Oxford, MS 215b]

The workes of heathen men not acceptable propter praemium ut unde principii. [C^2: transcript of notes in Corpus Christi College, Oxford, MS 215a]

The workes of heathen men not acceptable propter praemium agendi principium. [D^2: transcript of notes in Trinity College, Dublin, MS 119; ff. 19^r–70^r][61]

Of the variant readings, 'principium' is to be preferred to 'principii' on the textual authority of manuscript C^1, in Hooker's own italic hand. Since 'ut unde principium' makes no sense (and 'ut unde principii' little more), this would support the reading in manuscript D^2: 'agendi principium'. This would seem to be the case even though Booty notes that D^2 is in general a less accurate transcription than C^2.[62] One should also note that in the Aquinas commentary quoted by Hooker, the phrase used to refer to the sources of human action is the nearly identical 'principia agendi'.[63] A literal translation of D^2 might read as follows: 'The workes of heathen men not acceptable because of the reward, the source of the doing/action.' Hooker thus connects the acceptability of human actions with whether their 'source' (*principium*) deserves or justifies a reward. Heathen actions do not deserve a reward in his opinion because there is something defective about their origin or source.

For an understanding of what Hooker means here by 'source' (*principium*), one must examine the second note, which reads as follows: 'Morall works done in faith hope and charitie are accepted

[61] See *AN* 4:14.19–20. This note also contains a reference to Eucherius, bishop of Lyons, but not to any specific writing by him. As Booty observes, Keble points to the *Epistle to his Relative Valerian*, and Bayne to a passage about false philosophy. Hooker may perhaps have had in mind Eucherius's remark here that heathens went astray because they did not know God: this could be taken as implying that they lacked faith, and hence the correct principles for human action. Some of the remarks in this passage seem, though, to run counter to Hooker's arguments in favour of true heathen philosophy in the *Lawes* and elsewhere. See especially *Lawes*, 1:224.11–227.1 (III.8.8–9).

[62] See Booty, 'Introduction', *Folger*, iv. p. xlvii.

[63] See *DF* 4:109.g.18.

and rewarded with God, the want thereof punished with eternall death. No fornicator adulterer etc.'[64] It is thus the presence of the three theological virtues that make good works acceptable to, and rewardable by God. This is very close to the Aquinas commentator's statement that faith makes good works acceptable and pleasing to God. It is consequently the lack of the theological virtues that makes heathen works unacceptable. Two theories can be suggested for why this might be the case. First, assuming a forensic view of justification, one could argue that only those people who are justified by faith can perform works acceptable to God, since Christ covers the imperfections in their works. Secondly, one could argue, following Aquinas himself, that no human act is truly acceptable (*accepta*) and able to please (*potest placere*) God unless it is directed at humanity's last end, God, and this is not possible without the three theological virtues, of which faith is one:

> Natural reason is not entirely ruined in unbelievers by their unbelief; some knowledge of truth remains in them, and that enables them to perform deeds which are good of their kind.
>
> As for Cornelius, note that he was not really an infidel, else his actions would not have been acceptable to God, whom none can please without faith.[65]

Hooker certainly accepted the forensic theory of justification, but he may well have had the second theory in mind here. By speaking of 'morall works done in faith hope and charitie', rather than just faith itself, he seems to imply that such works are rewarded because of their intrinsic nature—since they stem from the theological virtues—rather than because faith has led their imperfections to be covered. One might think here of Hooker's distinction between mortal and venial sins; sanctification clearly has, in his opinion, a qualitative effect upon the actions that Christians can perform.

This would in turn suggest that heathen works are, in his opinion, not acceptable because their 'source' (*principium*) is defective, not lying in the theological virtues that direct humans towards God. One should note, though, that Hooker is not arguing here

64 See *DF* 4:14.21–3.

65 *ST* II-II.10.4: per infidelitatem non corrumpitur totaliter in infidelibus ratio naturalis, quin remaneat in eis aliqua veri cognitio, per quam facere possunt aliquod opus de genere bonorum. De Cornelio tamen sciendum est quod infidelis non erat; alioquin ejus operatio accepta non fuisset Deo, cui sine fide nullus potest placere. See also I-II.62.2–3; I-II.65.2, 5; II-II.23.7.

that all the works of heathens are sinful; that a person who fails to perform actions 'in faith hope and charitie' is therefore a 'fornicator' or an 'adulterer'. Hooker is alluding here to 1 Corinthians 6: 9, where Paul observes that 'nether fornicatours, nor idolaters, nor adulterers, nor wantons, nor bouggerers, Nor theves, nor covetous, nor drunkards, nor railers, nor extorcioners shal inherite the kingdome of God'. These remarks are made with reference to members of the Christian Church, since Paul has been considering the case of a Christian in Corinth who had reportedly been living with his father's wife. Paul's concern is to show that justification/sanctification do not remove the responsibility to lead a moral life. Hooker's reference to 1 Corinthians, and indeed the second note in general (as Booty observes), seems to be directed at Article 6 of the *Christian Letter*, and towards showing that faith and works, and not faith alone, are necessary for salvation:[66] as he mentions in another note on this article: 'how should workes be but necessary unto the last end seing the next and nerest cannot be attained without them'.[67] Hooker thus excludes Christian fornicators and adulterers from salvation due to their works, whatever their supposed faith; he does not here describe all the works of *mere natural persons* as sins.

Hooker was, therefore, in a position easily to demonstrate his orthodoxy with regard to Article 10 of the Thirty-Nine Articles. Although he argues in Book 2 of the *Lawes* that *mere natural persons* can glorify and obey God, and to some extent abstain from sin, this is perfectly compatible with the notion that such works are not acceptable to God, since only works originating from the theological virtues are meritorious and rewardable in heaven. As regards the problematic passage at the end of Book 2 cited by the *Christian Letter*, where Hooker speaks of the actions of *mere natural persons* being 'acceptable' in God's sight, this also could easily be defended. As Covel notes, in this passage Hooker merely affirms that actions performed according to natural law are in general acceptable to God, not acceptable in the technical sense of being rewardable in heaven.[68] None of this, however, proves Hooker's conformity with regard to the observation in Article 13 that works performed before 'the grace of Christ, and the inspiration of his Spirit' 'have

66 See Booty, 'Commentary', *Folger*, iv. p. 190.

67 See *DF* 4:22.23–4.

68 See *Lawes*, 1:188.28–31; *DF* 4:23.19–22; Covel, 'A Just and Temperate Defence', 489.

the nature of sin' (*peccati rationem habere*). This was potentially a more problematic point for Hooker, and one that will be returned to at the end of this chapter.

Having looked at Hooker's theory of grace, and his understanding of what actions are 'acceptable' to God, one is now finally in a position to analyse the opening part of the first essay of the *Dublin Fragments*.[69] It is here that Hooker examines the sense in which humans have the freedom to know and choose the good. This essay is, as the third essay implies, targeted specifically at showing Hooker's orthodoxy as regards Article 10, on free will:[70] significantly, he does not concern himself here with the accusations that the *Christian Letter* makes with respect to Articles 12 and 13. Since he defines 'good works acceptable and pleasant to God' as the works of sanctified Christians, this means he need only discuss his philosophy of mind and action in a manner that pertains to *divinely enhanced reason* and *divinely enhanced will*. His task is complicated, however, by the nature of the two passages that the *Christian Letter* uses to accuse him of contradicting Article 10. It will be recalled that in the first of these passages, which are both taken from the important seventh chapter of Book 1 of the *Lawes*, Hooker argues that 'There is in the will of man naturally that freedome, whereby it is apt to take or refuse any particular object whatsoever being presented unto it.'[71] In the second passage, he observes that 'There is not that good which concerneth us, but it hath evidence enough for it selfe, if reason were diligent to search it out.'[72] This chapter of the *Lawes*, and Hooker's philosophy of mind and action in general, does not assume the presence of sanctifying grace in relation to the operations of the human mind, except in discussions involving the theological virtues. These two remarks, therefore, pertain to *mere natural*

[69] See *DF* 4:101.1–109.4. For discussions of this opening part by the critics, see in particular: Stueber, 'Richard Hooker's Place in the History of Renaissance Christian Humanism', 375–7, 386–90; Hillerdal, *Reason and Revelation in Richard Hooker*, 138–40; Hill, 'The Doctrinal Background of Richard Hooker's *Lawes of Ecclesiastical Polity*, 143–6; Hill, 'Doctrine and Polity in Hooker's Laws', 178–81; Morrel, 'The Systematic Theology of Richard Hooker', 94–8; Thornburg, 'Original Sin, Justification and Sanctification in the Thought of Two Sixteenth Century English Divines: John Jewel and Richard Hooker', 149–52; Devine, 'Richard Hooker's Doctrine of Justification and Sanctification in the Debate with Walter Travers 1585–1586', 253–4; Neelands, 'The Theology of Grace of Richard Hooker', 168–74; Kirby, *Richard Hooker's Doctrine of the Royal Supremacy*, 46; Atkinson, *Richard Hooker and the Authority of Scripture, Tradition and Reason*, 29–30, 78.

[70] See *DF* 4:157.17–19.

[71] See *Lawes*, 1:79.27–9 (I.7.6); *DF* 4:17.20–18.1.

[72] See *Lawes*, 1:80.29–31 (I.7.7); *DF* 4:18.2–3.

persons as well as sanctified Christians, and in defending them one would expect Hooker to defend the ratiocinative and volitional capacities of both types of people. This is, indeed, what he in part does, but this is not immediately evident, and this essay of the *Dublin Fragments* can be read erroneously as a defence of the abilities of sanctified Christians alone. This situation is perhaps in part the result of Hooker's concern to show his agreement with Article 10, which does not deal with *mere natural persons*. Yet the chief problem seems to lie, as ever, with Hooker's lack of clarity about the nature of grace.

One might imagine that after the lengthy discussion on grace in this chapter, no further terminological problems could arise in this area. Unfortunately this is not the case, since the principal type of grace mentioned in this initial part of the first essay of the *Dublin Fragments*, with regard to the operations of the human mind, is called 'speciall' grace; a term he does not, of course, subsequently define. It is again possible that he did provide such a definition, and that it lay in the introduction to the first essay of the *Fragments*; since, however, this is now missing, it will be necessary to try to reconstruct the meaning of this term from the pages that do survive. I should like here to suggest the theory that 'speciall' grace is here synonymous with 'inward' grace, and that Hooker uses these terms in exactly the same way: 'speciall' grace would thus presumably earn its name for being either more than an 'ordinary' external grace, or more than the 'ordinary' help of the First Cause to secondary causes. Initially to support this idea, one might note how the commentator on Aquinas describes both common and sanctifying grace (both types of inward grace) as special graces, calling them respectively a 'special aid' (*Auxilium speciale*) and a 'special supernatural aid' (*Auxilium speciale supernaturale*).[73] One might also note Covel's terminology in his 'A Just and Temperate Defence', where he calls common grace a 'special favour of God', although he does not admittedly use this term with regard to sanctifying grace.[74] The only real way, however, to prove this theory is to look at the opening part of the first essay, and to see how Hooker uses this term in connection with his philosophy of mind and action.

73 See *DF* 4:109.g.7–12 and pp. 279–80 above.

74 See Covel, 'A Just and Temperate Defence', 474.

The first essay of the *Dublin Fragments* begins with a fragmentary remark on special grace, but there is no indication to what this term refers, or what it means. Hooker then proceeds, after a paragraph break, to curse those who disagree with Article 10 of the Thirty-Nine Articles, that prevenient and subsequent grace are necessary for 'the workes of pietie which are acceptable' to God.[75] Both these graces must in this context relate to forms of sanctifying grace, for the reasons that have been given above.

There then follows a discussion of the liberty of the will, in relation to the terms 'aptnes' and 'ablenes'.[76] The former of these terms is taken from the passage cited by the *Christian Letter* in which he argues that 'there is in the will of man naturally that freedome, whereby it is apt to take or refuse any particular object whatsoever being presented unto it'.[77] Hooker is here, therefore, in the position of defending this original remark. As noted in Ch. 3, the distinction between aptness and ableness is scholastic in its foundation: 'aptnes' refers to the will's innate capacity to choose freely, which cannot by definition be severed from it, while 'ablenes' refers to the will's capacity to actuate this choice for a particular end (such as choice of the good).[78] This is precisely the distinction he makes in the *Dublin Fragments*. With regard to aptness, Hooker argues that 'Aptnes freely to take or refuse things sett before it, is soe essentiall to the will, that being deprived of this it looseth the nature, and cannot possiblie retaine the definition of will.' With regard to ableness, he argues that the will is not 'able' of itself to choose the good; through 'a native evill habit' it will always of itself choose badly. He words this in the strongest possible terms, arguing that 'if Gods speciall grace did not aide our imbecilitie, whatsoever wee doe or imagine would be only and continuallie evill'. Special grace is necessary, therefore, for the will

[75] See *DF* 4:101.2–6. Hooker actually calls the second grace 'helping', which would refer to co-operating grace. Later in the *Dublin Fragments*, however, he speaks of prevenient and 'subsequent' grace (see *DF* 4:107.26–8). In either case the idea is basically the same, that prevenient or operating grace is necessary for people to have good desires/thoughts, whereas subsequent or co-operating grace is necessary for those good desires/thoughts to be put into effect. Subsequent grace has been used instead of co-operating grace throughout this chapter, as it is a more natural terminological partner to prevenient grace. Cf. *ST* I-II.111.2–3.

[76] See *DF* 4:101.6–102.8. There is a comparable discussion in Covel's 'A Just and Temperate Defence', 481–4. Cf. also Montague, *A New Gagg*, 107–9.

[77] See *Lawes*, 1:79.27–9 (I.7.6).

[78] See pp. 103–5.

to be 'able' to choose the good, as well as the bad. This is a distinction that is to some degree essential for any orthodox theologian who would assert the freedom of the will: he must make the choice of the good to some extent reliant upon grace, in order to avoid the heresy of Pelagianism. The fact that Hooker makes all human goodness reliant upon grace shows, in an unqualified sense, his acceptance of the Reformed doctrine of total depravity, not his rejection of metaphysical libertarianism.

What is at issue here, however, is not the distinction between aptness and ableness, but the nature of the special grace that en-ables the will. If special grace is identified with sanctifying grace then Hooker is here making a wholeheartedly Reformed assertion of humanity's absolute depravity (or at least the depravity of *mere natural persons*). This is how Kirby interprets a similar statement on sin and ableness in the third essay of the *Fragments*.[79] Yet Hooker is not speaking here about good works 'acceptable' to God, but about the distinction between aptness and ableness, with reference to the seventh chapter of Book 1 of the *Lawes*. These remarks are thus true of his philosophy of mind and action in general, which must create the strongest suspicion that special grace cannot merely refer to sanctifying grace. If it refers either to common or to 'inward' grace, then these observations fall in line with his views as articulated in the *Lawes* and the rest of the *Dublin Fragments*. The fact that Hooker has just discussed grace with regard to works 'acceptable' to God would suggest that special grace is synonymous with 'inward' grace; an inward aid given to help the mind in its operations, which embraces the concept of common as well as sanctifying grace. As has been argued in Ch. 3, while both Calvin and Hooker believe that all good actions by *mere natural persons* require the aid of common grace, Hooker considers this aid to be potentially much more efficacious than does Calvin.[80] While the theory of common grace merely modifies Calvin's concept of total depravity, for Hooker it means that humans as commonly encountered are not totally depraved. Thus despite initial appearances to the contrary, Hooker's observations in the *Dublin Fragments* on aptness and ableness, in a qualified sense, by no means commit him to a Reformed doctrine of total depravity.

[79] See Kirby, *Richard Hooker's Doctrine of the Royal Supremacy*, 46; *DF* 4:141.3–14.

[80] See pp. 108–9, 149–57.

Hooker ends this discussion of aptness and ableness with a quotation from Hilary of Poitiers's *De Trinitate* (The Trinity). I cite a translation, taken from the Fathers of the Church edition: 'even so the soul of man, if it has not breathed in the gift of the Spirit through faith, will, it is true, possess the faculty for understanding, but it will not have the light of knowledge'.[81] This is a perfect example of the complexities and ambiguities that this part of the *Dublin Fragments* has to offer. There can be little doubt that Hilary is here describing what Hooker would term sanctifying grace, since this 'gift' (*donum*) is received through faith. This might imply, therefore, that in Hooker's opinion, the will is able to choose the good only with the aid of this grace. One must recall, however, that Hooker is attempting to demonstrate his agreement with Article 10 at this point, which deals only with sanctifying grace. He thus illustrates his orthodoxy, as regards this article, by the citation of one of the Church Fathers, but thereby obscures his opinions on common grace. The weight of evidence in the late works shows, in spite of this, that Hooker did believe that non-Christians could both know and choose the good, with the help of common grace. One might consider, at this time, the following aide-memoire in Hooker's autograph notes on the *Christian Letter*:

> Remember heere to show the use of the law of nature in handling matters of religion. Are there not cases of salvation wherin ⟨the Church⟩ a man may have controversie with infidels which believe not the scriptures? And even with them which believe ⟨yeat⟩ scripture the law of nature notwithstanding is not without force ⟨so⟩ that any man ⟨ought⟩ to whome it is alleaged can cast it of as a thing impertinent.[82]

He continues to assume, as in the *Lawes*, that *mere natural persons* can know those parts of natural law that pertain to God, and thus presumably, at least to some extent, act according to their dictates. To this end he cites Aquinas's *Summa contra Gentiles* and Philippe du Plessis-Mornay (presumably, given the context, the *Traité de la Verité de la Religion Chrétienne Contre les Athées, Epicuriens, Payens, Juifs, Mahumedistes, et Autres Infideles*), both of which theologians describe how non-Christians can know a great deal about God through the

[81] *ita et animus humanus, nisi per fidem donum Spiritus hauserit, habebit quidem naturam Deum intelligendi, sed lumen scientiae non habebit.* See Hilary of Poitiers, *The Trinity*, trans. Stephen McKenna. *Fathers of the Church* 5 (New York, 1954), 63.

[82] See *AN* 4:13.14–20.

use of natural reason.[83] If Hooker really believed, with Calvin, that without sanctifying grace 'whatsoever wee doe or imagine would be only and continuallie evill', he would not have ascribed to *mere natural persons* the ability to have such an extensive knowledge of God and the divine will.

A similar discussion of aptness and ableness occurs in Hooker's autograph notes to the *Christian Letter*, although here the primary emphasis is upon reason and the 'light of divine grace' (*lumen divinae gratiae*), rather than the will.[84] This is a good example of Hooker's greater willingness to refer to the corruption of the reason in the late works, as opposed to in the *Lawes*. Significantly, though, Hooker does not define the type of grace involved. He does, however, refer in passing to Cyprian's conversion; a process that would logically have involved sanctifying grace.[85] This suggests to the reader that this entire note is concerned purely with this grace, as the one that can alone engender 'ableness' in the reason and the will. Hooker is again, though, defending his philosophy of mind and action in relation to Article 10 of the Thirty-Nine Articles, and this should not be taken as meaning that Christians are alone able to know and choose the good.

Hooker also cites three authorities, in his autograph notes, to support his views on aptness and ableness.[86] The first is Hilary, in the *De Trinitate*. The page of this work mentioned by Hooker does not seem particularly appropriate in this context. One must, therefore, join Bayne in wondering whether Hooker had in mind the passage that he quotes in the *Dublin Fragments*, which occurs on the previous page of the edition to which Hooker refers.[87] As this passage has been discussed above, there is no need to examine it again here.

The second authority is Philo of Alexandria. Two works are cited, the *Legum Allegoria* (Allegorical Interpretation) and *De Cherubim* (On the Cherubim) (though this latter citation is scored out). In both the passages to which Hooker refers, Philo argues forcefully that the human virtues, and right reason in particular,

[83] See ibid. 4:15.1–3. See also Booty, 'Commentary', *Folger*, iv. 190. Plessis-Mornay's *Traité* was published in Antwerp in 1581. Hooker also speaks in this note of 'Lactantius his proofes in matter of religion taken from nature.' Lactantius, in *De Opificio Dei* (The Workmanship of God) and *De Ira Dei* (The Wrath of God), would seem to ascribe somewhat less to the abilities of natural reason than either Aquinas or Plessis-Mornay.

[84] See *AN* 4:18.6–24.

[85] See ibid. 4:18.13–14: 'Vide Cyprianum de sua conversione.'

[86] See ibid. 4:17.21–2.

[87] See Booty, 'Commentary', *Folger*, iv. 193.

are planted in the mind by God.[88] To believe that such virtues have a human origin is, he argues, the very essence of foolishness and self-love: Pharaoh is taken as a paradigm of such self-love. Philo was, of course, a Jew living in first-century Alexandria, and he never converted to Christianity. The divine aid he describes cannot, therefore, be termed sanctifying grace, and his admonitory figure, Pharaoh, is the one Hooker uses in the third essay of the *Dublin Fragments* as an example of someone abandoned by 'inward'/common grace. This gives a strong indication that the grace that en-ables the will and the reason is not, in Hooker's opinion, merely sanctifying grace, but includes common grace as well.

The third authority is Dionysius the Pseudo-Areopagite. The passage to which Hooker refers, in the *De Divinis Nominibus* (The Divine Names), discusses how evil is merely a deficiency of good. Since this does not contribute to an understanding of Hooker's philosophy of mind and action and his views on grace, one need not bother to examine it here.

Returning to the *Dublin Fragments*, having discussed aptness and ableness, Hooker goes on to observe that 'Prescience, predestination and grace' do not compromise the freedom of the will.[89] He then reiterates his views on human depravity, stating that 'our nature . . . of itselfe . . . inclineth only unto evill.'[90] This corruption in the mental faculties is, he observes, cured by 'speciall grace', but he then goes on to associate this aid with sanctifying grace by talking of actions 'acceptable' to God that '*tende to the fruit of eternall life*'.[91] The reader is left to consider whether Hooker believes that all the actions of non-Christians are evil, or whether 'speciall grace' includes the concept of common grace but that this point is obscured, because Hooker is dealing here with this grace from a purely Christian perspective. Atkinson and Kirby both cite this passage to demonstrate Hooker's allegiance to the Reformed doctrine of total depravity, but one can see how in a qualified sense, once the presence of common grace is assumed, Hooker did not in these lines commit himself to this conclusion.[92]

[88] See *Philo*, trans. F. H. Colson and G. H. Whitaker (London, 1930), i. 175–81; ii. 51–5.

[89] See *DF* 4:102.9–103.9.

[90] See ibid. 4:103.9–12.

[91] See ibid. 4:103.12–17.

[92] See Atkinson, *Richard Hooker and the Authority of Scripture, Tradition and Reason*, 29–30, 78; W. J. Torrance Kirby, 'The Paradigm of Chalcedonian Christology in Richard Hooker's Discourse on Grace and the Church', *The Churchman* 114 (2000), 26.

After arguing briefly that grace does not compromise human freedom, Hooker then turns to discuss Pelagianism and Semi-Pelagianism. The parallels with the later examination of grace are apparent as he observes that such heretics acknowledge only 'outward grace', not 'inward grace'.[93] There has been, therefore, rather strangely, a transformation in Hooker's terminology, from the use of 'speciall' to 'inward' grace, in the same paragraph in the space of eighteen lines in the *Folger* edition. There is every indication that the concept referred to is precisely the same, but that Hooker has changed his terminology to accommodate his remarks on 'outward' grace. The binary distinction between 'speciall' and 'outward' grace would be unclear, whereas 'outward' and 'inward' grace are natural opposites. In fact, from this point onwards in the essays of the *Dublin Fragments* Hooker uses the term 'speciall grace' only once more, and employs the term 'inward grace' instead.[94] Perhaps if Hooker had had the opportunity to revise this work for publication he would have harmonized his terminology of grace. Since, however, 'speciall' grace and 'inward' grace are here used synonymously, and 'inward' grace, as later defined, clearly includes common as well as sanctifying grace, one can infer from this that common grace is a component part of Hooker's notion of 'speciall' grace. Thus, despite the earlier ambiguities, his remarks on works 'acceptable' to God and his quotation of Hilary of Poitiers, Hooker does still find that *mere natural persons* are to some extent able through grace to know and choose the good. This is merely obscured by his concern to show how one variety of 'speciall' or 'inward' grace is necessary for salvation, and to demonstrate his agreement with Article 10 of the Thirty-Nine Articles.

Having noted that grace, as it is given in this life, does not exclude the freedom to sin, Hooker then begins a commentary on the crucial seventh chapter of Book 1 of the *Lawes*.[95] He again emphasizes that knowledge of the good is not difficult to obtain: ignorance, therefore, is purely to be attributed to voluntary human sloth. Unlike the original chapter in the *Lawes*, however, he

[93] See *DF* 4:103.29–104.24.

[94] See ibid. 4:109.4. He talks here of 'Gods especiall grace' having not used the terms 'inward grace' and 'outward grace' for some time, and just prior to his lengthy discussion of these latter terms.

[95] See ibid. 4:105.10–108.7.

then explicitly associates diligence, which can alone overcome sloth, with grace:

Is our reason then by diligence although unasisted with Gods grace, yet able of itselfe to find out whatsoever doeth concerne our good? Some things there are concerning our good, and yet knowne even amongst them to whome the saving grace of God is not knowne. Butt noe saving knowledge possible, without the sanctifying spiritt of God.[96]

This is a perfect example of the ambiguous manner in which Hooker describes grace in the *Dublin Fragments*. Hooker asks initially whether reason can know the good without 'grace', but he does not answer this question directly. Rather, he states that the good (excluding saving knowledge) can be known without 'saving grace'. By referring, for the first time in the *Fragments*, to a specific type of inward/special grace ('saving grace'), he thus avoids describing how common grace is necessary for natural knowledge of the good. There can be no better illustration of his discomfort with the notion of common grace, so important a part of his theology, than these lines here.

Hooker then quotes from Tertullian's *Apologeticum* (Apology) to demonstrate how *mere natural persons* can, despite the difficulties, have knowledge of God, and then goes on to compare his own views with those of Calvin.[97] Calvin, he notes, also distinguishes between 'naturall and *supernaturall trueth* and *lawes*', and insists that grace is necessary for an understanding of both these, 'soe farre forth as they serve to our soules everlasting good'. This is again ambiguous. Hooker could be saying that he thinks, like Calvin, that no religious truths can be known without sanctifying grace. This would, as Ch. 3 has shown, be a misrepresentation of Calvin's position, for Calvin certainly does not believe that *mere natural persons* are totally without knowledge of the divine: rather, through common grace, they have sufficient knowledge to make themselves inexcusable.[98] Alternatively, and far more probably, Hooker could be indicating that, like Calvin, he believes that no religious truths can be known without grace, whether sanctifying or common. The latter interpretation would signal a degree of

96 *DF* 4:105.29–106.4.

97 See ibid. 4:106.2–15; Tertullian, 'Apology', *The Writings of Tertullian*, ed. A. Roberts and J. Donaldson. *The Ante-Nicene Fathers* 11 (Edinburgh, 1869), i. 86–7.

98 See pp. 149–55.

disingenuousness upon Hooker's part, for while it is certainly true that Calvin accepts common grace, he does not ascribe nearly so much to its efficacy as does Hooker in the *Lawes*.

Hooker then develops his theme on the nature of divine and natural laws by observing that the former can only be found in revelation, whereas the latter can be discovered by reason. This latter process, he reiterates, of course requires the help of grace:

> These trueths and lawes our first Parents were created able perfectly, both to have knowne and kept, which wee can now neyther fully attaine without the grace of God assisting us in the search, nor att all observe availablely to our salvation, except in the exercise thereof, both grace doe aide, and mercie pardon our manifold imperfections.[99]

This passage distinguishes between knowledge and observance of natural law. Knowledge is not directly associated with salvation; Hooker merely notes that grace is required for these laws to be fully known. This may well be a reference to the need for common grace, though it is worth recalling Hooker's observation in the *Lawes* that certain rare natural laws, such as the resurrection of the dead, can be read only in Holy Scripture, and hence can be accepted only with the aid of sanctifying grace.[100] As regards observance of natural law, Hooker is ambiguous. He does not say that *mere natural persons* cannot observe natural law, but rather that humans cannot 'att all observe availablely to our salvation' natural law without grace. Presumably only Christians can observe natural law in a salvific manner, but room is left for *mere natural persons* to observe natural law in a non-salvific way. The most probable rationale behind this tacit distinction lies in the concept of works pleasing and acceptable to God, since this is one of the central themes of this essay of the *Dublin Fragments*. Only sanctified Christians can in Hooker's opinion perform such works, which merit an eternal reward, because they alone possess the three theological virtues that sanctify human behaviour. *Mere natural persons* with the help of common grace may be able to perform moral works in accordance with natural law, but they cannot observe natural law 'att all observe availablely to our salvation'. Hooker thus in these lines emphasizes the need which Christians have for grace

[99] *DF* 4:107.2–7. [100] See pp. 122–3.

if they are to perform actions rewardable in Heaven, without denying the ability of *mere natural persons* to perform moral works. Yet as with his use of the words 'inward' and 'speciall', his terminology here obscures any such divide.

Hooker's next step is to consider the two passages that the *Christian Letter* cites from ch. 7 of Book 1 of the *Lawes* in an attempt to show his disagreement with Article 10. Regarding the first passage, concerning the 'aptness' of the will to choose freely, Hooker merely observes that this showed the nature of the will 'without consideration had eyther of sinne or of gods grace'.[101] He gives no indication that common as well as sanctifying grace might be involved in the choice of the good. One might also note that it is scarcely surprising that the *Christian Letter* should have mistaken Hooker over this matter, as grace is not discussed at all in this chapter of the *Lawes*. Hooker then distinguishes between prevenient and subsequent grace, in reference to Article 10. The former is described as initiating the reasoning/choosing process towards knowledge/choice of the good, while the latter is described as working with the reason/will to accomplish the desired act of knowledge/choice. This description is, of course, equally applicable to common as to sanctifying grace, even though Article 10 could be seen as referring only to the latter when speaking of 'the grace of God by Christ' (*gratia Dei, quae per Christum est*).

As this opening part of the first essay of the *Dublin Fragments* comes to an end, Hooker responds to the *Christian Letter*'s challenge that he explain how his philosophy of mind and action agrees with Romans 8: 7: '*The wisedome of the flesh is ennimitie against God, for it is not subject unto the law of God, neither in deed can be.*'[102] It will be recalled that the *Christian Letter* is probably referring here to Article 9 of the Thirty-Nine Articles, on original sin, which itself alludes to Romans 8: 7. Hooker defines 'the wisdome of the flesh' quite carefully as 'mans corrupt understanding and will not inlightned nor reformed by Gods spiritt'; in other words, the reason and the will acting without the aid of grace. He does not state whether this grace is common and/or sanctifying grace. With regard to natural law, he subsequently notes that people who follow the 'wisdome of the flesh' are ignorant of its dictates, and follow rather the

[101] See *DF* 4:107.18–22.

[102] See ibid. 4:107.31–109.4; *ACL* 4:19.11–16.

'judgement' of their sensitive appetites. He then makes this statement about divine law and revelation:

as the wisdome of the flesh, mans corrupt understanding and will not inlightned nor reformed by Gods spiritt is opposite and cannot submitt itselfe unto his lawe butt followeth the judgement of sensualitie contrarie to that which reason might learne by the light of the naturall lawe of God; Soe in matters above the reach of reason, and beyond the compasse of nature, where only faith is to judge, by Gods revealed lawe what is right or good, the wisdome of the flesh severed and devided from that spiritt which converteth mans heart to the liking of Gods trueth, must needes be here as formall adversaries to him, and as farre from subjection to his lawe as before.[103]

This obviously creates a problem in interpretation, for which there are two possible solutions. First, Hooker could be defining the 'wisdome of the flesh' as the mind unenlightened by sanctifying grace. From this it would follow that non-Christians can know nothing about natural law, and that common grace does not exist. Alternatively, one could acknowledge a deep ambiguity in Hooker's definition of this term. The 'wisdome of the flesh', as Hooker uses it, seems to apply to any opposition to God's laws, whatever its origin. As regards natural law, this opposition could be the result of a lack of common grace. As regards divine law, however, it would be the result of a lack of sanctifying grace. It would, therefore, be possible for Hooker to describe all non-Christians as having the 'wisdome of the flesh', without denying that some of them have knowledge of natural law. This second interpretation may seem rather complex, but it does correspond with the ambiguous use that Hooker makes of grace throughout the opening part of the first essay of the *Dublin Fragments*. To demonstrate its validity, however, it is necessary to compare Hooker's subsequent remarks with a passage from Book 3 of the *Lawes*.

In his following lines in the *Dublin Fragments*, Hooker observes that 'the wittiest, the greatest in account for secular and worldly wisdome, *Scribes, Philosophers, profounde disputers*' have been as much opposed to divine law as 'the carnall and more brutish sorte of men'.[104] He has thus changed his biblical reference text from Romans 8: 7 to 1 Corinthians 1: 19–20, which deals with such people and the

[103] *DF* 4:108.14–23. [104] See ibid. 4:108.24–6.

'wisdome of this worlde'. He then proceeds to give some examples of such learned heathens: 'Such in the *Primitive Church* were *Julian, Lucian, Porphyrie, Symachus*, and other of the like note, by whome both the naturall lawe of God was disobeyed, and the mysteries of supernaturall trueth derided.'[105] Hooker's four heathens all criticized Christianity in one way or another. They thus derided divine law, though it is not clear what their offences were as regards natural law. This should not be taken to mean, however, that in Hooker's opinion *mere natural persons* cannot know natural law. In Book 3 of the *Lawes* he attacks those who use 1 Corinthians 1: 19–20 to condemn all philosophy and natural reasoning.[106] He praises the mathematical wisdom of the Egyptians and Chaldeans, and the rational and oratorical wisdom of the Greeks. Regarding religious matters, he quotes Tertullian approvingly on how '*there are some things even knowne by nature, as the immortalitie of the soule unto many, our God unto all*'.[107] He also quotes Tertullian's observation that one may agree with Plato that the soul is immortal, but as regards those who disagree with him, one must remember that '*the very wisdome of the world is pronounced follie*'.[108] It is only against people that oppose the laws of God, therefore, that Hooker is prepared to cite Paul's texts on the 'wisdom of the world'. As he argues, in Book 3:

> But there are that beare the title of wise men and Scribes and great disputers of the world, and are nothing in deede lesse then what in shewe they most appeare. These being whollie addicted unto their owne wills, use their wit, their learning, and all the wisdome they have, to maintaine that which their obstinate harts are delighted with, esteeming in the phrentique error of their mindes the greatest madnes in the world to be wisdome, and the highest wisedom foolishnes. Such were both *Jewes* and *Graecians*, which professed the one sort legall, and the other secular skill, neither induring to be taught the mysterie of Christ.[109]

The passages in the *Dublin Fragments* are, therefore, an extension of the argument in the *Lawes* regarding the 'wisdome of the world'. Any opposition to God's laws is seen to merit this appellation, and since sanctifying grace is required for an understanding of divine law, all *mere natural persons* are theoretically in opposition to God's

[105] *DF* 4:108.26–9.
[106] See *Lawes*, 1:221.25–222.13 (III.8.4); 1:224.11–227.1 (III.8.8–9).
[107] See ibid. 1:225.3–5 (III.8.8).
[108] See ibid. 1:225.5–12 (III.8.8).
[109] Ibid. 1:226.15–24 (III.8.9).

laws. As the *Lawes* shows, however, this in no way means that Hooker considered all the reasoning of non-Christians to be worthy of the name 'the wisdom of the world/flesh'. With the aid of common grace, they are in his opinion capable of knowing a great deal about natural law and God. Hooker was, in the *Dublin Fragments*, therefore, able clearly to demonstrate his agreement with both Romans 8: 7 and 1 Corinthians 1: 19–20, without in any way revising his attitude to human nature.

After some concluding remarks, what has been termed the opening part of the first essay of the *Dublin Fragments* draws to a close, and Hooker turns to analyse the nature of grace in the passages that have been discussed above. He makes his views somewhat clearer, but it is hard not to feel that there is a distinct element of evasion on his part as regards common grace. Too many passages seem to be phrased deliberately to avoid a direct statement on the issue, and to veil this key part of his theology. The rather labyrinthine structure of this chapter is perhaps a good example of this problem, since it has been necessary to trace his arguments throughout the various parts of his late works, in order to track down his position on grace. As a defence of the *Lawes* in relation to Article 10 of the Thirty-Nine Articles, however, the *Dublin Fragments* are a great success. Hooker not only genuinely demonstrates the agreement between his theology and this standard of orthodoxy, but manages to sound far more characteristically Reformed than he actually is. A more open discussion of his views might have drawn further hostile criticism from such people as the authors of the *Christian Letter*, whereas here Hooker is able to represent his views in language superficially more amenable to his Reformed readers. Yet although the *Fragments* deal thoroughly with Article 10, and also deal effectively with the allusion to Romans 8: 7 in Article 9, Hooker says very little with regard to Articles 12 and 13, which also relate to his philosophy of mind and action. As a final part of this chapter, therefore, one may briefly consider whether he did defend himself from the charge that he held opinions contrary to these articles. To answer this, one must look further at his autograph notes in his edition of the *Christian Letter*.

The difficult part of Article 12 for Hooker is the observation, quoted by the *Christian Letter*, that although the good works of Christians 'are pleasing and acceptable' (*grata sunt et accepta*) to

God, they 'cannot endure the severity of God's judgement' (*divini iudicii severitatem ferre non possunt*).[110] Covel deals with this by arguing that the least transgression of God's law is sin, and since Christian good works are never wholly perfect, they always need to be forgiven to some extent.[111] Hooker does not appear to adopt this view, however. He remarks, in response to ch. 6 of the *Christian Letter*, that 'The very cause why good workes cannot justify is for that evell workes do exclude from salvation: And the most righteous in some things offend.'[112] By observing that the most righteous offend God in 'some things', he is far from saying that all the actions of Christians are in some way sinfully imperfect. This recalls the distinction, examined in Ch. 3, between *A Learned Discourse of Justification* where Hooker enquires whether any single human act has ever been completely pure, and *A Learned Discourse of the Nature of Pride* where Hooker condemns humanity because everyone has committed (at least) *one* sinful action.[113] Having made these comments on justification and evil works he then cites two authorities to illustrate his point. The first is Dionysius the Pseudo-Areopagite, and his *Ecclesiastical Hierarchy*. Here, Dionysius argues that the blemishes of the just are overlooked when they are received into heaven. The second is Philo, who argues in his work *Quod Deus Immutabilis Sit* (On the Unchangeableness of God) that 'there is no man who self-sustained has run the course of life from birth to death without stumbling'.[114] Neither passage in any way suggests that Christian good works are in some sense sinful.

In his subsequent note, 'On the imperfection of good works' (*De Imperfectione bonorum operum*), Hooker cites two further authorities.[115] The first reference is to Jerome's *Dialogus contra Luciferianos* (Dialogue against the Luciferians). The section to which Hooker actually refers does not seem particularly germane, but both Keble and Bayne point to a later passage that does deal with the imperfection of good works.[116] Here, Jerome makes the following remarks:

> To make my meaning plain, let us suppose a case:—I stand to pray; I could not pray, if I did not believe; but if I really believed, I should

[110] See *ACL* 4:23.11–12; *Documents of the English Reformation*, 291.

[111] See Covel, 'A Just and Temperate Defence', 490–1.

[112] See *AN* 4:23.7–9.

[113] See pp. 144–7.

[114] See *Philo*, iii 46–7: μηδενὸς ἀνθρώπων τὸν ἀπὸ γενέσεως ἄχρι τελευτῆς βίον ἄπταιστον ἐξ ἑαυτοῦ δραμόντος; Booty, 'Commentary', *Folger*, iv. 197.

[115] See *AN* 4:23.13–14.

[116] See Booty, 'Commentary', *Folger*, iv. 198.

cleanse that heart of mine with which God is seen, I should beat my hands upon my breast, the tears would stream down my cheeks, my body would shudder, my face grow pale, I should lie at my Lord's feet, weep over them, and wipe them with my hair, I should cling to the cross and not let go my hold until I obtained mercy. But, as it is, frequently in my prayers I am either walking in the arcades, or calculating my interest, or am carried away by base thoughts, so as to be occupied with things the mere mention of which makes me blush.[117]

Humans, in Jerome's opinion, rarely act perfectly, and all too easily fall into sinful actions or thoughts. Yet there is again nothing here to assert that good works are in themselves sinful.

Hooker's second reference concerning the imperfection of good works reads as follows: 'Genebrard. in Symb. Athanasii. p. 306.' Gilbert Génebrard (1535–97), a Benedictine monk and archbishop of Aix-en-Provence, was a learned Hebraist and a firm supporter of the anti-Protestant Holy League.[118] The work Hooker cites is a commentary on the Athanasian Creed, which was evidently published in Hooker's own lifetime. This particular edition has proved highly elusive, and the reference Hooker has in mind has never been located. The commentary was as Bayne notes, however, published in 1607 at the end of Génebrard's edition of the Psalms, and I have been able to consult a copy of this text in the British Library.[119] The only pages that seem relevant occur towards the end of the commentary, where Génebrard defends the concept of merit against 'schismatics' (*sectarios*).[120] Génebrard does not so much assert the imperfection of good works, as the fact that good works impose no obligation upon

[117] Jerome, 'The Dialogue Against the Luciferians', *St. Jerome: Letters and Select Works*, trans. W. H. Fremantle, G. Lewis, and W. G. Martley. *A Select Library of the Nicene and Post-Nicene Fathers of the Christian Church*, Second Series (Oxford, 1893) (*PL* 23:169–70), vi. 327: Verbi gratia dictum sit, ut quod volumus perspicuum fiat: ad orationem assisto; non orarem, si non crederem: sed si vere crederem, illud cor quo Deus videtur, mundarem, manibus tunderem pectus, genas lacrymis rigarem, corpore inhorrescerem, ore pallerem, jacerem ad Domini mei pedes, eosque fletu perfunderem, crine tergerem, haererem certe trunco crucis, nec prius amitterem, quam misericordiam impetrarem. Nunc vero creberrime in oratione mea, aut per porticus deambulo, aut de fenore computo, aut abductus turpi cogitatione, etiam quae dictu erubescenda sunt, gero.

[118] See Michael Ott, 'Gilbert Génebrard', *Catholic Encyclopedia*, vi. 412.

[119] See Booty, 'Commentary', *Folger*, iv. 198.

[120] Gilbert Génebrard, *Symbolum Athanasii Commentariis Huic Aeuo Accommodatis Illustratum* (Leiden, 1607), 94–9. I am most grateful to Claudia Simon for her translations of passages from this work.

God. Even though they stem from grace, he argues, as fruit from a tree or an effect from its cause, they do not make God a debtor:

Furthermore, there is a great difference between merits with respect to God and those with respect to humans. We make ourselves very meritorious towards humans, because we affect those humans through our action with some benefit. But we do not give God anything of this sort. Through our merit we oblige humans to us and we turn them into debtors. God, however, cannot be made a debtor by us personally, but only by Himself, either because He obliges Himself voluntarily to give us life, even though He owes us nothing, etc., or because He gives us necessary help, so that we achieve what He orders.[121]

It is also highly interesting that in his consideration of good works Génebrard carefully distinguishes between the meritorious works of Christians, which are 'acceptable and pleasing to God' (*Deo... gratae, & acceptae*), and the works of unbelievers, which may be virtuous but cannot be meritorious. This is very similar to the distinction made by Aquinas, the Aquinas commentator, and also, it would seem, Hooker himself:

Further, this scruple should be removed from the minds of those people who regard the name of Merit somewhat more harshly. As God crowns His gifts to us in His own way and as He rewards our good deeds from His own generosity and from the pact which He entered into with us, why do we usurp here the term of Merit and do not remember rather the sole term of grace? I answer that the term Merit is easily usurped between the deeds of Christians and the deeds of unbelievers. The actions of those [unbelievers] might be virtues. Nevertheless, they are not acceptable and pleasing to God in order to pursue eternal life which is not given through good deeds, except as I have said in so far as God is the effector, causer and acceptor of these. But our deeds are pleasing and welcome to God because they happen with Him, not I say as a companion, but with Him as the leader.[122]

[121] See Génebrard, *Symbolum Athanasii Commentariis*, 99: Alioqui latum discrimen inter merita erga Deum, & erga homines. De hominibus bene meremur, quia nostra actione afficimus illos aliquo commodo, nihil autem tale Deo praestamus. Merito nostro proprie homines nobis obstringimus, proprieque reddimus debitores. Deus autem a nobis debitor proprie nequit constitui, sed a se solum, vel quia sponte, cum nihil nobis deberet, sese obligauit daturum vitam, &c. vel quia suppeditat nobis auxilium quod est necessarium, ut quod iubet, perficiamus.

[122] See Génebrard, *Symbolum Athanasii Commentariis*, 97: Porro hic remouendus scrupus ex eorum animis, qui nomen Meriti paulo durius existimant. Cum Deus sua dona in nobis proprie coronet, ac nostra bona opera ex sua liberalitate, atque ex pacto, quod nobiscum iniit, remuneret, cur Meriti nomen hic usurpamus, & non potius gratiae solius meminimus? Respondeo & facile, meriti vocem, usurpari ad distinguendum inter

Yet again, therefore, as with the other authorities cited by Hooker, Génebrard is far from arguing that the good works of Christians (and non-Christians for that matter) should be considered as sins. Although it is difficult to state conclusively the nature of Hooker's views from these autograph notes, there were many other writers and passages he could have cited if he had wished to take a clearly Reformed stance on the sinfulness of Christian good works, such as Calvin himself. As it is, there are certainly grounds for believing, especially in the light of the citation of Jerome, that although Hooker indicates that his theology is in agreement with Article 12 of the Thirty-Nine Articles, he has distanced himself from a Reformed interpretation of it. If this is the case, then it is not surprising that he does not discuss his views on Article 12 in the *Dublin Fragments*, at least as they currently stand.

Hooker's success is more qualified, however, in rebutting the *Christian Letter*'s claim that his theology is contrary to Article 13, on works before justification. As his discussion of Article 10 makes clear, he has no difficulty in arguing that the works of *mere natural persons* are not 'pleasant and acceptable to God' (*Deo grata sint et accepta*). Article 13 also asserts, however, that works performed before 'the grace of Christ, and the inspiration of his Spirit' have the 'nature of sin' (*peccati rationem habere*), and this might seem to conflict with his argument in the *Lawes* that *mere natural persons* can to some extent abstain from sin through obedience to natural law. Hooker provides no autograph notes dealing with Article 13, and never retracts this opinion in any of his late works. This means that his conformity to this article is at least questionable. Some light can be thrown on this matter, though, by looking at the views of several other theologians who have considered the nature of 'acceptable' and pleasing, as well as sinful, works.

The first of these theologians is Covel, who was left with the task of defending Hooker's allegiance to Article 13. His usual method in the *Defence* is to work closely with Hooker's arguments in the *Lawes*, but in this case the only passages from the *Lawes* he mentions are those cited by the *Christian Letter* itself. The argument

Christianorum & incredulorum opera. Istorum actiones, utut virtutes sint. Deo tamen gratae, & acceptae non sunt ad vitam aeternam consequendam, quae non datur bonis operibus, nisi uti dixi, quatenus illorum Deus effector, causa, acceptatorque est. Nostrae autem, Deo, quia ipso non dico comite, sed duce fiunt, gratae sunt, & placent.

is primarily Covel's own, and it should therefore come as little surprise that it is distinctly different from that of Hooker. Covel begins by making a careful division between different types of human actions, which he classifies as either natural, civil, or religious. He then remarks, of the latter two classes:

> Secondly, Civil, which we call political, or moral, human actions; as to buy, sell, to learn any art, and to conclude any other action, which concerneth the politic, or private society of man: Thirdly, those which belong to the kingdom of God; to a perfect, happy, and true Christian life; as, to repent us of our sins, to believe in God, to call upon him, to obey his voice, to live after his precepts, and such like.[123]

This suggests that for Covel actions belonging to the kingdom of God are the concern of Christians, whereas non-Christians can properly only engage in civil actions. This is confirmed by his subsequent observation that the 'special favour of God', or common grace, is necessary for civil actions, whereas a 'grace of regeneration, or the grace of Christ, without which, there can be nothing performed of man truly good', is necessary for works of the kingdom.[124] He then proceeds to equate these works of the kingdom with the 'works of piety, pleasing and acceptable to God' referred to in Article 10.[125] Finally, when dealing with Article 13, he argues that the works of non-Christians are technically not only not acceptable to God but have the nature of sin: although through grace 'infidels' can externally obey natural law, their actions strictly considered are sinful because they spring from corrupt inner motives.[126] Unlike Hooker, Aquinas, and the Aquinas commentator, therefore, Covel conflates works not 'acceptable' to God with sinful works, in a manner similar to the *Christian Letter*. Although Covel's style and scholasticism may obscure the fact, his argument is close to that of Calvin examined in Ch. 3, though if anything Calvin is more positive about the religious actions of non-Christians.[127] In any case this is an excellent early example of a Reformed interpretation of Hooker's theory of human nature, with parallels in the present-day work of Kirby and Atkinson. It succeeds, though, by overlooking key elements of Hooker's thought.

[123] Covel, 'A Just and Temperate Defence', 474. [124] Ibid.
[125] Ibid. 482. [126] Ibid. 491. [127] See pp. 155–7.

An alternative view on this subject can be seen in Aquinas's *Summa Theologiae*. It will be recalled that Hooker quotes at length from a commentary on the *Summa*, which states that faith is necessary for works that are acceptable and pleasing to God. This is similar to the view of Aquinas himself that no human act is truly acceptable (*accepta*) and able to please (*potest placere*) God unless it stems from the theological virtue of charity. The article in which he observes this is, though, principally concerned with arguing that although unbelievers are incapable of acceptable and meritorious works, 'it does not follow that they sin in everything they do'.[128] For Aquinas, therefore, works that are not acceptable to God are not necessarily sins.

Is the view of Aquinas, however, compatible with Article 13? John Henry Newman appears implicitly to have thought it was. In *Tracts for the Times. No. 90* he provides a very careful interpretation of Article 13. He notes that despite its title, the substance of the article does not refer explicitly to works before justification, but rather to works done 'before the grace of Christ, and the inspiration of his Spirit' (*ante gratiam Christi, et Spiritus eius afflatum*). By interpreting 'the inspiration of his Spirit' as a reference to justification, and the non-technical phrase 'the grace of Christ' as a reference to grace in general, he is able to argue that the article condemns only those works performed before justification *and* without the receipt of grace. As he observes, of both Articles 12 and 13: 'They say that works *before* grace *and* justification are worthless and worse, and that works *after* grace *and* justification are acceptable, but they do not speak at all of works *with* GOD's aid, *before* justification.'[129] Since, in Newman's view, non-Christians may very well be given grace, this means that although their actions will not be acceptable to God they will not necessarily be sinful. This is just the sort of subtle distinction concerning non-Christian grace that is to be found in the *Dublin Fragments*. This does not mean, of course, that Hooker would necessarily have agreed with Newman's particular interpretation, but it does illustrate that it was possible to read Article 13 in a

[128] See *ST* II-II.10.4: Unde non oportet quod in omni suo opere peccent.

[129] See John Henry Newman, *Tracts for the Times. No. 90. Remarks on Certain Passages in the Thirty-Nine Articles*, 2nd edn. (London, 1841), 14–16, 81. See also E. J. Bicknell, *A Theological Introduction to the Thirty-Nine Articles of the Church of England*, 3rd edn., rev. H. J. Carpenter (London, 1955), 208. It is interesting to note that the rewording of Article 13 in the *Westminster Confession of Faith*, 16.7, serves to exclude such an interpretation.

way conducive to Hooker's views on *mere natural persons*. Given the hostile reception that Newman's tract received, one can perhaps appreciate the advantages that lay for Hooker in emphasizing his conformity in the *Dublin Fragments*, as opposed to making his precise views starkly clear.

Furthermore, by observing that Article 13 only condemns the concept of congruous merit as it refers to works before justification *and* the receipt of grace, Newman also argues that the article does not anathematize the view that non-Christians aided by grace can congruously merit further grace.[130] This would again have provided a route for Hooker to defend his orthodoxy regarding this article, for it is precisely this position with which he has been identified in Ch. 4. It should be noted that although he does not explicitly refer to congruous merit in the *Dublin Fragments*, least of all in connection with Article 13, he does implicitly refer to it in the second essay when speaking of the conditions necessary for justification, as has been observed in the previous chapter.[131]

Read as a whole the *Christian Letter* is in many respects an unskilful work of theology; it makes numerous errors of interpretation with regard to the *Lawes*, often as a result of an inadequate knowledge of scholastic theology. Yet in conclusion one can see that not all its accusations are wide of the mark, and those concerning Articles 10, 12, and 13 of the Thirty-Nine Articles certainly forced Hooker to become evasive and defensive. Hooker's views may have been consonant with the articles, but they were not necessarily consonant with a Reformed interpretation of them. In this the *Letter* correctly perceived the implications of Hooker's theology, as moving markedly away from the Reformed tradition in his view of human nature: a view of the *Letter* rejected in more general terms by Atkinson and Kirby, but not too dissimilar from Lake's more cautious recent assessment of this work.[132] It is not the case, as Hillerdal has argued, that the *Dublin Fragments* show that Hooker's position on grace was substantively confused.[133] Rather, the *Fragments* are confused in their presentation of theories that

[130] See Newman, *Tracts for the Times. No. 90*, 16.

[131] See pp. 180–5.

[132] See Atkinson, *Richard Hooker and the Authority of Scripture, Tradition and Reason*, 6; Kirby, 'Richard Hooker as an Apologist of the Magisterial Reformation in England', 220; Lake, 'Business as Usual? The Immediate Reception of Hooker's *Ecclesiastical Polity*', 457–62.

[133] See Hillerdal, *Reason and Revelation in Richard Hooker*, 137.

are (predestination perhaps excepted) in themselves quite logical and fully-formed. Doctrinal pressure appears to have made Hooker very wary of expressing his opinions, a problem compounded by his general lack of clarity as regards the subject of grace. The result is a body of late writings that must be approached with great care, especially the first essay of the *Dublin Fragments*. When one considers the subtle terminology of grace, as well as the discussions of justification, sanctification, and the distinction between mortal and venial sins outlined in the previous chapter, the final picture that emerges is distinctly different from the superficially Reformed image that Hooker may at times have been content to allow to appear.

Conclusion

Theologians of Hooker's eclectic nature are not simple to categorize: they do not fit easily into classificatory straitjackets. Was he, or was he not, a theologian of the Reformed tradition? Hooker himself does not explicitly answer this question: at most he describes the Church of England as one of the 'reformed Churches' in the *Lawes*, which says nothing about the precise orientation of his own theology, and he seldom quotes from or cites Continental Reformed writers.[1] One must, therefore, consider the theological development evident in his writing, such as that to be found by comparing *A Learned Discourse of Justification, Workes, and How the Foundation of Faith Is Overthrowne* with the *Lawes* and the late works on the subject of justification. Similarly, as regards assurance of election, one can compare *The First Sermon Upon Part Of S. Judes Epistle* and the Latin letter to John Rainolds with his subsequent writings. From the evidence available, Hooker in the early sermons on Jude looks clearly Reformed, the good student of Rainolds, his puritan tutor at Corpus Christi College, Oxford. The situation is, however, much more complex by the time of the *Lawes* and the late writings.

Hooker, right through his life, can be identified more or less clearly with certain Reformed positions. In the *Dublin Fragments* he argues that all those who are truly justified are elect and therefore granted the grace of final perseverance, which Seán F. Hughes has described in general as 'a genuinely distinctive Reformed position'.[2] Although for the most part after his earliest writings he distanced himself from the common Reformed view that the elect can be assured of their salvation, it has been argued in Ch. 4 that there is evidence in the *Lawes* that this belief lingered on in his thought in connection with Holy Communion. Critics have also argued that his doctrine of predestination lies notionally midway

[1] See *Lawes*, 1:333.22–336.15 (IV.13.9–14.1); Gibbs, 'Introduction: Books II, III & IV', *Folger*, vi. 148. Cf. Atkinson, *Richard Hooker and the Authority of Scripture, Tradition and Reason*, p. xx, who quotes Hooker selectively on this matter.

[2] See p. 182.

between Calvin and Arminius, though whether this takes Hooker part-way out of the Reformed tradition depends upon whether one regards Arminius as a Reformed theologian.[3] Hooker's sacramentalism, it has also been argued, while it was highly innovative in the context of the Reformed England of his day, did not greatly distance him from Calvin or separate him from the Reformed tradition as a whole.[4] There is good evidence, then, that Hooker was at least in part a Reformed theologian. In the mature theology of the *Lawes* and late works, however, as this study has shown, many other beliefs can be identified with him that distance him from the Reformed tradition. His metaphysical libertarianism, at the root of much of his theology, was a radical break with sixteenth-century Reformed theology, though whether it was hostile to the Reformed tradition *per se* depends in part again on how one views Arminianism. More generally, it has been argued that his attitude to human nature, as it is aided by grace, is distinctly different from the picture of humanity characteristic of Reformed theology. *Mere natural persons* are, in Hooker's opinion, free in both the civil and the religious realms, through diligence and divine grace (which is resistible) to know and to perform to some degree works that glorify and are obedient to God, and hence to abstain from sin. Natural law is thus still for such persons a way, albeit imperfectly, to know and to obey God the Creator, if not God the Redeemer. Humans as commonly encountered are not totally depraved, and Hooker, in the *Lawes* at least, places relatively little emphasis upon original sin, while still affirming humanity's absolute depravity without divine aid. For *divinely enhanced persons* (i.e. justified Christians) Hooker in his mature theology holds fast to the concept of forensic justification *per fidem propter Christum*. He makes

[3] See pp. xvii, 6.

[4] See p. 6; Peter Lake, 'Lancelot Andrewes, John Buckeridge, and Avant-Garde Conformity at the Court of James I', *The Mental World of the Jacobean Court*, ed. L. L. Peck (Cambridge, 1991), 181; 'The Laudian Style: Order, Uniformity and the Pursuit of the Beauty of Holiness in the 1630s', *The Early Stuart Church, 1603–1642*, ed. K. Fincham (Basingstoke, 1993), 113; Lake, 'Business as Usual? The Immediate Reception of Hooker's *Ecclesiastical Polity*', 484–5. Perhaps, however, more should be made of the differences between Hooker and Calvin as regards the sacramental role of Holy Communion. As noted in Ch. 4, Hooker probably regards Holy Communion as the instrumental cause of post-baptismal justification, and in one passage of the *Lawes* intimately connects knowledge of election to reception of this sacrament: both these views are distinctly un-Calvinist. Conversely, while Calvin argues that the sacraments are only efficacious when a sermon is preached to the congregation, Hooker rejects this view. See pp. 186–7, 247–9 and Ch. 4 n. 218.

justification, however, an action that must be congruously merited through a person co-operating freely with grace, and something that can be lost through mortal sin and then subsequently regained. Through co-operation people can earn a heavenly reward, and through performing works of supererogation (vulgarly defined) they can increase the extent of that reward. Hooker views sanctification as having a qualitative effect on human behaviour, enabling Christians to abstain from all mortal sins though not of course all venial sins. He gives reason a role quite alien from that to be found in Calvin's theology, placing it as a barrier or filter between the believer and the Holy Spirit. Hooker opposes the view that Holy Scripture must be authenticated and interpreted by the direct inner witness of the Holy Spirit, giving this role instead to demonstrative reasoning (as it is aided by grace). This finds its culminating expression in his triple view of religious authority, which consists (in a qualified sense) of scripture, reason, and tradition, in that order. Throughout the *Lawes* he evinces a marked hostility to the Reformed (and more generally Protestant) concept of *sola scriptura*. This is powerful evidence indeed that Hooker, in his later years, though still having one foot in the Reformed tradition, had also taken one step decisively outside it.

How one describes such a position is arguably rather subjective, but in my opinion it is unhelpful and misleading to describe the mature Hooker as a Reformed theologian. There are too many aspects of his thought in which he systematically opposes Reformed ideas for this to form an accurate assessment of his overall mature view, even though one can nonetheless state that he continued in his later life to hold a range of distinctively Reformed beliefs. My evaluation of Hooker is thus quite different from that to be found in the work of Kirby, Atkinson, McGrath, and many other writers of the last twenty years, and is a good deal closer to Lake's assessment of Hooker in *Anglicans and Puritans?*. There seems little need for a revision of this assessment in terms of a statement that while Hooker may have broken with the English Reformed tradition he still remained in some sense Reformed, for the conclusions of this study have been based on an analysis of Hooker not only from the perspective of English Reformed theology but from Continental Reformed theology as well.[5] One can appreciate, however, why numerous writers from the early seventeenth century onwards have identified Hooker as a thoroughly Reformed theologian. Since Hooker's theological development has been largely unappreciated, critics have been able to cite Hooker's earlier opinions, such as those on justification, as if they represented his position as a whole. As regards his mature work, the *Lawes* purports to be a critique of presbyterianism in particular and puritanism more generally, not an attack on aspects of Reformed theology. Hooker was not a Peter Baro or a Jacob Arminius, let alone a Martin Luther, prepared openly to assail the theological norms of his contemporaries. Despite the very real radicalism of his theological development, his method suggests a conservative desire to influence people indirectly of the veracity of his ideas. He suggests in the *Lawes*, for instance, that when learned theologians talk about the action of the Holy Spirit in the authentication of Holy Scripture they are really referring to reason as it is aided by the Spirit: the Reformed position on this matter is valorized in this process, and covertly ripped up as Hooker presents himself as a moderate figure of the centre opposing the views of puritan and Anabaptist extremists concerning the direct action of the Spirit. Perhaps, though, Hooker's conservatism obliged him to be too cautious a rhetorician in the *Lawes*, for his indirect approach resulted in his more radical principles being missed by many of his readers. This is a fate that Richard Montague did not suffer in *A New Gagg* in 1624, which adopts a similar strategy of condemning as puritan distinctively Reformed ideas, under the justification in this case that the genuine doctrines of the Church of England had been deliberately distorted by Roman Catholic polemicists. Montague's unsubtle approach ensured that his book became a national issue, whereas the no less radical Hooker was quoted by opponents of Montague, such as William Prynne in his *Anti-Arminianisme*, as an authority for orthodox Reformed ideas.[6] Hooker's approach is especially clear in the

[5] See p. 8.

[6] See Wallace, *Puritans and Predestination: Grace in English Protestant Theology, 1525–1695*, 84–6; White, *Predestination, Policy and Polemic*, 138. Significantly, of Prynne's five citations of Hooker in *Anti-Arminianisme*, four are from the early tractates and sermons. See William Prynne, *Anti-Arminianisme, or The Church of Englands Old Antithesis to New Arminianisme*, 2nd edn. (London, 1630), 88, 97, 203–4. For connections between the ideas of Montague and Hooker, see Ch. 4 nn. 56, 122, 139; Ch. 5 n. 76.

first essay of the *Dublin Fragments*, where he demonstrates his rhetorical skill by giving a fairly Reformed appearance to his decidedly un-Reformed interpretations of some of the Thirty-Nine Articles. A number of his more advanced opinions are also expressed in highly abbreviated form in his surviving work, such as the distinction between mortal and venial sins, so it is little wonder that they have so often been overlooked in the past. Finally, Hooker died at the age of 46 without having published a defence of the *Lawes* or having had a chance to develop his theological views any further. Even the last three books of the *Lawes* were published only in the middle of the next century. He was dead before the Hampton Court Conference of 1604 and long before the Caroline monarchy created an environment where dissent from Reformed theology could be expressed more openly. Though the comparison should not be pushed too hard, it is nevertheless interesting to reflect that at the age of 46 William Laud was still only dean of Gloucester, and that his real influence came subsequently in his later years. As it was Hooker died a relatively obscure parish priest, never having been preferred to a bishopric or even a royal chaplaincy, unlike so many conformist theologians of his day.

Once one has described Hooker as having taken one step outside the Reformed tradition, it is natural to enquire where this step took him. Peter Lake has been at the forefront of work on this subject in recent years, though one should stress that he has considered how Hooker was moving away from the English Reformed tradition, not the Reformed tradition as a whole. He has identified two movements that Hooker can be seen as having genuinely anticipated in certain respects: Arminianism and Laudianism. Hooker's proto-Arminianism has been canvassed earlier, both in the consideration of Hooker's metaphysical libertarianism and with respect to the work that Neelands and others have done showing Hooker's partial movement away from Calvin in his theory of predestination. Hooker's proto-Laudianism is a more complex matter, as Laudianism is not so easily defined in the way that the Remonstrance sets out a clear description of Arminian doctrine. Lake has, however, convincingly connected a range of elements in Hooker's theology, that were uncharacteristic of the Elizabethan and Jacobean Church, with the style of piety that is associated with

Laud.[7] This covers the strong sacramentalism of Hooker's theology, with its emphasis on the positive religious role of ritual, liturgy, and ceremony, and the beauty of holiness, and the growth of the mystical body of Christ through the consumption of Christ's body and blood. Prayer is magnified at the expense of preaching, as the exegesis of the Word becomes the means for which prayer and reception of the sacraments are the end. Lake also refers to the broad-based notion of the godly community to be found in Hooker's work, in opposition to a polarized division between the godly and the profane. Through Hooker's influence on such theologians as Lancelot Andrewes and John Buckeridge he traces the path of these ideas through to Laud and radicals such as Montague, who in varying degrees adopted Hooker's method of identifying as puritan and extremist doctrines that were distinctive of the English Reformed tradition.

It is doubtful, though, whether Arminianism and Laudianism in themselves fully encompass all that is distinctive about Hooker's development away from the Reformed tradition of his day. This is an area where more research is needed, but the fact that Lake can present Hooker as proto-Arminian and proto-Laudian, and yet also as in some sense Reformed, is itself suggestive of this view. Laud, for instance, appears to have held opinions on reason and religious authority markedly different from those of Hooker.[8] If one wishes to understand Hooker's place more generally in the English Church, he is probably best seen as being at or near the head of the movement away from the Reformed tradition in the Church, of which Arminianism and Laudianism were only in certain respects an expression. Ironically, however, for those who have travelled down this path further than Hooker, he is unlikely in his entirety to prove a wholly acceptable figure, even setting aside his early tractates and sermons. He kept one foot in the Reformed tradition throughout his life, and his belief in the existence of a golden chain stretching from regeneration through to final perseverance that

[7] See Lake, *Anglicans and Puritans?*, 245; 'Lancelot Andrewes, John Buckeridge, and Avant-Garde Conformity at the Court of James I', 113–14; 'The Laudian Style: Order, Uniformity and the Pursuit of Holiness in the 1630s', 163–81; 'Business as Usual? The Immediate Reception of Hooker's *Ecclesiastical Polity*', 482–6. See also Julian Davies, *The Caroline Captivity of the Church. Charles I and the Remoulding of Anglicanism 1625–1641* (Oxford, 1992), 10, 52–4.

[8] See E. C. E. Bourne, *The Anglicanism of William Laud* (London, 1947), 85–6; Davies, *The Caroline Captivity of the Church*, 60.

guarantees the salvation of the justified, and his forensic theory of justification by faith alone which was for him such a crucial part of the Gospel, may well make him seem rather alien to such persons, as a theologian who had failed to be radical enough. Similarly, for those looking at Hooker from the perspective of Reformed theology, he is also unlikely in his entirety to prove an especially conducive theologian, holding as he does a multiplicity of beliefs that firmly distance him from this tradition. Given the authority with which Hooker has become invested in the English Church, it is little wonder that he has been rewritten so often in the past as either thoroughly 'Anglican' or as thoroughly Reformed. Hooker should be taken on his own terms, in all his complexity, as a major if somewhat enigmatic contributor to the theological self-understanding of the Anglican Communion.

APPENDIX
Original Sin and Inherited Guilt

Although Hooker's views on original sin have been discussed at some length, there has as yet been no consideration of the related question of inherited guilt. It is worth looking briefly at this topic at the end of this study, not only in itself, but for the important lessons it conveys both about Hooker's views on human freedom, and his sense of theological caution. According to the theory of inherited guilt, the whole of humanity acted, in some sense, with Adam when our forefather committed the primordial sin: as a result of this, all humans bear a direct guilt for this action, in addition to the punishment of having a corrupt mind and body. Many traditional theologians accepting this notion would wish to add that, because of this guilt, people are actually born sinful, rather than merely falling into this state with the first transgression which they commit during their lives. This subject becomes of more than theoretical interest in the case of infants who die without being baptized. If these infants are in a state of sin because of inherited guilt, it becomes questionable whether they will in fact be saved. This is obviously a highly emotive issue, and one that seems to have been especially difficult for Hooker. He speaks about inherited guilt in the *Lawes*, and certainly suggests that non-Christian infants will not be saved without baptism. Yet the logic of his legal theory points to a less Augustinian conclusion regarding their fate, especially given the emphasis he places upon the voluntary nature of sin. The results of this theory can arguably be seen in one of his private manuscripts, written shortly before his death, where he takes a rather different approach to inherited guilt from that to be found in the *Lawes*.

The following discussion will begin with a general comparison of the views of Hooker and Thomas Cartwright on infant baptism, since Hooker was responding to the views of his puritan contemporary as regards this issue. One may then examine the implications of Hooker's legal theory, before concluding with his final observations on inherited guilt in the so-called *Notes towards a Fragment on Predestination*.

Cartwright's prime concern regarding baptism, in his various replies to Whitgift in the Admonitions controversy,[1] is to demonstrate that it is completely unacceptable that this sacrament should be performed by private individuals. God, he argues, ordained that people should be baptized in church by a minister, and this order should under no circumstances be

[1] See p. 15 above.

changed. The reason usually given for private baptisms was, of course, necessity; the fear that an infant might die unbaptized and be excluded from heaven as a consequence.[2] Cartwright, therefore, takes considerable pains to show that baptism with water is not essential to salvation, dealing with the key text John 3: 5: 'except that a man be borne of water and of the Spirit, he can not enter into the kingdome of God'. He argues that 'water' in this verse signifies 'by a translation or borowed speech... the spirite of God, the effect whereof it shadoweth out'. Physical water is thus only a sign of baptism, and is not essential to the actual process. It is perfectly possible, he finds, for God to baptize infants in the Spirit without the need for water, and as a result those infants who die unbaptized by human hands need not be considered damned. It is possible, however, that he wished to restrict this exemption to the children of Christian parents: at one point he observes that 'if he be not a Christian, before he come to receiv bapti[s]m: bapti[s]m can make him no Christian, which is onely the seal of the grace of God before received', which would militate against the fate of non-Christian infants.[3]

Hooker vigorously criticizes Cartwright's arguments, seeing them as far too permissive, and at the same time uncharitable. He emphasizes the necessity of outward baptism with water, although it is important to observe the twofold distinction he makes when so doing. He begins by stressing the necessity of outward baptism for salvation, faulting Cartwright for his non-literal reading of John 3: 5. Humans must quite literally, he argues, '*be borne againe of water*', since the material element is 'a necessarie outward meane to our regeneration'.[4] Cartwright and Hooker, it would seem, could not be further apart. Yet this distance is perhaps in part a rhetorical strategy of Hooker, for once having rebutted Cartwright, and having established the necessity of outward baptism, he goes on to modify his stance very significantly. On the basis of equity, he accepts that martyrdom may remove the requirement of outward baptism: indeed, the case of the good thief in Luke 23: 39–43 required no less. Equity also induces Hooker to extend this argument to embrace faithful adults who die before receiving the sacrament.[5] Finally, when considering the case of infants, he does accept that 'grace is not absolutely tyed unto sacramentes', since God may grant people dispensations through His infinite mercy.[6] This implies, of course, that water is not absolutely necessary for

[2] Women (especially midwives), as well as men, could legally baptize children in cases of emergency in this period. On this subject, and infant baptism more generally, see J. D. C. Fisher, *Christian Initiation: The Reformation Period* (London, 1970), 73–145; David Cressy, *Birth, Marriage, and Death: Ritual, Religion, and the Life-Cycle in Tudor and Stuart England* (Oxford, 1997), 64, 114–22.

[3] See in particular *Replye*, 143–6; *The Rest of the Second Replie*, 134.

[4] See *Lawes*, 2:251.21–253.1 (V.59.1–4); 2:254.14–18 (V.60.1).

[5] See ibid. 2:258.18–259.15 (V.60.5).

[6] See ibid. 2:260.1–261.9 (V.60.6).

salvation, a major restatement of his position that brings him much closer to Cartwright. Yet Hooker ends by insisting on a second type of necessity, not accepted by his opponent. The Church, he argues, is required by God to ensure that all receive the sacrament of baptism wherever humanly possible; if this entails breaking the normal orders and regulations of the Church, then this is an acceptable sacrifice. As he observes:

a necessitie there is of receivinge and a necessitie of administring the sacrament of baptisme; the one peradventure not so absolute as some have thought, but out of all peradventure the other more streight and narrowe, then that the Church which is by office a mother unto such as crave at her handes the sacred mysterie of theire nue birth should repell them and see them dye unsatisfied of these their ghostlie desires, rather then give them theire soules rites with omission of those thinges that serve but onlie for the more convenient and orderlie administration thereof.

our merciles strictnes may be our own harme, although not theires towardes whome wee showe it; and wee for the hardnes of our hartes may perish, albeit they through Gods unspeakeable mercie doe live.[7]

It is this second form of necessity that marks the real substantive difference between Cartwright and Hooker, although it must be said that Hooker does also place more importance on the causative properties of water in baptism. As regards inherited guilt, however, it is highly significant that Hooker clearly restricts the dispensation from outward baptism to infants born of Christian parents.[8] If Hooker will condemn other infants who die without baptism, it would seem that he must have held to some theory of inherited guilt, which he believed was sufficient in itself to exclude from salvation.[9] This conclusion is substantiated by the fact that he argues, in ch. 60 of Book 5, that the grace bestowed during baptism 'taketh away all former guiltines'.[10] He quotes from Tertullian,

[7] Ibid. 2:261.10–18 (V.60.7); 2:262.5–8 (V.60.7).

[8] See e.g. ibid. 2:260.28–261.7 (V.60.6): 'seinge that to all professors of the name of Christ this preheminence above infidels is freely given, the fruite of theire bodies bringeth into the world with it a present interest and right to those meanes wherewith the ordinance of Christ is that his Church shalbe sanctified, it is not to be thought that he which as it were from heaven hath nominated and designed them unto holines by speciall priveledge of theire verie birth, will him selfe deprive them of regeneration and inward grace, onlie because necessitie depriveth them of outward sacramentes.' Hooker thus argues that those who God has privileged with being born into a Christian family will also be privileged in cases where baptism is unavailable.

[9] Interestingly, though, Hooker does not in the *Lawes* speak of these infants as being punished in hell. In the *Dublin Fragments* he describes a form of eternal punishment that involves only the loss of the joys of heaven; this was traditionally the fate of those sent to Limbo, amongst whom were unbaptized infants. See *DF* 4:147.5–7.

[10] See *Lawes*, 2:255.10 (V.60.2). See also 2:260.24–6 (V.60.6); *Just.* 5:109.17–20.

Eusebius Gallicanus, and Gregory of Nazianzus to illustrate this point, and indeed the latter two writers speak explicitly, in the passages Hooker cites, of people being born sinful.

This might in itself seem a fairly acceptable account of Hooker's views on inherited guilt. Yet if one looks in detail at his legal philosophy, then the situation appears to be not quite so clear. Of central interest is his understanding of the legal concept of *mens rea*; the mental process involved in specific human actions. Although he did not use this term, he was certainly familiar with the idea, as he shows in his chapter on baptism by women: 'Wherein appeareth also the difference betwene humane and divine lawes, the one of which two are content with *opus operatum*, the other require *opus operantis*; the one doe but claime the deed, the other especiallie the minde. So that accordinge to lawes which principallie respect the harte of men, workes of religion beinge not religiouslie performed cannot morallie be perfect.'[11] One might refer, as an example, to Paul's observation in 1 Corinthians 13: 3: 'And thogh I fede the poore with all my goods, and thogh I give my bodie, that I be burned, and have not love, it profiteth me nothing.' It is the intention, or *mens rea*, as well as the action itself, that is important.

Hooker's chief interest in this concept is in relation to the freedom of the will. On several occasions he remarks that it is unjust to blame someone for evil actions that have been performed involuntarily. The only exception is when people are at fault for rendering their actions involuntary, as in the case of a drunken person. This shows a concern for *mens rea*, since Hooker wishes to judge people not only by their deeds, but also by the mental processes behind them. As he observes, quoting from the Digest of the *Codex Justinianus*: 'From the sundrie dispositions of mans will, which is the roote of all his actions, there groweth varietie in the sequele of rewards and punishments, which are by these and the like rules measured: *Take away the will, and all actes are equall*.'[12] Of the categories of involuntary action recognized by Hooker, the most relevant concerns those beings who lack the rational ability to choose freely. He remarks concerning these that: 'sith creatures which have no understandinge can shew no will; and where no will is, there is no sinne; and onlie that which synneth is subject to *punishment*; which waye should anie such creature be *punishable* by the lawe of God?'[13]

[11] See *Lawes*, 2:281.3–18 (V.62.15). Hooker's remarks do not seem, here, to represent satisfactorily the position of the common law in his day: see W. S. Holdsworth, *A History of English Law*, 3rd edn. (London, 1923), iii. 372–3; viii. 434–45.

[12] *Lawes*, 1:94.34–95.2 (I.9.1). See also 1:94.7–34 (I.9.1); *Pride*, 5:339.10–14.

[13] *Lawes*, 2:62.26–9 (V.17.3) (though this passage refers specifically to inanimate idolatrous objects). One might also consider cases of invincible ignorance: see *Pride*, 5:312.12–18; *Lambeth Palace Library MS (Fairhurst) 2006, ff. 6r–15v*, *Folger*, v. 276.

Madmen and the severely mentally impaired, amongst others, fall into this category, as of course do infants.[14] This immediately raises important questions, of course, about Hooker's views on inherited guilt. It is hard to square this doctrine with his concern for *mens rea* and free will, for according to his legal philosophy no one should be punished for acts over which they have had no control. Significantly, Hooker never describes how all humanity acted with Adam in Eden and hence deserve eternal punishment purely for original sin. Yet it is clear, from his remarks on infant baptism, that he believed in the notion of inherited guilt, and the deleterious effect it could have upon non-Christian infants. There would appear, therefore, to be a tension or inconsistency between Hooker's theology on the one hand, and his legal philosophy on the other. He evidently felt very strongly about the need for baptism, and worried that those who lacked it might not be saved. Yet his belief in the freedom of the will, and the importance of an equitable legal system, seem to question the logic of an inherited guilt that leads to the punishment of apparently innocent infants.

Hooker was not, however, unaware of this tension. In the *Notes towards a Fragment on Predestination*, written shortly before his death and published for the first time in the *Folger* edition in 1982, Hooker reveals, in his private manuscripts, that this was something that concerned him.[15] There are two relevant passages, both of which take the form of a question, and then an answer. One may begin with the first of these, quoting Booty's translations of Hooker's Latin: 'Is Original Sin, of which the whole race of man is guilty, the cause of perdition of those who perish through retributive justice? This cannot be. Rather the antecedent evil in the damned is the cause of damnation.'[16] Hooker clearly accepts here the existence of inherited guilt, but appears to deny that anyone can be excluded from heaven purely on this basis. Some other, more tangible form of evil, is required for such a punishment, which is in line with his remarks upon *mens rea* in the *Lawes*. Yet Hooker seems to have had difficulty in accepting the radicalism of this conclusion, as the following fascinating lines illustrate: 'Does Original Sin cause no one to perish eternally? This also is ⟨difficult to believe⟩ ⟨uncertain⟩ uncertain. There are, however, those who think so.'[17]

Despite the logic of his previous observation, Hooker does not state here decisively that no one is excluded from heaven because of original sin. Rather, he demonstrates considerable uncertainty, twice crossing out

[14] See *Lawes*, 1:79.9–20 (I.7.4); 1:94.13–18 (I.9.1).

[15] See *Pred.* 4:95.17–31.

[16] An omnibus qui pereunt per justitiam vindicativam causa perditionis sit originale peccatum ⟨pecc-⟩ cujus universa hominis natura est rea. Hoc fieri non potest. Imo quicquid antecedit mali in perditis est causa perditionis.

[17] An culpa originalis nulli causa sit ut pereat in aeternum. Et hoc ⟨difficile creditur⟩ ⟨incertum⟩ incertum. Sunt tamen qui sic existimant.

his own words. It is tempting to wonder what other phrases he considered using, before writing 'incertum' for a second time. He was certainly right in indicating that there were those who held such a position; not least of all Zwingli, amongst the Protestant Reformers.[18] It is hard, as a result of this, not to feel that Hooker tends here towards a more permissive position, removing even non-Christian infants from the threat of punishment due to original sin. Yet a possible mixture of conservatism, and deeply held views over baptism, seems to have prevented him from taking a definite stance. One must inevitably question why such uncertainty was not expressed in the *Lawes*. It is possible that Hooker's views on this subject underwent a development, perhaps as a result of reflections upon his legal philosophy. Alternatively, due perhaps to a desire for polemical advantage, or simply as a result of doubts over the catholicity, veracity, and/or acceptability of his speculations, he elected to take a more Augustinian approach in the *Lawes*, in tension with his ideas on *mens rea* and the freedom of the will. It is, nevertheless, interesting to observe Hooker thinking in this passage, deliberating in a way barely hinted at in his more polished great work.

[18] See W. P. Stephens, *The Theology of Huldrych Zwingli* (Oxford, 1986), 194–6, 204.

BIBLIOGRAPHY

PRIMARY SOURCES

[ANONYMOUS], 'A Christian Letter of Certaine English Protestantes . . . unto that Reverend and Learned man, Maister R. Hoo[ker]', in *The Folger Library Edition of The Works of Richard Hooker*, ed. W. S. Hill (Cambridge, Mass., 1982), iv. 1–79.

ARMINIUS, JACOBUS, *Iacobi Arminii . . . Opera Theologica* (Leiden, 1629).

—— *The Works of James Arminius*, ed. J. Nichols (London, 1825–75).

AUGUSTINE, *Augustins Enchiridion*, ed. O. Scheel (Tübingen, 1903).

—— *Faith, Hope, and Charity*, trans. Louis A. Arand, Ancient Christian Writers, The Works of the Fathers in Translation, 3 (Westminster, Md., 1947).

—— *Aurelii Augustini Opera* (*Corpus Christianorum*, Series Latina, 27–57; Turnhout, 1954–).

—— *Concerning the City of God Against the Pagans*, trans. H. Bettenson (Harmondsworth, 1972).

BRAY, Gerald (ed.), *Documents of the English Reformation* (Cambridge, 1994).

CALVIN, JOHN, *Ioannis Calvini Opera Quae Supersunt Omnia*, ed. G. Baum, E. Cunitz, and E. Reuss (*Corpus Reformatorum*, 29–87; Brunswick, 1863–1900).

—— *Joannis Calvini Opera Selecta*, ed. P. Barth and G. Niesel (Munich, 1926–36).

—— *Calvin's Commentaries: The Epistles of Paul the Apostle to the Romans and to the Thessalonians*, trans. R. Mackenzie (Edinburgh, 1960).

—— *Calvin's Commentaries. The First Epistle of Paul the Apostle to the Corinthians*, ed. D. W. Torrance and T. F. Torrance, trans. J. W. Fraser (Edinburgh, 1960).

—— *Institutes of the Christian Religion*, ed. J. T. McNeill, trans. F. L. Battles (Philadelphia, 1960).

—— *Institution de la Religion Chrestienne*, ed. Jean-Daniel Benoit (Paris, 1960).

—— *Concerning the Eternal Predestination of God*, trans. J. K. S. Reid (London, 1961).

—— *Calvin's Commentaries: The Second Epistle of Paul the Apostle to the Corinthians and the Epistles to Timothy, Titus and Philemon*, ed. D. W. Torrance and T. F. Torrance, trans. T. A. Smail (Edinburgh, 1964).

—— *Calvin's Commentaries: The Acts of the Apostles*, ed. D. W. Torrance and T. F. Torrance, trans. J. W. Fraser (Edinburgh, 1966).

CALVIN, JOHN, *The Bondage and Liberation of the Will: A Defence of the Orthodox Doctrine of Human Choice against Pighius*, ed. A. N. S. Lane, trans. G. I. Davies (Grand Rapids, Mich., 1996).

CARTWRIGHT, THOMAS, *A Replye to an answere made of M. Doctor Whitegifte againste the admonition to the Parliament* (Hemel Hempstead?, 1573). *STC* 4711.

—— *The Second Replie of Thomas Cartwright: against Maister Doctor Whitgiftes second answer, touching the Church Discipline* (Heidelberg, 1575). *STC* 4714.

—— *The Rest of the Second Replie agaynst maister Whitgifts second Answer* (Basle, 1577). *STC* 4715.

—— *Christian Religion: Substantially, Methodicallie, Plainlie, and Profitablie Treatised* (London, 1611). *STC* 4707.5.

—— *A Brief Apologie* (Middelburg, 1596; facsimile edn., Amsterdam, 1970).

—— *A Confutation of the Rhemists Translation* (Leiden, 1618; facsimile edn., Amsterdam, 1971).

Certain Sermons or Homilies, ed. Ronald B. Bond (Toronto, 1987).

COCHRANE, A. C. (ed.), *Reformed Confessions of the 16th Century* (London, 1966).

COVEL, WILLIAM, 'A Just and Temperate Defence of the Five Books "Of Ecclesiastical Polity" Written by Mr. Richard Hooker', in *Hooker's Ecclesiastical Polity and Other Works*, ed. B. Hanbury (London, 1830), ii, 439–568. This edition of 'A Just and Temperate Defence' has recently been republished: see following entry. Taylor comments in the Editor's Preface, p. v: 'Hanbury produced a text that serves scholars just as well as the 1603 edition, and that serves casual readers better than that 1603 edition, yet that loses nothing.'

—— *A Just and Temperate Defence of the Five Books of Ecclesiastical Polity*, ed. J. A. Taylor (Lewiston, NY, 1998).

DUNS SCOTUS, JOHN, *Duns Scotus on the Will and Morality*, selected and trans. Allan B. Wolter (Washington, DC, 1986).

—— *Philosophical Writings: A Selection*, trans. A. Wolter (Indianapolis, 1987).

Geneva Bible, The. A Facsimile of the 1560 Edition (Madison, 1969).

GÉNEBRARD, GILBERT, *Symbolum Athanasii Commentariis Huic Aeuo Accommodatis Illustratum* (Leiden, 1607).

HILARY OF POITIERS, *The Trinity*, trans. Stephen McKenna, Fathers of the Church 5 (New York, 1954).

HOOKER, RICHARD, *The Workes of . . . Mr. Richard Hooker*, 7th edn., ed. John Keble, rev. R. W. Church and F. Paget (Oxford, 1888).

—— *The Folger Library Edition of The Works of Richard Hooker*, ed. W. Speed Hill, 7 vols. (i–v, Cambridge, Mass., 1977–90; vi, Binghamton, NY, 1993; vii, Tempe, Ariz., 1998).

JEROME, 'The Dialogue Against the Luciferians', *St. Jerome: Letters and Select Works*, trans. W. H. Fremantle, G. Lewis, and W. G. Martley, A Select Library of the Nicene and Post-Nicene Fathers of the Christian Church, Second Series 6 (Oxford, 1893), 319–34.

JUSTIN MARTYR, 'The Dialogue with Trypho', *Writings of Saint Justin Martyr*, trans. T. B. Falls (New York, 1948), 139–366.

MONTAGU, RICHARD, *A Gagg for the New Gospell? No: A New Gagg for an Old Goose* (London, 1624; facsimile edn. Amsterdam, 1975).

NEWMAN, JOHN HENRY, *Lectures on Justification* (London, 1838).

—— *Tracts for the Times, No. 90: Remarks on Certain Passages in the Thirty-Nine Articles*, 2nd edn. (London, 1841).

Oxford English Dictionary, The, 2nd edn., prepared by J. A. Simpson and E. S. C. Weiner (Oxford, 1989).

Patrologiae Cursus Completus, Series Latina, ed. J. P. Migne (Paris, 1844–64).

PERKINS, WILLIAM, *A Golden Chaine*, trans. [R. Hill] (London, 1591). *STC* 19657.

—— *A Case of Conscience* (London, 1592). *STC* 19665.

Philo, trans. F. H. Colson and G. H. Whitaker (London, 1930).

PROSPER OF AQUITAINE, ST, *The Call of All Nations*, trans. and annotated P. De Letter, Ancient Christian Writers. The Works of the Fathers in Translation 14 (Westminster, Md., 1952).

PRYNNE, WILLIAM, *Anti-Arminianisme, or The Church of Englands Old Antithesis to New Arminianisme*, 2nd edn. (London, 1630). *STC* 20458.

TERTULLIAN, 'Apology', *The Writings of Tertullian*, ed. A. Roberts and J. Donaldson, The Ante-Nicene Fathers 11 (Edinburgh, 1869), i.

THOMAS AQUINAS, *The Summa Contra Gentiles of Saint Thomas Aquinas*, trans. English Dominican Fathers (London, 1924–9).

—— *Summa Theologiae*, Latin text with English trans., Blackfriars edn. (London, 1964–81).

TRAVERS, WALTER, *A Full and Plaine Declaration of Ecclesiasticall Discipline owt of the word of God*, trans. T. Cartwright (Heidelberg, 1574). *STC* 24184.

—— 'A Supplication made to the Privy Council by Master Walter Travers', in *The Folger Library Edition of The Works of Richard Hooker*, ed. W. S. Hill (Cambridge Mass., 1990), v. 189–210.

WHITGIFT, JOHN, 'The Defence of the Answer to the Admonition', in *The Works of John Whitgift*, ed. J. Ayre (Cambridge, 1851–3), i–iii.

SECONDARY SOURCES

ALLEN, J. W., *A History of Political Thought in the Sixteenth Century*, 3rd edn. (London, 1951).

ALLISON, C. F., *The Rise of Moralism: The Proclamation of the Gospel from Hooker to Baxter* (London, 1966).

ALMASY, RUDOLPH, 'The Purpose of Richard Hooker's Polemic', *Journal of the History of Ideas* 39 (1978), 251–70.

ATKINSON, NIGEL, *Richard Hooker and the Authority of Scripture, Tradition and Reason* (Carlisle, 1997).

——'Hooker's Theological Method and Modern Anglicanism', *The Churchman* 114 (2000), 40–70.

AVIS, P. D. L., 'Richard Hooker and John Calvin', *The Journal of Ecclesiastical History* 32 (1981), 19–28.

BANGS, CARL, *Arminius: A Study in the Dutch Reformation* (Nashville, 1971).

——'Arminius as a Reformed Theologian', *The Heritage of John Calvin. Heritage Hall Lectures 1960–1970*, ed. J. H. Bratt (Grand Rapids, Mich., 1973), 209–22.

BAUCKHAM, RICHARD, 'Hooker, Travers and the Church of Rome in the 1580s', *Journal of Ecclesiastical History* 29 (1978), 37–50.

——'Richard Hooker and John Calvin: a Comment', *The Journal of Ecclesiastical History* 32 (1981), 29–33.

BAVINCK, HERMAN, 'Calvin and Common Grace', *Calvin and the Reformation* (London, 1909), 99–130.

BETTONI, EFREM, *Duns Scotus: The Basic Principles of his Philosophy*, trans. and ed. B. Bonansea (Washington, DC, 1961).

BICKNELL, E. J., *A Theological Introduction to the Thirty-Nine Articles of the Church of England*, 3rd edn., rev. H. J. Carpenter (London, 1955).

BONANSEA, BERNADINE M., 'Duns Scotus' Voluntarism', *John Duns Scotus, 1265–1965*, ed. J. K. Ryan and B. M. Bonansea (Washington, DC, 1965), 83–121.

BOOTY, JOHN E., 'Introduction', *The Folger Library Edition of The Works of Richard Hooker*, ed. W. Speed Hill (Cambridge, Mass., 1982), iv. pp. xiii–xlviii.

——'Commentary', *The Folger Library Edition of The Works of Richard Hooker*, ed. W. Speed Hill (Cambridge, Mass., 1982), iv. 183–267.

——'Introduction: Book V', *The Folger Library Edition of The Works of Richard Hooker*, ed. W. Speed Hill (Binghamton, NY, 1993), vi. 183–231.

——'Commentary: Book V', *The Folger Library Edition of The Works of Richard Hooker*, ed. W. Speed Hill (Binghamton, NY, 1993), vi. 653–832.

——*Reflections on the Theology of Richard Hooker: An Anglican Addresses Modern Anglicanism* (Sewanee, Tenn., 1998).

BOURKE, VERNON J., *Will in Western Thought* (New York, 1964).

BOURNE, E. C. E., *The Anglicanism of William Laud* (London, 1947).

BOUWSMA, WILLIAM J., 'Hooker in the Context of European Cultural History', *Richard Hooker and the Construction of Christian Community*, ed. A. S. McGrade (Tempe, Ariz., 1997), 142–58.

BRYDON, MICHAEL A., 'The Evolving Reputation of Richard Hooker: An Examination of Responses to the *Ecclesiastical Polity*, 1640–1714' (Ph.D. thesis, Univ. of Durham, 1999).

BUREN, PAUL VAN, *Christ in Our Place: The Substitutionary Character of Calvin's Doctrine of Reconciliation* (London, 1957).

COLLINSON, PATRICK, *The Elizabethan Puritan Movement* (Oxford, 1967).

—— *The Religion of Protestants: The Church in English Society 1559–1625* (Oxford, 1982).

—— 'England and International Calvinism 1558–1640', M. Prestwick (ed.), *International Calvinism* (Oxford, 1985), 197–223.

—— 'Hooker and the Elizabethan Establishment', A. S. McGrade (ed.), *Richard Hooker and the Construction of Christian Community* (Tempe, Ariz., 1997), 149–81.

COOLIDGE, JOHN S., *The Pauline Renaissance in England. Puritanism and the Bible* (Oxford, 1970).

COPLESTON, FREDERICK, *A History of Philosophy*, ii. *Mediaeval Philosophy* (London, 1950).

COUSINS, A. D., 'Playing with Reason: Aspects of Hooker's Rhetoric in *Lawes* I–V', *Journal of English and Germanic Philology* 97 (1998), 177–89.

CRAGG, GERALD, R., *Freedom and Authority: A Study of English Thought in the Early Seventeenth Century* (Philadelphia, 1975).

CRESSY, DAVID, *Birth, Marriage, and Death: Ritual, Religion, and the Life-Cycle in Tudor and Stuart England* (Oxford, 1997).

CROXFORD, LESLIE, 'The Originality of Hooker's Work', *Proceedings of the Leeds Philosophical and Literary Society*, 15/2 (1973), 15–57.

D'ENTRÈVES, ALEXANDER PASSERIN, *The Medieval Contribution to Political Thought* (Oxford, 1939).

—— *Natural Law: An Introduction to Legal Philosophy* (London, 1951).

DAVIES, JULIAN, *The Caroline Captivity of the Church: Charles I and the Remoulding of Anglicanism 1625–1641* (Oxford, 1992).

DEVINE, JOSEPH G., 'Richard Hooker's Doctrine of Justification and Sanctification in the Debate with Walter Travers 1585–1586' (Ph.D. thesis, The Hartford Seminary Foundation, 1976).

DONAGAN, ALAN, 'Thomas Aquinas on Human Action', *The Cambridge History of Later Medieval Philosophy*, ed. N. Kretzmann, A. Kenny, and J. Pinborg (Cambridge, 1982), 642–54.

DOWEY, EDWARD A., JR, *The Knowledge of God in Calvin's Theology* (New York, 1952).

EDELEN, GEORGES, 'Textual Introduction', *The Folger Library Edition of The Works of Richard Hooker*, ed. W. Speed Hill (Cambridge, Mass., 1977), i. pp. xxix–xxxviii.

FAULKNER, ROBERT K., 'Reason and Revelation in Hooker's Ethics', *The American Political Science Review* 59 (1965), 680–90.

FISHER, J. D. C., *Christian Initiation: The Reformation Period* (London, 1970).

FORSTMAN, H. JACKSON, *Word and Spirit: Calvin's Doctrine of Biblical Authority* (Stanford, Calif., 1962).

FORTE, PAUL E., 'The Achievement of Richard Hooker, 1554–1600' (Ph.D. thesis, State Univ. of New York at Buffalo, 1980).

—— 'Richard Hooker's Theory of Law', *The Journal of Medieval and Renaissance Studies* 12 (1982), 133–57.

FRANK, WILLIAM A., 'Duns Scotus' Concept of Willing Freely: What Divine Freedom Beyond Choice Teaches Us', *Franciscan Studies* 42 (1982), 68–89.

—— 'Duns Scotus on Autonomous Freedom and Divine Co-Causality', *Medieval Philosophy & Theology* 2 (1992), 142–64.

FREDDOSO, ALFRED J., 'Introduction', in Luis de Molina, *On Divine Foreknowledge (Part IV of the Concordia)*, trans. with an introduction and notes by A. J. Freddoso (Ithaca, NY, 1988).

GERRISH, B. A., *Grace and Gratitude: The Eucharistic Theology of John Calvin* (Edinburgh, 1993).

GIBBS, LEE W., 'Richard Hooker's *Via Media* Doctrine of Justification', *Harvard Theological Review* 74 (1981), 211–20.

—— 'Introduction: Book I', *The Folger Library Edition of The Works of Richard Hooker*, ed. W. Speed Hill (Binghamton, NY, 1993), vi. 81–124.

—— 'Commentary: Book I', *The Folger Library Edition of The Works of Richard Hooker*, ed. W. Speed Hill (Binghamton, NY, 1993), vi. 477–521.

—— 'Richard Hooker's *Via Media* Doctrine of Scripture and Tradition', *Harvard Theological Review* 95 (2002), 227–35.

GREGG, WILLIAM OTIS, 'Richard Hooker's 'Of the Lawes of Ecclesiasticall Polity I–V': A Theology of Sacramentality' (Ph.D. thesis, Univ. of Notre Dame, 1993).

GRISLIS, EGIL, 'Richard Hooker's Image of Man', *Renaissance Papers 1963* (The Southeastern Renaissance Conference, 1964), 73–84.

—— 'The Role of *Consensus* in Richard Hooker's Method of Theological Inquiry', *The Heritage of Christian Thought: Essays in Honor of Robert Lowry Calhoun*, ed. R. E. Cushman and E. Grislis (New York, 1965), 64–88.

—— 'The Hermeneutical Problem in Richard Hooker', *Studies in Richard Hooker: Essays Preliminary to an Edition of his Works*, ed. W. S. Hill (Cleveland, 1972), 159–206.

—— 'Introduction to Commentary', *The Folger Library Edition of The Works of Richard Hooker*, ed. W. Speed Hill (Cambridge, Mass., 1990), v. 619–55.

—— 'Commentary', *The Folger Library Edition of The Works of Richard Hooker*, ed. W. Speed Hill (Cambridge, Mass., 1990), v. 683–850.

—— 'Index of Scriptural References', *The Folger Library Edition of The Works of Richard Hooker*, ed. W. Speed Hill (Cambridge, Mass., 1990), v. 851–909.

—— 'The Anglican Spirituality of Richard Hooker', *Toronto Journal of Theology* 12 (1996), 35–45.

—— 'The Assurance of Faith According to Richard Hooker', in A. S. McGrade (ed.), *Richard Hooker and the Construction of Christian Community* (Tempe, Ariz., 1997), 237–49.

HACKING, IAN, *The Emergence of Probability: A Philosophical Study of Early Ideas about Probability, Induction and Statistical Inference* (Cambridge, 1975).

HAUGAARD, WILLIAM P., 'The Scriptural Hermeneutics of Richard Hooker: Historical Contextualization and Teleology', in D. S. Armentrout (ed.), *This Sacred History: Anglican Reflections for John Booty* (Cambridge, Mass., 1990), 161–74.

—— 'Introduction: The Preface', *The Folger Library Edition of The Works of Richard Hooker*, ed. W. Speed Hill (Binghamton, NY, 1993), vi. 1–80.

—— 'Introduction: Books II, III & IV', *The Folger Library Edition of The Works of Richard Hooker*, ed. W. Speed Hill (Binghamton, NY, 1993), vi. 125–81.

—— 'Commentary: The Preface', *The Folger Library Edition of The Works of Richard Hooker*, ed. W. Speed Hill (Binghamton, NY, 1993), vi. 403–75.

—— 'Commentary: Book II', *The Folger Library Edition of The Works of Richard Hooker*, ed. W. Speed Hill (Binghamton, NY, 1993), vi. 523–51.

HELM, PAUL, *Faith and Understanding* (Edinburgh, 1997).

HENDRY, GEORGE S., *The Holy Spirit in Christian Theology*, rev. edn. (London, 1965).

HESSELINK, I. JOHN, *Calvin's Concept of the Law* (Allison Park, Pa., 1992).

HILL, W. SPEED, 'The Doctrinal Background of Richard Hooker's *Laws of Ecclesiastical Polity*' (Ph.D. thesis, Harvard Univ., 1964).

—— 'Doctrine and Polity in Hooker's Laws', *English Literary Renaissance* 2 (1972), 173–93.

—— Review of Peter Lake, *Anglicans and Puritans? Presbyterian and English Conformist Thought from Whitgift to Hooker*, *Seventeenth-Century News* 47 (1989), 39–40.

HILLERDAL, GUNNAR, *Reason and Revelation in Richard Hooker* (Lund, 1962).

HOLDSWORTH, W. S., *A History of English Law*, 3rd edn. (London, 1923).

HOOPES, ROBERT, *Right Reason in the English Renaissance* (Harvard, 1962).

HUGHES, JOHN G., 'The Theology of Richard Hooker' (Ph.D. thesis, Univ. of Leeds, 1979).

HUGHES, PHILIP E., *Faith and Works: Cranmer and Hooker on Justification* (Wilton, Conn., 1982).

HUGHES, SEÁN F., 'The Problem of "Calvinism": English Theologies of Predestination c.1580–1630', in S. Wabuda and C. Litzenberger (eds.), *Belief and Practice in Reformation England: A Tribute to Patrick Collinson from his Students* (Aldershot, 1998), 229–49.

KAPITAN, TOMIS, 'Free Will Problem', *The Cambridge Dictionary of Philosophy*, ed. R. Audi (Cambridge, 1995), 280–2.

KAVANAGH, ROBERT, 'Reason and Nature in Hooker's Polity' (Ph.D. thesis, Univ. of Wisconsin, 1944).

KEARNEY, H. F., 'Richard Hooker: a Reconstruction', *The Cambridge Journal* 5 (1952), 300–11.

KEBLE, JOHN, 'Editor's Preface', in Richard Hooker, *The Workes of... Mr. Richard Hooker*, 7th edn., ed. J. Keble, rev. R. W. Church and F. Paget (Oxford, 1888), i. pp. i–cxiii.

KENDALL, ROBERT TILLMAN, *Calvin and English Calvinism to 1649* (Oxford, 1979).

KENNY, ANTHONY, 'Descartes on the Will', *The Anatomy of the Soul. Historical Essays in the Philosophy of Mind* (Oxford, 1973), 81–112.

—— *Aquinas on Mind* (London, 1993).

KIRBY, W. J. TORRANCE, *Richard Hooker's Doctrine of the Royal Supremacy* (Leiden, 1990).

—— 'Richard Hooker as an Apologist of the Magisterial Reformation in England', in A. S. McGrade (ed.), *Richard Hooker and the Construction of Christian Community* (Tempe, Ariz., 1997), 219–33.

—— 'Richard Hooker's Theory of Natural Law in the Context of Reformation Theology', *Sixteenth Century Journal* 30 (1999), 681–703.

—— 'The Paradigm of Chalcedonian Christology in Richard Hooker's Discourse on Grace and the Church', *The Churchman* 114 (2000), 22–39.

KLEMPA, WILLIAM, 'John Calvin on Natural Law', *Calvin Studies* 4 (1988), 1–24.

KOROLEC, J. B., 'Free Will and Free Choice', in N. Kretzmann, A. Kenny, and J. Pinborg (eds.), *The Cambridge History of Later Medieval Philosophy* (Cambridge, 1982), 629–41.

KUIPER, HERMAN, *Calvin on Common Grace* (Goes, 1928).

KUYPER, ABRAHAM, *Calvinism. Being the Six 'Stone' Lectures Given at Princeton Theological Seminary, U.S.A.: A New Edition* (London, 1932).

LAKE, PETER, *Anglicans and Puritans? Presbyterian and English Conformist Thought from Whitgift to Hooker* (London, 1988).

—— 'Lancelot Andrewes, John Buckeridge, and Avant-Garde Conformity at the Court of James I', in L. L. Peck (ed.), *The Mental World of the Jacobean Court* (Cambridge, 1991), 113–33.

—— 'Defining Puritanism—Again?', in F. J. Bremer (ed.), *Puritanism. Transatlantic Perspectives on a Seventeenth-Century Anglo-American Faith* (Boston, 1993), 3–29.

—— 'The Laudian Style: Order, Uniformity and the Pursuit of the Beauty of Holiness in the 1630s', in K. Fincham (ed.), *The Early Stuart Church, 1603–1642* (Basingstoke, 1993), 161–85.

—— 'Predestinarian Propositions', *Journal of Ecclesiastical History* 46 (1995), 110–23.

—— 'Business as Usual? The Immediate Reception of Hooker's *Ecclesiastical Polity*', *Journal of Ecclesiastical History* 52 (2001), 456–86.

LANE, A. N. S., 'Did Calvin Believe in Freewill?', *Vox Evangelica* 12 (1981), 72–90.

LEWIS, C. S., *Poetry and Prose in the Sixteenth Century* (Oxford, 1954).

LONERGAN, BERNARD J. F., in J. P. Burns (ed.), *Grace and Freedom: Operative Grace in the Thought of St. Thomas Aquinas* (London, 1971).

MACCULLOCH, DIARMAID, *The Later Reformation in England 1547–1603* (Basingstoke, 1990).

—— 'Richard Hooker's Reputation', *English Historical Review* 117 (2002), 773–812.

MCGRADE, ARTHUR S., 'The Coherence of Hooker's *Polity*: The Books on Power', *Journal of the History of Ideas* 24 (1963), 163–82.

—— 'Hooker's *Polity* and the Establishment of the English Church' *Richard Hooker: Of the Laws of Ecclesiastical Polity*, ed. A. S. McGrade and B. Vickers (London, 1975), 11–40.

—— 'Introduction: The Last Three Books and Hooker's Autograph Notes', *The Folger Library Edition of The Works of Richard Hooker*, ed. W. Speed Hill (Binghamton, New York, 1993), vi. 233–47.

MCGRATH, ALISTER E., *Iustitia Dei. A History of the Christian Doctrine of Justification*, 2nd edn. (Cambridge, 1998).

—— *Christian Theology. An Introduction* (Oxford, 1994).

MCGUINESS, I., 'Sin (Theology of)', *New Catholic Encyclopedia* (New York, 1967), xiii. 241–5.

MCNEILL, JOHN T., 'Natural Law in the Teaching of the Reformers', *The Journal of Religion* 26 (1946), 168–82.

MAHON, VINCENT, 'The "*Christian Letter*": Some Puritan Objections to Hooker's Work; and Hooker's "Undressed" Comments', *The Review of English Studies* 25 (1974), 305–12.

MALONE, MICHAEL T., 'The Doctrine of Predestination in the Thought of William Perkins and Hooker', *Anglican Theological Review* 52 (1970), 103–17.

MANLEY, LAWRENCE, *Convention 1500–1750* (Cambridge, Mass., 1980).

MANUSZAK, DAVID, 'Authority in Hooker's *Polity*' (Ph.D. thesis, Univ. of Michigan, 1976).

MARSHALL, J. S., *Hooker and the Anglican Tradition: An Historical and Theological Study of Hooker's Ecclesiastical Polity* (London, 1963).

MONAHAN, ARTHUR P., 'Richard Hooker: Counter-Reformation Thinker', in A. S. McGrade (ed.), *Richard Hooker and the Construction of Christian Community* (Tempe, Ariz., 1997), 203–17.

MORREL, GEORGE W., 'The Systematic Theology of Richard Hooker' (Th.D. thesis, Pacific School of Religion, 1969).

MOSER, PAUL K., 'Epistemology', *The Cambridge Dictionary of Philosophy*, ed. R. Audi (Cambridge, 1995), 233–8.

MULLER, RICHARD A., *God, Creation, and Providence in the Thought of Jacob Arminius: Sources and Directions of Scholastic Protestantism in the Era of Early Orthodoxy* (Grand Rapids, Mich., 1991).

MUNZ, PETER, *The Place of Hooker in the History of Thought* (London, 1952).

NEELANDS, W. DAVID, 'The Theology of Grace of Richard Hooker' (D.Th. thesis, Trinity College and the University of Toronto, 1988).

NEELANDS, W. DAVID, 'Hooker on Scripture, Reason and "Tradition" ', in A. S. McGrade (ed.), *Richard Hooker and the Construction of Christian Community* (Tempe, Ariz., 1997), 75–94.

NEW, JOHN F. H., *Anglican and Puritan: The Basis of their Opposition, 1558–1640* (London, 1964).

NICHOLS, AIDAN, *The Panther and the Hind: A Theological History of Anglicanism* (Edinburgh, 1993).

NIESEL, WILHELM, *The Theology of Calvin*, trans. H. Knight (London, 1956).

NORMORE, CALVIN, 'Future Contingents', in N. Kretzman, A. Kenny, and J. Pinborg (eds.), *The Cambridge History of Later Medieval Philosophy* (Cambridge, 1982), 358–81.

O'BRIEN, T. C., Commentary, in Thomas Aquinas, *Summa Theologiae* (London, 1964–81), p. xxxi.

—— 'Appendix 4', in Thomas Aquinas, *Summa Theologiae* (London, 1964–81), p. xxxi.

O'NEIL, A. C., 'Sin', *The Catholic Encyclopedia* (New York, 1912), xiv. 4–11.

OTT, MICHAEL, 'Gilbert Génebrard', *The Catholic Encyclopedia* (New York, 1909), vi. 412.

PAGET, FRANCIS, *An Introduction to the Fifth Book of Hooker's Treatise of the Lawes of Ecclesiastical Polity* (Oxford, 1899; 2nd edn., 1907).

PAINTER, BORDEN W., 'Anglican Terminology in Recent Tudor and Stuart Historiography', *Anglican and Episcopal History* 56 (1987), 237–49.

PARK, KATHARINE, 'The Organic Soul', in C. B. Schmitt, Q. Skinner, and E. Kessler (eds.), *The Cambridge History of Renaissance Philosophy* (Cambridge, 1988), 464–84.

PEGIS, ANTON C., 'Molina and Human Liberty', *Jesuit Thinkers of the Renaissance* (Milwaukee, 1939), 75–132.

PELIKAN, JAROSLAV, *Reformation of Church and Dogma (1300–1700)* (Chicago, 1983).

PERROTT, M. E. C., 'Richard Hooker and the Problem of Authority in the Elizabethan Church', *The Journal of Ecclesiastical History* 49 (1998), 29–60.

POHLE, JOSEPH, 'Merit', *The Catholic Encyclopedia* (New York, 1911), x. 202–8.

—— 'Molinism', *The Catholic Encyclopedia* (New York, 1911), x. 437–41.

PRESBYTERIAN CHURCH (USA), 'The Nature of Revelation in the Christian Tradition from a Reformed Perspective', in D. K. McKim (ed.), *Major Themes in the Reformed Tradition* (Grand Rapids, Mich., 1992), 35–50.

REVENTLOW, HENNING GRAF, *The Authority of the Bible and the Rise of the Modern World*, trans. J. Bowden (London, 1984).

SCHMITT, CHARLES B., *John Case and Aristotelianism in Renaissance England* (Kingston, 1983).

SECOR, PHILIP B., *Richard Hooker: Prophet of Anglicanism* (Tunbridge Wells, 1999).

SHAPIRO, BARBARA J., *Probability and Certainty in Seventeenth-Century England* (Princeton, 1983).

SHEERIN, F. L., 'Molinism', *New Catholic Encylopedia* (New York, 1967), ix. 1011–13.

SHUGER, DEBORA K., *Habits of Thought in the English Renaissance. Religion, Politics, and the Dominant Culture* (Berkeley and Los Angeles, 1990).

—— ' "Society Supernatural": The Imagined Community of Hooker's *Lawes*', in C. McEachen and D. Shuger (eds.), *Religion and Culture in Renaissance England* (Cambridge, 1997), 116–41.

SPINKS, BRYAN D., *Two Faces of Elizabethan Anglican Theology: Sacraments and Salvation in the Thought of William Perkins and Richard Hooker* (Lanham, Md., 1999).

STANLEY, VERNON, *Richard Hooker* (London, 1907).

STANWOOD, P. G., 'Richard Hooker's Discourse and the Deception of Posterity', in N. Rhodes (ed.), *English Renaissance Prose: History, Language and Politics* (Tempe, Ariz., 1997), 75–90.

STEPHENS, W. P., *The Holy Spirit in the Theology of Martin Bucer* (Cambridge, 1970).

—— *The Theology of Huldrych Zwingli* (Oxford, 1986).

STUEBER, MARIE S., 'Richard Hooker's Place in the History of Renaissance Christian Humanism' (Ph.D. thesis, St Louis Univ., 1954).

THOMPSON, W. D. J. CARGILL, 'The Philosopher of the "Politic Society": Richard Hooker as a Political Thinker', in W. S. Hill (ed.), *Studies in Richard Hooker: Essays Preliminary to an Edition of his Work* (Cleveland, 1972), 3–76.

THORNBURG, CHARLES M., 'Original Sin, Justification and Sanctification in the Thought of Two Sixteenth Century English Divines: John Jewel and Richard Hooker' (Ph.D. thesis, The Hartford Seminary Foundation, 1975).

TUCK, RICHARD, 'Hooker's Political Thought', Richard Hooker 400th Anniversary Lectures (Examination Schools, Oxford, 17 November 2000).

TYACKE, NICHOLAS, *Anti-Calvinists: The Rise of English Arminianism c. 1590–1640* (Oxford, 1987; repr. pbk 1990).

VAN LEEUWEN, HENRY G., *The Problem of Certainty in English Thought 1630–1690* (The Hague, 1963).

VAN ROO, WILLIAM A., *Grace and Original Justice According to St. Thomas*, Analecta Gregoriana, 75 (Rome, 1955).

VOAK, NIGEL, 'Reason, Will and Grace in the Works of Richard Hooker' (D.Phil. thesis, Univ. of Oxford, 1998).

WALLACE, DEWEY D., JR., *Puritans and Predestination: Grace in English Protestant Theology, 1525–1695* (Chapel Hill, NC, 1982).

WEIL, LOUIS, 'The Gospel in Anglicanism', in S. Sykes and J. Booty (eds.), *The Study of Anglicanism* (London, 1988), 51–76.

WENDEL, FRANÇOIS, *Calvin: The Origins and Development of his Religious Thought*, trans. P. Mairet (London, 1963).

WESTBERG, DANIEL, *Right Practical Reason: Aristotle, Action, and Prudence in Aquinas* (Oxford, 1994).

WHITE, PETER, *Predestination, Policy and Polemic: Conflict and Consensus in the English Church from the Reformation to the Civil War* (Cambridge, 1992).

—— 'The *Via Media* in the Early Stuart Church', in K. Fincham (ed.), *The Early Stuart Church, 1603–1642* (Basingstoke, 1993), 211–30.

WILLIAMS, GEORGE HUNTSTON, 'Erasmus and the Reformers on Non-Christian Religions and *Salus Extra Ecclesiam*', in Theodore K. Rabb and Jerrold E. Seigel (eds.), *Action and Conviction in Early Modern Europe* (Princeton, 1969), 319–70.

WILMER, RICHARD H., JR., 'Hooker on Authority', *Anglican Theological Review* 33 (1951), 102–8.

WIPPEL, JOHN F., *Metaphysical Themes in Thomas Aquinas* (Washington, DC, 1984).

WOLTER, ALLAN B., *The Philosophical Theology of John Duns Scotus* (Ithaca, NY, 1990).

YEANDLE, LAETITIA, 'Textual Introduction: *Two Sermons Upon S. Judes Epistle*', *The Folger Library Edition of The Works of Richard Hooker*, ed. W. Speed Hill (Cambridge, Mass., 1990), v. 1–7.

—— 'Textual Introduction: *A Learned and Comfortable Sermon of the Certaintie and Perpetuitie of Faith in the Elect*', *The Folger Library Edition of The Works of Richard Hooker*, ed. W. Speed Hill (Cambridge Mass., 1990), v. 59–68.

—— 'Textual Introduction: *A Learned Discourse of Justification, Workes, and How the Foundation of Faith Is Overthrowne*', *The Folger Library Edition of The Works of Richard Hooker*, ed. W. Speed Hill (Cambridge Mass., 1990), v. 83–104.

—— 'Textual Introduction: *A Learned Sermon of the Nature of Pride*', *The Folger Library Edition of The Works of Richard Hooker*, ed. W. Speed Hill (Cambridge, Mass., 1990), v. 299–308.

ZAHL, PAUL F. M., *The Protestant Face of Anglicanism* (Grand Rapids, Mich., 1998).

INDEX

The Early Reformation on the Continent
Owen Chadwick
Oxford History of the Christian Church

Reformation in Britain and Ireland
Felicity Heal
Oxford History of the Christian Church

Buildings, Faith, and Worship
The Liturgical Arrangement of Anglican Churches
1600–1900
Nigel Yates